E-BUSINESS AND E-CHALLENGES

Emerging Communication

Studies in New Technologies and Practices in Communication

Emerging Communication is publishing state-of-the-art papers that examine a broad range of issues in communication technology, theories, research, practices and applications.
It presents the latest development in the field of traditional and computer-mediated communication with emphasis on novel technologies and theoretical work in this multidisciplinary area of pure and applied research.
Since *Emerging Communication* seeks to be a general forum for advanced communication scholarship, it is especially interested in research whose significance crosses disciplinary and sub-field boundaries.

Volume 4

Earlier published in this series

Vol. 1. G. Riva and F. Davide (Eds.), Communications Through Virtual Technologies: Identity, Community and Technology in the Communication Age
Vol. 2. G. Riva and C. Galimberti (Eds.), Towards CyberPsychology: Mind, Cognition and Society in the Internet Age
Vol. 3. L. Anolli, R. Ciceri and G. Riva (Eds.), Say Not to Say: New Perspectives on Miscommunication

ISSN: 1566-7677

E-Business and E- Challenges

Edited by

Veljko Milutinović

University of Belgrade, Belgrade, Yugoslavia

and

Frédéric Patricelli

Telecom Italia, Rome, Italy

Foreword by

Jerome Friedman

MIT, Nobel Laureate

IOS Press

Ohmsha

Amsterdam • Berlin • Oxford • Tokyo • Washington, DC

ISBN 1 58603 276 3 (IOS Press)
ISBN 4 274 90526 8 C3055 (Ohmsha)

Publisher
IOS Press
Nieuwe Hemweg 6B
1013 BG Amsterdam
The Netherlands
fax: +31 20 620 3419
e-mail: order@iospress.nl

Distributor in the UK and Ireland
IOS Press/Lavis Marketing
73 Lime Walk
Headington
Oxford OX3 7AD
England
fax: +44 1865 75 0079

Distributor in the USA and Canada
IOS Press, Inc.
5795-G Burke Centre Parkway
Burke, VA 22015
USA
fax: +1 703 323 3668
e-mail: iosbooks@iospress.com

Distributor in Germany, Austria and Switzerland
IOS Press/LSL.de
Gerichtsweg 28
D-04103 Leipzig
Germany
fax: +49 341 995 4255

Distributor in Japan
Ohmsha, Ltd.
3-1 Kanda Nishiki-cho
Chiyoda-ku, Tokyo 101-8460
Japan
fax: +81 3 3233 2426

PRINTED IN THE NETHERLANDS

Preface

This book is related to the tutorials of the SSGRR conferences held in the years 2000, 2001, and 2002.

Each of the SSGRR conferences featured a set of tutorials on hot topics in e-Business on the Internet. This book includes chapters resulting from a 1:1 correspondence with the tutorial talks.

After SSGRR, these tutorials were presented many more times for industry and academia in the USA and Europe.

Veljko Milutinović (University of Belgrade)
Frédéric Patricelli (Learning Services/SSGRR)

June 20, 2002

SCUOLA SUPERIORE
G. REISS ROMOLI

TELECOM ITALIA
LEARNING SERVICES

Zivoslav Adamovic
Andreja Cvetanovic
Milos Cvetanovic
Dusan Dingarac
Dragan Domazet
Zeljko Duricic
Zoran Horvat
Natasa Ilic
Momcilo Inic
Miodrag Ivkovic
Mladenka Jakovljevic
Nemanja Jovanovic
Marko Jovic
Nikola Klem
Petar Kocovic
Milos Kovacevic
Gvozden Marinkovic
Nikola Milanović
Valentina Milenkovic
Bratislav Milic
Marjan Mihanovic
Darko Milutinovic
Sonja Mrvaljevic
Jasmina Pilipovic
Aleksandra Popovic
Zaharije Radivojevic
Milan Savic
Nikola Skundric
Milan Simic
Miodrag Stefanovic
Goran Timotic
Djordje Trifunovic
Aleksandra Vranes
Ivana Vujovic

E-Business and E-Challenges

Edited by

Veljko Milutinovic

and

Frédéric Patricelli

Foreword by

Jerome Friedman (MIT),

Nobel Laureate

Foreword

The development of Homo Sapiens has been a history of innovations, from the earliest crude tools to the modern technological society of today. The growth of science and technology has been exponential during the last century; and under the right circumstances, this rapid growth can be expected to continue.

The major innovations of the future – those that will shape the society of the future – will require a strong foundation of both basic and applied research. It is ironic that quantum mechanics, one of most abstruse conceptual frameworks in physics – one that was developed to explain atomic spectra and the structure of the atom, lies at the foundation of some of our most important technological developments, because it provided the understanding of semiconductors that was essential for the invention of the transistor. Quantum mechanics thus contributed directly to the development of technologies that gave us world wide communication, computers with their applications to all phases of modern life, lasers with many diverse uses, consumer electronics, atomic clocks, and superconductors – just to mention a few. The internet and the world wide web, which are profoundly reshaping the way that we communicate, learn, and engage in commerce, owe their origins in a deep sense to the physicists of the past who worked to understand the atom. In modern industrial nations, quantum mechanics probably lies at the basis of a sizable fraction of the gross national product. This is but one example, and there are many others in all areas of science that demonstrate this point.

It is clear that innovation is the key to the future and the human drive to understand nature is the key to future innovation. Society must do all that it can to preserve, nurture and encourage curiosity and the drive to understand.

Jerome Friedman,
MIT, Cambridge, Massachusetts, USA,
Nobel Laureate in Physics

January 20, 2002

Contents

E-Business and E-Challenges
V. Milutinović and F. Patricelli (Eds.)
IOS Press, 2002

CHAPTER I
B2C: MAKING YOUR OWN E-COMMERCE SITE, STEP BY STEP

E-Commerce site is a way of selling products using electronic mediums, especially Internet, and it also includes business planning, analyzing customer profile, online payment, etc. The basic requirements and techniques for creating a web store or shopping mall will be shown in this chapter. We will also discuss the methods for completing credit card transactions and the security problems concerning them.

1.1. Introduction to E-commerce

E-Commerce is a part of E-business, computer-driven business and economy. Most of e-Commerce goes through the Internet. This is realized through World Wide Web (WWW), intranet, extranet, Virtual Private Network (VPN), Secure Socket Layer (SSL) encryption, etc.

The benefits of doing business over the Internet are:

- Today around 30 000 000 people are using Internet (this number is increasing), and they are all potential customers, so the market is virtually the whole world
- A number of countries and companies marginalized by their geographical position can move to the center of the virtual geography with e-commerce, and compete with the best situated companies based on the quality of their products and marketing
- The working hours of e-Commerce are 24 hours a day, 7 days a week, 365 days a year
- The costs are reduced: the running costs (room, electricity, salesmen) are no longer necessary, instead You need to pay for shopping cart software, web space, server, digital certificate (and this costs less).
- The information of the customers are more accessible, so You can make better customer profiles

For a successful e-Commerce You need to:

- Create an e-Commerce Site, usually a web store or a shopping mall, realized through shopping cart software
- Implement security systems for credit card processing by obtaining a digital certificate and using SSL
- Consider Planning and Marketing

1.1.1 Creating a Web Store

Web store is a place where you can exhibit and sell goods to the Internet users.

In order to have a Web store you need to:

a) Get an **Internet Merchant Bank Account** - this is an account that enables credit card transactions over the Internet, which is nowadays the basic payment method (and most often the only one) at the Web store. In the US, many banks offer the Internet Merchant Accounts, and in other countries it may be a problem. The solution is that, because in

Internet business you can have an account anywhere in the world, you can register in the country where banks support Internet Merchant Accounts. Remember that the regular merchant account takes up to a month to get through, and that your account must be able to handle 'Card Not Present' transactions.

b) Get **Web Hosting** (WWW domain) at an Internet Service Provider, in order to set and host the store. When choosing a Web hosting company you need to consider that they provide: upload stream as fast as possible; good technical support; fast server-side connection to the Internet; throughput proportional to number of customers (or otherwise it will seem slow to the customers); staff that is knowledgeable about e-commerce; classified statistics of access to your Web site

c) Find a **Provider of Online Transactions** - the go-between between the customer and merchant's bank. This is an additional security measure, which prevents the merchant from misusing the credit cards. The responsibility of credit card processing is entirely on the Provider of Online Transactions. When choosing this provider consider how many transactions do you expect to be completed in a month, how many products do you have to put on your web site, how complex does the software need to be, how much are you willing to spend. Most of them are situated in the US, so international merchants can get US merchant account, find a local Online Transaction Provider, or utilize one of the few companies that services the international market.

d) Develop or purchase **Shopping Cart Software** - a software that creates an e-Commerce site (You can also use catalog software or a flat order form, but they are very simple and with little options). Creating a Shopping Cart software is usually done with proper tools, or obtained from Online Transaction Providers that have shopping cart software offered along with their service. In general there are three types of Shopping Cart softwares: for small, medium and large businesses. Later in this chapter we will introduce in our opinion best tools for each type: Yahoo! Store (for small businesses), ecBuilder (for medium businesses) and Microsoft Commerce Server 2000 (for large businesses).

1.1.2 Obtaining a Digital Certificate

A digital certificate (SSL Server Certificate) enables Security Socket Layer SSL on the Web server. SSL prevents anyone unauthorized from obtaining or changing confidential information, such as credit card number.

Digital Certificate is in a way your digital ID: it guaranties on the Internet that you are who you say, and it also gives you a set of keys for encrypting data, so you can safely transmit them over the Internet. This transmission is done with SSL. Any e-commerce company will require you to have SSL before you can use their services. you can usually use the certificate owned by the Web hosting company where your page resides. You can obtain Your own Digital Certificate from: Verisign (http://www.verisign.com) or Thawte (http://www.thawte.com).

1.1.3 Credit Cards and Electronic Cash

Mostly purchasing over the Internet is done with the credit card. The consumer finds the merchants Web site, and decides to buy something. Then, he or she is moved to the Online Transaction Server, which contacts the bank.. Transaction (credit card billing) is passed through private gateway (SSL) to a CC Processing Network, where it is completed (or denied). If it is accepted, OTP transfers the customers money temporarily to a separate account. When the goods is delivered, Online Transaction Server transfers the money to the merchants account.

Electronic cash is the informational equivalent of physical banknotes and coins. It can offer anonymity to the buyer, global acceptance, etc. But it is still not developed enough, because it needs very efficient technical infrastructure and a large number of users. Some of the on-line electronic cash systems based on the digital bills are E–Cash (DigiCash firm) and NetCash.

1.1.4 Marketing and Planning

Here are some advices you may find useful: Submit your site to as many search engines as possible; Find Web sites with similar contence and make deals to create reciprocal links; Use advertising banners ; Put your URL in the signature file of your email and the header of all business correspondence; Use e-mail to contact people, tell as much people as you can about your business; Investigate the Web sites that are possible rivals; If you anticipate a lot of growth in the amount of orders coming through your site, be sure you can handle them.

1.2 Yahoo! Store

Yahoo! Store is a tool for building small e-commerce sites. You can access it at http://store.yahoo.com.

The advantages of using this tool are low cost for small stores, interface which is very easy to use, results are visible immediately, powerful support provided by other Yahoo! Services, statistics, customer ratings.

The disadvantages, on the other hand, are that you can't create original look of the e-commerce site because the sites are made from one template, company still needs its own server in order to use the most advanced capabilities of Yahoo! Store, such as custom functions for tax and shipment calculation, the options in design and trading are limited, the price of the product can only be in US dollars.

Before creating Yahoo! Store you need Yahoo ID and password (the same for all Yahoo services) and credit card.

There are three interfaces for editing the Yahoo! Store: Simple, Regular and Advanced, depending on the variety of options they offer and their complexity. The editing is done through changing the Variables like background color, font, button color, etc.

Each Yahoo! Store has the front page (where You find the name and description of the company), and on this main page there are links to the section pages, that represent different group of products. On each section page there are appropriate products that are being sold in this Store (and also the image of the product). When a customer clicks on the product, an item page is loaded, with the description and price of the product, and the order button, that enables the customer to buy the product. Some of the options you can use in Yahoo! Store are making one item special (showing it on the front page), selling accessories together with certain items, etc.

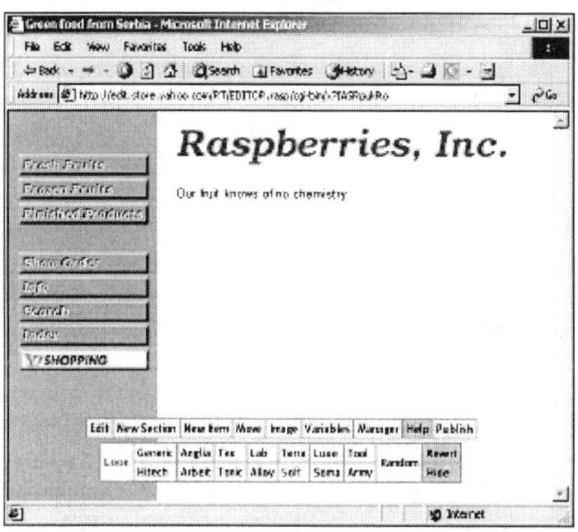

Figure 1.1 The example of Yahoo! Store

For more information refer to [Tutorial].

1.3 The ecBuilder

EcBuilder is a software package coming from MultiActive Software, Inc, designed for creating small and medium business sites. It has much more options than Yahoo! Store, including order processing, cataloging items, customer feedback, etc. It is based on embedded Java Script and Cookie technologies. The price of this package is 495$ (on January 1st, 2000), and there are no additional hardware or software demands.

You can find it at http://www.ecbuilder.com.

Security issues are provided through a special ecBuilder's server named ecPlace (independent from merchant's site and merchant's ISP), maintained by MultiActive, Inc. This is an interface with the Online Transaction Provider.

The creating of the site is done by following 16 steps in the wizard. They are Site Structure, Company Address, Site Builder Profile (person responsible for maintaining the site), Contact Person Profile (person responsible for handling the orders), Business Classification, Company Identity, Payment Methods (like credit card), Online Payment Processing (information on Your OTP), Catalog, Advertising and Statistics, Order and Inquiry Fields (customer feedback), Site Design and Preview, Security Options, Search Engines, and Upload Your Site.

The ecOrderDesk is one interesting application in ecBuilder, that allows user to track and manage the orders received from the ecBuilder Web site. EcOrderDesk supports three types of records: orders, item inquiries, and general inquiries.

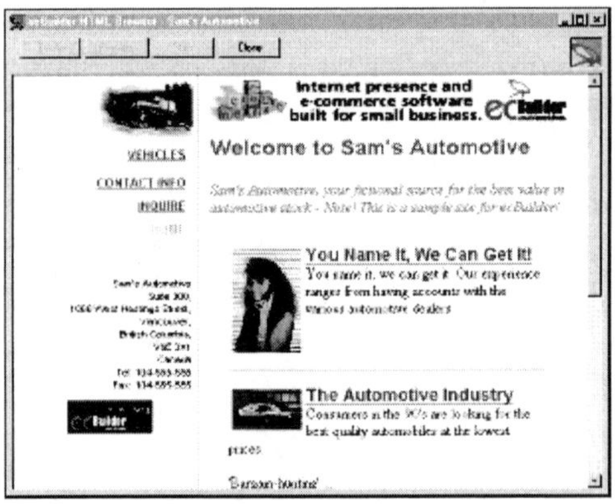

Figure 1.2 One possible look of the finished site

For more information refer to [Tutorial].

1.4 Secure Socket Layer (SSL)

This is one of the most widely accepted ways of protection of sensitive data while transferring from the customer to the server on which the store is situated. It is originating from Netscape Communications.

The basic idea behind the SSL protocol application is to insert a new level between HTTP and TCP communication software levels, which would encrypt the data. It consists of at least two layers, and those are: (1) SSL Handshake Protocol (provides an agreement during which the secret data needed for encryption and decryption keys and signature calculation are determined, based on the keys form the Digital Certificate), and (2) SSL Record Protocol (does the actual encryption and decryption of the sensitive data). This is done through various symmetrical and asymmetrical algorithms, such as DES and RSA.

1.5 Microsoft Site Server Commerce Edition

SSCE is a very effective tool for making complex e-commerce sites, and is intended for very large businesses, and can fulfill all of their demands. Most of the pages on one SSCE.Web site are ASP pages with the server side script that manipulates the set of COM (Component Object Model) objects, usually most of them coming from the SSCE package. Software uses these objects to collect information from the customer, to find and/or save information by using the ODBC/DAO queries and to process the tasks through the OPP.

The advantages of this package are obvious even from the basic concepts and tools inside Microsoft Site Server Commerce Edition 3.0 package: *Site Builder Wizard* with several finished sites provided as examples; *Dynamic Merchandising* is the support for the easy real-time product and prices catalog administration from any standard Web browser, using Promotion Wizard; **Order Processing Pipeline** (OPP) is the concept that serves all the operations in the background, as collecting the information needed for the product catalog, prices forming, tax calculation, etc, and writing them to another object called Order Form. OPP is the fundamental concept that stands behind the design and the work of e-commerce sites created using SSCE package; Integration with *Microsoft Transaction Server* (MTS); *Dynamical catalog creation*, *Rich Object Model* which comes inside SSCE provides a wide range of operations concerning processing the information about products, shoppers, and orders; *Direct Mailer*, a simple tool for creating the personalized TDEM (Target Directed e-mail Marketing) campaigns based on shopper profiles and their affinities; SSCE tools for the analyzing are creating the reports needed to analyze the customers traffic on the site.

Figure 1.3 Example of OPP: typical set of stages

For more information refer to [Tutorial].

1.6 Microsoft Commerce Server 2000

Microsoft Commerce Server 2000 builds on the Site Server 3.0 Commerce Edition, improving some issues, like tighter integration among the key systems, reduced development time, and greater business functionality. [Comparison]

Commerce Server is comprised of five systems: the Business Analytics System, the Product Catalog System, the Targeting System, the Profiling System, and the Business Process Pipelines System.

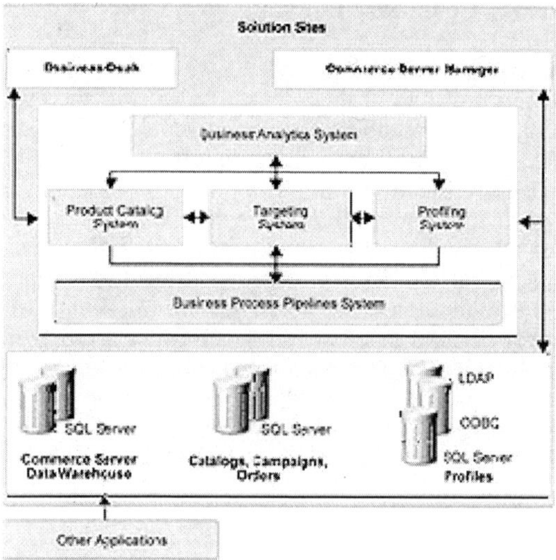

Figure 1.4 Commerce Server architecture

Commerce Server is designed to operate together with other Microsoft .NET Enterprise Servers. You can find out more at http://www.microsoft.com/commerceserver.

1.7 The Automatic Credit Card Payment Within the ASP Applications

One possible way to achieve the credit card payment is to use the ActiveX COM objects provided by the E-xact Transactions Ltd. E-xact serves as a Transaction Gateway Provider in this case. Find out more on www.E-xact.com. In general, five institutions must be involved to process transactions in this way: the customer with a credit card; merchant with an e-commerce site; Transaction Gateway Provider; merchant possesses an account at a bank, with the permission to accept credit card payments; There is an institution that has provided the customer with the credit card account, which is capable to authorize the credit cards and transactions.

1.8 Conclusion

Considering the constant growth of the use of Internet, it is logical to assume that in the future, a large percent of world wide business will be e-Business.

There are a lot of tools for making an e-Commerce site, and they all vary in their price, complexity and the variety of options they offer. The biggest problem is the security issues. Most security measures, as shown in this chapter, are very reliable, but there is still doubt among the customers.

REFERENCES

[Overview] "Commerce Server 2000 Resource Kit — Ch. 1, Overview and Scenarios," (http://www.microsoft.com), 20 December 2001

[CaseStudy] "Case Study — Starbucks Technical Deployment Guide," (http://www.microsoft.com),20 December 2001

[Tutorial] Milutinović, V., "Infrastructure for E-Business on the Internet," Copyright by Kluwer, 2001

CHAPTER 2
B2B

Mladenka Jakovljevic and Veljko Milutinović

At least two major research areas will affect the growth or nongrowth of the Internet businesses over the next three to five years:
- Wireless technology,
- Security.

Wireless Application Protocol (WAP) will help define information exchange over wireless and mobile links (promotes interoperability of wireless networks, devices, and applications by using a common set of applications and protocols).

2.1 Introduction

The most popular e-Commerce channel is the Internet. The Internet has become today's most important business platform, enabling connectivity to all your e-Business constituents — customers, partners, suppliers, and employees [CA01].

By 2004, Internet use will grow to over 700 million users. They will conduct over $2.6 trillion a year in commerce over the Net. That's over $4.9 million a minute, 24 hours a day, 7 days a week, 365 days a year.

2.1.1 Types of E-Commerce

There are two major types of e-Commerce:
- Business-to-consumer (B2C) - in which consumers purchase products and services from businesses,
- Business-to-business (B2B) - in which businesses buy and sell among themselves.

The key to a successful e-Business is high-availability of the network, servers, applications, and data. The e-Business challenge is twofold:
- Satisfy your customers better than your competitors can,
- Run a superior, technological infrastructure that can support, and enhance your e-Business potential.

The first generation of e-Business focused on navigation and speed. Next generation demands security, reliability, availability, and performance [Shim00].

2.1.2 Standards for E-Commerce Transactions

Business conduct e-Commerce transactions through standards such as Electronic Data Interchange (EDI) and the Extensible Markup Language (XML). EDI is the electronic exchange of structured documents between trading partners. Its primary goal is to minimize the cost, effort and time incurred by paper-based business transactions. EDI is complex and difficult to implement. It has required special proprietary software, but there are now moves to enable EDI data to travel inside XML [Shim00].

XML is a markup language for documents containing structured information. The XML specification defines a standard way to add markup to documents. XML was created so that richly structured documents could be used over the Web.

2.1.3 Top Ten Barriers

The top ten barriers to e-Commerce are: Security and encryption;

Trust and risk; Lack of qualified personnel; Lack of business models; Culture; User authentication and lack of public key Infrastructure; Organization; Fraud and risk of loss; Internet/Web is too slow and not dependable; Legal issues.

The most significant barrier to the growth of e-Commerce continues to be concerns about security [CA01].

2.1.4 Framework

A typical business depends on other businesses for several of the direct and indirect inputs to its end products. B2B e-Commerce automates and streamlines the process of buying and selling these intermediate products. It provides more reliable updating of business data. B2B makes product information available globally and updates it in real time. For procurement transactions, buyers and sellers can meet in an electronic marketplace and exchange information.

Market researchers predict that B2B transactions will amount to a few trillion dollars in the next few years, as compared to about 100 billion dollars' woryth of B2C transactions.

B2B involves engineering the interactions of diverse, complex enterprises. All services and resources on the Web are treated as business objects that can be combined in novel ways to build virtual companies, markets, and trading communities. A business can be viewed as a set of processes. A process can be anything from work order generation to human resources development. Company planners capture business processes in models and implement them as enterprise applications. The trend has been to include more and more outside entities such as customers and suppliers in process engineering.

The most popular frameworks for e-Business are:

- OBI; eCo; and RosettaNet.

2.1.5 What is Interoperability?

Interoperability is a key issue in B2B. Not dependent on specific hardware products or operating systems environments. Use of accepted standards enables accessibility and usability across different technology platforms.

"Interoperability" means the ability of separate systems to be linked together and then operate as if they were a single entity.

2.2 XML

Extensible Markup Language (XML) has been a subject of technical conversations for quite some time. XML was developed by an XML Working Group formed under the auspices of the World Wide Web Consortium (W3C) in 1996. XML is a markup language for documents containing structured information. A markup language is a mechanism to identify structures in a document. The XML specification defines a standard way to add markup to documents. XML was created so that richly structured documents could be used over the Web [XML98].

2.2.1 Why XML?

From a business perspective, XML technologies bring innovation and interoperability to the document authoring, indexing, and management processes. XML is a text-based metalanguage format for data exchange, it provides a pathway to transfer data easily between dissimilar applications and servers. The only viable alternatives, HTML and SGML, are not practical for this purpose. A simplified version of SGML, XML is a less complicated markup language framework that can be used to develop a customized solution to manage specific information.

Different from Hypertext Markup Language (HTML), XML encapsulates the structured data within a document, but does not include any code related to how the data should be displayed in the user interface. Based upon the simple concept of using tags to describe information so that the data can be easily accessed across any network and between dissimilar applications, XML is referred to as a metalanguage. XML is specifically focused on defining the content of a document, rather than how the data will look. Because of its ability to interoperate with a variety of systems, XML is supported by computing software and hardware companies such as Sun Microsystems, IBM, Oracle, and Microsoft.

Document content structured with XML can be delivered over the HTTP protocol as easily as HTML.

2.2.2 XML Will

Enable internationalized media-independent electronic publishing. Allow industries to define platform-independent protocols for the exchange of data, especially the data of electronic commerce. Deliver information to user agents in a form that allows automatic processing after receipt. Make it easier to develop software to handle specialized information distributed over the Web. Make it easy for people to process data using inexpensive software. Allow people to display information the way they want it, under style sheet control. Make it easier to provide metadata — data about information — that will help people find information and help information producers and consumers find each other.

2.2.3 The Design Goals

The design goals for XML are:

- XML shall be straightforwardly usable over the Internet.
- XML shall support a wide variety of applications.
- XML shall be compatible with SGML.
- It shall be easy to write programs which process XML documents.
- XML documents should be human-legible and reasonably clear.
- The XML design should be prepared quickly.
- The design of XML shall be formal and concise.
- XML documents shall be easy to create.
- Terseness in XML markup is of minimal importance.

2.2.4 Document-Type Definition

A DTD is specifying the structure of an XML file. It gives the names of the elements, attributes, and entities that can be used, and how they fit together. A DTD is a file (or several files to be used together), written in XML's Declaration Syntax, which contains a formal description of a particular type of document. XML allows designers to write their own document-type definition – DTD [Pitts00].

DTDs are rules that define which markup element can be used to describe the document. If you want to create your own markup you have to define it in DTD. There are thousands of XML DTDs already in existence in all kinds of areas. Many of them can be downloaded and used freely or you can write your own. Some DTDs:

- PGML (Precision Graphics Markup Language),
- CDF (Channel Definition Format),
- CML (Chemical Markup Language),
- OSD (Open Software Description).

2.2.4.1 DTD for HTML

HTML will become one more DTD in collection of XML vocabularys. Different specifications of HTML that W3C has publicated and some others elements and attributes that was established by Microsoft and Netscape are actually DTDs.

Example: You know that you have put text inside <b> and </b> if you want the text be bold. If you use <bold> and </bold> you don't get bold text.

These roules and many others are a part of DTD for HTML 4.0.

2.2.4.2 Logical and Physical Structure

Each XML document has both a logical and a physical structure. Physically, the document is composed of units called entities. Logically, the document is composed of declarations, elements, comments, character references, and processing instructions, all of which are indicated in the document by explicit markup.

An XML **element** is used to describe a concrete piece of data and may contain children text nodes and other element nodes. An element usually contains two different kinds of tag a start-tag and an end-tag, with text or more markup between them. XML lets you decide which elements you want in your document and then indicate your element boundaries using the appropriate start- and end-tags for those elements. Elements are deffined in DTDs and their markups are used to represent these elements in documents.

An XML **attribute**, however, is typically only used to further describe an element and does not contain children text nodes. Attributes are used to associate name-value pairs with elements. Attribute specifications may appear only within start-tags and empty-element tags.

2.2.4.3 DTD and Document

DTDs define markup that you use to describe content of your document. XML lets users to create their own DTD. In fact DTD is part of document evan if it is been in different file. DTDs and documents are one unit divided in two parts. XML document is divided because that two parts content different type of information, and each of them have different role to play.

DTD contents: Element declaration, Attribute-list declaration, Content model, Entity declaration

Basic document structure: Prolog, Document element, Elements, Attributes, Content, Comment, Processing instructions.

2.2.5 Example

In the next example I present you:

- **gallery.dtd** and **paintings.xml**

document used to catalogized all paintings in some gallery. In the Figure 2.1 you can see a content of gallery.dtd.

- PAINTING define painting record
- TITLE describe title of painting
- PAINTER define author of painting
- TECHNIQUE describe painting technique
- PRICE define price of painting
- RATING according to rank between one and five
- COMMENTS comment about painting

Figure 2.1. Gallery.dtd

In the Figure 2.2 you can see the first step in element declaration. EMPTY elements don't contain any text. They have attributes to describe content.

```
<!ELEMEN painting>
<!ELEMENT title>
<!ELEMENT painter>
<!ELEMENT technique EMPTY>
<!ELEMENT price>
<!ELEMENT rating EMPTY>
<!ELEMENT comments>
```

Figure 2.2. Element declaration

In the Figure 2.3 you can see attributes that we use to describe elements in this example.

TECHNIQUE: CLASS. Velues for the CLASS are oil, watercolor, crayon, and graphics.

RATING: NUMBER. Values for the NUMBER are 1, 2, 3, 4, and 5.

Figure 2.3. Attributes

In the Figure 2.4 you can see attribute-list declaration.

```
<!ATTLIST TECHNIQUE CLASS ( OIL | WATERCOLOR |
CRAYON | GRAPHICS ) "OIL" #REQUIRED>
<!ATTLIST RATING NUMBER ( 1| 2 | 3 | 4 | 5 ) "3" #REQUIRED>
```

Figure 2.4 Attribute-list declaration

All possible values of attributes are put between (and). They are separate with |. "OIL" and "3" go without saying. Labela #REQUIRED means that the attribute is required every time when element is used in the document.

2.2.5.1 Element Content

An element type has **element content** when elements of that type must contain only child elements (no character data), optionally separated by white space (characters matching the nonterminal).

There are tree types of content in XML:

- Data content - text characters (#PCDATA),
- Element content - contain some other elements and describe the way they come,
- Mixted content - contain both text and elements.

In the Figure 2.5 you can see parent-child element.

PAINTING
- title
- painter
- technique
- price
- rating
- comments

Figure 2.5. Parent-child element

In Figure 2.6 you can see how the new element declaration looks.

```
<!ELEMENT painting ( title, painter, technique, price, rating,
comments?)>
<!ELEMENT title (#PCDATA)>
<!ELEMENT painter (#PCDATA)>
<!ELEMENT technique EMPTY>
<!ELEMENT price (#PCDATA)>
<!ELEMENT rating EMPTY>
<!ELEMENT comments (#PCDATA)>
```

Figure 2.6. Element declaration

Elements title, painter, technique, price, rating have to be inside painting element in that order. Element comment can be skiped because it is marked with (?).

In Figure 2.7 you can see the finale product gallery.dtd.

```
<!ELEMENT painting ( title, painter, technique, price, rating,
comments?)>
<!ELEMENT title (#PCDATA)>
<!ELEMENT painter (#PCDATA)>
<!ELEMENT technique EMPTY>
<!ATTLIST TECHNIQUE CLASS ( OIL | WATERCOLOR |
CRAYON | GRAPHICS ) "OIL" #REQUIRED>
<!ELEMENT price (#PCDATA)>
<!ELEMENT rating EMPTY>
<!ATTLIST RATING NUMBER ( 1| 2 | 3 | 4 | 5 ) "3" #REQUIRED>
```

Figure 2.7. Gallery.dtd

2.2.5.2 Prolog

Prolog contains all relevant informations about the document and it is not part of content or markup. Prolog contains XML declaration, document-type declaration, and processing instructions.

XML documents should begin with an **XML declaration** which

specifies the version of XML are used and tells application which process document to process just document or to process both document and DTD.

In Figure 2.8. you can see how common XML declaration looks.

```
<?XML VERSION="1.0" RMD= "ALL" ?>
```

a) (?)- this is processing instruction;

b) RMD (Required Markup Declaration);

- ALL - all DTDs have to be processed together with document;
- INTERNAL - just internal DTD has to be processed;
- NONE - none of the DTDs have to be processed;

Figure 2.8. XML declaration

2.2.5.3 Internal DTD

You can add DTD that you made for your document inside of the document, but be vary careful. This internal subset of DTD is usefull because you can identificate entities which are unique for that document. When you want to use DTD just for one document you can put it in your document (now you can use that DTD only in that document!). If you put DTD in separate file you can use it in as many documents as you want.

In Figure 2.9 you can see document-type declaration for **paintings.xml** document.

<!DOCTYPE gallery SYSTEM “gallery.dtd”>

a) <!DOCTYPE - declaration of document’s type begines with this;
b) gallery – document-element name;
c) SYSTEM - DTD is placed somewhere in computer system and its name is gallery.dtd.

Figure 2.9 Document-type declaration

In Figure 2.10 you can see how document looks when DTD is a part of the document.

```
<!DOCTYPE gallery [
<!ELEMENT painting ( title, painter, technique, price, rating,
comments?)>
<!ELEMENT title (#PCDATA)>
<!ELEMENT painter (#PCDATA)>
<!ELEMENT technique EMPTY>
<!ATTLIST TECHNIQUE CLASS ( OIL | WATERCOLOR |
CRAYON | GRAPHICS ) “OIL” #REQUIRED>
<!ELEMENT price (#PCDATA)>
<!ELEMENT rating EMPTY>
<!ATTLIST RATING NUMBER ( 1| 2 | 3 | 4 | 5 ) “3” #REQUIRED>
<!ELEMENT comments (#PCDATA)>
]>
```

Figure 2.10 Paintings.xml document

2.2.5.4 Processing Instruction

Processing instructions (PIs) allow documents to contain instructions for applications. XML declaration is actualy the PI. PIs begin with <? and end with ?>. You can use PI in any place in the document but most offen in prolog.

Document element defined in internal DTD has top priority. That element is presumed to be the ‘root’ element, which encloses everything else in the document, solt contents all other elements.

In Figure 2.11 you can see document element for paintings.xml.

```
<GALLERY>...</GALLERY>
```

Figure 2.11 Document element

Elements are main components of the markup language and they are defined in DTD. Elements appear in the document like markups. Non-empty elements are made up of a start-tag, the element's content, and an end-tag.

Empty elements are a special case that may be represented either as a pair of start- and end-tags with nothing between them or as a single empty element tag that has a closing slash to tell the parser 'don't go looking for an end-tag to match this.

EMPTY elements are used to insert entities in document — like IMG in HTML.

In Figure 2.12 you can see code that describe painting in paintings.xml document using gallery.dtd.

```
<PAINTING>
        <TITLE>Smoking</TITLE>
        <PAINTER>Drasko Klikovac</PAINTER>
        <TECHNIQUE CLASS="CRAYON" />
        <PRICE>???</PRICE>
        <RATING NUMBER="5" />
        </COMMENTS>
</PAINTING>
```

Figure 2.12 Description of the painting

```
        <TECHNIQUE>
        <CLASS>Oil</CLASS>
        </TECHNIQUE>

        <RATING>
        <NUMBER>5</NUMBER>
        </RATING>
```

Figure 2.13 Element definition

Attributes give you more informations about element. Instead of the attributes we can use elements. In that case we have to define two more elements in our example: CLASS and NUMBER and you can see these definition in Figure 2.13.

In Figure 2.14 you can see the final product paintings.xml document.

```
<?XML VERSION="1.0"' RMD= "ALL" ?>
<!DOCTYPE gallery SYSTEM "gallery.dtd">
<GALLERY>
<PAINTING>
<TITLE>Smoking</TITLE>
                <PAINTER>Drasko Klikovac</PAINTER>
        <TECHNIQUE CLASS="CRAYON" />
        <PRICE>???</PRICE>
        <RATING NUMBER="5" />
        </COMMENTS>
</PAINTING>
</GALLERY>
```

Figure 2.14 Paintings.xml

2.2.6 Well-Formed and Valid XML Document

All XML documents must be well-formed:

- If there is no DTD in use, the document should start with a Standalone Document Declaration (SDD) saying so: <?xml version="1.0" standalone="yes"?>
- All tags must be balanced: that is, all elements which may contain character data must have both start- and end-tags present (omission is not allowed except for empty elements).
- All attribute values must be in quotes.
- Any EMPTY element tags (*eg* those with no end-tag like HTML's <IMG>, <HR>, and <BR> and others) must either end with '/>' or you have to make them appear non-EMPTY by adding a real end-tag.
  Example:
 would become either <BR/> or
</BR>.
- There must not be any isolated markup-start characters (< or &) in your text data.
- Elements must nest inside each other properly, well-formed documents with no DTD may use attributes on any element, but the attributes are assumed to be all of type CDATA.

An XML document is **valid** if it has an associated document type declaration and if the document complies with the constraints expressed in it. They must already be well-formed [XML98].

2.2.7 Xlink and Xpointer

The linking abilities of XML systems are much more powerful than those of HTML. Existing HREF-style links will remain usable, but the new linking technology is involving hypertex which let you manage bidirectional and multi-way links, as well as links to a span of text (within your own or other documents) rather than to a single point.

An XPointer is always preceded by one of #, ?, or |. The # and ? mean the same as in HTML applications. The | means the sub-resource can be found by applying the XPointer to the resource, but the method of doing this is left to the application.

2.2.8 XML Processor

A software module called an **XML processor** is used to read XML documents and provide access to their content and structure. It is assumed that an XML processor is doing its work on behalf of another module, called the **application**.

2.2.9 XSL

XSL is a stylesheet language for XML. Working in conjunction with XML, Extensible Style Language (XSL) is a generic XML-to-XML transformation language that is also expressed in XML. XSL is used to convert an XML file into well-formed HTML, potentially with cascading style sheet decorations. Figure 2.15 shows that transformation.

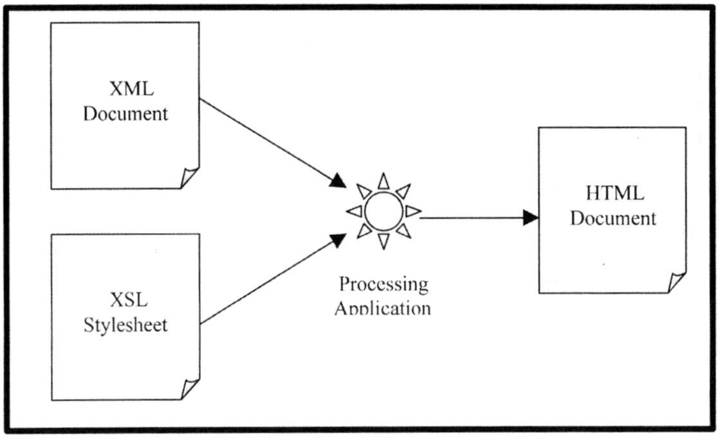

Figure 2.15 Using XML with XSL

The resulting output can then be displayed within a browser interface. This extensible presentation method is one of the keys to the interest in XML technologies because it only requires a change to the XSL template to revise the presentation of all XML documents using that template. XSL can also present information in an order different from how it is stored and can perform other data manipulation transformations prior to display.

Microsoft Internet Explorer 5.0 contains the ability to parse XML documents. Microsoft Office 2000 uses XML embedded within HTML files to store information that cannot otherwise be held in HTML, such as a document's properties. In addition, with native XML support planned for Microsoft SQL Server 7.5, additional XML features, such a improved search capabilities and content categorization, should be widely available in the new millennium.

The publicly-released Netscape code (**Mozilla**) and the almost indistinguishable Netscape6 have extensive XML support, based on James Clark's **expat** xml parser. The Opera browser now supports XML, CSS, and XSL on MS-Windows and Linux and is the most complete implementation so far. The browser size is tiny by comparison with the others, but features are good and the speed is excellent.

2.3 OBI

The OBI standard is an open design for business-to-business Internet commerce solutions. OBI is not a product or a service. It is a freely available standard which any organization can obtain and use. It is a freely available design, a framework, for business-to-business Internet commerce solutions [OBI01].

The standard contain an architecture, detailed technical specifications and guidelines, and compliance and implementation information. Copies of the standard may be obtained through the OBI Consortium's World Wide Web site at www.openbuy.org.

2.3.1 OBI Architecture

Buying organizations are responsible for:

- Requisitioner profile information,
- Account codes,
- Tax status, and

- Approvals.

Selling organizations are responsible for:

- Electronic catalogs and the associated price,
- Order entry, and
- Inventory mechanisms.

2.3.2 OBI Transaction Flow

In the Figure 2.16 you can see the OBI transaction flow.

1. The requisitioner is the person who actually places the order. The requisitioner is affiliated with a Buying Organization. Requisitioner views Home Page on Purchasing Server.

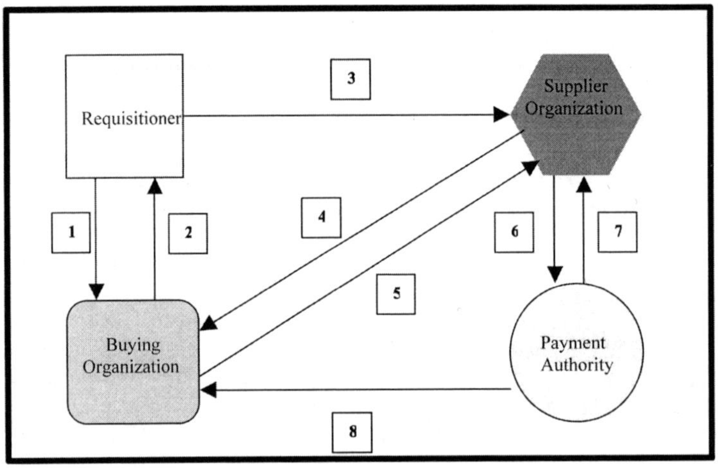

Figure 2.16 Transaction flow

2. Requisitioner obtains link to the Supplier Merchant Server on-line catalog with desired goods. Buying Organization checks relevant informations about Requisitioner.

3. After assurance that Requisitioner is from Buying Organization, Requisitioner browses catalog, selects items, and confirms order contents.

4. If requisitioner places order, supplier transmits OBI order-request securely to buying organization server for added information and approval.

5. Administrative information is added, requisitioner completes order form, order is "approved", and completed order is returned securely to Supplier.

6. Supplier authorizes transaction with the appropriate payment authority.

7. Order enters Supplier's fulfillment process and is delivered to Requisitioner.

8. Buying organization receives billing statement and generates check.

2.3.3 Requisitioner

The requisitioner represents the end-user of the system. The requisitioner is affiliated with a buying organization. The requisitioner is assumed to have access to a desktop machine, with a World Wide Web browser and a corporate Intranet and the Internet. The requisitioner also has a digital certificate, issued by a trusted certificate authority.

2.3.4 Buying Organization

The buying organization represents the purchasing management and the information systems which support purchasing. These include systems for handling the requisitioner profile information, trading partner information, workflow, approvals, account, and tax status information necessary to complete an order. These systems include an OBI server for receiving OBI Order Requests and returning OBI Orders.

OBI Order Request - partially completed electronic order that is sent from supplier to buying organization for completion and approval after requisitioner selects items and "checks out".

OBI Order - order that is sent from the buying organization to supplier after administrative information is added and order is processed and approved.

The buying organization also negotiates and maintains contractual relationships with preferred selling organizations.

2.3.5 Selling Organization

The selling organization maintains a dynamic electronic catalog that presents accurate product and price information. Product and price information reflects the contract with a buying organization.

The selling organization's catalog must be integrated effectively with inventory and order management systems. It also must be integrated with an OBI server for sending OBI Order Requests and receiving OBI Orders. Selling organizations must be able to authorize certain transaction types with the appropriate payment authority.

2.3.6 Payment Authorities

Payment authorities provide authorization for the payment vehicle presented by the requisitioner. Payment authorities must provide payments to selling organizations and a timely invoice to the buying organization. Payment authorities may include a variety of financial institutions. The OBI standard is intended to support a variety of payment vehicles.

2.3.7 Security

The OBI standard includes precise technical specifications for security, transport, and contents of OBI Order Requests and OBI Orders. The OBI standard uses the SSL (Secure Sockets Layer) protocol to secure communications on the Internet.

Digital certificates based on the ITU-T's X.509v3 standard (the most popular form of digital certificate) are used for authentication of requisitioners as well as servers.

Digital signatures can be applied to OBI Order Requests and OBI Orders to provide high levels of assurance of the identity of the originator of an order, as well as order integrity. Exchange of OBI Order Requests and OBI Orders is accomplished via HTTP over SSL. Within OBI, HTTP is also used for transmission of order documents between servers. Contents of OBI Order Requests and OBI Orders are based on the ANSI ASC X.12's 850, a standard for an EDI purchase Order.

2.4 eCo Framework

The eCo Specification is an architectural framework that enables businesses to discover each other on the World Wide Web and determine how they can do business. The idea behind the eCo Framework architecture is that it lets marketmakers on the Internet create markets, within which businesses offer services to one another by exchanging documents [eCo99].

2.4.1 Architectural Model

This architectural model is intended to provide a common basis for two parties to negotiate an understanding of how they will do business. The details of how their systems are implemented "behind the scenes" are up to them. Business communities and marketplaces can be expected to adopt specific interfaces and protocols for conducting business.

eCo is a XML based , object-oriented interoperability framework. In that framework all services and resources on the Web are treated as business objects. That objects can be combined in novel ways to build virtual companies, markets, and trading communities.

eCo will enable innovative commerce services that use software agents to compare, aggregate, integrate, and translate data in Web documents, databases, and applications.

Future eCo market places will feature multiple sellers or sources of products and services and, on the other side, many buyers that want to compare these products, their prices and alternatives in order to make the best purchase decision.

Sources will include multiple types of product content from multiple seller sources. The seller sources are made up of multiple database types with multiple data constructs and data libraries.

2.4.2 Agents

The most obvious impact will come from smart shopping agents, which will level the playing field in their dealings with merchants. Intelligent Business Registries are a source for product, service, location or process context. These agents will be able to locate sources for specific products, services or processes using Business Registries. They can then query them in parallel to locate the best deals or relationships.

Most merchant sites will provide agent-searchable catalogs that can supply product descriptions, as well as information about price and availability. Some merchants will also provide sales agents that can negotiate with shopping agents and generate customized offers in response to their solicitations.

The shopping agent can then prioritize the offers it receives according to criteria set forth by its owner, e.g., the cheapest flight, the most convenient departure time, the roomiest aircraft, and so on.

2.4.3 Commerce Net's eCo Framework

The primary focus of CommerceNet's eCo Framework Project is to demonstrate the value of the integration of three common component-based electronic commerce services. These services are:

- Semantic integration of multiple database types with multiple data constructs and data libraries,
- Trusted open registries, and
- Agent-mediated buying.

The central problem faced when considering e-Commerce interoperability stems from the wide variety of way in which e-Commerce is carried out.

A business only needs to spend an hour to fill out and post an information document on its website to become Business Level Compliant. Others can then access this document and discover how to conduct business together.

With full eCo compliance, a prospective trading partner can learn all that is required to interoperate with an organization in almost any market environment by examining the eCo documents on its website.

The purpose of this specification is to:

- Define a conceptual architecture through which information on e-Commerce systems can be communicated,
- Define a method of querying that information,

- Define the structure that will be used to return that information.

There is a basic requirement that trading partners be able to:

- Discover other businesses on the Internet,
- Determine whether they want to do business and how they can participate within a market,
- Determine what Services are provided and consumed by other businesses,
- Determine the underlying interactions and the documents and information used by interactions,
- Determine if and how their e-Commerce systems can communicate,
- Determine what modifications need to be implemented to ensure interoperability between their systems,
- Establish communications through other channels than the Internet.

Through the conceptual framework defined by the eCo Architecture, businesses can define, publish, and exchange meta-data descriptions on their e-Commerce systems. The goal of this meta-data is to:

- Allow interested parties to gain an understanding of the various aspects of the e-Commerce system being represented,
- Provide the information needed to satisfy the above requirements and enable interoperability.

In order for this exchange of meta-data to occur between two interested parties, they need to:

- Share a common understanding of the basic components that make up an e-Commerce environment, and
- How those components relate,
- Have a common way of exposing information about of each of these components.

The organizer of the community will be the "market maker" for a particular market-space. These are community-focused markets. Data types and agent-mediated open registries are semantic integrated. They will serve as the basis for the development and operation of these markets.

2.4.4 eCo Specification

The eCo **Architectural Specification** presents information about an e-Commerce system in 6 layers.

The eCo **Semantic Specification** provides a sample set of business documents that can be used inside the eCo framework. They can be used as-is, or extended and modified to meet specific needs. Their use is not mandatory.

Each layer presents information about itself. By examining this information, others can:

- Locate the system understand what it is for,
- Recognize what market(s) it participates in,
- Identify protocols the system uses to communicate,
- Discover what documents the system uses to conduct business,
- Learn how to interoperate with the system.

2.4.5 Architectural Layers

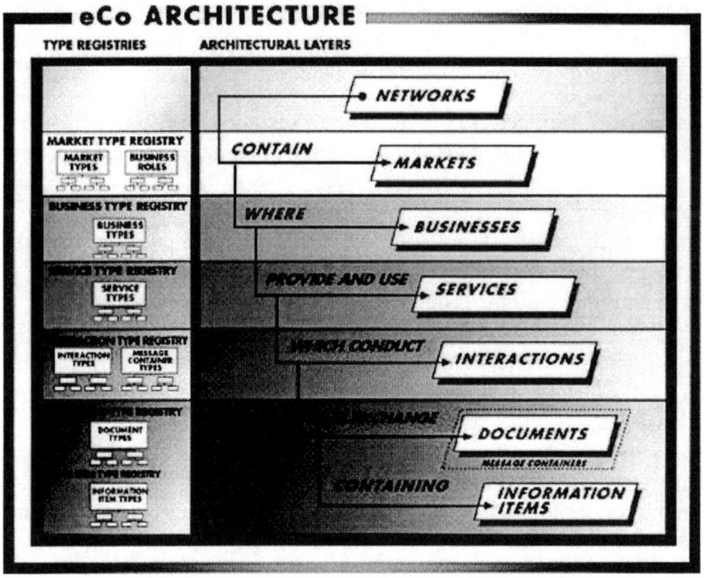

Figure 2.17 Architectural layers

Each layer relates to the next layer in a defined way. Information or properties of each layer are described separately through various "Type Registries" associated with each layer of the Architecture. Each layer, and its Registries, are intended to provide some aspect of information about the electronic commerce environment and enable an interested party to obtain information at each layer to potentially use offerred services, or join the marketplace and either provide new services, or interoperate as a trading partner with other businesses in that marketplace. The typical topology is demonstrated in Figure 2.17.

2.4.5.1 Networks

The topmost layer, the **Network**, represents one or more physical networks (e.g. Internet) in which electronic commerce systems can exist. These "Networks" will contain various marketplaces, or "Markets," for providing or obtaining specific goods and services. The network operator may choose to organize the network according to any principle appropriate to the purpose of that network.

For example, the network could be an index of markets in a specific ontology, much as the popular search engines index Web sites.

2.4.5.2 Businesses

Each "Market" in the Network may be independent, and may have its own rules, procedures, and protocols for participation within that Market. Markets themselves are made up of one or more businesses that are described by the **"Businesses"** layer of the eCo Architecture.

For example, this layer might identify the type of business, its location, Web page, and other business-related information. Any one business may participate in multiple markets. Any activities or functions within the business could participate in a market dedicated to satisfying the needs of those activities. These markets could be specific to one business or could be operated among multiple businesses.

For example, a business might wish to make a market for all of the companies that participate in its supply chain. That same business could participate in third party supply chain markets for the specific vertical industry of that business.

2.4.5.3 Services

The next layer of the eCo Architecture, the **"Services"** layer, enables each business to describe the types of business services offerred, their interfaces, and other information needed to use a particular service offerring.

That could include catalog browsing, ordering products, making payment, checking order status, product life cycle, new product introduction and so on. The interface for each business service offered would be described by the "Services" layer of the Architecuture.

2.4.5.4 Interactions

Relationships among services are described in the **"Interactions"** layer, and are normally hidden from the service-user. In one sense, this layer describes a "choreography" of interactions that may take place when a service is invoked. The exact sequence of events in this choreography may be pre-determined, or it may be event-driven by the user's selection of specific options offered by the service.

This layer is used to describe the types of interactions behind each service, and the types of messages which are exchanged during each interaction.

2.4.5.5 Documents

Each message may contain one or more types of documents or information needed during that interaction. The document types exchanged in an interaction are described by the **"Documents"** layer of the eCo Architecture.

A business may define their own data elements and documents. A business could also use the data elements and documents that have been defined by a third party.

2.4.5.6 Information Items

Finally, the **"Information Items"** layer of the eCo Architecture describes the type of information items (e.g. data elements and attributes) comprising each type of document used by an interaction.

2.4.6 Querying

The eCo Architecture further defines interfaces for querying or accessing the set of information or properties described at each Layer. By querying a Layer's published information and examining its property set, an interested party can obtain information about that Layer, and determine enough information about the Layer to interoperate with it.

By examining all the Layers implemented by a fully eCo compliant system, a trading partner can determine all the necessary information needed to interact with that system.

2.4.7 Type Registries

The eCo Architecture defines a set of Type Registries associated with each Layer of the Architecture that are used to establish type information describing the various document and element type components in an e-commerce system.

Each Registry can provide information on one or more specific sets of types appropriate to that Registry. For example, the Business Registry provides a set of type definitions required by the Business Layer, and so on. Using Type Registries, it is possible to determine the equivalency of two types that are defined within the same Registry, retrieve the definition of a type, and determine the relationships that exist between types.

Each Registry exposes a Published Interface in much the same way as the eCo Layers do. These Published Interfaces allow the Registry to be queried for information. eCo confines the scope of its Registry Interfaces to the retrieval of type information.

2.4.8 eCo Architecture Relationships

In the Figure 2.18, two companies are represented as eCo Businesses (implementations of the eCo Business Layer). These Businesses exist together in an eCo Market that provides a venue for the type of e-Commerce that they are conducting.

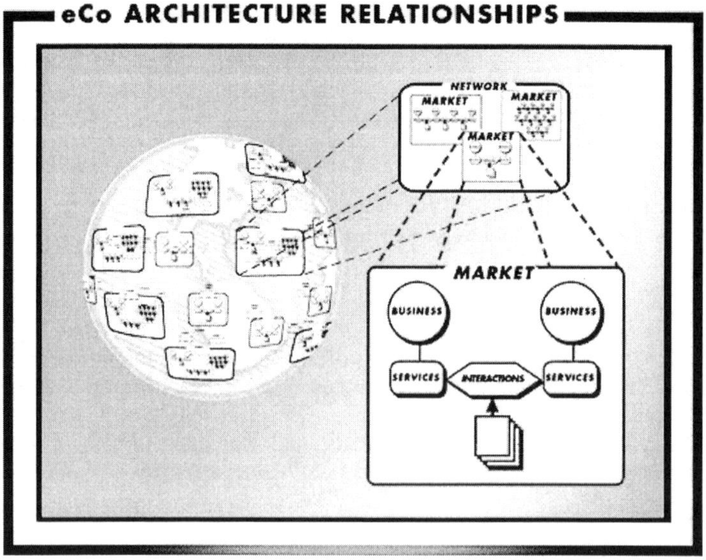

Figure 2.18 eCo architecture relationships

The eCo Market is indexed within a Network of Markets so that it can be located on the Internet. Each of these Businesses offers a set of e-Commerce "Services" to each other. Each Service represents an interface to a business process. A Service is composed of a set of document exchanges. We call these exchanges "Interactions". An Interaction occurs when a request is sent from one Business to another and a response is received. The Documents that are exchanged as part of any Interaction consist of discrete elements of information. These "Information Elements" are the building blocks from which Documents are composed.

2.4.9 Registry Schemas

Registry schemas and data elements will be based on a set of XML-based Commerce Libraries. These registries will allow sellers to register their products/services and authenticate themselves and their service policies. Their products will be accurately compared with those of other sellers. Buyers will be able to register their preferences, profiles, and authorization boundaries privately.

XML-Based Commerce Libraries should consist of information models for generic business concepts including:

- Business description primitives like companies, services, and products,
- Business forms like catalogs, purchase orders, and invoices,
- Standard measurements, date and time, location,
- Classification codes.

This information should be represented as an extensible, public set of XML building blocks that companies can customize and assemble to develop XML applications quickly.

2.4.10 Published Interface

The mechanism that is used to query a Published Interface is a simple URL based protocol. Each Published Interface is identified by a unique URI. This URI can be resolved to a "Base URL" for that Interface.

The response to any query is always in the form of an XML document that is formatted in accordance with a pre-defined Document Type Definition (DTD). This method was chosen to minimize the need for server-side scripting.

The Published Interface offered by a Layer can be extended to include queries over and above the base set defined by this document. In order for an interested party to discover what queries are available through a given Interface a "QueryInterface" query is defined at each Layer. The names of all Interface Extension queries must begin with an underscore character ('_').

In order to inform a casual visitor that a given Web site is host to an eCo Published Interface, the owner of that site may optionally place a document called "eco.xml" (case sensitive) at the root level of the site. This document should be structured in accordance with the eCoInterfaceList DTD. With this information, the search engine could then proceed to index the Business on its eCo Properties.

2.5 RosettaNet Framework

RosettaNet is an independent, self-funded, non-profit consortium of major Information Technology (IT), Electronic Components (EC), and Semiconductor Manufacturing (SM) vendors. A pioneer to the field of XML based open business-to-business e-Commerce standards [RosettaNet99].

RosettaNet normalizes and specifies the common business processes between trading partners (known as PIPs), and an open and interoperable protocol for the networked applications that execute the business processes.

RosettaNet standardization efforts can be divided into three broad groups:

- RosettaNet Dictionaries,
- RosettaNet PIPs,
- RosettaNet Implementation Framework.

2.5.1 RosettaNet Dictionaries

RosettaNet dictionaries define common set of properties for use by the business process (PIP) specifications and associated business documents and guidelines.

RosettaNet dictionaries are classified as Business Dictionaries and Technical Dictionaries.

The RosettaNet Business Dictionary designates the properties for defining business transactions between trading partners. These are:

- Business Properties (e.g. business address),
- Business Data Entities (e.g. ActionIdentity) and
- Fundamental Business Data Entities (e.g. BusinessTaxIdentifier, AccountNumber) etc.

There is only one business dictionary that encompasses all supply chains (EC, IT etc). Technical dictionary defines properties for products, components, and services that span the EC, IT and other supply chains. Formerly distinct EC Technical Dictionary and the IT Technical Dictionary are now integrated into the RosettaNet Technical Dictionary.

2.5.2 Partner Interface Processes

RosettaNet Partner Interface Processes™ (PIPs™) define the specific sequence of steps required to execute a business processes between supply-chain partners. Examples of such processes include purchase order management and distribution of new product information. RosettaNet PIP specification includes specification of structure and content format of the business documents exchanged (XML DTDs and guidelines) and the time, security, authentication and performance constraints on these interactions.

Specification of the PIPs is limited to publicly visible interactions and interfaces between the trading partners.

Hence these are also referred to as the public processes. Private processes are business processes within an enterprise that trigger the execution or are triggered by the execution of the public processes or the PIPs. Each PIP specification includes a business document with the vocabulary. A business process with the choreography of the message dialog is included. PIPs apply to the following core processes:

- Administration,
- Partner, Product and Service Review,
- Product Introduction,
- Order Management,
- Inventory Management,
- Marketing Information Management,
- Service and Support, and
- Manufacturing.

The RosettaNet PIP architecture comprises two fundamental parts:

- **A business process model**. This model captures business roles and their interactive functional activities, the information that is exchanged when performing these interactive activities, and the sequence in which these interactions take place.
- **A distributed information system design**. This design specifies the agent and service software components and information exchange and message protocols.

RosettaNet distributes PIPs to the trading partners, who use these guidelines as a road map to develop their software applications. By following the PIP, two different organizations in the supply chain can standardize their interfaces and extend them over an existing framework. RosettaNet developed its framework by adopting existing standards wherever possible.

2.5.3 Implementation Framework

The RosettaNet Implementation Framework or RNIF required to execute business processes between the trading partners, in an open, interoperable, secure, and platform&implementation independent way. RNIF defines:

- The RosettaNet business message format for exchange of the business documents,
- Elements to support authentication, authorization, encryption and non-repudiation,
- Details of the bindings for the transfer protocols (e.g. HTTP), and
- The specification for a reliable exchange of messages between partners.

2.6 Solutions

For procurement transactions, buyers and sellers can meet in an electronic marketplace and exchange information. This is the most advanced and efficient form of B2B. The marketplaces are build on:

- A common Internet platform,
- WWW browsers,
- Advanced security technologies,
- The latest payment systems, and
- Experience from other approaches.

There are two solutions that will be represented in this chapter, and they are:

- Commerce One and
- TIBCO.

2.6.1 Commerce One

Commerce One has developed two distinct e-Marketplace solutions: **MarketSet™** and **Net Market Maker™**. They share the robust infrastructure of the **MarketSite™** operating environment [CommerceOne01].

2.6.1.1 MarketSite

MarketSite provides the operating environment needed to connect buyers, suppliers, and service providers. It supports e-Marketplace interoperability.

MarketSite is the core technology at the center of all complete Commerce One e-Marketplace solutions. It can power the largest public e-Marketplace. It is flexible enough to adapt to the individual business needs of a private e-Marketplace. You can create a powerful e-Marketplace for service-based companies such as banks, retailers, and telecommunications providers.

The Commerce One MarketSite™ has three major components:

- MarketSite Transaction Platform,
- MarketSite Builder, and
- MarketSite Business Services Framework.

MarketSite Transaction Platform provides messaging, routing, addressing, transaction, security, connectivity, components, and services required to create business-to-business e-Marketplace.

MarketSite Builder gives you the tools to create, maintain, and scale your online community. It enables you to create your own branded marketplace, register and manage users, and target content and services to those users.

MarketSite Business Services Framework is a set of services, interfaces, tools, methodologies, and documentation that makes it easy to integrate complementary business applications and services.

2.6.1.2 MarketSet

MarketSet allows trading partners to:

- Get efficiencies throughout the entire procurement process,
- Connect to more markets and sources,
- Cut procurement cycle times,
- Reduce supply chain costs,
- Reduce inventory buffers,

- Extend existing enterprise capabilities,
- Decrease time-to-market.

MarketSet provides a set of services:

- Auction Services,
- Content Services,
- Procurement Services,
- Order Management Services,
- Planning Services,
- Design Services, and
- Analysis Services.

Every business cycle through these critical processes as part of the supply chain - from design through delivery. The operating environment and business applications that make up MarketSet streamline the entire supply chain by transforming these linear processes into parallel processes.

2.6.1.3 Net Market Maker Solution

Net Market Maker Solution is a solution that will help your e-Marketplace:

- Achieve the fastest time to market,
- Create unique branding that sets your e-Marketplace apart from the rest,
- Generate multiple revenue streams through value added services,
- Leverage expertise and resources from the Commerce One Global Trading Web™.

Transaction services are the core technologies that support e-Marketplace-based transactions. On a basic level, these technologies include all the hardware and software necessary to check pricing and availability, issue purchase orders, track fulfillment, and present bills.

On a more advanced level, these technologies include localization (financing or taxes, for example).

The best business decisions are based on more complete information. The best e-Marketplaces are the ones that provide that additional information. Information services can be divided into two categories:

- Catalog and
- Editorial content.

Catalog content is a list of products and services provided by the Web site's subscribing suppliers.

Editorial content consists of information that adds value to the trading community. Editorial content can include analyst articles, business trends, and summaries of leading business indicators.

2.6.1.4 Auction Services

Commerce One Auction Services are based on an Applications Service Provider (ASP) model. Commerce One Auction Services offers international language, multi-currency, and local time zone support for multinational e-Commerce.

B2B Portals such as Commerce One.net allow you to dynamically establish new trading relationships with trading partners worldwide in a trusted and secure online environment.

Auction Services give corporations full control of their B2B Internet auctions. The standard implementation time is less than two weeks and once the system is in place, it takes auction originators just a few minutes to set up any auction. The browser-based, point and click system is user-friendly and easy-to-understand for both the auction originator and bidder.

Bidders can use multi-variable bidding, multi-level bidding, quick-bidding, and proxy bidding for a dynamic bidding environment.

The conditions are determined by the auction originator before the start of an auction. Auctions can be customized with attachments in multiple formats graphics (such as EPS, JPEG), multimedia files (such as MPEG, AVI), or documents (such as Excel, Word, or Word Perfect).

Commerce One also supports the most popular auction formats, including English, Yankee, Dutch, and Sealed Bids. Originators may generate reports on open, paused, closed, or deleted auctions.

There are three modules in the system and they are:

- Administrator,
- Originator, and
- Bidder.

They are all browser based.

Commerce One.net is enabling to conduct business across e- Marketplaces. It supports trade between buyers and suppliers across multiple e-Marketplaces and it is open to any application and technology standard.

2.6.2 TIBCO

To achieve real-time B2B integration, businesses have to realize two types of requirements: **human interactions** and **system-to-system interactions**. To setisfay the first requirement business must has a portal, through which a partner can access all the content and application services that they need to execute their jobs. To satisfy the second requirement business must has a technical infrastructure that allows the partners applications to talk to its applications [TIBCO01].

2.6.2.1 Product Lines

TIBCO's three product lines are:

- **TIBCO ActiveEnterprise®**,
- **TIBCO ActiveExchange**, and
- **TIBCO ActivePortal**.

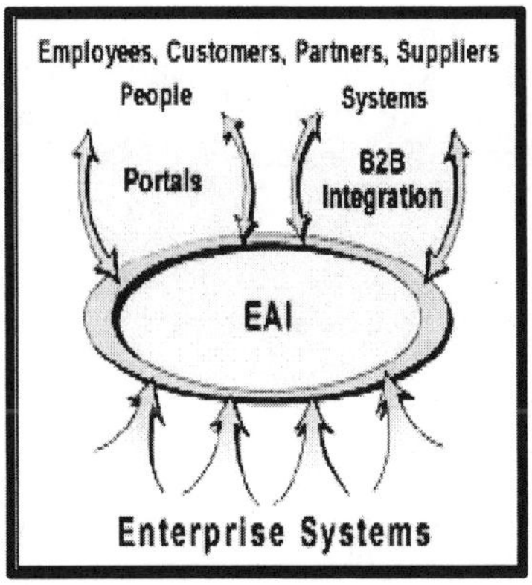

Figure 2.19 Fundamental areas

There are three fundamental areas of e-Business and they are showed at the Figure 2.19:

- **EAI integrates** internal systems and processes,

- **Portals extend** those systems and processes to people,
- **B2B integration connects** them with other businesses.

2.6.2.2 TIBCO ActiveEnterprise

TIBCO ActiveEnterprise's messaging system is a way of connecting enterprise applications. Includes adapters for leading applications and databases. Automatically transforms messages as they move through the system. Keeps e-Business systems running smoothly at all times.

The most visible parts of e-Business are Portals and B2B commerce. Foundation of e-Business is the integration of behind-the-scenes systems, known as Enterprise Application Integration. EAI makes businesses more efficient by letting internal applications work together and automating routine processes. EAI also improves the way businesses interact with the outside world by enabling interactive portals and B2B connections.

TIBCO's innovative "information bus" gives each application a single point of contact with the rest of the system. Each application has the connection with the messaging system. That connection is called an "adapter". Adapters let applications "plug in" to the messaging system.These adapters convert events inside the application into messages. Messages then can be easily exchanged with other applications via the messaging system. Adapters also can turn incoming messages into operations to be performed.

Once applications are plugged in to the messaging system, they can send and receive messages. Applications often use data formats that are incompatible. To resolve these differences, the messages must be transformed.

A business can be viewed as a set of processes. Letting applications work together makes it possible for companies to automate their business and become more efficient. The most processes involve both applications and people. The coordination of businesses processes requires a system that can manage both electronic and human operations.

E-Business systems present unique challenges in terms of system administration. Any problems should be resolved immediately and automatically, with alerts letting administrators know about any exceptional situations that they need to address. TIBCO ActiveEnterprise lets administrators monitor application parameters, behavior, loading activities throughout local or wide-area networks.

The message bus architecture allows new services to be easily added to the system. This lets new components communicate with existing applications throughout the system without requiring point-to-point connections between each one.

Quality service has become a key element of success for all businesses. This need for timely information drives the need for an e-Business infrastructure that delivers information to every place where it is needed (both inside and outside the organization) as soon as it is generated.

There are three common types of interactions used in messaging:

- Request/Reply,
- Broadcast Request/Reply,
- Publish/Subscribe.

Request/Reply: One application requests information from another, and a reply is provided.

Broadcast Request/Reply: An application broadcasts one message to multiple recipients, and they each send back a reply.

Publish/Subscribe: An application posts a given message to the network just once, and all components that are "subscribed" to that message's subject receive it.

2.6.2.3 TIBCO ActivePortal

Enables the complete personalization of portals by users and administrators. Lets users of all kinds interact with business applications like PeopleSoft, SAP, and Oracle. Lets users access portals through both the Web and wireless devices. Portals give people personalized access to content and services from inside businesses and from external sources. Portals basically present a summary of the interesting activity within other sources such as software applications, databases and external content sources. Portals let users personalize their own view. They see only the information that they need. Portal administrators can define which users are allowed to see which content, ensuring the security of sensitive information.

Businesses are using portals to give employees, customers and partners personalized interfaces to their systems. Businesses of all kinds benefit by letting people interact in real-time with business systems and processes. Employees are more productive and make better decisions. Customers are more satisfied. Supply chain interactions are more efficient. Users have to be able to access portals at any time from any place using wireless devices. Users need to be able to define which information is accessible through which devices. They also need to be able to manage the distribution of alerts so they aren't bothered by notifications about events that don't require immediate action.

TIBCO ActivePortal provides:

- Out of the box support for integration with web page content (page scraping),
- Web-based applications,
- XML documents,
- Database content,
- Any application adapted to TIBCO's information bus.

TIBCO ActivePortal is based on an easy to use integration wizard interface. No programming is necessary. Creating or editing a portal category usually takes less than five minutes.

TIBCO ActivePortal fully separate the collection of data from the delivery of that information. TIBCO ActivePortal then supports multiple delivery formats and protocols including HTML/HTTP for web page delivery, WML/WAP or SMS for wireless device delivery, SMTP for e-mail delivery.

2.6.2.4 TIBCO ActiveExchange

Provides a complete B2B integration solution. Lets businesses securely exchange documents with other businesses. Makes the supply chain more efficient by automating complex cross-company processes. Lets businesses expand their network of trading partners by connecting with businesses of all sizes. Supports the highest levels of security available. Lets businesses connect their systems with their trading partners more quickly and easily.

When businesses buy or sell things, they use things like POs and invoices to make sure the right process is followed. When they are buying and selling over the Internet, these documents must be sent securely. XML is the most common format for B2B commerce, but others will continue to be used to meet the needs of specific industries and partners. Documents are usually exchanged via HTTPS, FTP or e-mail.

Buyers need to make sure money is available and purchases have been approved. Sellers need to handle things like product availability and billing. It is important for businesses to communicate the same way every time. This means that both parties must follow specific processes for every transaction. Once these cross-company processes have been established, it's possible to make them more efficient by automating them.

For most companies, small and medium businesses represent the majority of their trading partners. They need to be able to connect with partners of all sizes. They must be able to give small and mid-size businesses ways of connecting. This can be done by distributing a client-side application. They let them conduct transactions through their Web browser.

B2B integration solutions need to give businesses a convenient way of defining and managing the relationships they have with each partner. They must be able to manage things like which partners can participate in a given process and which documents a given partner is allowed to send and receive.

Another important aspect of B2B integration is security. Private messages need to be encrypted so unauthorized parties can't read them. Users have to be validated to make sure users are who they say they are. Each transaction needs to be logged so nobody can deny that it took place.

2.7 Conclusion

Electronic business is one of the most visible trends in today's business world. This is not only thanks to the great attraction of the Internet, but also because electronic business is redefining virtually every business process - from the back office to supply chains, financial reporting and customer support. It is changing conventional concepts and rules about strategic alliances, outsourcing, competition, industry specialisation and customer relationships.

Far sooner than most of us expect, electronic business will be an integral part of doing business. There will be no further need to distinguish between business and electronic business. The two key drivers for the adoption of electronic business are:

- Increased efficiency through improved business processes,
- Access to new market opportunities, both nationally and internationally.

The electronic marketplace is an open solution for electronic document exchange, bringing together multiple suppliers and multiple buyers who are connected through a common technology platform utilising the Internet. This is the most advanced and efficient form of B2B.

In 2010, it is expected that about 75% of B2B transactions will be conducted electronically in the US. Most electronic transactions will be carried out via electronic marketplaces, accounting for 57% of the total transaction volume. In absolute terms, this signifies USD 11.9 trillion of B2B transactions over the market places, according to Forrester Research.

Early forms of B2B electronic business were based on EDI (Electronic Data Interchange), which allows exchange information through a standard set of transactions over value-added-networks (VAN). Other examples of B2B electronic business include sell-side and buy-side electronic business solutions. These are environments which are dominated by sellers or buyers, respectively.

The next stage for such solutions involves marketplaces developing and facilitating online trading communities which consist of many sellers and many buyers. The marketplaces build on a common Internet platform, WWW browsers, advanced security technologies, the latest payment systems and experience from other approaches. They provide a new class of opportunities over the older, proprietary and expensive VANs or narrow, focused sell-sides and buy-sides.

The central problem faced when considering e-Commerce interoperability stems from the wide variety of way in which e-Commerce is carried out.

Having all above in mind, in this chapter an effort was made to shed more light on a number of problems of importance for the field of electronic business on the Internet (EBI).

REFERENCES

[CA01] Products, (http://ca.com/b2b), Computer Associates, **2001.**

[CommerceOne01] Products, (http://www.commerceone.com), CommerceOne, **2001.**

[eCo99] The eCo Specification, (http://eco.commerce.net), The CommerceNet, **September 1999.**

[OBI01] The Open Buying on the Internet, OBI Specification, (http://www.openbuy.org), The OBI Consortium, **2001.**

[Pitts00] Pitts, N., "In Record Time XML," Authorized translation from English language edition published by Sybex, Serbia, Yugoslavia, **Copyright 2000.**

[RosettaNet99] The RosettaNet Specifications, (http://www.rosettanet.org), The RosettaNet, **December 1999.**

[Shim00] Shim, S., Pendyala, V., Sundaram, M., Gao, J., "Business-to-Business E-Commerce Frameworks," Computer, **October 2000.**

[TIBCO01] Products, (http://www.tibco.com), TIBCO, **2001.**

[XML98] The Extensible Markup Language (xml) 1.0 Specification, (http://www.w3.org), The World Wide Web Consortium, **February 1998.**

E-Business and E-Challenges
V. Milutinović and F. Patricelli (Eds.)
IOS Press, 2002

CHAPTER 3
E-BUSINESS MANAGEMENT AND WORKFLOW TECHNOLOGIES

Željko Đuričić and Veljko Milutinović

This chapter covers briefly the most relevant issues in the area of workflow technologies. It describes the *workflow* point of view on work processing. Also, it helps to point out the basic understanding and abstract from the details of individual *workflow management system*.

3.1 What is Workflow?

Workflow instance (shortly workflow) describes the current execution of a single business process (Figure 3.1) and a workflow management system is an execution platform for such workflow.

Workflow contains:

- A set of tasks to be carried out,
- Roles to carry out each task,
- Data (usually specified as documents) to be used in each task,
- A schedule that defines the sequence for carrying out the tasks.

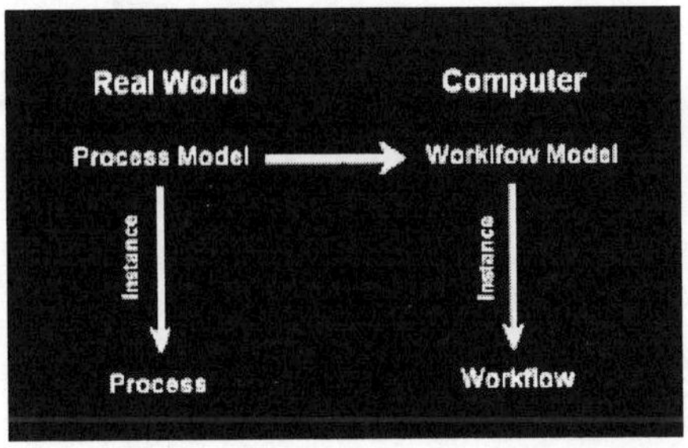

Figure 3.1 Processes and Workflows

During workflow, documents, information or tasks are passed from one participant to another in a way that is governed by rules, routes, and roles [WfMC01].

1) Rules govern the actions of the participants responsible for the assigned tasks.
2) Routes are paths that tasks flow from one participant to the next in the business process.
3) Roles are associated with certain participants responsible for completing the individual tasks that make up a business process.

3.1.1 The Workflow Meta Model

This section points out an extensible meta model of the Workflow Management Coalition that represents the essential building blocks of every workflow (Figure 3.2). The meta model also introduces the relevant workflow terminology commonly used [WfMC96a].

This meta model identifies six elementary building blocks comprising *workflow processes*, decomposed into *process activities*, *transitions* between activities, *workflow relevant data* used by activities, and *participants* and *applications* performing activities [WfMC96b].

- A **Workflow Process Definition** describes the process itself specifying which tasks need to be executed, in what order, and by whom. A workflow process definition consists of many logical steps of the so-called workflow process activities.
- A **Workflow Process Activity** is a description of a piece of work. They are related to one another via transition information. An activity may be implemented as **atomic** (a logical working unit in the sense that it is the smallest processable unit within a workflow) or as a **sub process** (a couple of logical working units).

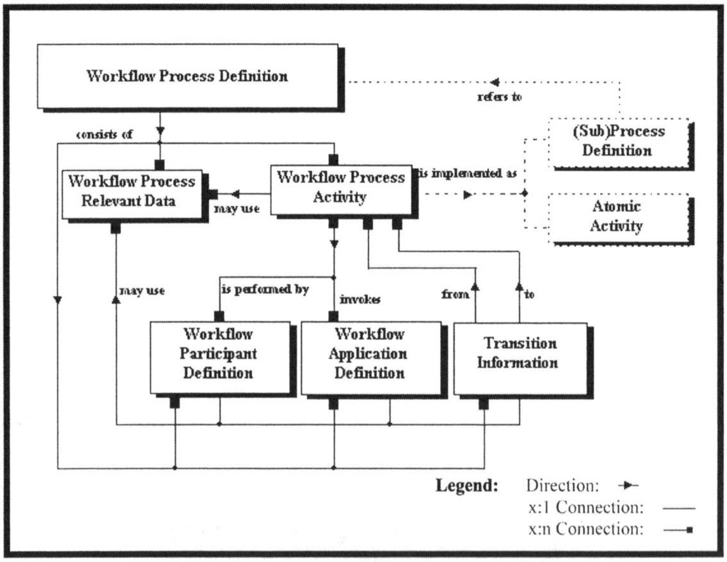

Figure 3.2 The Extensible Workflow Meta Model as Proposed for Standardization by the Workflow Management Coalition

The activity can be assigned:

1. To workflow participants who are allowed to perform the activity, or
2. To an application, which will be invoked during run time to automate the activity.

Usually, a common term is used for both, workflow (human) participants and applications, and that is – **actors.**

- **Transition Information** describes the flow of control between different process activities. Workflow can be a sequential progression of activities or a set of activities each taking place concurrently, eventually impacting each other according to a set of rules, routes, and roles.

- A **Workflow Participant Definition** describes the performer of an activity. The definition of a performer does not necessarily refer to a single person, but also to any business organizational entity (a team or a department).

- **Workflow Application Definition.** Process definition describes automated applications assigned to an activity. These applications will be invoked during run time by the workflow management engine.

- **Workflow Process Relevant Data** are data that have to be made available to a subsequent activity, invoked application or transition information. If there are lots of possible routes in a workflow, choice of the next activity to be executed may depend on availability of these data.

With the outlined building blocks we can specify workflows consisting of coordinated chains or networks of activities connected in a specific order to achieve a common goal (Figure 3.3).

The basic idea is that changes in the flow of work are mostly independent from changes concerning individual activities. For instance, using additional or alternative paths as well as changing the order does not necessarily affect the implementation of an activity.

Workflows can be decomposed hierarchically in subworkflows. Activities may be assigned to one or more actors. The term actor summarizes human beings, organizational units, but also machines, and computers. There are manual and automated (workflow) activities. Workflow management considers both types of activities. Human actors perform manual and partly automated activities. Computers (automated actors) execute automated activities in the form of application programs (actor layer, figure 7.3). Activities are not necessarily bound to be performed by a particular actor. Allocation strategies help to find an appropriate actor during run time. For instance, roles and capabilities of human actors are relevant characteristics that influence allocation strategies.

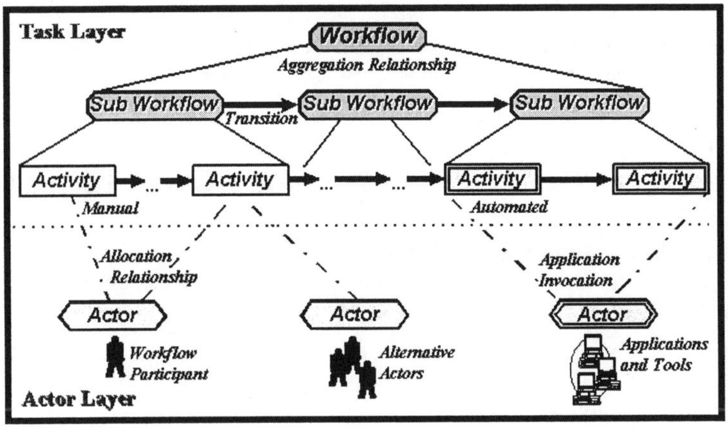

Figure 3.3 The Workflow Point of View on Work Processing - an Overall Illustration

3.1.2 Real and Virtual Workplaces

From a workflow point of view, the processing of business tasks in an enterprise can conceptually be divided into three parts: (1) Decomposing business tasks into activities in such a way that the activities can be managed and performed autonomously by one or more actors, (2) the coordination of activities and (3) processing activities at workplaces. The first is clearly a human task that is done through workflow modeling or business process reengineering (BPR), which goal is a planning better organization. Thus it is a matter of build time. The second and third are matters of run time and they can be automated to a great extend by workflow management systems. The third directly addresses workplaces and will be considered later.

An enterprise consists of one or more workplaces cooperatively working on business tasks.

A **real workplace** (i.e. a **physical workplace**) is commonly defined as a place where work is done. The kind of work being processed at a workplace differs within and between enterprises. Still there are some common characteristics of real workplaces when focusing on *how work is done* (what is the main concern of WFMS) instead on *which work is done*:

- **Work items** (i.e. activity instances) that represent elementary units of work to be processed. In order to be performed, they are assigned to workplaces. Examples for work items are tasks such as information processing or manufacturing of goods.
- **Actors** which perform the work at a workplace. The term actor is normally applied to a human participant, but from a work processing point of view it also includes machines and computers. Thus, human and machine based resources are conceptually regarded as equivalent for carrying out work.
- Access to **tools** and **applications**, which are applied when work items are executed. Examples for tools and applications are text processing software or communication media such as telephones and fax.
- Access to **business objects** being manipulated during the execution of work items. Examples for business objects are any documents and products.

The term **virtual workplace** aims at the autonomy of workplaces. A workplace can be described as virtual if one or more of the following aspects apply:

- **Independence of space.** One does not have to know **where** is the workplace where a work item is performed.
- **Independence of time.** One does not have to know **when** a work item is performed at a workplace.
- **Independence of actors.** One does not have to know **who** is performing the work at the workplace.
- **Independence of implementation.** One does not have to know **how** a work item is performed at a workplace. Often the implementation depends on the type of the participating actor.

The concept of virtualization allows a dynamic and flexible assignment of virtual workplaces to real (i.e. physical) workplaces. A physical workplace behind a virtual workplace can migrate, additional physical workplaces can be added, and other workplaces may vanish without affecting the work of running workflows. Thus, virtual workplaces are much more independent of each other in spite of cooperatively working on business tasks.

3.2 Workflow Management Systems

The continued process of re-organizations, integrations and process redesigns can lead to a complex spiderweb of business information (Figure 3.4).

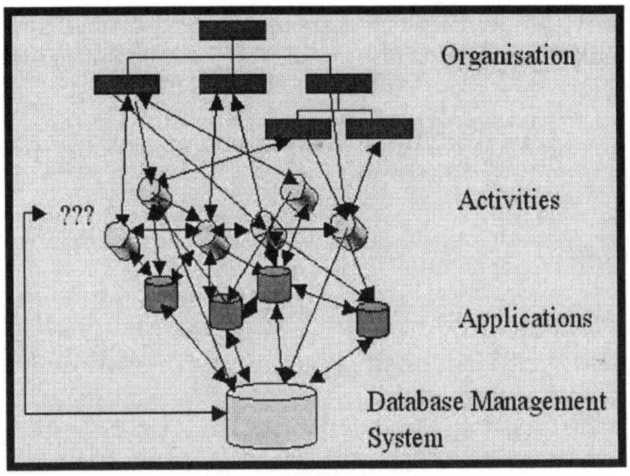

Figure 3.4 Complex Spiderweb of Information

If you want to tame this chaos, you should use a workflow management system. It can control the exchange of the information and also manage application integration (Figure 3.5). WFMS exchange data with your applications, but also can exchange data directly with the database (Figure 3.6).

3.2.1 Definition

To be competitive in today's business world, companies must automate the flow of work throughout the organization. Implementing a workflow management system allows an organization to automate and track their dynamic business processes (workflows).

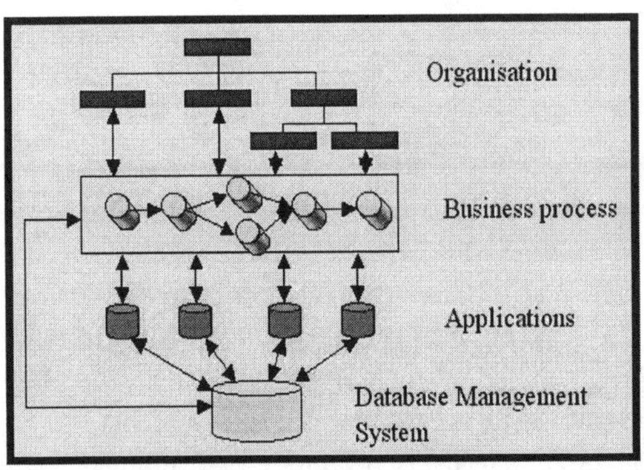

Figure 3.5: Using of WFMS

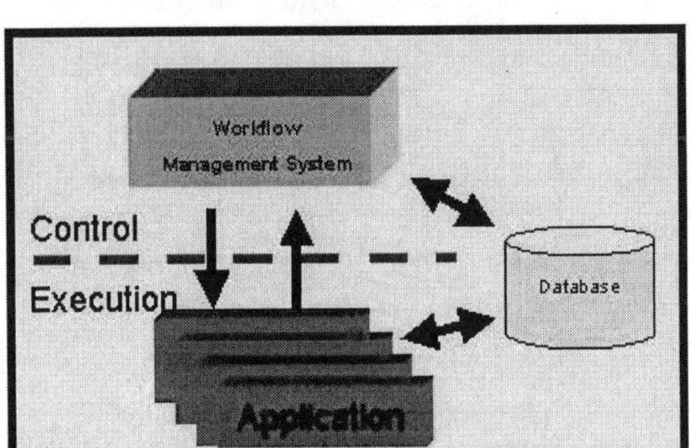

Figure 3.6 Communication between WFMS, Database, and Applications.

Workflow management system (WFMS) is a group of software systems designed to provide computerized support for modeling (the build time) and executing (the run time) workflows.

To understand the spectrum of automation support commonly provided by WFMS, the Reference model of the Workflow Management Coalition will be described in the following.

3.2.2 The Reference Model

The Workflow Management Coalition (WfMC) is an international organization whose mission is to promote workflow and establish standards for workflow management systems (to standardize terminology and define standard architecture and interfaces). One of the results achieved by the WfMC is the definition of a reference model for the architecture of a workflow system (Figure 3.7).

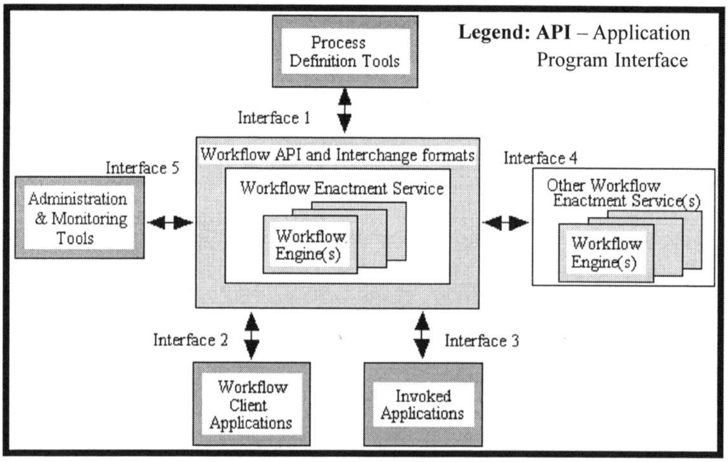

Figure 3.7 The Reference Model for WFMS as Proposed for Standardization by the Workflow Management Coalition

The reference model describes generic workflow architecture and a set of interfaces based on a two-tier client-server model [WfMC94]. The core of any workflow system is the workflow enactment service or workflow server.

The **workflow enactment service** (workflow server) provides the run-time environment which takes care of the creation, managing, and execution of the workflow (process) instances. The workflow enactment service utilizes one or more workflow management engines.

A **workflow engine** handles selected part(s) of the workflow instance. This means that engine is responsible for interpreting a part or whole process definition, creation of process instance and management of its execution, navigation between activities and creating work items for their processing, interacting with the external resources necessary to process the various activities, etc.

The **process definition tools** are used to define, model, document, and analyze a business process and for resource classifications. These tools are used at design time. The final output from the process modeling and design activity is a process definition, which can be interpreted at run time by the workflow engine. Most workflow management systems provide three process definition tools: (1) process definition language or a tool with a graphical interface to model flow of work, (2) a tool to specify resource classes (organizational model), and (3) a simulation tool to analyze and estimate the performance of the specified workflow.

The end-user communicates with the workflow system via the workflow client applications. Generally speaking, **workflow client application** is an application which interacts with a workflow engine, requesting facilities and workflow services from the engine, for performing **manual activities.** More precisely, this is the GUI application used to view and manage the content of a user's worklist on the server. The interaction between the client application and the workflow engine occurs through a well-defined interface 2, embracing the concept of a worklist - the queue of work items assigned to a particular actor by the workflow engine. Via that interface work items are offered to the end user. By selecting a work item, the user can execute a task for a specific case. Also, this interface allows a Workflow Client Application from one vendor to interact with a Workflow Server from another vendor.

If necessary, the workflow engine invokes applications via interface 3. So, an **invoked application** is a workflow application that is invoked by the WFMS (not user) to perform **automated** activity - fully or in part - or to support a workflow participant in processing a work item.

The **administration and monitoring tools** are used to monitor and control the workflow. These tools are used to register the progress of cases and to detect bottlenecks. Moreover, these tools are used to set parameters, allocate people and handle abnormalities.

Via interface 4, the workflow system can be connected to other workflow systems. So, there is ability **(workflow interoperability)** for two or more workflow engines to communicate and work together in order to coordinate their work.

To standardize the five interfaces shown in Figure 3.3, the WfMC aims at a common Workflow Application Programming Interface (WAPI). The WAPI is envisaged as a common set of API calls (to support functions between a workflow engine and applications or other system components) and related interchange formats (to support interoperability between different workflow engines) which may be grouped together to support each of the five interfaces.

3.2.2.1 The Workflow Interoperability

The management of large sets of workflows, especially complex workflows across enterprises, cannot be handled by a single WFMS. Thus, the biggest challenge for reference model is to provide a standard for interoperability among the workflow systems, and on this way to enable support for **distributed** or **decentralized** workflows (Figure 3.8).

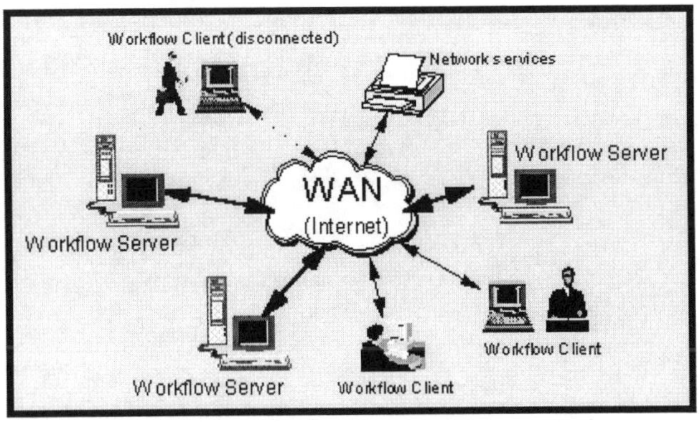

Figure 3.8 Distributed Workflows: Heterogeneous Servers, Participants, and Applications on a WAN

Distributed workflows can be defined as process-based applications that can easily execute in a wide area network environment (such as the Internet) across heterogeneous platforms and environments [Paul97]. A typical distributed workflow is described below.

Consider a virtual team of IT consultants from different companies, scattered across the globe. The team is working on a special project that requires the use of a specific workflow to ensure the quality of project. The consultants themselves may be mobile and intermittently connected to the network via portable computers. Irrespective of his location, the project leader may want to monitor and alter the workflow at any time. Similarly, irrespective of location, specific work items assigned to a participant must appear on his worklist during workflow execution. The workflow may contain automated steps that involve updating of network databases, sending email and faxes, and printing documents on printers that are physically accessible to mobile participants. The workflow may also interact with a variety of other subworkflows, running on heterogeneous machines on the network, either by the way of nesting or simple triggering. Finally, each participant in this workflow may also be simultaneously participating in many other workflows on the network.

3.2.3 Typical Features

Workflow management systems allow organizations to ***define*** and ***control*** the various activities associated with a business process. In addition, many management systems also allow the opportunity to ***measure*** and ***analyze*** the execution of the process so that continuous improvements can be made. Such improvements may be short-term (e.g., reallocation of tasks to better balance the workload at any point in time) or long-term (e.g., redefining the workflow process to avoid bottlenecks in the future). Most workflow systems also ***integrate*** other systems used by the organization: document management systems, databases, e-mail, etc. This integration provides structure to a process which employs a number of otherwise independent systems.

Listed below are some typical features associated with many workflow management systems.

- ***Process Definition Tool***: A graphical or textual tool for defining the business process. The defining facilities of WFMS focus on the answers to the following question: **What** is done (workflows), **how** (the activities and flow of work between activities), **by whom** (the participating human and automated actors) and **with what means** (the tools). A number of process-modeling techniques are available to define the detailed routing and processing requirements of a typical workflow. Figures 3.9 and 3.10 show examples of using modeling tools in the software package COSA Workflow (COSA Solutions).

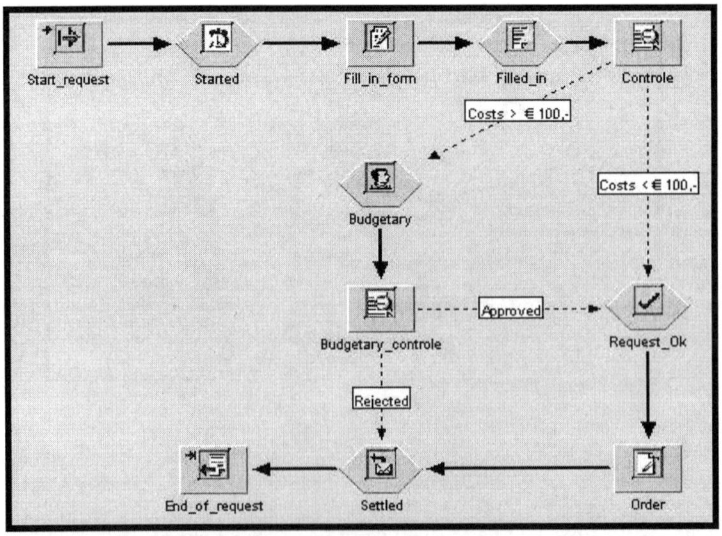

Figure 3.9 Modeling Business Processes Using Network Editor (COSA Workflow) [Cosa00]

- ***Simulation, Prototyping and Piloting**:* With some WFMS we can simulate workflow model or create prototype and pilot versions of a particular workflow so that it can be tried and tested on a limited basis before it goes into production. The WFMS FlowMark of IBM for example, allows a discrete, dynamic, and stochastic simulation. Before the simulation of a given workflow specification can start, some relevant data have to be added: the variation in start intervals for each workflow and subworkflow, the variation in the duration time for each task, the probability of a transition between tasks, the available capacities of resources, the required capacity of the resources, etc. The WFMS-based simulation allows an animation of process models as well as the calculation of capacities and performance.

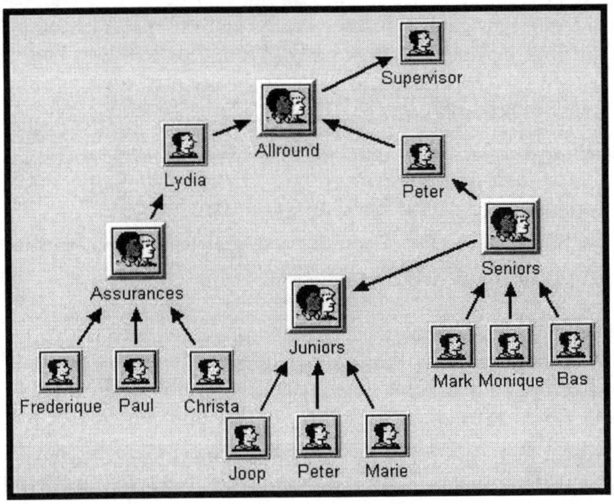

Figure 3.10 Describing Roles and Teams Using User Editor (COSA Workflow)

- ***Task Initiation and Control**:* The business process defined above is initiated and the appropriate human and IT resources are scheduled and engaged to complete each activity as the process progresses.
- ***Rules Based Decision Making**:* Rules are created for each step to determine how workflow-related data is to be processed, routed, and tracked. As an example, one rule might generate email notifications when a condition has been met. Another rule might implement conditional routing of documents and tasks based on the content of fields. Still another might invoke a particular application to view data.
- ***Document Routing**:* This might be accomplished by passing a file or folder from one recipient to another (e.g. an email attachment). Of course, each person in the process can add his own comment without affecting the original document.
- ***Invocation of Applications to View and Manipulate Data**:* Word-processors, spreadsheets, etc. can be invoked to allow workers to create, update, and view data.
- ***Worklists**:* These allow each worker to quickly identify their current tasks along with such things as due date, goal date, priority, etc. Some systems are able to analyze where jobs are in the workflow and how long each step should take, and then estimate when various tasks will reach an individual's desk.
- ***Task Automation**:* Computerized tasks can be automatically invoked. This might include such things as letter writing, email notices, or execution of certain applications.

- ***Event Notification***: Staff and managers can be notified when certain milestones occur, when workload increases, etc.
- ***Process Monitoring***: The system can provide valuable information on current workload, future workload, bottlenecks (current or potential), missed deadlines, etc.
- ***Access to Information over the World Wide Web***: Some systems provide Web interfacing modules in order to provide workflow information to remote customers, suppliers, collaborators, etc.
- ***Tracking and Logging of Activities***: Information about each step can be logged. This might include such things as start and completion times, person(s) assigned to the task, and key status fields. This information might later be used to analyze the process or to provide evidence that certain tasks were in fact completed. Reports on the status of each task during the business process provide knowledge to help ensure continuous improvement in the workflow and helps to locate any strains in the system that may slow the business process.
- ***Administration & Security***: A number of functions are usually provided to identify the participants and their respective privileges as well as to administer routines associated with any application (e.g., file back-ups, archiving of logs).

3.2.4 Administrational Actions at Workplaces

The instantiation of a workflow generates one or more work items, which together constitute the task to be performed by the actors. The work items are normally presented to the actor via a **worklist**, which maintains details of the work items allocated to a workplace, and a **worklist handler**, which interacts with the worklist on behalf of the actor.

In general, several work items are performed at a workplace. Because of this, additional **administrational actions** are needed beyond **core business actions** that directly contribute to the business objectives. Administrational actions at a workplace are for instance: selecting an appropriate work item to deal with next, invoking supporting tools and applications or carrying out any after treatment (e.g. archiving or bookkeeping).

Workflow management systems directly aim at the support of administrational actions at workplaces (Figure 3.11). The administrational actions of work items can be classified into **actions during preparation**, **actions during aftertreatment,** and **actions between work processing**:

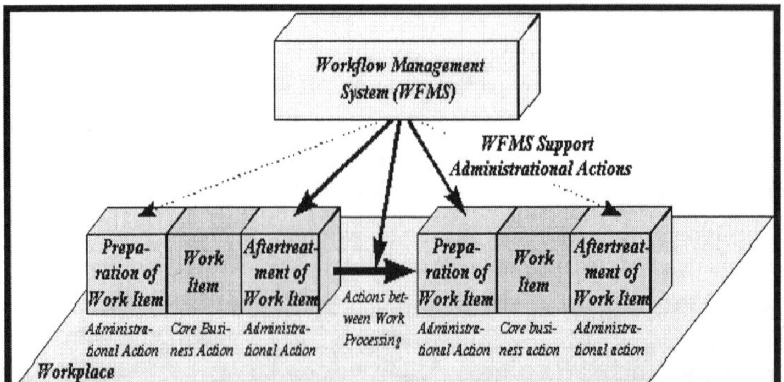

Figure 3.11 Workflow Management Systems Automate Administrational Actions at Workplaces

- During preparation:
  - **Managing worklists.** A WFMS helps to manage a list of work items that can be executed at a workplace. Also, the question that has to be answered for each workplace is with which work item to proceed.
  - **Providing the workflow relevant data**. A WFMS provides access to information required for work processing. If necessary, the amount of information and the format may change (e.g. by decompression, decoding).
  - **Invocation of tools and applications**. Tools or applications may be invoked either to support the work performed by a human actor or to completely automate work processing. *Thus, only invoked applications perform core business actions (task automation), whereas WFMS provides administrational support (workflow automation).*
  - **Supporting suspension and resumption of work.** Even though a work item was assigned to a workplace the work item execution may not take place at once. Maybe it has to be suspended for a while because of unfulfilled requirements. Here a WFMS can help to check the conditions and requirements and depending on results suspend or resume work.
- Between work processing:
  - **Reassigning work**. Non-available actors (e.g. caused by the vacation or illness of human actors or a failure of a machine/computer) do not necessarily hinder time critical workflows.
  - **Workload balancing**. Knowing the workload (e.g. number of work items to perform) of equivalent workplaces, helps to balance the workload of all workplaces. The allocation of virtual workplaces in combination with workload balancing and reassigning work allows a dynamic and flexible real workplace allocation.
  - **Transmission of workflow relevant data**. Information and workflow relevant data can be moved electronically between workplaces.
- During after treatment:
  - **Archiving monitored data**. The administration and monitoring tools of a WFMS help to answer the question of who has worked when, how long and with what result on a work item or a workflow. This information can be given for automated as well as for manual activities.
  - **Transformation of workflow relevant data**. If necessary the information relevant for further workflow activities gets compressed and encoded.

3.2.5 Virtual Workplaces and WFMS

WFMS helps to conceal from the participants of a workflow (e.g. clients, managers and actors) on which (real) workplace, when, where, by whom and with what implementation a work item is processed. For this, virtual workplaces are specified during build time. During run time a WFMS has to map an addressed virtual workplaces on one or more physical workplaces (Figure 3.12).

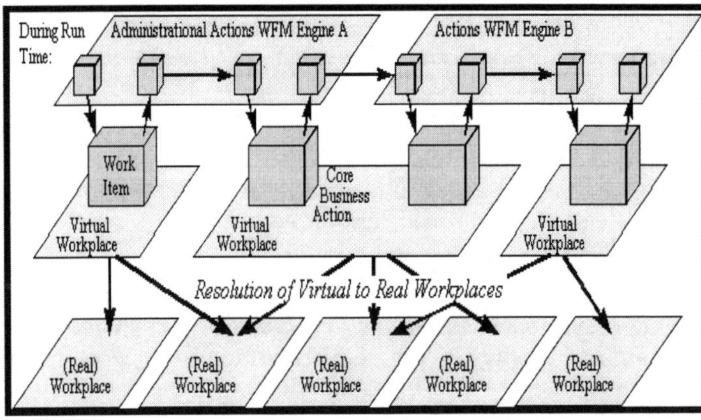

Figure 3.12 Resolution of Virtual Workplaces to Real Workplaces

Why are virtual workplaces of interest? With virtual workplaces activities are performed while physical properties of workplaces can be neglected to some extend. For instance, virtual workplaces can comprise office, stationary (home) and mobile workplaces.

The obvious advantages for human participants are mobility and flexibility in working hours and in the organization of work, thus contributing to an arrangement of profession and family.

The potential for the enterprise may comprise cost reduction (e.g. reducing fixed office space), more efficiency of the working resources, greater choice in enterprise locations, etc.

3.2.5.1 A Virtual Enterprise Scenario

To illustrate the applicability of WFMS for virtual workplaces, a virtual enterprise scenario is introduced. **Virtual enterprises** are temporary networks of legally independent enterprises, with goal to achieve maximum flexibility in respond to market demands. Such networks are especially attractive for Small and Medium Enterprises (SME) to compete with large enterprises.

Next scenario depicts a craftsmen virtual enterprise consisting of a central administration and a number of participating craftsmen. The craftsmen are specialized in different services (e.g. plumber, tiler, bricklayer). Depending on the kind of customer order, one or more craftsmen services are combined. Because of the character of the virtual enterprise the customer does not necessarily know which craftsmen will carry out his order.

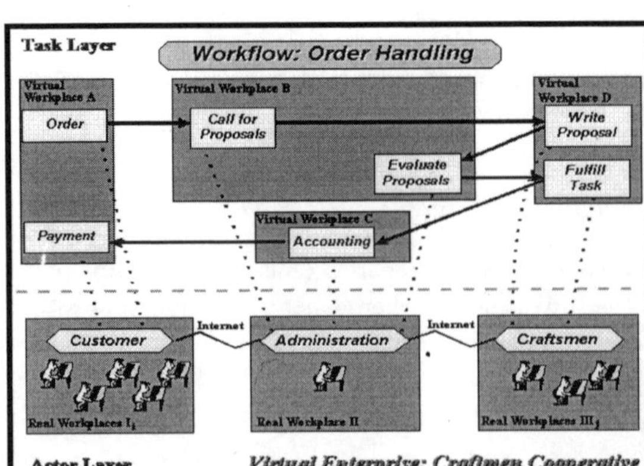

Figure 3.13 Example of a Workflow in a Virtual Enterprise

Figure 3.13 shows the order handling workflow in the virtual enterprise scenario. This workflow consists of seven tasks distributed to four virtual workplaces. A customer (workplace A) awards an order to the craftsmen cooperative. The order is received by the administration (workplace B) which classifies orders and initiates a bid procedure. The order is sent to those craftsmen (workplace D) who provide appropriate services. The call for proposal might be addressed to just a single craftsman or to a group of craftsmen. The craftsmen who want to compete for an order send back a proposal to the administration. There it is evaluated and the order is awarded to the craftsman or group of craftsmen with the best proposal. After fulfilling the work, accounting takes place at workplace C and the customer has to pay.

To support this workflow by a WFMS, the virtualization of workplaces in this scenario is suitable because of several reasons. The customer is integrated in this workflow through the Internet. The order is transmitted electronically; the payment is done by a credit card. By this, for each customer is provided a workplace independent of time and space. The virtual workplaces B and C are mapped to a single real workplace, the administration. By the specification of two different virtual workplaces it is possible to assign them to different real workplaces in the future. Based on the Internet the virtual workplace D is mapped to a set of craftsmen.

The example demonstrates that a WFMS enables virtual workplaces in every aspect of virtualization mentioned earlier. The customer as well as the craftsmen perform their activities to some extends independent of space, time, implementation and actors.

3.2.6 Workflow Oriented Information Systems

In some cases, managing workflows yields special requirements: workflows must be able to cope with continuous changes without having to stop the business process, they must be scalable and integrate existing or create new applications that provide the implementation for one or more automated or partly automated tasks of an enterprise.

New applications are developed when the development efforts are justified in the long run by the benefits of automation. This is the case for well-understood routine work with a high repetition rate. But, the application development as well as application migration (e.g. adapting an application to new requirements) requires intense efforts and is very time-consuming. This results in applications that are not very flexible to adapt to changes – legacy applications.

The term **legacy application** denotes applications which cannot be modified easily due to various reasons (see [Brodie95]).

The **application landscape** of an enterprise consists of a set of applications where each application automates a set of closely related activities.

The term **information system** comprises the application landscape and all other components of an enterprise that deal with information processing.

The lasting high application development efforts reveal the demand for a new architecture of information systems, which is proposed in the following.

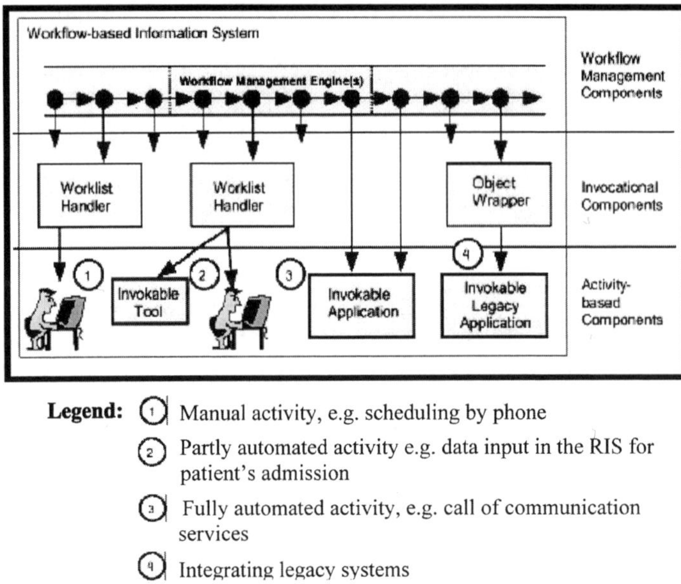

Figure 3.14 Architecture of Workflow Oriented Information System

Workflow oriented architecture of information systems consists of three layers (Figure 3.14). The layers conceptually separate the components of an information system into workflow management components, invocational components and activity-oriented component.

Workflow management components deal with the flow of work of one or more workflows. At the one extreme a workflow may consist of only one activity. At the other extreme a workflow may consist of activities spanning one or more organizational units or enterprises. This layer may consist of one or more workflow management engines.

Invocational components deal with the invocation of human participants that have to perform manual activities, with the invocation of participants and supporting tools that have to perform partly automated activities, and with the invocation of applications that have to perform fully automated activities.

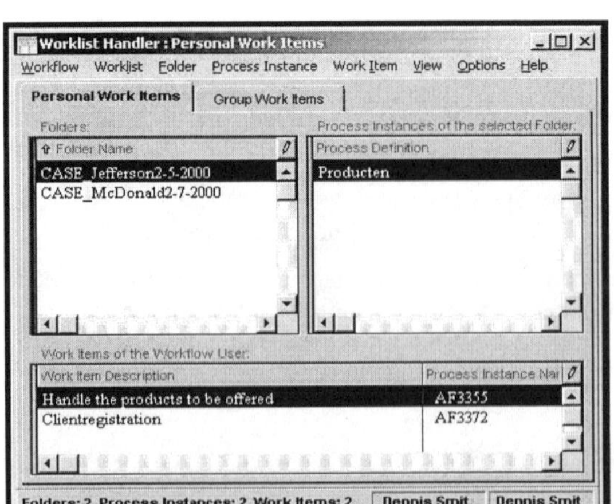

Figure 3.15 Worklist Handler in the COSA Workflow

To deal with human participants worklist handler components are needed. A worklist handler generates worklists that are shown to the end-user (Dennis Smit on figure 3.15). They may be printed on paper, displayed on screen or provided by a mailing system.

Applications that are designed to interact with a workflow management engine do not need any further consideration.

When legacy applications should be integrated then, for instance, object wrappers are applicable as interfaces between the workflow engines and applications. If the programming effort for a wrapper is too high, it is better to call the legacy system manually.

Activity-oriented components provide the implementations of partly or fully automated activities to be performed at a workplace. From the workflow point of view also human actors can be conceptually regarded as such components. The user can start a manual task (e.g., a phone call) or an application on his PC (e.g., spreadsheet or scheduling program). Automated activities trigger a computer-based invocation of applications.

3.2.6.1 Main Benefits

The approach outlined above has three main benefits:

- Workflow-oriented information systems further shift the automation boundary, because assignment to human actors and invocation of tools and applications are computerized.
- Workflow-oriented information systems may be adapted to changes in the workflows and in the workplaces more easily than "conventional" information systems. This is the case because the flow of work is separated from the elementary steps, the activities. For example, the flow of work (i.e. where in a workflow an activity is performed) may change without affecting the implementation of activities.
- This approach provides facilities for integration of legacy application systems in a heterogeneous application landscape. Instead of replacing legacy systems, using them in isolation or completely reimplementing the functionality of a legacy system (a revolutionary strategy) the workflow approach enables a evolutionary migration strategy: A legacy application that are suitable with no or minor changes in the interface, can further be used through e.g. object wrappers.

3.2.6.2 An Example: Design of a Hospital Information System

At the University Hospital of Saarland, Homburg, Germany, some typical clinical workflows were analyzed [Graeber95]. Wards and service units (e.g. department of radiology) have to cooperate and to exchange information for the treatment of patients. The service (e.g. a radiological examination) is ordered by the ward (i.e. by the responsible physician) and is delivered by the service unit.

This workflow is broken up roughly into patient management, performance of examination, and transfer of findings. 1) The patient management consists of an appointment between the ward and the department (manually) and an entry in the department information system (partly automated) (see legend of figure 3.14). 2) The examination (manually using medical devices) and its documentation (partly automated: dictation and print-out using a word processor) trigger the transfer of findings to the ward. 3) This transfer is performed automatically by a communication server [Graeber96].

A pilot-project is being carried out between wards and the department of radiology, equipped with a radiology information system (RIS). All workplaces are equipped with PCs and integrated in a network. The complete workflow is controlled by a WFMS (the workflow management component). 1) The appointment is supported by printed worklists (generated by a worklist handler, i.e. an invocational component). For admission in the department of radiology the RIS is started for data entry (invokable application). 2) The examination is again controlled by a worklist that contains what have to be done. For the recording of findings a word processor is started (invokable tool) with a suitable template. The RIS and the word processor communicate via OLE (Object Linking and Embedding). So data, which are entered using word processor, are automatically stored in the RIS. 3) After that the findings are transferred to a communication server using NFS (Network File system). And finally, an API is used for the transmission of findings to the workstations of the wards.

3.2.7 Benefits

The implementation of workflow management tools should be seen as an opportunity to improve both the underlying business process and the existing organizational structure.

Opportunities for Organizational Change: Workflow management systems can help companies to achieve the organizational changes necessary to operate effectively in today's world. These changes might include the move to a *flatter organizational structure* and *greater team orientation*. Managing the business process is much easier, because of routes, roles, and rules built into the system. In addition, improved communications provided by notifications and document sharing can lead to increased collaboration among team members and across teams and business units.

Opportunities for Process Change: Workflow systems force organizations to examine and define their business processes, what usually leads to *business process reengineering* (BPR) In fact, it is essential that an underlying process be analyzed and improved prior to workflow system implementation. Investments in workflow tools will not solve underlying problems in the business process, if the tool is simply used to automate existing bad processes. James G. Kobielus in Workflow Strategies [Kobielus97] suggests that an organization optimize a process with any of three goals in mind: "minimizing process time, maximizing value-added process content, or maximizing flexibility at the initial point of customer contact." He provides some guidelines for achieving each of these:

- To minimize process time:
  - Reduce the number of participants in a process,
  - Reduce the maximum completion time of each task (automate tasks, notify staff of approaching due dates),
  - Reduce "handoff" time to transfer work among participants,
  - Reduce maximum queuing time (prioritize items that have been awaiting action for a long time),
  - Increase the number of tasks running in parallel.
- To maximize value added content (i.e. improve the quality of product or reduce its price):
  - Apply standard workflow routes, roles, and rules automatically to each new case; deviate from the standard only when certain predefined thresholds are crossed (exceeds dollar limit) or certain flags are raised (customer complaint),
  - Provide participants with immediate, on-line access to all information bases,
  - Enable continual tracking and notification,
  - Eliminate costs associated with paper documentation (scan and index as soon as it enters the workflow).
- To maximize flexibility at the initial point of contact:
  - Provide multiple access options,
  - Capture customer data only once,

- Support distributed transaction processing,
- Enable ad-hoc, flexible workflow to tailor the process to the customer's needs.

Improved Access to Information: Workflow management systems build corporate knowledge. Information that may have been scattered among various staff members is now combined and available to all employees. This is especially useful to newer employees. For any particular project, more information about both the history and the current status of the process is now available for any staff member to view.

Improved Security and Reliability: Workflow management unites data from many different applications, provides secure storage and provides this data with organization and integrity. Using mechanisms such as role privileges (determines who can access and change information), process control (e.g. a document may need management approval before moving on to the next step), and system back-ups, WFMS makes data more reliable.

3.2.8 Trade-Offs & Dangers

Issues to consider before implementing any workflow system include the following.

Worker Resistance: Human-factor issues represent the greatest obstacle to the acceptance of workflow. Many workers will see workflow management as a mechanism for removing their decision-making power. Others will resent being monitored and feel that the system is an invasion of their privacy. Still others will miss the interpersonal give-and-take which might now be replaced by an automated system.

Overmanagement: Workflow processes can be defined at any level of detail. A system which attempts to dictate and monitor every detail of the process, may be excessive and incur unnecessary overhead. For instance, exceptions may be modeled, but this modeling requires a high effort and becomes very complex.

Loss of Flexibility: Using WFMS to automate business processes that require workers to remain flexible and use personal judgment, can lead to loss of flexibility. These processes are generally not good candidates for workflow management.

Technical Implementation Costs: Workflow management systems can be complex, requiring a variety of resources to implement and manage. Costs include development and maintenance of the network, the purchase price of the workflow software products, application development and implementation.

Costs of Defining Complex Processes: The business process itself may be difficult to define and even more difficult to reengineer. A reliable workflow definition requires a detailed understanding of the underlying business process. Success depends on management and staff commitment and can be expected to take a considerable amount of time.

Creation of New Work: Everything mentioned above create additional work, which must be offset by anticipated savings or benefits.

3.2.9 Choosing the Right Process

Processes which will benefit most from managed workflow are those that will find advantage in a automation and control as well as profit from the integration of those processes across enterprise. Typical candidates are processes which are document intensive, include lots of hand-offs among participants, and require high process integrity. However, simple and ad-hoc processes can also benefit from managed workflow if they are supported with a corresponding simple and flexible workflow management system. The following factors for determining processes which might benefit from workflow management, have been suggested by James G. Kobielus in *Workflow Strategies* [Kobielus97].

- ***Speed:*** Prolonged processes are often the first to get attention. Complaints from customers, suppliers and managers ("Why does this take so long?") often provide the incentive for improvement.
- ***Cost:*** Costs to be aware of include high labor costs and frequent routing of simple tasks to high-priced personnel.
- ***Accuracy:*** Signals might include complaints about process integrity as well as problems pertaining to accurate record keeping.
- ***Quality:*** Is the quality of the end-product inconsistent?
- ***Customer Satisfaction:*** Does the process generate a steady stream of complaints?

Once candidates for process reengineering are identified, priority can be given to those which will most positively impact the organization. Other method is to prioritize an organization's critical success factors (perhaps from the above list) and then obtain consensus on which projects will address the highest ranked items.

3.2.10 Steps of Implementing a WFMS

Recommended practices for successful implementing workflow management systems [Kobielus97]:

Focus on Business Objectives: Spend some time studying the organization and determine which potential workflow management benefits are most important to overall success.

Focus First on Projects that are Well Understood: For initial implementations, choose projects with clearly understood process activities.

Use Metrics: Take baseline measurements so that expected benefits can be quantified. Once implemented, track these metrics in order to spot favorable or unfavorable trends. Examples of metrics are: labor hours to complete the process, number of errors, time used to access data, and generated revenues.

Obtain Support of Upper Management: It is important that this support be available and visible for planning, implementing, and refining and not just for project approval.

Obtain Support of Staff: The staff must be involved in the redesign process and understand that the new process will fail without their commitment. Reassure staff that the new process will automate tasks in order to free up their time for more productive work. Although more structure is being added to the process, critical tasks will still be dependent on employee knowledge and effort. Staff should also know that they will receive adequate training and will be given enough time to learn the system before benefits are expected to accrue.

Integrate with Current Systems and New Systems: Many of the advantages of workflow management systems are the result of its integration with existing systems already being used in the business process. The purpose of workflow is to integrate these systems and add integrity to the process. In addition, many of the goals of business reengineering can only be obtained as a result of new systems being implemented along with workflow management. These might include document management systems or Internet/Intranet access.

Implement in Phases: Start with a small first-phase with just a few users and/or a limited number of activities. In later phases, expand the number of users and expand the system's functionality (but do not expand both in one phase).

3.3 Technical Overview

3.3.1 Four Main Categories of Workflow

Figure 3.16 shows four main broad categories of workflow systems:

- Production Workflow Systems
- Administrative Workflow Systems
- Ad-hoc Workflow Systems
- Collaborative Workflow Systems

The business value defines the importance of a workflow to the company's business. A process of high business value is at the core of a company. Repetition measures how often a particular process is performed in the same manner. It's an indicator of whether the process is worth being modeled. This indicator is important since modeling a process for the first time is often difficult and time-consuming, what makes it typically expensive.

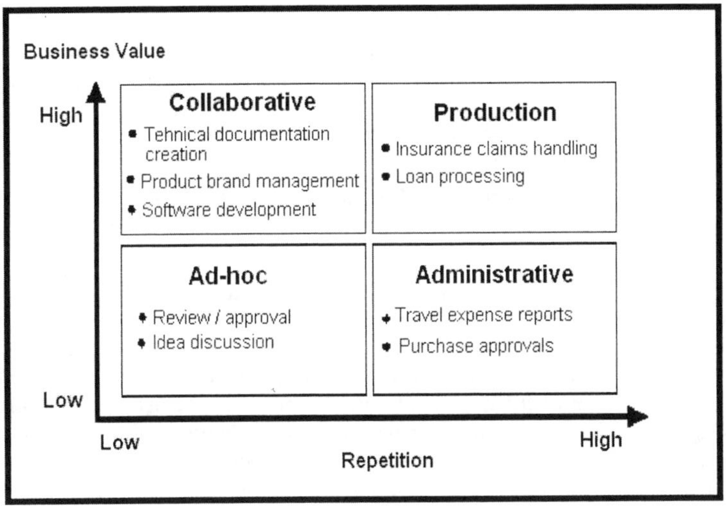

Figure 3.16 Categories of Workflow Systems [Leymann 01]

3.3.1.1 Production (Transaction) Workflow Systems

This is the largest market category, both in vendors and revenues, and comprises software designed to automate business-critical applications that work full time on repetitive operations. These systems evolved from the first systems on the market, FileNet and ViewStar. They are sometimes referred to as filestore-based systems, document-image processing systems, and forms management systems, because they route folders consisting of one or more forms or different types of documents though the organization and store them in a central repository.

Production workflow shows high repetition factor and high business value (Figure 3.16), what means that this workflow implements the core business of company. Generally, production WFMS automates complex business processes that tend to be repetitive, highly structured with almost no variations (Figure 3.18), and which are characterized by high transaction rate of work items moving through the process. This type of workflow needs to cope with many process instances per day. Typical examples would be mortgage loan processing in banking and financial markets (Figure 3.17), insurance underwriting and claims processing.

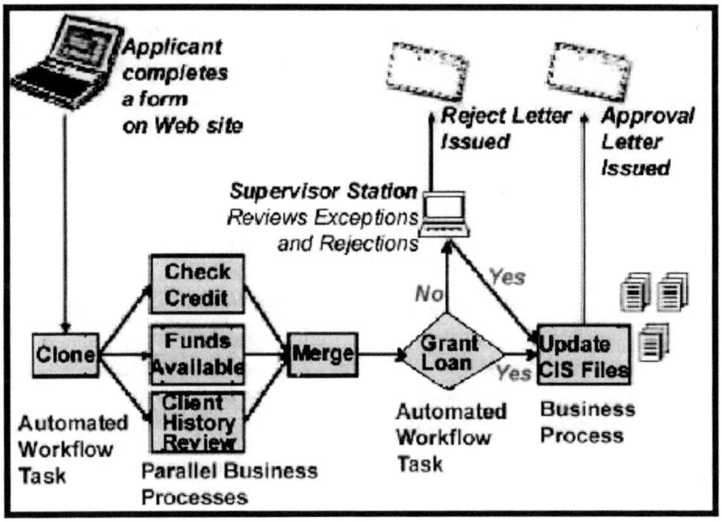

Comment: After an application form is filled, it is cloned so many activities can be executed in the parallel. The logic in the workflow engine is able to automatically decide whether a loan should be granted or not. A supervisor is required only to review exceptions and rejections.

Figure 3.17 Loan Processing

Workflow systems are similar in their desire and need to reduce the volume of back-office paperwork in daily operations. Systems in this category are based on the idea that an organization should only have to touch a paper document once, when it is received by the organization and scanned into electronic form. Thereafter, it is routed through the phases needed to finish the treatment of the document (such as making a decision, calculating the tax, etc.). An insurance claim is a prime example. The workflow product insures that the appropriate persons review the claim form in the appropriate sequence to complete the processing of the claim. The major benefit of digitizing paper documents and routing them through the computer network, turns out not to be saving storage space, but a huge acceleration of the business process. But automation of high-volume paper-driven processes was only the earliest application of workflow technology.

Production workflow systems was only initially focused on document-image processing and the routing of documents or scanned images though the organization. Today document-centric and image-centric products are replaced with more general-purpose workflow environments that have the ability to route any data through the organization, whether this data is an image, a document or a transaction. Workflow providing certain customer service is a good example. When the customer calls in, a dispatcher log the call and then let the workflow engine first assign it to specialists, obtain management review, then generate a response (e-mail message), and finally submit the case to a billing system to determinate a bill. This type of application contains two dimensions that go beyond the capabilities of document-based workflow. First, the business process may need to interface to electronic subsystems (e.g., the e-mail server or the billing system). Second, the process probably needs to execute in real business time (e.g. while the customer is on the phone or on-line) where the hand-offs between individual steps need to occur with high levels of performance and reliability.

These systems generally support a lot of functions and obtain high level of quality and accuracy, allow great customization, and run in a wide range of network and computing environments. Usually, human input is required only to handle exceptions (work items that fall outside of pre-determined process tolerances).

However, these systems have some disadvantages. For example, they are generally more expensive than other systems. They usually require expensive application development and integration services from an external consultant.

The core capabilities supported in most of today's production workflow solutions are: database management, document management, forms management, computer-aided software engineering (CASE), electronic messaging, Internet/Intranet services, electronic commerce services, etc.

This category is closely aligned to the Workflow Management Coalition (WfMC's) Reference Model mentioned above.

3.3.1.2 Administrative Workflow Systems

Administrative workflow shows a low business value, but the repetition factor is high.

Administrative workflow corresponds to case-driven processes, but which have well-defined structure. So, administrative workflows have a predefined structure which is instantiated each time the workflow is performed. Although the structure is predefined, alternative routing is possible, but needs to be predefined, too.

The products contained herein are stand-alone tools that primarily route documents (electronic forms and file attachments) over existing email systems. This is enough because performance requirements are less stringent than in production workflows. This category started with the FormFlow product.

Advantages: Messaging is usually based on an existing email system, and because of that products in this category are usually low-cost. The implementation and use of the products are designed to work with a minimum of training and customization.

Disadvantages: Systems in this category are not as comprehensive and flexible as systems in the production workflow systems category.

Usually, administrative workflow systems can be split into three parts: electronic messaging technology, forms management, and database management. Electronic messaging is done via the email system. The people comprising the process use the email system to route forms and messages between each other. The forms are usually created with a standalone tool, and these forms are sent between people, allowing them to change and update fields. When a form has reached its end-point, where the process is done with it, it is written to the database.

These workflow systems typically take care of internal administrative processes such as expense account or purchase order processing. In the case of travel expense account processing, the employee fills out a form, the employee's manager approves it, and the expense account department verifies the charge and issues the appropriate bank order.

3.3.1.3 Ad-Hoc Workflow Systems

Ad-hoc workflow is characterized by having a low business value and low repetition rate. Workflow systems in this category are designed to support ad-hoc business processes that are characterized by:

- Minimal preplanning because their structure cannot be predicted,
- Few participants,
- Simple routing rules that are being redefined from day-to-day depending on what works.

These processes are not defined (completely) in advance, because next steps are determined by each user involved in the process. Thus, these systems can be suitable to support largely unstructured processes (see figure 7.18) that facilitate several users interacting on a shared piece of work, e.g. several users might collaborate on producing a certain report.

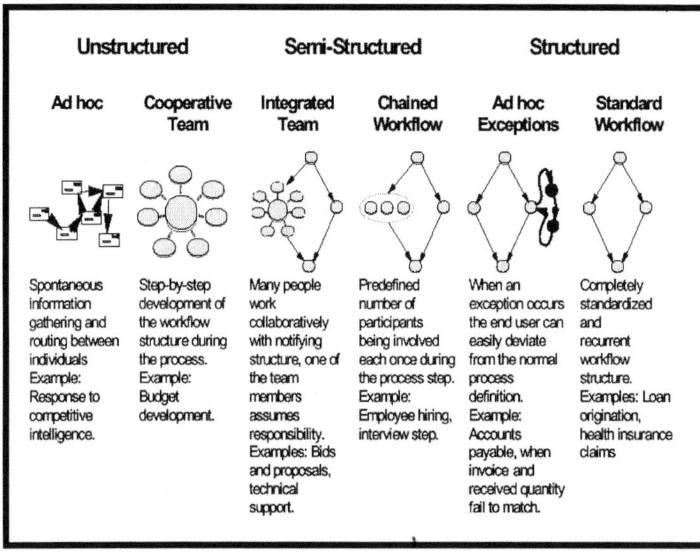

Figure 3.18 Types of Processs Depending on Structure
(Source: Hilpert and Nastansky, 1994)

Ad-hoc workflow systems allow individual users to create and modify process definitions (during the operation of the process) very quickly and easily to meet circumstances as they arise. So, they maximize flexibility in areas where throughput and security are not major concerns. Whereas in production workflow, the organization clearly owns the process, ad-hoc workflow users own their own processes (table 3.1 compares production and ad-hoc workflow). Because of a large number of possible process definitions, these systems must support rapid definition and easy activation of business processes.

	AD-HOC	PRODUCTION
Infrastructure	E-Mail	Transactions
Flow Structure	Ad-hoc	Structured, some ad-hoc
Transaction Rates	Low	Medium to High
Scope	Workgroup/Dept	Dept/Enterprise
Target Users	Human only	Human and Machine
Example Products	Lotus Notes	Staffware

Table 3.1 Comparison: Production and Ad-hoc Workflow Systems

Ad-hoc relies on e-mail as a transport mechanism for routing work. In this kind of workflow typical is a "for-your-information" routing. Example, routing for comments or approvals: a manager sends a note to all his department members with information deemed important for them. The receivers can do whatever they want with the note, including routing it to others who should see the information. Such a process terminates if nobody routes the note to anyone else.

3.3.1.4 Collaborative Workflow Systems

Collaborative workflow is characterized by a high business value, but infrequent execution. Vendors of collaborative workflow systems are focused on the automation of team-based processes that are usually unstructured (Figure 3.18), or in the best case, are semi-structured (i.e. they involve some unstructured activities within a larger structured framework).

These systems handle a lot of, but still one or two orders of magnitude less process instances per hour than production workflow systems. Here, flexibility is more important than productivity.

Typically, there are many workflow instances running concurrently and they involve groups of employees sending messages and sharing information towards achieving a common goal. Groups can vary from small, project-oriented teams to widely dispersed people with interests in common. These systems must include a mechanism for sharing documents, data and user comments on work in progress, thus the information get routed faster, more securely, and with less effort. But in a collaborative environment, automating work routing is often less important than other aspects of work management, such as:

- Activity execution with possibility to delegate activity, to accept, reject and resubmit activity mechanisms,
- Pushing timely information to the user so that they can act upon it,
- Deadline management (rerouting work when deadlines are missed),
- Status reporting, etc.

Software development is an example of business process that can be well supported by collaborative workflow systems. This complex process depends on the cooperation of multiple departments within the company. Here speed, efficiency and strict process controls are the most critical. The use of the Internet to support team communications across enterprises is also a critical success factor to most organizations.

Effective use of collaborative workflow systems to support team working is now considered a vital element in the success of enterprises of all kinds. Thus, this category has the highest growth potential and is where many production-oriented workflow vendors are moving to.

3.3.2 Division Based upon Transport Mechanism

Distinguishing by the transport mechanism used to route the work items, workflow products can belong to one or more of the following major categories:

- ***Document Based:*** Document management technology is concerned with searching and routing of electronic documents between individuals that are participated in performing the business procedure. SERfloware (SER) and WFX (Eastman Software) are typical representatives of document based workflow products.
- ***E-mail Based:*** Systems in this category employ the power of electronic mail mechanism to distribute information between participants. InTempo from JetForm and Microsoft Exchange are typical examples.

- ***Groupware Based:*** This category of products support and improve the interaction between teams via group discussion processes, accessing bulletin board, etc. For example, Lotus Notes, TeamWARE Flow (Fujitsu), and Microsoft Exchange are products in this category.
- ***Transaction Based:*** This category incorporate transaction management facilities and database management software to support certain classes of business transactions. Eastman Software Enterprise Workflow is a typical example of transaction based workflow product.
- ***Internet (Web) Based*:** This category of products is designed for use on the Internet. From the definition tool, HTML forms are automatically generated and can be redrawn graphically using any HTML editor. Maybe, the most important advantage of using the WWW for workflow systems is the feature of fill-in forms in HTML, which allows a form based interaction between the user and a tasks. Such systems aim to serve for Internet-based business operations over distributed and heterogeneous environments. Bizflow 2000, Visual Workflow, COSA and W4 fall into this category. This category will be describe more precisely in the next section.

3.3.3 Web-Based Workflow Systems

3.3.3.1 Introduction

Systems in this category utilize Web clients and servers to deliver their functionality. In order to exploit the potential of the Web, companies offering workflow products now provide a **Web interface** to WFMSs. This allows both the employees and the customers of a company to interact with the WFMS through the Web. Employees can access their worklist via a Web browser instead of using a special client application as in traditional WFMSs. Thus employees can interact with the WFMS wherever they are located, as long as they have access to a Web browser. Also, a customer submits an order via a Web form, and after that appropriate workflow is automatically triggered to handle the customer order.

3.3.3.2 Advantages

Many organizations already have some of the technology and networking capabilities needed to implement these systems. Thanks to the extent of the WWW, these workflow products facilitate telecommuting and other flexible work arrangements.

Whereas the other categories of workflow products operate over application infrastructures that incorporate a wide range of protocols and application services, web-based workflow only requires:

- WWW Internet/Intranets/Extranets,
- Web servers (offer the workflow services serving the HTML pages and Java applets),
- Web browsers (on the user's desktop),
- Workflow engines (determines routing and processing of work items).

3.3.3.3 Disadvantages and Possible Improvements

The level of skill needed to develop and deploy the work process is higher than for "messaging-based" systems and end-users cannot be expected to develop forms or Java applications, necessary elements of Web-based workflow systems. The security of these systems is the major concern, especially when the global Internet is used to transport documents and forms.

Usually, these WFMSs lack facilities for workflows whose steps directly access and update data from Web servers. In short, they support customer-to-business transactions over the Web, but not business-to-business transactions. So, there is a necessity to support workflows whose steps are business-to-business transactions executed by Web servers. Possible solution can be providing WFMS with additional knowledge about the Web, its protocols and data format such that workflows can directly access information by interacting with Web servers. This can allow companies to automate their business processes on the Web, by allowing steps to automatically query/update information from Web servers located both within and outside the organization. The additional knowledge required is provided by the workflow system developer and the workflow designer.

Combining workflow management and Web technologies in this manner offer immense benefits for conducting business over the Web. The most important is possibility of creating virtual enterprise. The formation of such a virtual enterprise makes it possible to implement JIT (Just In Time) method of inventory control to save money on inventory, warehousing and handling costs. Thus a company manufacturing a product, can use Web workflows to place orders for the individual components needed to make the product immediately after it receives an order for the product.

Most important problems that can arise in implementing workflows on the Web are:

- Unreliability of the Web in the form of server/network failures and delays,
- Insufficient efficiency

First, for the reliable execution of workflows on the Web there is a necessity for a special protocol to ensure that an update request is processed by a server exactly once, despite network/server failures. Second, to ameliorate the effects of network delays and failures, vendors can provide an optimizer that, using the data and control flow information associated with the workflow schema, will compile a workflow schema and parallelize the steps in the workflow to the maximum possible extent. Third, to improve efficiency, we can prefetch some steps using emerging Web technologies (like Java) and utilize standard enhancements that have been proposed for the Web infrastructure (e.g. for the HTTP protocol by the Internet Engineering Task Force - IETF). The goal is reducing the number of messages exchanged (both within the organization and to other organizations through the organizations gateway) and reducing the load at the workflow engine.

3.3.4 Endnote on Categories

There is no single best category of workflow systems. The right system depends on the nature of the processes to be supported with a workflow tool.

By now, workflow management technology and its underlying concepts are in their infancies. Typically, only individual and well- understood (production) workflows can be sufficiently modeled and adequately supported by WFMS. Also, there are problems because no standards have yet been developed except for production workflow category. The Workflow Management Coalition (WfMC's) Reference Model defines a generalized target architecture driving the development of most production workflow solutions.

3.4 Existing Products

Although workflow management systems still have a long way to go until they can be considered mature technology, the first generation of commercial systems has started to find wide acceptance. Some of them are [Waria01]:

- Bizflow 2000 (Handysoft)

- COSA Workflow (COSA Solutions)
- TeamWARE Flow (Fujitsu)
- Dolphin (Fujitsu)
- InTemp (JetForm)
- MQ/Series Workflow (IBM)
- SERfloware (SER)
- Staffware (Staffware Corp.)
- TIB/InConcert (TIBCO)
- Visual Workflow (FileNet)
- W4 (W4)

3.5 The Future of Workflow Management Systems

In the late 1990's, workflow systems were changing the way that businesses manage the flow of work, and therefore heavily influenced changes in today's business. But changes in today's structure of organizations and the environment, are directly changing the structure and objectives of management workflow systems themselves. The major areas affecting the future of workflow management systems are:

- Customization
- Structure of the Organization
- E-Mail
- Virtual Corporations
- Web
- E-Commerce

3.5.1 Customization

The Workflow Management Coalition (WfMC) states customization as one of the primary reasons for causing changes in workflow applications.

More and more companies are realizing the benefits of implementing a workflow management system. Therefore, the demand from various types of organizations for a customized workflow system is increasing. As a result, there is a continuous increase in the number and types of systems in the market today.

3.5.2 Structure of the Organization

Modern companies are more integrated than in the past. Many organizations are moving away from organizational departments that make independent decisions and instead are emphasizing mutual decisions made across the organization. So, they are demanding a change in workflow from department-oriented to full organization-oriented. This means that companies are demanding instant information to all parts of the organization. Therefore, one of the biggest changes in workflow systems results from the demand to meet the organizations communication demands.

3.5.3 E-Mail

E-mail is becoming much more widely used in current workflow systems to help solve the cross-organization problem. Messaging-based workflow is becoming more popular because they can use e-mail protocols as their transport. E-mail based workflow is ideal due to its low costs to deploy and maintain.

For example, a bank may have a production workflow system to process loan applications. When an exception occurs - for example, a customer seeking an unusually large loan - the loan officer can choose a button to initiate a workflow exception. A system-produced form can then be routed via e-mail to the vice president who may review it and re-route it back to the loan officer online.

3.5.4 Virtual Corporations

Organizations whose employees work out of home from PC's need workflow transmitted through a medium to reach all pertinent employees. No single workflow system has been designed to satisfactorily solve this problem as of yet. Part of the problem has been met as workflow can be transmitted through the web and e-mail.

3.5.5 Web

Bringing the web technology and workflow together creates huge opportunities for extending the benefits of workflow even further. From reduction of internal administration costs to pushing services right out to customers desktops.

3.5.6 E-Commerce

Forrestor Research estimates that 78% of total dollars spent on e-Commerce in 1999. were business-to-business transactions, totaling $17 billion. It is estimated that in 2002, it will be $327 billion. Changes in workflow will be brought about from organizations demanding workflow systems that enable them to integrate their business processes with those of other organizations with whom they do business.

3.6 Summary

Workflow technology coordinates a company's human and electronic resources and processes. Enterprises should incorporate such modern technology because it provides competitive advantages by facilitating management and freeing the company's intellectual resources from routine and administrational work. Workflow automation can contribute to the competitiveness of an enterprise, because released extra time could be used by the intellectual resources to interact with customers and suppliers, to better understand market and analyze trends that affect their work and reactively initiate changes in their work.

This emphasizes that the intellectual asset is a very precious resource for an enterprise (see e.g. [Beer81], [Espejo89]). To be competitive, every intellectual resource at every workplace has to adapt rapidly to the changing environmental conditions and must quickly make decisions based on all the information available. This guarantees effectiveness (doing the right things) and efficiency (doing the things right).

3.7 Problems

1. What are the essential parts of every workflow, and what do they serve for?
2. Are there possibilities to change actors or routes of tasks, without impact on the implementation of activities? If there is a possibility, why is it possible?
3. What are the essential blocks of the workflow management systems?
4. What could be the biggest problems in the workflow interoperability?
5. Give an example of a virtual enterprise, and think what could be personal and organizational benefits.
6. Imagine your own example of an organization information system, and describe its major parts.
7. What are the best ways to improve a business process?
8. What are the possible dangers that can be caused by automation of processes?
9. For each type of WFMS, give an example of a process that can be supported.
10. What are the possible problems that can arise in the implementation of the web-based workflow management systems? How could they be solved?

References

[Beer81] Beer, S., "The Brain of the Firm," Wiley, Chichester, UK, **1981.**

[Brodie95] Brodie, M.L., Stonebraker, M., "Migrating Legacy Systems," Morgan Kaufmann, San Francisco, USA, **1995.**

[Cosa00] Workflow Overview, (http://www.cosa.nl/demo_uk.asp), COSA Solutions, Vianen, Netherlands, **2000.**

[Espejo89] Espejo, R., Harnden, R., "The Viable System Model," Wiley, Chichester, UK, **1989.**

[Graeber95] Graeber S., "Object-Oriented Modeling of Hospital Information Systems," In: Greenes RA, Peterson HE, Protti DJ, eds. MEDINFO 95, Amsterdam, Netherlands, **1995,** pp. 494-497.

[Graeber96] Graeber S., "Communications Services for a Distributed Hospital Information System," Methods Inf Med **1996,** pp. 35-230 – 35-241.

[Kobielus97] Kobielus, G.J., "Workflow Strategies," IDG Books Worldwide, **1997.**

[Leymann01] Leymann, F., Roller, D., "Understanding Workflow," The Business Integrator Journal, **Fall 2001.**

[Paul97] Paul, S., Park, E., Chaar, J., **"**Essential Requirements for a Workflow Standard," IBM T.J. Watson Research Center, OOPSLA, Yorktown Heights, New York, USA, **1997.**

[Waria01] Product Descriptions, (http://www.waria.com/books/study-products.htm), Workflow and Reengineering International Association, **August 2001.**

[WfMC01] About Workflow Management Coalition, (http://www.wfmc.org/about.htm), The Workflow Management Coalition, **2001.**

[WfMC94] The Workflow Reference Model. TC-1003 (Status 1.1), Workflow Management Coalition (WfMC), Brussels, Belgium, **1994.**

[WfMC96a] Terminology and Glossary. TC-1011 (Status 2.0), Workflow Management Coalition (WfMC), Brussels, Belgium, **1996.**

[WfMC96b] Interface 1 - Process Definition Interchange. TC-1016 (Status 6.0), Workflow Management Coalition (WfMC), Brussels, Belgium, **1996.**

E-Business and E-Challenges
V. Milutinović and F. Patricelli (Eds.)
IOS Press, 2002

CHAPTER 4
DATA MINING

Jovanovic Nemanja

In this chapter we would like to introduce the reader to the topic of data mining and related issues. We would like to encourage those who have tried to find "data mining" *in the dictionary and failed. Everything is OK, the word is spelled correct, and the only problem why you couldn't find it is that the term is brand new.*

First we would give the definition of DM. Then we point out differences between DM and related techniques. We will discuss different problem types and focus on CRISP-DM process model.

4.1 Introduction

The amount of information in the world is estimated to double every 20 months. It is spread among data warehouses all around the world in different formats, on different security level etc. Data warehouses today can range in size up to terabytes. Somewhere within these masses of data lies hidden information of strategic importance. The main question is how to find this needle in the haystack.

The newest solution to this problem is *Data mining* (DM). It is a result of a long process of research and product development but it is not a magic wand. It won't supervise your data warehouse and notify you when it espies an interesting pattern. On the other side it doesn't eliminate the need to know your problem as well as understand your data or analytical methods. It's just an assistant that can help you classify your data, predict later behavior, extract association rules or detect sequences. But with the efficient use of DM in your projects you could also reduce costs and increase revenues.

Data mining can be defined as automated extraction of predictive information from various data sources. It's a powerful technology with great potential to help users focus on the most important information stored in data warehouses or streamed through communication lines. DM can answer questions that were to time consuming to resolve in the past. Also DM can predict future trends and behaviors, allowing us to make proactive, knowledge-driven decisions.

4.1.1 DM vs. Knowledge Discovery in Databases

The term "*data mining*" is used somewhat indiscriminately and is often applied to describe all of the tools employed to analyze and understand data. More specifically, however, DM is a part of a larger process called *Knowledge Discovery in Databa*ses (KDD). KDD incorporate several techniques: searching, statistical analysis, On-Line Analytical Processing (OLAP) and data mining.

4.1.2 DM vs. OLAP

Data mining is also frequently identified with *On-Line Analytical Processing* (OLAP). As we shall see, they are very different techniques that can complement each other.

OLAP is part of the spectrum of decision support tools. Traditional query and report tools describe WHAT is in a database. OLAP goes further; it's used to answer WHY certain things are true. The user forms a hypothesis about a relationship and verifies it with a series of queries against the data. For example, an analyst might want to determine the factors that lead to loan defaults. He or she might initially hypothesize that people with low incomes are bad credit risks and analyze the database with OLAP to verify (or disprove) this assumption. In other words, the OLAP analyst generates a series of hypothetical patterns and relationships and uses queries against the database to verify them or disprove them.

The question is: How to form this hypothesis? It is a deductive process that is based on essential understanding of data and relations among them. What happens when the number of variables being analyzed is in the dozens or even hundreds? It becomes much more difficult and time-consuming to form a good hypothesis.

Data mining is different from OLAP because rather than verify hypothetical patterns, it uses the data itself to uncover such patterns. It is essentially an inductive process. For example, suppose the analyst who wanted to identify the risk factors for loan default were to use a data mining tool. The data mining tool might discover that people with high debt and low incomes were bad credit risks (as above), but it might go further and also discover a pattern the analyst did not think to try, such as that age is also a determinant of risk.

Here is where data mining and OLAP can complement each other. OLAP can be used to verify the results of data mining process. To achieve performance and useful output this cycle should to be supervised by analyst. This is important because the better you understand your data, the more effective the knowledge process will be.

4.2 Data mining problem types

The goal of data mining is to produce new knowledge that the user can act upon. It does this by building a model of the real world based on data collected from a variety of sources which may include corporate transactions, customer histories and demographic information, process control data, and relevant external databases such as credit bureau information or weather data. The result of the model building is a description of patterns and relationships in the data that can be confidently used for prediction.

Before we select appropriate models and algorithms we have to focus on our goal: what is the ultimate purpose of mining this data? The next step is deciding on the type of prediction that's most appropriate. Usually, data mining project involves a combination of different problem types, which together solve the problem.

4.2.1 Data description and summarization

Data Description and Summarization aims at the concise description of characteristics of the data, typically in elementary and aggregated form. This gives the user an overview of the structure of the data. Sometimes, data description and summarization alone can be an objective of a data mining project. For instance, a retailer might be interested in the turnover of all outlets broken down by categories. Changes and differences to a previous period could be summarized and highlighted. This kind of problem would be at the lower end of the scale of data mining problems.

However, in almost all data mining projects data description and summarization is a sub goal in the process, typically in early stages. At the beginning of a data mining process, the user often knows neither the precise goal of the analysis nor the precise nature of the data. Initial exploratory data analysis can help to understand the nature of the data and to find potential hypotheses for hidden information. Simple descriptive statistical and visualization techniques provide first insights in the data. For example, the distribution of customer age and their living areas gives hints about which parts of a customer group need to be addressed by further marketing strategies.

Data description and summarization typically occurs in combination with other data mining problem types. For instance, data description may lead to the postulation of interesting segments in the data. Once segments are identified and defined a description and summarization of these segments is useful. It is advisable to carry out data description and summarization before any other data mining problem type is addressed. In this document, this is reflected by the fact that data description and summarization is a task in the data understanding phase.

Summarization also plays an important role in the presentation of final results. The outcomes of the other data mining problem types (e.g., concept descriptions or prediction models) may also be considered summarizations of data, but on a higher conceptual level.

Many reporting systems, statistical packages, OLAP and EIS systems can cover data description and summarization but do usually not provide any methods to perform more advanced modeling. If data description and summarization is considered a stand alone problem type and no further modeling is required, these tools are also appropriate to carry out data mining engagements.

4.2.2 Segmentation

The data mining problem type *segmentation* aims at the separation of the data into interesting and meaningful subgroups or classes. All members of a subgroup share common characteristics. For instance, in shopping basket analysis one could define segments of baskets depending on the items they contain.

Segmentation can be performed manually or (semi-) automatically. The analyst can hypothesize certain subgroups as relevant for the business question based on prior knowledge or based on the outcome of data description and summarization. However, there are also automatic clustering techniques that can detect previously unsuspected and hidden structures in data that allow segmentation.

Segmentation can be a data mining problem type of its own. Then the detection of segments would be the main purpose of data mining. For example, all addresses in zip code areas with higher than average age and income might be selected for mailing advertisements on home nursing insurance.

Often, however, very often segmentation is a step towards solving other problem types. Then, the purpose can be to keep the size of the data manageable or to find homogeneous data subsets that are easier to analyze. Typically, in large datasets various influences overlay each other and obscure the interesting patterns. Then, appropriate segmentation makes the task easier. For instance, analyzing dependencies between items in millions of shopping baskets is very hard. It is much easier (and more meaningful, typically) to identify dependencies in interesting segments of shopping baskets, for instance high-value baskets, baskets containing convenience goods or baskets from a particular day or time.

Note: In the literature there is a confusion of terms. Segmentation is sometimes called clustering or classification. The latter term is confusing because some people use it to refer to the creation of classes, while others mean the creation of models to predict known classes for previously unseen cases. In this document, we restrict the term classification to the latter meaning (see below) and use the term segmentation for the former meaning, though classification techniques can be used to elicit descriptions of the segments discovered.

Appropriate techniques:

- Clustering techniques.
- Neural nets.
- Visualization.

Example:

A car company regularly collects information about its customers concerning their socio-economic characteristics like income, age, sex, profession, etc. Using cluster analysis, the company can divide its customers into more understandable subgroups and analyze the structure of each subgroup. Specific marketing strategies are deployed for each group separately.

4.2.3 Concept descriptions

Concept description aims at an *understandable* description of concepts or classes. The purpose is not to develop complete models with high prediction accuracy, but to gain insights. For instance, a company may be interested to learn more about their loyal and disloyal customers. From a concept description of these concepts (loyal and disloyal customers) the company might infer what could be done to keep customers loyal or to transform disloyal customers to loyal customers.

Concept description has a close connection to both segmentation and classification. Segmentation may lead to an enumeration of objects belonging to a concept or class without any understandable description. Typically, there is segmentation before concept description is performed. Some techniques, for example conceptual clustering techniques, perform segmentation and concept description at the same time.

Concept descriptions can also be used for classification purposes. On the other hand, some classification techniques produce understandable classification models, which can then be considered as concept descriptions. The important distinction is that classification aims to be complete in some sense. The classification model needs to apply to *all* cases in the selected population. On the other hand, concept descriptions need not be complete. It is sufficient if they describe important parts of the concepts or classes. In the example above, it may be sufficient to get concept descriptions of those customers who are clearly loyal.

Appropriate techniques:

- Rule induction methods.
- Conceptual clustering.

Example:

Using data about the buyers of new cars and using a rule induction technique, a car company could generate rules that describe its loyal and disloyal customers. Below are examples of the generated rules:

If SEX = male and AGE > 51 then CUSTOMER = loyal

If SEX = female and AGE > 21 then CUSTOMER = loyal

If PROFESSION = manager and AGE < 51 then CUSTOMER = disloyal

If FAMILY STATUS = bachelor and AGE < 51 then CUSTOMER = disloyal

4.2.4 Classification

Classification assumes that there is a set of objects – characterized by some attributes or features – which belong to different classes. The class label is a discrete (symbolic) value and is known for each object. The objective is to build classification models (sometimes called classifiers), which assign the correct class label to previously unseen and unlabeled objects. Classification models are mostly used for predictive modeling.

The class labels can be given in advance, for instance defined by the user or derived from segmentation.

Classification is one of the most important data mining problem types that occur in a wide range of various applications. Many data mining problems can be transformed to classification problems. For example, credit scoring tries to assess the credit risk of a new customer. This can be transformed to a classification problem by creating two classes, good and bad customers. A classification model can be generated from existing customer data and their credit behavior. This classification model can then be used to assign a new potential customer to one of the two classes and hence accept or reject him.

Classification has connections to almost all other problem types. Prediction problems can be transformed to classification problems by binning continuous class labels, since binning techniques allow transforming continuous ranges into discrete intervals. These discrete intervals are then used as class labels rather than the exact numerical values and hence lead to a classification problem. Some classification techniques produce understandable class or concept descriptions. There is also a connection to dependency analysis because classification models typically exploit and elucidate dependencies between attributes.

Segmentation can either provide the class labels or restrict the dataset such that good classification models can be built.

It is useful to analyze deviations before a classification model is built. Deviations and outliers can obscure the patterns that would allow a good classification model. On the other hand, a classification model can also be used to identify deviations and other problems with the data.

Appropriate techniques:

- Discriminant analysis.
- Rule induction methods.
- Decision tree learning.
- Neural nets.
- K Nearest Neighbor.
- Case-based reasoning.
- Genetic algorithms.

Example:

Banks generally have information on the payment behavior of their credit applicants. Combining this financial information with other information about the customers like sex, age, income, etc., it is possible to develop a system to classify new customers as good or bad customers, (i.e., the credit risk in acceptance of a customer is either low or high, respectively).

4.2.5 Prediction

Another important problem type that occurs in a wide range of applications is *prediction*. Prediction is very similar to classification. The only difference is that in prediction the target attribute (class) is not a qualitative discrete attribute but a continuous one. The aim of prediction is to find the numerical value of the target attribute for unseen objects. In the literature, this problem type is sometimes called regression. If prediction deals with time series data then it is often called forecasting.

Appropriate techniques:

- Regression analysis.
- Regression trees.
- Neural nets.
- K Nearest Neighbor.
- Box-Jenkins methods.
- Genetic algorithms.

Example:

The annual revenue of an international company is correlated with other attributes like advertisement, exchange rate, inflation rate etc. Having these values (or their reliable estimations for the next year) the company can predict its expected revenue for the next year.

4.2.6 Dependency analysis

Dependency analysis consists of finding a model that describes significant dependencies (or associations) between data items or events. Dependencies can be used to predict the value of a data item given information on other data items. Although dependencies can be used for predictive modeling, they are mostly used for understanding. Dependencies can be strict or probabilistic.

Associations are a special case of dependencies, which have recently become very popular. Associations describe affinities of data items (i.e., data items or events which frequently occur together). A typical application scenario for associations is the analysis of shopping baskets. There, a rule like "in 30 percent of all purchases, beer and peanuts have been bought together" is a typical example for an association.

Algorithms for detecting associations are very fast and produce many associations. Selecting the most interesting ones is a challenge.

Dependency analysis has close connections to prediction and classification, where dependencies are implicitly used for the formulation of predictive models. There is also a connection to concept descriptions, which often highlight dependencies.

In applications, dependency analysis often co-occurs with segmentation. In large datasets, dependencies are seldom significant because many influences overlay each other. In such cases it is advisable to perform a dependency analysis on more homogeneous segments of the data.

Sequential patterns are a special kind of dependencies where the orders of events are considered. In the shopping basket domain, associations describe dependencies between items at a given time. Sequential patterns describe shopping patterns of one particular customer or a group of customers over time.

Appropriate Techniques:

- Correlation analysis.

- Regression analysis.
- Association rules.
- Bayesian networks.
- Inductive Logic Programming.
- Visualization techniques.

Example 1:

Using regression analysis, a business analyst has found that there is a significant dependency between the total sales of a product and its price and the amount of the total expenditures for the advertisement. Once the analyst discovered this knowledge, he can reach the desired level of the sales by changing the price and/or the advertisement expenditure accordingly.

Example 2:

Applying association rule algorithms to data about car accessories, a car company has found that if a radio is ordered, an automatic gearbox is ordered as well in 95 percent of all cases. Based on this dependency, the car company decides to offer these accessories as a combination which leads to cost reduction.

4.3 Data mining process model

A systematic approach is essential to successful data mining. Many process models were designed to guide the analyst through a sequence of steps that will lead to good results. For example SPSS Clementine uses the 5A's (Assess, Access, Analyze, Act and Automate) and SAS Enterprise Miner uses SEMMA (Sample, Explore, Modify, Model and Assess). A consortium of vendors and users of DM tools has been developing a specification called CRISP-DM (*Cross-Industry Standard Process for Data Mining*).

4.3.1 History of CRISP-DM

CRISP-DM was conceived in late 1996 by three "veterans" of the young and immature data mining market. DaimlerChrysler (then Daimler-Benz) was already experienced, ahead of most industrial and commercial organizations, in applying data mining in its business operations. SPSS (then ISL) had been providing services based on data mining since 1990 and had launched the first commercial data mining workbench – Clementine – in 1994. NCR, as part of its aim to deliver added value to its Teradata data warehouse customers, had established teams of data mining consultants and technology specialists to service its clients' requirements.

At that time, early market interest in data mining was showing signs of exploding into widespread uptake. This was both exciting and terrifying. All of them had developed their approaches to data mining as they went along. Were they doing it right? Was every new adopter of data mining going to have to learn, as they had initially, by trial and error? And from a supplier's perspective, how could they demonstrate to prospective customers that data mining was sufficiently mature to be adopted as a key part of their business processes?

A standard process model, they reasoned, non-proprietary and freely available, would address these issues for them and for all practitioners.

A year later they had formed a consortium, invented an acronym (CRoss-Industry Standard Process for Data Mining), obtained funding from the European Commission and begun to set out their initial ideas. As CRISP-DM was intended to be industry-, tool- and application-neutral, they knew they had to get input from as wide a range as possible of practitioners and others (such as data warehouse vendors and management consultancies) with a vested interest in data mining. They did this by creating the CRISP-DM Special Interest Group ("The SIG", as it became known). Consortium launched the SIG by broadcasting an invitation to interested parties to join them in Amsterdam for a day-long workshop.

The workshop surpassed all expectations. Three things stood out:

- Twice as many people turned up as had been initially expected.
- There was an overwhelming consensus that the industry needed a standard process and needed it now.
- As each attendee presented their views on data mining from their project experience, it became clear that although there were superficial differences – mainly in demarcation of phases and in terminology – there was tremendous common ground in how they viewed the process of data mining.

Over the next two and a half years, consortium worked to develop and refine CRISP-DM. They ran trials in live, large-scale data mining projects at Mercedes-Benz and at their insurance sector partner, OHRA. They also worked on the integration of CRISP-DM with commercial data mining tools. The SIG proved invaluable, growing to over 200 members and holding workshops in London, New York and Brussels.

By the end of the EC-funded part of the project – mid-1999 – they had produced a good-quality draft of the process model. Those familiar with that draft will find that a year on, although now much more complete and better presented, CRISP-DM 1.0 is by no means radically different.

Over the past year, DaimlerChrysler had the opportunity to apply CRISP-DM to a wider range of applications. SPSS' and NCR's Professional Services groups have adopted CRISP-DM and used it successfully on numerous customer engagements covering many industries and business problems.

CRISP-DM has not been built in a theoretical, academic manner working from technical principles, nor did elite committees of gurus create it behind closed doors. Both these approaches to developing methodologies have been tried in the past, but have seldom led to practical, successful and widely–adopted standards. CRISP-DM succeeds because it is soundly based on the practical, real-world experience of how people do data mining projects.

4.3.2 CRISP-DM methodology

4.3.2.1 Hierarchical breakdown

The CRISP-DM data mining methodology is described in terms of a hierarchical process model, consisting of sets of tasks described at four levels of abstraction (from general to specific): phase, generic task, specialized task and process instance.

At the top level, the data mining process is organized into a number of phases; each phase consists of several second-level generic tasks. This second level is called generic, because it is intended to be general enough to cover all possible data mining situations. The generic tasks are intended to be as complete and stable as possible. Complete means covering both the whole process of data mining and all possible data mining applications. Stable means that the model should be valid for yet unforeseen developments like new modeling techniques.

The third level, the specialized task level, is the place to describe how actions in the generic tasks should be carried out in certain specific situations. For example, at the second level there might be a generic task called clean data. The third level describes how this task differed in different situations, such as cleaning numeric values versus cleaning categorical values or whether the problem type is clustering or predictive modeling.

The description of phases and tasks as discrete steps performed in a specific order represents an idealized sequence of events. In practice, many of the tasks can be performed in a different order and it will often be necessary to repeatedly backtrack to previous tasks and repeat certain actions. CRISP-DM does not attempt to capture all of these possible routes through the data mining process because this would require an overly complex process model.

The fourth level, the process instance, is a record of the actions, decisions and results of an actual data mining engagement. A process instance is organized according to the tasks defined at the higher levels, but represents what actually happened in a particular engagement, rather than what happens in general.

4.3.2.2 Mapping generic models to specialized models

The data mining context drives mapping between the generic and the specialized level in CRISP-DM. Currently, we distinguish between four different dimensions of data mining contexts:

- The application domain is the specific area in which the data mining project takes place.
- The data mining problem type describes the specific class(es) of objective(s) that the data mining project deals with.
- The technical aspect covers specific issues in data mining that describe different (technical) challenges that usually occur during data mining.
- The tool and technique dimension specifies which data mining tool(s) and/or techniques are applied during the data mining project.

A specific data mining context is a concrete value for one or more of these dimensions. For example, a data mining project dealing with a classification problem in churn prediction constitutes one specific context. The more values for different context dimensions are fixed, the more concrete is the data mining context.

We distinguish between two different types of mapping between generic and specialized level in CRISP-DM:

- Mapping for the present.

If we only apply the generic process model to perform a single data mining project and attempt to map generic tasks and their descriptions to the specific project as required, we talk about a single mapping for (probably) only one usage.

- Mapping for the future:

If we systematically specialize the generic process model according to a pre-defined context (or similarly systematically analyze and consolidate experiences of a single project towards a specialized process model for future usage in comparable contexts), we talk about explicitly writing up a specialized process model in terms of CRISP-DM.

Which type of mapping is appropriate for your own purposes depends on your specific data mining context and the needs of your organization. The basic strategy for mapping the generic process model to the specialized level is the same for both types of mappings:

- Analyze your specific context.
- Remove any details not applicable to your context.
- Add any details specific to your context.

- Specialize (or instantiate) generic contents according to concrete characteristics of your context.
- Possibly rename generic contents to provide more explicit meanings in your context for the sake of clarity.

4.3.3 CRISP-DM process model: Phases

The current process model for data mining provides an overview of the life cycle of a data mining project. It contains the phases of a project, their respective tasks and relationships between these tasks. At this description level, it is not possible to identify all relationships. Essentially, relationships could exist between any data mining tasks depending on the goals, the background and interest of the user and most importantly on the data.

The life cycle of a data mining project consists of six phases. The sequence of the phases is not rigid. Moving back and forth between different phases is always required. It depends on the outcome of each phase which phase or which particular task of a phase, has to be performed next.

Data mining is not over once a solution is deployed. The lessons learned during the process and from the deployed solution can trigger new, often more focused business questions. Subsequent data mining processes will benefit from the experiences of previous ones.

In the following, we outline each phase briefly:

4.3.3.1 Business understanding

This initial phase focuses on understanding the project objectives and requirements from a business perspective, then converting this knowledge into a data mining problem definition and a preliminary plan designed to achieve the objectives.

4.3.3.2 Data understanding

The data understanding phase starts with an initial data collection and proceeds with activities in order to get familiar with the data, to identify data quality problems, to discover first insights into the data or to detect interesting subsets to form hypotheses for hidden information.

4.3.3.3 Data preparation

The data preparation phase covers all activities to construct the final dataset (data that will be fed into the modeling tool(s)) from the initial raw data. Data preparation tasks are likely to be performed multiple times and not in any prescribed order. Tasks include table, record and attribute selection as well as transformation and cleaning of data for modeling tools.

4.3.3.4 Modeling

In this phase, various modeling techniques are selected and applied and their parameters are calibrated to optimal values. Typically, there are several techniques for the same data mining problem type. Some techniques have specific requirements on the form of data. Therefore, stepping back to the data preparation phase is often necessary.

4.3.3.5 Evaluation

At this stage in the project you have built a model (or models) that appear to have high quality from a data analysis perspective. Before proceeding to final deployment of the model, it is important to more thoroughly evaluate the model and review the steps executed to construct the model to be certain it properly achieves the business objectives. A key objective is to determine if there is some important business issue that has not been sufficiently considered. At the end of this phase, a decision on the use of the data mining results should be reached.

4.3.3.6 Deployment

Creation of the model is generally not the end of the project. Even if the purpose of the model is to increase knowledge of the data, the knowledge gained will need to be organized and presented in a way that the customer can use it. It often involves applying "live" models within an organization's decision making processes, for example in real-time personalization of Web pages or repeated scoring of marketing databases. However, depending on the requirements, the deployment phase can be as simple as generating a report or as complex as implementing a repeatable data mining process across the enterprise. In many cases it is the customer, not the data analyst, who carries out the deployment steps. However, even if the analyst will not carry out the deployment effort it is important for the customer to understand up front what actions need to be carried out in order to actually make use of the created models.

4.3.4 CRISP-DM process model: Tasks

4.3.4.1 Business understanding

Determine business objectives

The first objective of the data analyst is to thoroughly understand, from a business perspective, what the client really wants to accomplish. Often the client has many competing objectives and constraints that must be properly balanced. The analyst's goal is to uncover important factors, at the beginning, that can influence the outcome of the project. A possible consequence of neglecting this step is to expend a great deal of effort producing the right answers to the wrong questions.

Assess situation

This task involves more detailed fact-finding about all of the resources, constraints, assumptions and other factors that should be considered in determining the data analysis goal and project plan. In the previous task, your objective is to quickly get to the crux of the situation. Here, you want to flesh out the details.

Determine data mining goals

A *business goal* states objectives in business terminology. A *data mining goal* states project objectives in technical terms. For example, the business goal might be "Increase catalog sales to existing customers." A data mining goal might be "Predict how many widgets a customer will buy, given their purchases over the past three years, demographic information (age, salary, city, etc.) and the price of the item."

Produce project plan

Describe the intended plan for achieving the data mining goals and thereby achieving the business goals. The plan should specify the anticipated set of steps to be performed during the rest of the project including an initial selection of tools and techniques.

Initial assessment of tools and techniques

At the end of the first phase, the project also performs an initial assessment of tools and techniques. Here, you select a data mining tool that supports various methods for different stages of the process, for example. It is important to assess tools and techniques early in the process since the selection of tools and techniques possibly influences the entire project.

4.3.4.2 Data understanding

Collect initial data

Acquire within the project the data (or access to the data) listed in the project resources. This initial collection includes data loading if necessary for data understanding. For example, if you apply a specific tool for data understanding, it makes perfect sense to load your data into this tool. This effort possibly leads to initial data preparation steps. If you acquire multiple data sources, integration is an additional issue, either here or in the later data preparation phase.

Describe data

Examine the "gross" or "surface" properties of the acquired data and report on the results. Describe the data which has been acquired, including: the format of the data, the quantity of data, for example number of records and fields in each table, the identities of the fields and any other surface features of the data which have been discovered. Does the data acquired satisfy the relevant requirements?

Explore data

This task tackles the data mining questions, which can be addressed using querying, visualization and reporting. These include: distribution of key attributes, for example the target attribute of a prediction task; relations between pairs or small numbers of attributes; results of simple aggregations; properties of significant sub-populations; simple statistical analyses. These analyses may address directly the data mining goals; they may also contribute to or refine the data description and quality reports and feed into the transformation and other data preparation needed for further analysis.

Verify data quality

Examine the quality of the data, addressing questions such as: is the data complete (does it cover all the cases required)? Is it correct or does it contains errors and if there are errors how common are they? Are there missing values in the data? If so how are they represented, where do they occur and how common are they?

4.3.4.3 Data preparation

Select data

Decide on the data to be used for analysis. Criteria include relevance to the data mining goals, quality and technical constraints such as limits on data volume or data types. Note that data selection covers selection of attributes (columns) as well as selection of records (rows) in a table.

Clean data

Raise the data quality to the level required by the selected analysis techniques. This may involve selection of clean subsets of the data, the insertion of suitable defaults or more ambitious techniques such as the estimation of missing data by modeling.

Construct data

This task includes constructive data preparation operations such as the production of derived attributes, entire new records or transformed values for existing attributes. Derived attributes are new attributes that are constructed from one or more existing attributes in the same record. Examples: *area = length * width.*

Integrate data

These are methods whereby information is combined from multiple tables or records to create new records or values.

Merging tables refers to joining together two or more tables that have different information about the same objects. Example: a retail chain has one table with information about each store's general characteristics (e.g., floor space, type of mall), another table with summarized sales data (e.g., profit, percent change in sales from previous year) and another with information about the demographics of the surrounding area. Each of these tables contains one record for each store. These tables can be merged together into a new table with one record for each store, combining fields from the source tables.

Merged data also covers aggregations. Aggregation refers to operations where new values are computed by summarizing together information from multiple records and/or tables. For example, converting a table of customer purchases where there is one record for each purchase into a new table where there is one record for each customer, with fields such as *number of purchases, average purchase amount, percent of orders charged to credit card, percent of items under promotion, etc.*

Format data

Formatting transformations refer to primarily *syntactic* modifications made to the data that do not change its meaning, but might be required by the modeling tool.

Some tools have requirements on the order of the attributes, such as the first field being a unique identifier for each record or the last field being the outcome field the model is to predict. It might be important to change the order of the records in the dataset. Perhaps the modeling tool requires that the records be sorted according to the value of the outcome attribute. A common situation is that the records of the dataset are initially ordered in some way but the modeling algorithm needs them to be in a fairly random order. For example, when using neural networks it is generally best for the records to be presented in a random order although some tools handle this automatically with-out explicit user intervention.

Additionally, there are purely syntactic changes made to satisfy the requirements of the specific modeling tool. Examples: removing commas from within text fields in comma-delimited data files, trimming all values to a maximum of 32 characters.

4.3.4.4 Modeling

Select modeling technique

As the first step in modeling, select the actual modeling technique that is to be used. Whereas you possibly already selected a tool in business understanding, this task refers to the specific modeling technique, e.g., decision tree building with C4.5 or neural network generation with back propagation. If multiple techniques are applied, perform this task for each technique separately.

Generate test design

Before we actually build a model, we need to generate a procedure or mechanism to test the model's quality and validity. For example, in supervised data mining tasks such as classification, it is common to use error rates as quality measures for data mining models. Therefore, we typically separate the dataset into train and test set, build the model on the train set and estimate its quality on the separate test set.

Build model

Run the modeling tool on the prepared dataset to create one or more models.

Assess model

The data mining engineer interprets the models according to his domain knowledge, the data mining success criteria and the desired test design. This task interferes with the subsequent evaluation phase. Whereas the data mining engineer judges the success of the application of modeling and discovery techniques more technically, he contacts business analysts and domain experts later in order to discuss the data mining results in the business context. Moreover, this task only considers models whereas the evaluation phase also takes into account all other results that were produced in the course of the project.

The data mining engineer tries to rank the models. He assesses the models according to the evaluation criteria. As far as possible he also takes into account business objectives and business success criteria. In most data mining projects, the data mining engineer applies a single technique more than once or generates data mining results with different alternative techniques. In this task, he also compares all results according to the evaluation criteria.

4.3.4.5 Evaluation

Evaluate results

Previous evaluation steps dealt with factors such as the accuracy and generality of the model. This step assesses the degree to which the model meets the business objectives and seeks to determine if there is some business reason why this model is deficient. Another option of evaluation is to test the model(s) on test applications in the real application if time and budget constraints permit.

Moreover, evaluation also assesses other data mining results generated. Data mining results cover models which are necessarily related to the original business objectives and all other findings which are not necessarily related to the original business objectives but might also unveil additional challenges, information or hints for future directions.

Review process

At this point the resultant model hopefully appears to be satisfactory and to satisfy business needs. It is now appropriate to do a more thorough review of the data mining engagement in order to determine if there is any important factor or task that has somehow been overlooked. This review also covers quality assurance issues, e.g., did we correctly build the model? Did we only use attributes that we are allowed to use and that are available for future analyses?

Determine next steps

According to the assessment results and the process review, the project decides how to proceed at this stage. The project needs to decide whether to finish this project and move on to deployment if appropriate or whether to initiate further iterations or set up new data mining projects. This task includes analyses of remaining resources and budget that influences the decisions.

4.3.4.6 Deployment

Plan deployment

In order to deploy the data mining result(s) into the business, this task takes the evaluation results and concludes a strategy for deployment. If a general procedure has been identified to create the relevant model(s), this procedure is documented here for later deployment.

Plan monitoring and maintenance

Monitoring and maintenance are important issues if the data mining result becomes part of the day-to-day business and its environment. A careful preparation of a maintenance strategy helps to avoid unnecessarily long periods of incorrect usage of data mining results. In order to monitor the deployment of the data mining result(s), the project needs a detailed plan on the monitoring process. This plan takes into account the specific type of deployment.

Produce final report

At the end of the project, the project leader and his team write up a final report. Depending on the deployment plan, this report may be only a summary of the project and its experiences (if they have not already been documented as an ongoing activity) or it may be a final and comprehensive presentation of the data mining result(s).

Review project

Assess what went right and what went wrong, what was done well and what needs to be improved.

Summarize important experiences made during the project. For example, pitfalls, misleading approaches or hints for selecting the best suited data mining techniques in similar situations could be part of this documentation. In ideal projects, experience documentation covers also any reports that have been written by individual project members during the project phases and their tasks.

4.4 Choosing software for DM

In evaluating data mining tools you must look at a whole constellation of features, described below. You cannot put data mining tools into simple categories such as "high-end" versus "low-end" because the products are too rich in functionality to divide along just one dimension.

There are three main types of data mining products. First are tools that are analysis aids for OLAP. The next category includes the "pure" data mining products. These are horizontal tools aimed at data mining analysts concerned with solving a broad range of problems. The last category is analytic applications that implement specific business processes for which data mining is an integral part. For example, while you can use a horizontal data mining tool as part of the solution of many customer relationship management problems, you can also buy customized packages with the data mining imbedded. However, even packaged solutions require you to build and tune models that match your data.

Depending on your particular circumstances — system architecture, staff resources, database size, problem complexity — some data mining products will be better suited than others to meet your needs. Evaluating a data mining product involves learning about its capabilities in a number of key areas.

4.5 Summary

Data mining offers great promise in helping us to uncover patterns hidden in the data that can be used to predict the behavior of customers, products and processes. However, data mining tools need to be guided by users who understand the business, the data, and the general nature of the analytical methods involved.

It's vital to properly collect and prepare the data, and to check the models against the real world. Choosing the right data mining products means finding a tool with good basic capabilities, an interface that matches the skill level of the people who'll be using it, and features relevant to your specific problems.

REFERENCES

[Nilsen90] Hecht-Nilsen, R., Neurocomputing, Addison-Wesley, **1990**

[Fayyad96] Fayyad, U., Shapiro, P., Smyth, P., Uthurusamy, R., Advances in Knowledge Discovery and Data Mining, MIT Press, **1996**

[Pyle99] Pyle, D., Data Preparation for Data Mining, Morgan Kaufman, **1999**

[CROW99] Introduction to Data Mining and Knowledge Discovery, (http://www.twocrows.com), **1999**

[CRISP00] CRISP-DM Process Model, (http://www.crisp- dm.org), **2000**

E-Business and E-Challenges
V. Milutinović and F. Patricelli (Eds.)
IOS Press, 2002

CHAPTER 5
E-BANKING

Skundric Nikola, Milutinović Veljko, Kovacevic Milos and Klem Nikola

Electronic communication is infiltrating into the every aspect of our lives. The number of people using some sort of e-channels for various services is constantly increasing and of course among the most popular ones is the Internet. Traditional banking business, as all other businesses, is also adapting to these changes and new demands. This chapter will lead you through the world of electronic banking (especially Internet banking) from the very beginning to the point where you will learn how to set up your own Internet bank channel. Security and banking business are inseparable; of all e-Businesses, the security is here maybe the most important. Therefore, one whole section of this chapter is devoted to security issues. You will learn what the main security problems in Internet communications are; you will familiarize yourself with the solutions to these problems such as Digital Signatures and Digital Certificates (including ITU-T X.509 Certificates); and you will see a real-life implementation of these techniques through a Secure Sockets Layer in your browser.

Finally, you will see an Internet bank demo, and for the very end some useful tips on searching for the financial information on the Web.

5.1 Introduction to E-Banking

For a start, we shall make a brief overview of e-Business today; after that we shall answer the question "What is an e-Bank?" and explain the benefits of e-Banking. Finally, you will see some facts about e-Banking in Europe and the USA.

5.1.1 E-Business in Brief

Imagine the following situation: It is Monday and you have to do a lot of things:

- Reserve airplane tickets for your vacation
- Buy gifts for your child's birthday
- Pay bills for the current month (such as electricity, telephone, etc.)
- Check the bank account information
- Inform relatives about family gathering next weekend

Some time ago, this would be almost impossible to do in just one day – or at least you would waste a lot of valuable time. But, thanks to the development of E-Business, you can do all of the above from your home, or even from your car.

Every day more and more people are getting on the Internet. (Wireless access is becoming very popular too.) In the year 2000, there were about 414 million Internet users, and roughly 10% were using wireless access. At the end of 2001, there were already 673 million users and more then a third of them were using wireless access. According to eTForecasts, these numbers will rise by the end of the 2005 to a level of almost 1.2 billion users from which 62% will be wireless users (**Figure 5.1**).

Along with the increase of the Internet population, e-Commerce turnover is increasing too. For example, two years ago, Europeans had spent 770 million $ on-line, last year the turnover was 1970 million $, and at the end of 2001 it was more then 3.3 billion $.

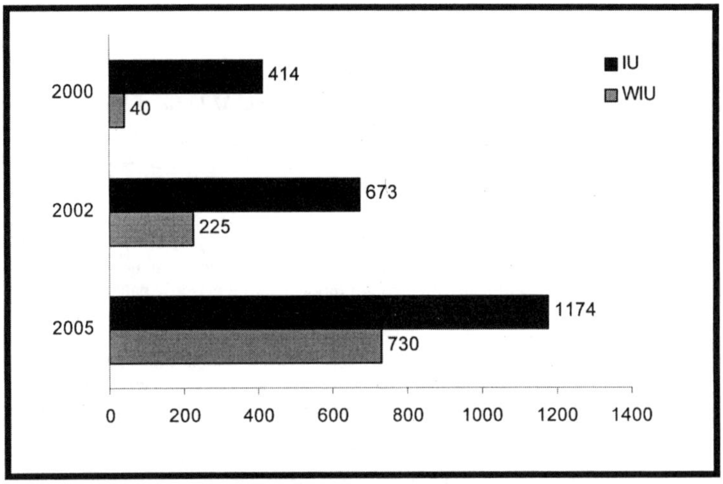

Legend: IU – Internet users **WIU** – Wireless Internet users

Comment: We are living in a connected world.

Figure 5.1 Worldwide Internet and Wireless Internet users, in millions (source: [eTForecasts01])

The growth is even larger in e-Business arena. During the 2002, only in Europe, B2B turnover will breach the level of 200 billion $.

Also, recent tragic terrorist attacks had one rather unexpected effect; according to some companies in the USA, in the last quarter of 2001 electronic bill payment has increased by almost 20%, but the full picture is yet to be seen.

Anyhow, e-Banking is no exception to these worldwide trends, but first, let's see what exactly an e-Bank is?

5.1.2 What Is an E-Bank?

Traditional banking business assumes that we have to have customer desk at bank's building, and that we have the office hours from 8.00 AM to 7.00 PM. On the other hand, our customers have their jobs during the day, and they have family activities after the job. As you can see, there is obvious collision between customers' demands and our capabilities.

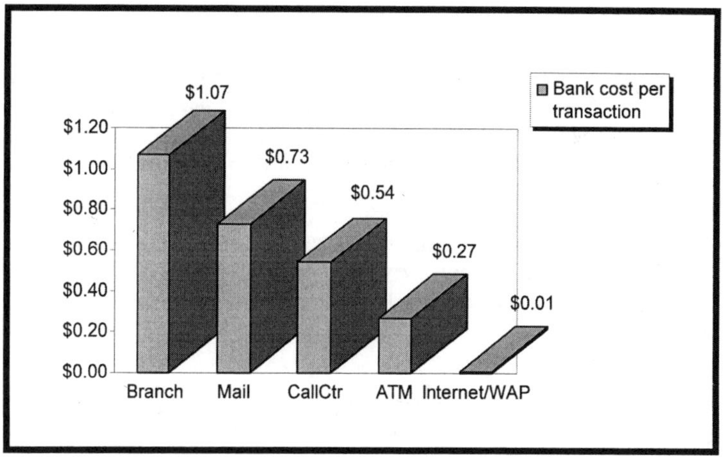

Legend: **CallCtr** – Phone banking
Internet/WAP – PC, PDA, WAP or Web TV

Figure 5.2 Bank cost per transaction (source: [ABA99])

E-Bank is transforming banking business into e-Business through utilizing various e-Channels. E-channels are:

- Internet,
- WAP based mobile network,
- Automated telephone,
- ATM network,
- SMS and FAX messaging,
- Multipurpose information kiosks,
- Web TV and others…

These e-Channels enable financial transactions from anywhere, and they allow a non-stop working time. If we remember that customers require non-stop working time, and that they want to be able to use services from anywhere, we can clearly see that in e-Banking business we now have a perfect match between their requests and our capabilities.

Of course, this is not the only advantage of e-Banking. You also have the possibility to extend your market (even out of country) because, among other things, you do not need any more an office in every single town. Also, you have the possibility to process more financial transactions, and last, but not the least, you have the possibility to lower your transaction cost.

Figure 5.2 on the previous page, shows the bank cost per transaction for various types of channels. As you can see, whilst the cost per transaction in ordinary branch is $1.07, in e-Banking business that cost can be lowered to only 1 cent per transaction by using Internet or WAP access through a PC, PDA, WAP mobile device or Web TV.

Now it is time to review some facts about status of Internet banking in the Europe and in the USA.

5.1.3 Some Facts about E-Banking in Europe and the USA

In Europe, there are already more then 12 million Internet bankers. The undisputed leader is Germany where 51% of the Internet users utilize e-Banking services. First runner-up is, a bit surprisingly, Sweden where that figure is 36%. The average for Europe today is about 10% with projected growth to 15% (that is 20 million) by the end of 2003 (sources: [Jupiter00], [eStats99]).

In the USA, bankers are well aware of benefits of Internet banking. In the year 2000, investments in the e-Banking technology were at a level of about half a billion $, and it is planned that such investments rise to a level of more then 2 billion $ by the end of 2005 (source: [Greenspam00]).

Powerful banks in the States are more present on the Web. According to FDIC (Federal Deposit Insurance Corporation), only 5% of banks with assets less then 100 million $ have some sort of online presence (source: [FDIC01]).

This percentage raises with financial power, so the most powerful banks with assets more then 10 billion $ have an excellent 84% online presence **(Figure 5.3).**

Assets	Number of Banks	Online Presence
Less then $100M	5,912	5%
$100M to $500M	3,403	16%
$500M to $1B	418	%34
$1B to $3B	312	42%
$3B to $10B	132	52%
More then $10B	94	84%

Comments: Powerful banks in the USA are more present.

Figure 5.3 Online banking presence (source: [FDIC00])

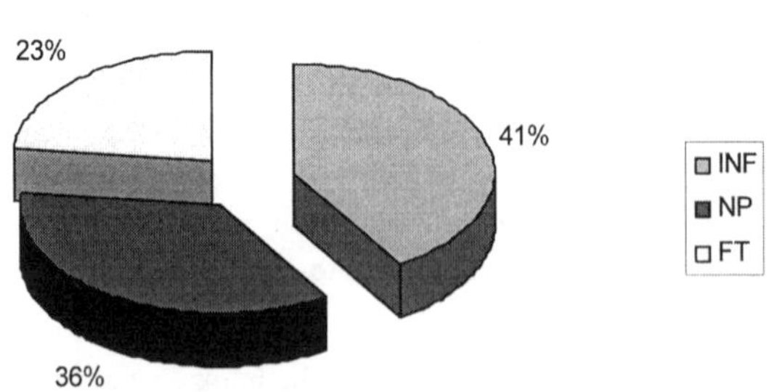

Legend: **INF** – Information only
NP – No presence
FT – Full transactional

Figure 5.4 Online status of the top 100 U.S. banks (source: [FDIC00])

Note that "online presence" does not necessarily denote banks' ability to perform online transactions. Online presence can also refer to various types of information published on the Web by the bank. At the end of the year 2000, about 1,100 U.S. banks, large and small, had been providing full-fledged transactional banking online. In the next two years additional 1,200 transactional online banks are expected, and by the 2005, the number of such banks should increase to more than 3,000.

The usage of Internet as an e-Channel, especially through WWW service, makes financial services available to wide population. Anyone who has access to Internet can easily make financial transactions simply by using browser and visiting appropriate Web locations. Of course, the usage of Internet, as well as other e-Channels, poses some security risks, both for the users and for the banks. That is the subject of the following section.

5.2 Security Issues

By now, you became aware of all the opportunities electronic banking can provide; above all improved efficiency and convenience. However, these benefits and opportunities come with a price – they can pose significant risk to a financial institution as well as to an individual. Naturally, those risks can be mitigated by adopting comprehensive risk management program.

5.2.1 Overview of Security Problems

People often hear a lot of different stories and have too much confidence in information picked up in the Hollywood movies, so the next section will try to give you a rather brief, yet informational, view on a problem of security in Internet communications. After reading it, you should have a decent knowledge about that subject.

Electronic banking, as you understood by now if you have not known already, relies on a networked environment. A computer network is simply an arrangement in which multiple computers are connected so that information, applications, and equipment can be shared. By design, networks can increase efficiency, convenience and access, but at the same time, the design also limits the degree to which the environment can be controlled. Network access can be performed through a combination of devices such as personal computers, telephones, interactive television equipment, and card devices with embedded computer chips. The connections are completed primarily through telephone lines, cable systems, and in some instances wireless technology. Whether the system is informational or transactional, these systems facilitate interaction between the bank and the user, often with the support of third-party service providers.

It is important to note that not all networks carry the same degree of risk; not all networks are equally vulnerable; not all networks are equally critical; and not all networks contain data that is equally sensitive.

Internal attacks are potentially the most damaging because a bank's personnel, which can include consultants as well as employees, may have authorized access to critical computer resources. Combined with detailed knowledge relating to the bank's practices and procedures, an internal attacker could access value transfer systems directly, or exploit trusted relationships among networked systems to gain a level of access that allows him to circumvent established security controls. After that, the attacker could potentially transfer money or other assets inappropriately. That is why the first thing you should do is to review and evaluate the security of internal networks.

The use of public networks poses additional risk to those of internal networks. It is important to note that the use of dedicated or leased lines may provide inappropriate sense of security relating to the confidentiality of data transmitted over them. These lines use the infrastructure of public networks; therefore, they are vulnerable to same attacks as the public networks themselves. Risks include line tapping and the possible interception and alteration of data. Therefore, it is wise to encrypt sensitive data transmitted via public networks.

The Internet is a public network of networks that can be accessed by any computer equipped with a modem – so like with any pubic network, the communication path is non-physical and may include any number of eavesdropping and active interference possibilities. Also, it is an open system where the identity of the communicating partners is not easy to define. Thus, as Ed Gerck nicely said "the Internet communication is much like anonymous postcards, which are answered by anonymous recipients." However, these postcards, open for anyone to read – and even write in them – must carry messages between specific end-points in a secure and private way [Gerck00]. Having all that in mind, in e-Banking business we can define three main problems:

1. **Spoofing** – "How can I reassure customers who come to my site that they are doing business with me, not with a fake setup to steal their credit card numbers?
2. **Eavesdropping** – "How can I be certain that my customers' account number information is not accessible to inline eavesdroppers when they enter into a secure transaction on the Web?"
3. **Data alteration** – "How can I be certain that my personal information is not altered by online eavesdroppers when they enter into a secure transaction on the Web?"

Generally, what we have to achieve is following:

- **Authentication** – to prevent spoofing.
- **Privacy** – to prevent eavesdropping.
- **Data integrity** – to prevent data alteration.
- **Non-repudiation** – to prevent the denial of a previous act.

The solution is to use Digital Certificates and Digital Signatures for Web servers, to provide authentication (that is to provide that communication is happening between the desired endpoints), data integrity and non-repudiation service; and to use cryptography algorithms to provide privacy. All these concepts will be explained in a little while. After that, you will see how Secure Sockets Layer in your Internet browser uses these techniques to achieve trusted communication.

5.2.2 Cryptography Basics

The purpose of the cryptography is to provide privacy, and that is achieved through utilization of various cryptography algorithms. Mathematical basis of these algorithms exceeds the scope of this chapter; here you should understand the basic principles of encrypted communication.

Figure 5.5 shows the simplified flowchart of the secure transmission of some message (that is, any data).

Generally, a sender takes a plain message and encrypts it with some encryption algorithm and some keys. Then he freely sends it over an insecure channel to a receiver, who then uses appropriate decryption algorithm and appropriate keys for the decryption of the message thus returning it into its original form.

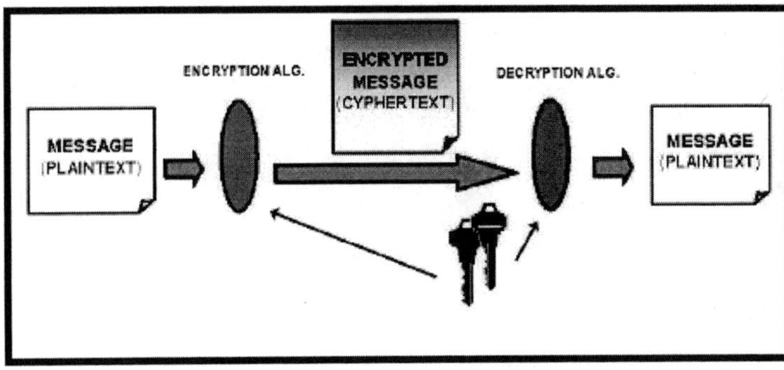

Comment: A pair of keys is used in the process of encryption and decryption. The correlation of that pair depends on the approach we take.

Figure 5.5 Simplified flowchart of the encrypted transmission

Relating to the keys used in the encryption/decryption process we can make a distinction between three approaches:

- Symmetric approach
- Asymmetric approach
- Hybrid approach

In symmetric approach, both sides use the same key for the encryption and decryption. This approach is useful for bulk data encryption because it is computationally faster then other methods, but we have a problem of key distribution. The best-known symmetric algorithms are DES (Data Encryption Standard, IBM & National Bureau of Standards, 1977), DESX (slightly strengthen version of DES) and IDEA.

In asymmetric approach, the sender uses the public key for the encryption and the receiver uses the private key for the decryption. This approach is more convenient for short data encryption because it is computationally slower then other methods, but here we do not have a problem with key distribution because the public key can be freely distributed over any channel, including insecure ones. However, we have other sort of the problem – how to securely bind that pubic key and its owner. The most popular asymmetric algorithms are RSA (Rivest, Shamir & Adleman, 1977) and Diffie-Hellman (1976).

The hybrid approach combines the good sides of both fore mentioned methods. It uses symmetric approach for data encryption (thus attaining good speed) and asymmetric approach for passing the symmetric key. This approach is applied in SSL. We shall talk more about SSL a bit later.

As you see, no matter what approach we choose, we have a problem with key management. In the symmetric approach, there is a problem with key distribution because we still have to have some sort of secure channel (not necessarily e-Channel) for sending the symmetric key. In asymmetric approach, on the other hand, although the public key can be distributed over any insecure channel we have a problem with secure binding of the public key and its owner. As you will see, that binding is done through the Digital Certificates. We will come back to that in a little while.

5.2.3 Digital Signatures

You have learned that cryptography provides privacy but there is a still opened question of the security. From a security point of view, we have to achieve three important things in our electronic communication (as mentioned before in section 5.2.1):

- **Origin authentication** – verification whether the message was sent by a declared sender,
- **Data-integrity authentication** – verification whether the message was changed after it was sent, and
- **Non-repudiation** – prevention of a denial of a previous act.

This is all accomplished through Digital Signatures – they were designed exactly for that purpose: to provide authentication and data integrity of electronic documents, as well as the non-repudiation service.

How do they work? Rather simply as you are about to see.

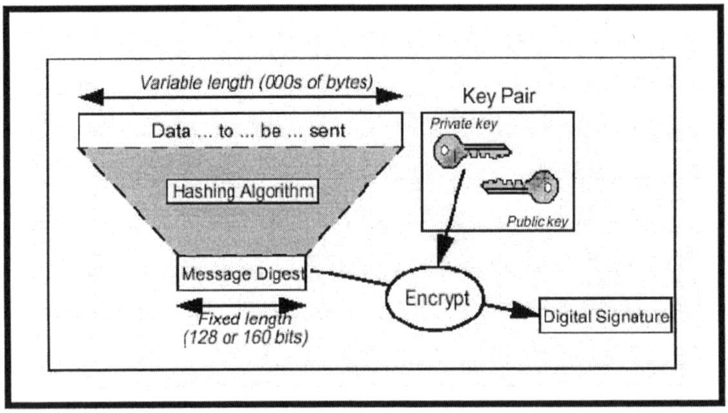

Comment: Digital Signature differs for different chunks of data it signs. The unique (and thus more similar to the real-life signature) is the key pair.

Figure 5.6 Generation of Digital Signature

Figure 5.6 shows the process of generation of the Digital Signature. Starting point is a variable length message, which we would like to sign digitally. First step is creating a message digest using one way hashing algorithm (like RSA-MD2, RSA-MD5, NIST-SHS, etc.) - these algorithms are designed to provide digests with a fixed length, usually 128 or 160 bits. After that, we encrypt the message digest with our private key, and the resulting sequence of bytes is what we call a Digital Signature.

OK, we created a Digital Signature, now what? Like in the real life, when we sign some document at the bottom of the paper, this signature is sent together with the message through an insecure channel. With that, as a sender, you have done what you could.

Now it is on the receiver to use that Digital Signature for authentication and integrity check of the message. How it is achieved, you can see on the **Figure 5.7**.

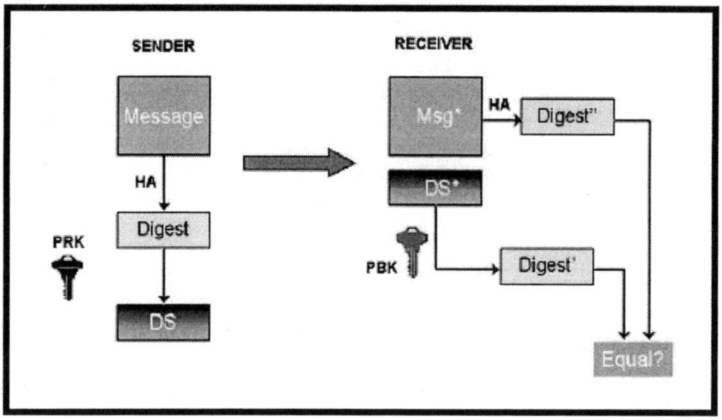

Legend: **PRK** – Private Key
PBK – Public Key
HA – Hashing Algorithm
DS – Digital Signature
Msg* – Received message (possibly corrupted)
DS* – Received Digital Signature

Figure 5.7 Authentication of the message using a Digital Signature

The receiver gets a packet with a message and a Digital Signature. First he uses a public key of the sender to decrypt the Digital Signature back into the message digest, which we shall call Digest'. At the same time, the receiver makes another message digest, but this time from the received message, using the same hashing algorithm as on the sender's side. That other message digest we shall call Digest''. Now all he have to do is to compare Digest' and Digest''. If they are equal, received message was really sent by the declared user, and we are certain that it was not tampered with.

Beside data integrity and authentication service, we have mentioned that the digital signatures mechanism also supports the important non-repudiation service. A. Menezes defines non-repudiation as "a service that prevents the denial of a previous act" [Menezes97]. That is, we can prevent the denial by a user of having participated in part or all of a communication. The non-repudiation service actually provides proof of the integrity and origin of the data in an unforgeable relationship that can be verified by any third party at any time. In e-Banking, this is extremely important.

The whole system of Digital Signatures relies on the capability to bind the public key and its owner. In other words, we can ask ourselves following two questions:

Q1: "How can I be sure that the public key my browser uses to send account number information is in fact the right one for that Web site, and not a bogus one?"

Q2: "How can I reliably communicate my public key to the customers so they can rely on it to send me encrypted communications?"

As we already mentioned, the solution to this problem is the Digital Certificates.

5.2.4 Digital Certificates

The problems that may be caused by a false certification or no certification mechanism can range from a "man-in-the-middle" attack in order to gain knowledge over controlled data, to a completely open situation to gain access to data and resources. It is important to note that these problems do not disappear with encryption or even a secure protocol. If the user connects to a spoofing site, which appears to be what he wants, he may have a secure connection to a thief and that will not make it safer. The identity certification or authentication is a must. We already said in previous section that Digital Signatures provide such authentication, but we also said that we have a problem with public key binding.

The certificates provide strong binding between the public key and some attribute (name or identity). They introduce tamperproof attributes used to help someone receiving a message decide whether the message, the key and the sender's name are what they appear to be – *without asking a sender*. Of course, absolute certification methods are logically impossible because a certificate cannot certify itself. A person relying on the certificate must verify its digital signature by referring, in turn, to another certificate, and so on along the chain of certificates until reaching a valid certificate digitally signed by a primary certification authority, whose digital signature is reasonably reliable – ultimately there must be a final "relying party"; some sort of "master" certificate you trust.

Digital Certificate is actually an electronic file that uniquely identifies communication entities on the Internet. Their purpose is to associate the name of an entity with its public key. Digital Certificates are issued and signed by the Certification authority. Everybody trusts Certification authority, and the Certification authority is responsible for entity name – public key binding.

De-facto standard for digital certification is ITU-T recommendation X.509 [ITU01]. The X.509 recommendation defines the framework for the provision of authentication services under a central control paradigm represented by "Directory". The "Directory" is implemented by a **Certification Authority** (CA), which issues certificates to **subscribers** (CA Clients) in order for such certificates to be verifiable by **users** (the public in general). These are the three main entities recognizable in X.509 certification procedures.

Certification Authority is a general designation for any entity that controls the authentication services and the management of certificates. This entity is also called **issuer**. Certification Authorities are in general independent, even in the same country. Certification authority can be:

- Public (a bank)
- Commercial (VeriSign, Thawte)
- Private (a company for private needs)
- Personal (you, me)

The legal and technical relationship between Certification authority and its subscribers and users are governed by a Certification Practice Statement (CPS) issued by the Certification authority. X.509 recommendation references several items to be defined in the CPS, but it's internally defined by each Certification authority within broad limits and lies outside the scope of X.509.

Subscriber is an entity that supplies to the Certification authority the information that is to be included in the entity's own certificate, signed by the CA. The subscriber is a commercial client to a Certification authority. Usually, as defined in the Certification authority's Certification Practice Statement, the information supplied by the subscriber is "endorsed" by the issuer. It is important to note that here *endorsed* stands for *copied as received.* Certification authority copies the subscriber's information to the certificate, but neither denotes nor confirms it, so **there is no warranty**.

User is an entity which relies upon a certificate issued by a Certification authority in order to obtain information on the subscriber. User is also sometimes called **verifier** and may use any Certification authority or any number of Certification authorities, depending on their location and ease of access. The user is party who is relying on the information and is at risk.

Naming Authority (NA) is not usually outwardly perceived, but is the actual entity. Naming authority defines the naming scheme used by the Certification authority. Certification authority can double as a Naming authority but they provide two different functions. Semantically, the Certification authority refers to a name; however, it does not denote it. The Naming authority denotes it.

An interesting and important issue is the naming scheme in X.509 certificates. A certificate actually associates the public key and unique distinguished name (DN) of the user it describes – the authentication relies on each user possessing a unique distinguished name. The Distinguished Name is denoted by a Naming authority and accepted by a Certification authority as a unique *within* the Certification authority's domain, where the Certification authority can double as a Naming authority. It's interesting to note that the same user can have different distinguished names in different Certification authorities, or can have the same distinguished name in different Certification authorities even if the user is **not the first** to use it in any of the Certification authorities. In other words, the different distinguished name in different Certification authorities does not necessarily mean different users (person/company/bank) and vice versa – the same distinguished name in different Certification authorities does not necessarily mean same users. That is the reason why we said earlier that the CA certificate only refers to a name and does not denote it.

What exactly is X.509 certificate? Section 3.3.3 of the X.509v3 defines a certificate as:

user certificate; public key certificate; certificate;

the public keys of a user, together with some other information, rendered unforgebale by encipherment with the private key of the certification authority which issued it.

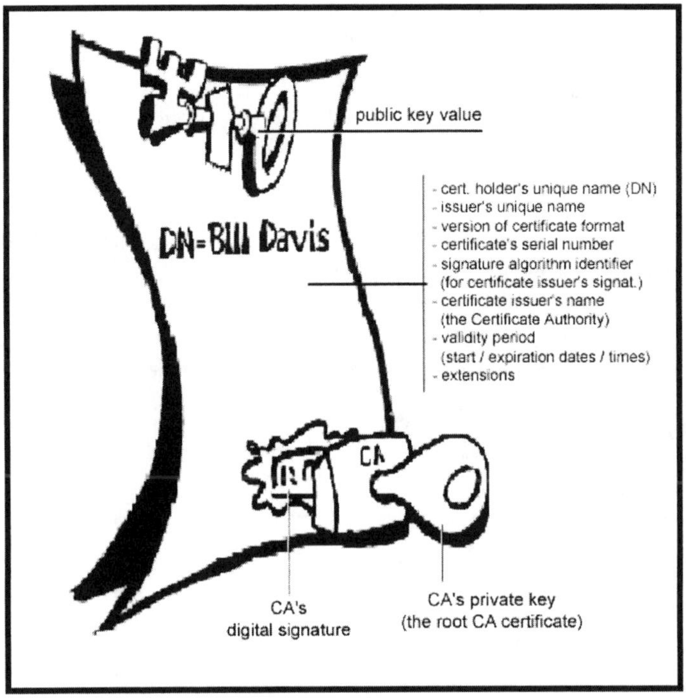

Figure 5.8 How X.509 Certificate Looks Like

The procedure of issuing the X.509 certificates consists of seven steps:

1. **Key Generation.** First step a potential subscriber has to do is to generate private/public key pair that will be used for his Digital Signature. (The public key from that pair will become part of the issued certificate.)
2. **Matching the Policy Information.** Then, you have to choose the Certification authority to which you want to apply for the certificate and collect all the necessary information required by that authority.
3. **Sending of Public Keys and Information.** The next step is to submit the application, together with public keys and other required information. After this, an applicant can just sit and wait.
4. **Verification of Information.** The Certification authority now verifies the information provided by the applicant. If everything appears to be in order, we can continue to the next step. (We shall talk more about this later. For now, just take with reserve the exact meaning of the phrase "verification of information".)
5. **Certificate Creation.** As we said just now, if the Certification authority is satisfied with the information you provided, now is the moment to actually create a certificate.
6. **Sending/Posting the Certificate.** When the certificate is created, the Certification authority sends it to the applicant.
7. **Loading of the Certificate.** Everything the applicant now has to do is to upload the acquired certificate into a computer and start using it.

Figure 5.8 shows the general contents of issued X.509 certificate. It contains the following information:

- The certificate holder's public key value
- The certificate holder's unique name (DN)
- Version of the certificate format
- Certificate serial number
- Signature algorithm identifier (for certificate issuers signature)
- Certificate issuer's name (the Certification authority)
- Validity period (start/expiration dates/times)
- Extensions

Finally the whole certificate is digitally signed by the Certification authority with its private key (which is also called the root CA certificate).

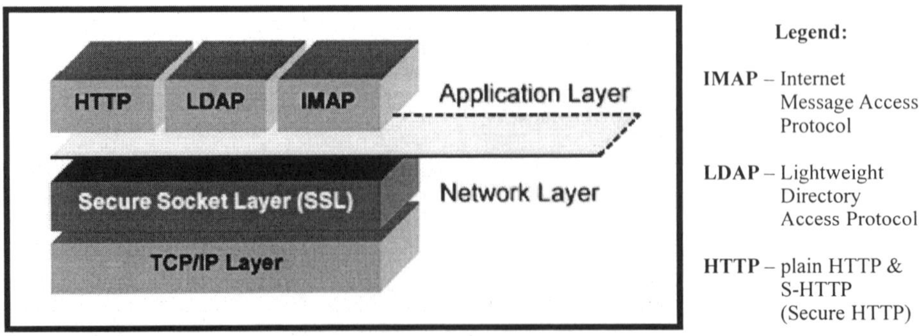

Figure 5.9 Location of the SSL in the OSI layered model

Soon, we shall see how Digital Certificates are verified in the user's browser, as well as some common mistakes and potential weaknesses. But first, we have to understand one important link in the security chain – the Secure Sockets Layer.

5.2.5 Secure Sockets Layer (SSL)

Secure Sockets Layer (SSL) is perhaps the widest used security protocol on the Internet today. It allows for encryption and certification functionality in a TCP/IP environment. SSL is the basis for every e-Business trust infrastructure, including e-Banking.

Modern computer telecommunications have a layered structure. OSI (Open System Interconnection) model defines three main layers: Application Layer, Network Layer and Physical Layer. (Actually, there are seven layers: Application Layer, Presentation Layer, Session Layer, Transportation Layer, Network Layer, Data-link Layer and Physical Layer. However, this detailed division is not always necessary.) These layers communicate through strictly defined 'interfaces' (you can think of them as gates between the layers). In that way, we accomplish the layer abstraction, which is very important because we can independently change and develop various layers without worrying how that will affect the other layers (the same idea of abstraction is one of the corner stones of Object Oriented Programming – OOP).

As you can see on the **Figure 5.9**, the Secure Sockets Layer (in the less detailed model we are using) is inserted as a topmost sub layer in the Network Layer.

Here we have to make an important observation. People easily make the mistake and regard HTTPS and S-HTTP (Secure HTTP) as identical – which is not the case. When a Web address begins with https:// it only denotes that we are connecting to a secure Web server through a SSL connection (the little yellow padlock in the system line of your browser indicates that the secure connection has been established); so, HTTPS is related to SSL. On the other hand, S-HTTP is a superset of HTTP. It is an independent protocol and the part of the Application Layer, unlike SSL, which is the part of the Network Layer. S-HTTP was designed by E. Rescorla and A. Schiffman of EIT to secure HTTP connections. It provides a wide variety of mechanisms to provide for confidentiality, authentication, and integrity. The system is not tied to any particular cryptographic system, key infrastructure, or cryptographic format – it allows messages to be encapsulated in various ways. Encapsulations can include encryption, signing, or MAC based authentication. This encapsulation can be recursive, and a message can have several security transformations applied to it. S-HTTP also includes header definitions to provide key transfer, certificate transfer, and similar administrative functions. S-HTTP does not rely on a particular key certification scheme. It includes support for RSA, in-band, out-of-band and kerberos key exchange. Key certifications can be provided in a message, or obtained elsewhere [Shostack95a]. As we said at the beginning, S-HTTP is part of an application, not part of a network socket connection.

Layered Structure of the SSL

Secure Sockets Layer is a protocol designed to work, as the name implies, at the socket layer, to protect any higher-level protocol built on sockets, such as telnet, ftp, or HTTP (including S-HTTP). As such, it is ignorant of the details of higher-level protocols, and what is being transported – higher-level protocols can layer on top of the SSL transparently.

SSL protocol is composed of two layers: the *Record Layer* and the *Handshake Layer*. A multitude of ciphers and secure hashes are supported, including some explicitly weakened to comply with export restrictions.

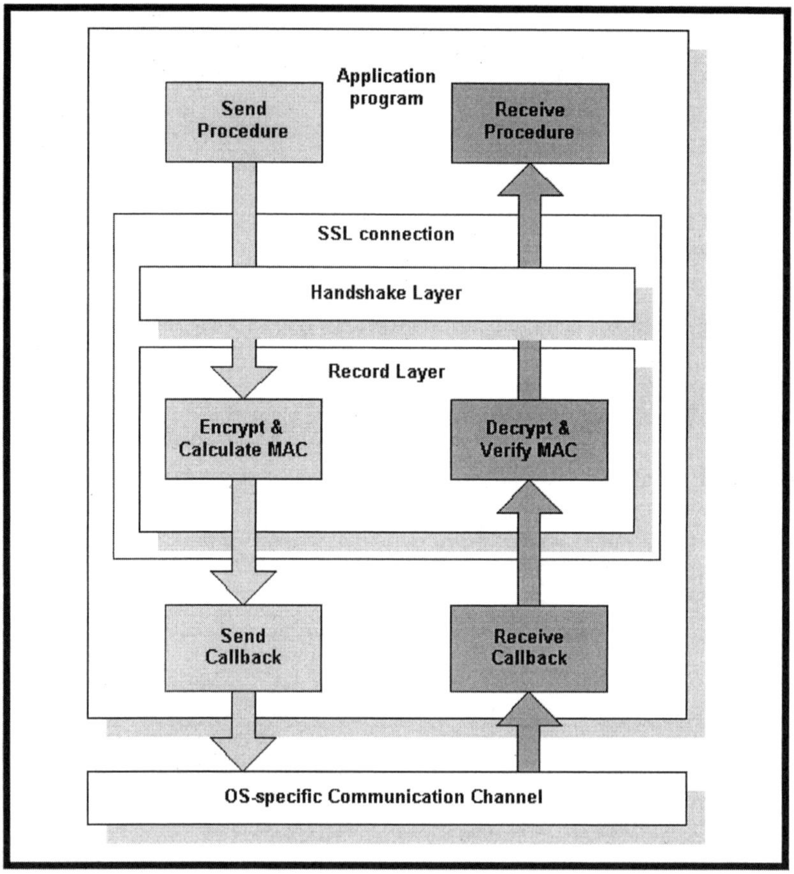

Figure 5.10 SSL connection and communication channel

SSL Record Layer

At the lowest level, layered on top of some reliable transport protocol (e.g., TCP), is the Record Layer. It provides connection security using data encryption with symmetric cryptography and message integrity check with keyed MAC (Message Authentication Code). The Record Layer takes messages to be transmitted, fragments the data into manageable blocks, optionally compresses the data, applies a MAC, encrypts, and transmits the result. (Effectively the Record Layer digitally signs the message using the same procedure as explained in the section 5.2.3 *Digital Signatures*. As a public key for encryption, for every SSL session we create a randomly generated temporary master key – marked as SSK on the pictures. The process of adopting a SSK is described in the Handshaking Layer.) Received data is decrypted, verified, decompressed, and reassembled, then delivered to higher-level clients.

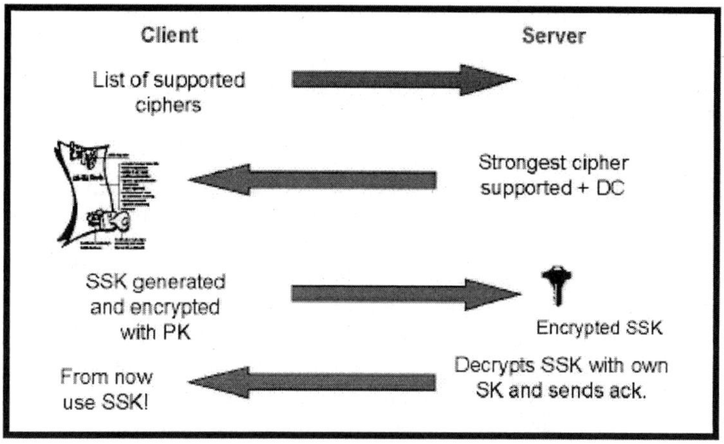

Legend: **DC** – Server's Digital Certificate
PK – Server's Public Key
SSK – Randomly Generated Master Key (Secure Socket Key for that SSL session)
SK – Server's Private Key

Figure 5.11 SSL Handshaking Phase (simplified)

Failures to authenticate, decrypt, or otherwise get correct answers in a cryptographic operation result in I/O errors, and a close of connection.

SSL Handshake Layer

A handshake occurs when a machine tries to *use* a SSL connection. The connection may has already been opened, but for security reasons if no session exists "recently" (recently is not explicitly defined, but suggested to be under 100 seconds - SSL, C.8), we have to make a new handshake. The other type of a handshake is when client authentication is desired.

When a client wishes to establish a secure connection, it sends a CLIENT-HELLO message, including a challenge, along with the information on the cryptographic systems it is willing or able to support. The server responds with a SERVER-HELLO message, which is connection id, its key certificate (that is server's Digital Certificate), and information about the cryptosystems it supports. The client is responsible for choosing a cryptosystem it shares with the server.

The client then verifies the server's public key, and responds with a CLIENT-MASTER-KEY message, which is a randomly generated master key, encrypted or partially encrypted with the server's public key. The client then sends a CLIENT-FINISHED message. This includes the connection-id, encrypted with the client-write-key. (All these keys will be explained separately in a little while.) The server then sends a SERVER-VERIFY message, verifying its identity by responding with the challenge, encrypted with the server write key. The server got its server-write-key sent to it by the client, encrypted with the server's public key. The server must have the appropriate private key to decrypt the CLIENT-MASTER-KEY message, thus obtaining the master-key, from which it can produce the server-write-key.

If client authentication is in use, then the server must at some point, send a REQUEST-CERTIFICATE message, which contains a challenge (called challenge') and the means of authentication desired. The client responds with a CLIENT-CERTIFICATE message, which includes the client certificate's type, the certificate itself, and a bunch of response data. The server then sends a SERVER-FINISH message.

There are a number of keys used over the course of a conversation. There is the server's public key, a master key, a client-read-key and a client-write-key. (The standard uses the term server-write-key as another name for client-read-key, and server-read-key as another name for client-write-key.)

Client-write-key and client-read-key are derived via a secure hash from the master key, an ordinal character, the challenge, and connection-id. Of this input, only the master key is sent encrypted (with the server's public key.) The master key is reused across sessions, while the read- & write- keys are generated anew for each session.

Once the handshaking is complete, the application protocol begins to operate. This is also called the data-exchange phase. All the security related work is done in the Record Layer, as we previously described and showed on **Figure 5.10**. The SSL specification is not clear at what point the SSL connection is considered to be done with a connection, or what to do with the keys at that point. There is an implication that the session is done when the TCP connection is torn down, and keys should be kept for roughly 100 seconds after that, but this is not explicitly defined. More information on SSL can be found in [Shostack95b] and [MS-DN00].

About SSL Strength

There are two variants of SSL: 40-bit and 128-bit (this refers to master key length). According to RSA labs, it would take a trillion trillion years to crack 128-bit SSL using today's technology! However, SSL being a low-level protocol does little to protect you once your host is compromised. Until recently there was also a problem related to certificate revocation. Now days Certificate authorities supply lists of revoked certificates in so called Revocation Lists – CRLs. (CRLs are in fact a will to revoke but not an actual revocation. It's like stolen credit card numbers list – it's up to you to check them.) Older SSL protocols implementations were not consulting those lists (because such lists had not existed at their design time). However, all relatively new SSL protocol implementations support revocation lists (or at least so is claimed).

US export restrictions apply to issued Digital Certificates and browser implementations (support for 128-bit SSL), but from recently VeriSign (a commercial Certification authority) is allowed to issue Global Digital Certificates that work both in the US and export versions of browsers (and to use 128-bit SSL).

SSL represents a strong link in the security chain that is not likely to loosen. However, as we all know, the chain is as strong as its weakest link, which brings us back to the question of verification of the Digital Certificates.

5.2.6 Verification of DCs in the user's browser

Figure 5.12 shows the procedure of verification of Digital Certificates in the user's Internet browser.

When the browser receives some Digital Certificate, it has to do several things. First, it checks whether the today's date is within the validity period of a certificate and whether the certificate has been revoked. Then it tries to locate an issuer's distinguished name in the list of trusted Certification Authorities (compiled by the user), whereby checking if the issuing Certification authority is a trusted Certification authority. If that is the case, then the browser checks whether the issuing Certification authority's public key validate issuer's digital signature. Finally, it checks does the domain name specified in the server's distinguished name match the server's actual domain name. With that the process of verification is done.

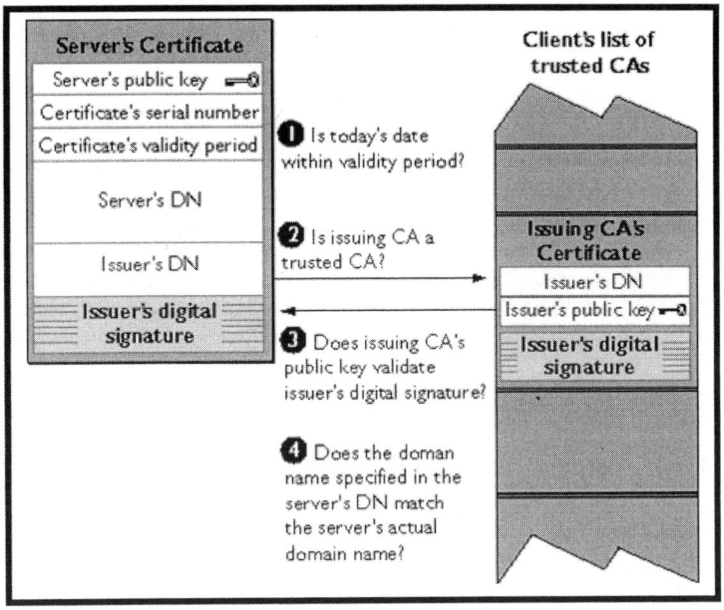

Figure 5.12 Verification of Digital Certificates in the user's browser

It is worth noting that most of the servers (that use Certification authority certificates) force the client to accept certain Certification authority's signatures - for the top level Certification Authorities - which are often "hardwired" into the software.

The Certification Authorities' public key may be the target of an extensive decryption attack. That is why Certification Authorities should use very long keys and change these keys regularly. Top-level Certification Authorities unfortunately are exceptions. It may not be practical for them to change keys frequently because their keys may be written into the software (such as browser) used by a large number of verifiers. Certification Authorities that may be the most probable targets are the ones that offer the smallest protection level. Like Ed Gerck said: "Protection, in this case, is an inverse function of worth" [Gerck00].

5.2.7 Final Words on Digital Certificates

Let's review the disclaimer, generally **not visible** in the certificate itself. For example:

VERISIGN DISCLAIMS ANY WARRANTIES WITH RESPECT TO THE SERVICES PROVIDED BY VERISIGN HEREUNDER INCLUDING WITHOUT LIMITATION ANY AND ALL IMPLIED WARRANTIES OF MERCHANTABILITY OR FITNESS FOR PARTICULAR PURPOSE. VERISIGN MAKES NO REPRESENTATION OR WARRANTY THAT ANY CA OR USER TO WHICH IT HAS ISSUED A DIGITAL ID IN THE VERISIGN SECURE SERVER HIERARCHY IS IN FACT THE PERSON OR OGRANIZATION IT CLAIMS TO BE WITH RESPECT TO THE INFORMATION SUPPLIED TO VERISIGN. VERISIGN MAKES NO ASSURANCES OF THE ACCURACY, AUTHENTICITY, INTEGRITY, OR RELIABILITY OF INFORMATION CONTAINED IN DIGITAL IDs OR IN CRLs COMPILED, PUBLISHED OR DISSEMINATED BY VERISIGN OR THE RESULTS OF CRYPTOGRAPHIC METHODS IMPLEMENTED.

The disclaimer does not say that VeriSign has no warranty on its services or that it takes no liability on them. It only says that VeriSign has no warranties and accepts no liability for services that VeriSign does **not** recognize it provides.

We mentioned earlier in the section 5.2.4 when we talked about issuing X.509 certificate that the statement "verification of information" should be taken with a reserve. Regarding the validation procedures for the user's identity, X.509 states that "*a certification authority shall be satisfied of the identity of a user before creating a certificate for it*", which means that identity validation procedures are to be satisfied in the Certification Authorities' own frame of reference, as defined in their Certification Practice Statements, which can be entirely different for different Certification Authorities. Furthermore, commercial Certification Authorities' CPSs generally accept indirect references when issuing certificates, such as using an ID as identity proof, which can be easily subject to fraud and lead to public risks. Unwary user, or non-technical user which is the majority, is led to believe that the words "authority" or "certificate" carry the same weight as their dictionary entries would imply, which, as we have seen, is not the case.

Every CA, effectively, must provide the following:

- That the subject's public key has a working private key counterpart elsewhere (with no warranties that the public/private key pair is not artificially weakened, that it is actually in the possession of the named subject and that no one else has obtained a copy of it).
- That the subject's distinguished name is unique to *that* Certification authority (with no warranties that such distinguished name contains the actual subject's name, location or that the subject even exists or has a correctly spelled name).

The issue whether a user's distinguished name actually corresponds to identity credentials that are linked to a person or simply to an e-mail address, and how such association was verified, is outside the scope of X.509 and depends on each Certification authority's self-defined CPS and on each Naming authority. You should always remember that X.509 certificate is essentially a bag of bytes, which meaning and validity strongly depends on the Certification authority.

In general, there is no such thing like ultimate list of all trusted Certification Authorities so those certificates can be entered in one's browser. Trust must be evaluated relative to the user, who is the party at risk, in his own domain, references and terms.

Two excellent Certification Authorities are:

- **VeriSign** (www.verisign.com)
- **Thawte** (www.thawte.com)

If you are interested in the details on how to apply for a digital certificate, these two addresses are what you need. (VeriSign is an issuer of digital certificate for Microsoft Corporation.)

5.3 Bankers Point of View

Now we shall take a look on the e-Banking from a banker's point of view. Here you will find out how to set up an Internet bank channel, you will see an Internet bank demo, and at the end find out how to search for financial information on the Web.

5.3.1 Setting up an Internet Bank Channel

In this first section you will familiarize yourself with the Internet bank architecture, you will see how planning phase in the set up process looks like, get to know the strategic and technology partners, and you will see what are the required tasks after initial introduction of a new channel.

5.3.1.1 Internet Bank Architecture

General Internet bank architecture is shown on **Figure 5.13.** Every modern bank has some sort of back office system to which the branch office terminals are connected. If we want to give our customers the possibility to perform their banking transactions over the Internet, it goes without saying that we cannot let them access our back office system directly. We have to make some sort of electronic user desk for our customers.

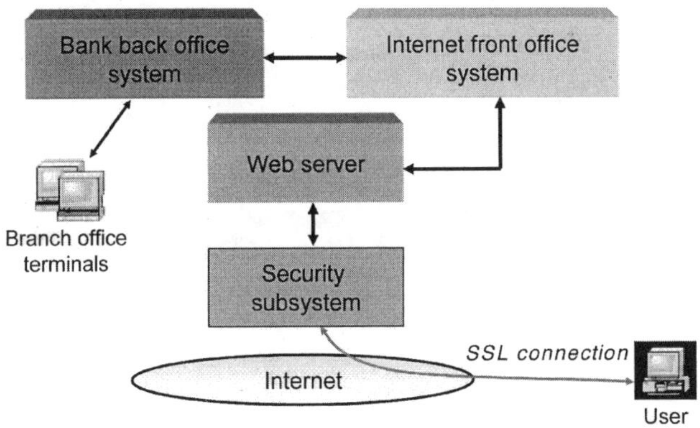

Figure 5.13 Internet Bank Architecture

The system that performs that task is called Internet front office system. Internet front office system, is then, connected to a Web server. With the help of security subsystem, we can achieve secure communications by using Secure Sockets Layer (which was explained in detail in previous section). Of course, this is just a rough sketch.

The above system can be implemented as *in-house* or *out-of-house* architecture. In the in-house architecture all components of the system are on-site (in the bank); in the out-of-house approach some components are still located at the bank (generally only the core server and data-transfer server) while the rest of system components are located elsewhere (at the Application Service Provider – we shall talk about them latter). The picture is worth a thousand words, so let us examine CustomerLink primer (**Figure 5.14**).

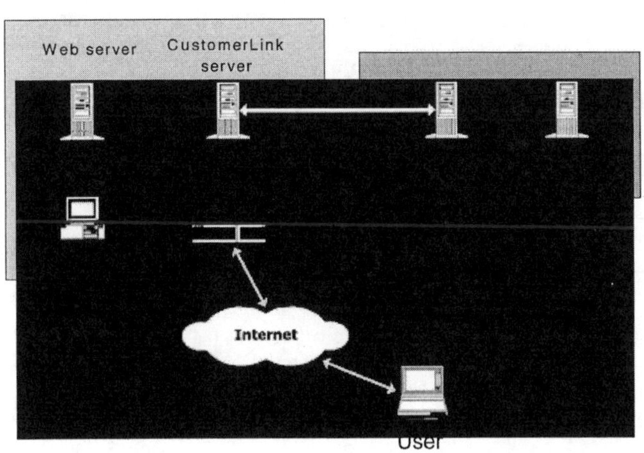

Figure 5.14 Out-of-house Architecture [Equifax01]

As you can see, if the out-of-house architecture is used, bank only has to provide a core server and a data-transfer server (and of course to sign a contract with some Application Service Provider – ASP). Also, note that with this approach a bank no longer has a direct connection with a user – all communication is handled by an ASP. Alternatively, if we choose to use in-house architecture, we have to provide complete functionality. In that case, we would no longer need a data-transfer server, but beside core server, we would have to provide a CustomerLink server, in-house Web server, security firewall, and a router – all of them on-site.

The choice between in-house and out-of-house architecture is basically the choice whether we are going to use services from an Application Service Provider or not. It is an important decision in our planning phase, and we shall come back to that later.

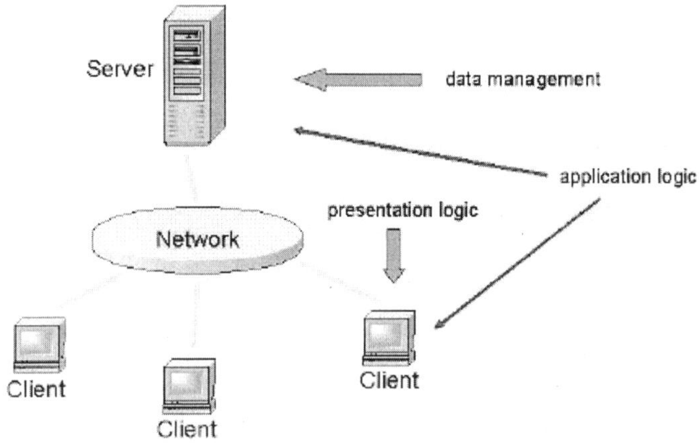

Figure 5.15 Banking Software Architecture: Client-Server System

Before Internet revolution, banking software systems were dominantly of client-server type (**Figure 5.15**). Client-server relation in general represents the network configuration where the work potential defined with processing abilities or accessible information is distributed between several machines. Some machines – the clients – can demand services or information from other machines – servers. Server, for example, can access huge databases and perform searches in behalf of the client. In this constellation, at least some part of the processing is done by the server. Applications which can be run in the client-server environment are divided into a part closer to user (Front End) executed by the client, and a part farther from user (Back End) executed by the server. Client-server computing allows several types of relations between client and server. In the banking software systems designed in such manner, usually the front end application provides presentation logic and partially application logic: it accepts commands from the user, makes the requests to a server and displays the results, and in certain cases even does some computation locally. Back end application, on the other side, provides data management and request processing as well as communication with front end application (so actually the largest part of the application logic is located in the back end application) [Novell95].

In the Internet era, banking software system became n-tier client/server (where n > 2). Typical n-tier software system is shown in **Figure 5.16**. In this configuration we have a slightly different picture. First of all, there is no longer just one server. Instead, we have several servers each (more or less) specialized for certain service, which altogether form some sort of a chain link to the client (that is where the name n-tier comes from).

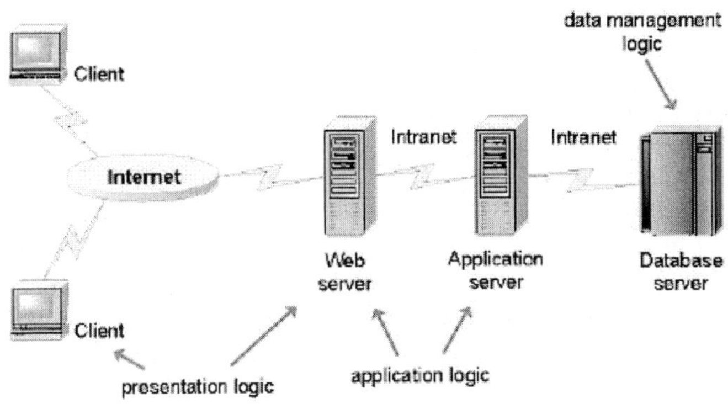

Figure 5.16 Banking Software Architecture: N-tier Client/Server

In this approach, we have a so-called thin client, which is connected to a Web server, usually using HTTPS (which is essentially HTTP + SSL, as we described in section 5.2.5). Web server hosts Java Server Pages (Şervelts) or Active Server Pages that forms the HTML code and interact with the application tier. The sole purpose of the thin client is basically to interpret received HTML code (in the Internet browser) and to act as a communication link between the user and the rest of the system.

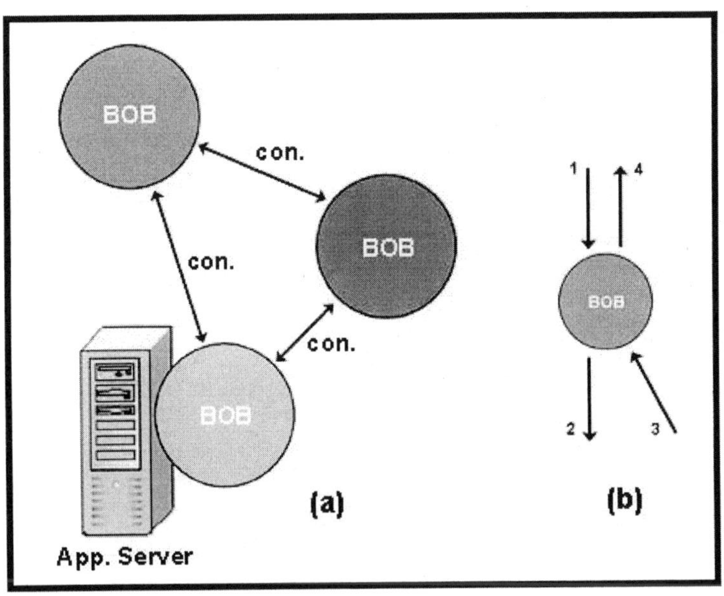

Legend: **BOB** – Business Object
Con. – Object Interconnection

Comment: Figure (a) shows the relation of business objects within the application server.
Figure (b) shows the sequence of events after a BOB receives the request for service. Detailed description of that sequence is given in the text.

Figure 5.17 Application Tier: The Application Server

Business objects (**Figure 5.17a**) can be on a single or multiple application servers. They are written in C/C++, Java (Enterprise Java Beans - EJB), Delphi, COBOL or some other programming language. Business objects communicate with each other using CORBA (Common Object Request Broker Architecture), DCOM (Distributed Component Object Model), RMI (Remote Method Invocation, used for Java-to-Java object communication) or some similar distributed object system.

When a business object receives the request for service (**Figure 5.17b**, marked as 1), it generates a SQL query through a JDBC/ODBC to data tier (2). Upon completion of a query data tier sends required data to business object (3), which then generates data response back to the client (4). As we can see, the whole data management logic is separated in the data management server (the data tier).

5.3.1.2 Application Service Providers (ASPs)

Now when you know how Internet bank generally works, you can begin the setup process. First step in that process is making a plan (at least it should be). During this planning phase we need to answer the following questions:

1. What are the services to be installed?
2. What services we (the bank) could implement in-house?
3. What services we could implement through Application Service Providers (out-of-house)?
4. Who are technology partners?

We already mentioned ASPs earlier when we were speaking about in-house and out-of-house Internet bank architecture. It is time to see what an ASP really is.

"If you're a CIO with a head for business, you won't be buying computers anymore. You won't buy software either. You'll rent all your resources from a service provider"

- Scott McNealy, CEO of Sun Microsystems

Application service provider offers standardized packages of applications, necessary infrastructure, and certain degree of service. Main characteristic of ASPs is that they offer applications that are already purchasable. ASP offers one-to-many solution, which is less expensive then a classis IT one-to-one solution.

Advantages of using ASPs are:

- Thin client
- Renting instead of buying
- Only effective time used is charged
- Cost planning is more reliable
- Total cost of ownership is decreased
- You need less IT workforce
- You save installation/upgrading time
- Reaction time is reduced
- You have one single business partner

Of course, using ASPs have some disadvantages too: you need a broad bandwidth for data synchronization between your server and ASP; there is always a question of data security on the Internet; not all applications have Internet compatible surfaces yet; and you loose your company's independence.

The setup of the Internet bank channel is rather a complex problem. You need to think about telecommunications infrastructure, you have to think about security, you have to think about multi-tier software structure, and there is a question of maintenance. Because of all this *we recommend using ASPs for setting up a new Internet channel in case of mid- and small size banks*. The biggest banks should reconsider which services to delegate to ASPs.

We mentioned at the beginning of this section that in the planning phase we need to decide what services are going to be installed. As for the ASPs, they offer an extensive list of services:

- Online personal banking (such as account information, transfers, deposits, etc.)
- Online cash management for companies
- Bill payment
- Check payment
- Card payment solutions
- Insurance services
- Web presentation design
- Web presentation hosting
- Web presentation administration
- Security services
- Testing of electronic business software
- Remote administration of bank's servers
- And more…

Choosing the right Application Service Provider is the most important task in the setup process. An ASP we choose as our partner must be an expert for Internet access and it has to have experience in electronic business. It is of **utmost importance** that ASP has a secure and fault-tolerant LAN (Local Area Network). An ASP of our choice also has to have a good software solution and well-educated IT staff accessible 24 hours a day, 365 days a year.

As a help for choosing strategic and technology partners, here is the list of some good Application Service Providers:

For personal banking and cash management (name, web address, software solution):

- Equifax, www.equifax.com, www.efx-ebanking.com; CustomerLink
- Digital Insight, www.digitalinsight.com, AXIS
- Vifi, www.vifi.com, InternetBanker

Bill payment:

- CheckFree, www.checkfree.com

Card Payment Processing:

- RS2 Software Group, www.rs2group.com, BankWorks

Web Hosting:

- Digex, www.digex.com

Web design for banking

- DiamondBullet, www.diamondbullet.com, www.bankingwebsites.com

5.3.1.3 Required Tasks after Initial Introduction of a New Channel

After introduction of a new Internet channel, you need to perform some activities to get that channel going. You need to educate the bank's staff, you need to organize permanent marketing campaign and you should obtain information about competition and potential customers (investors).

Education of Staff

Studies show that the education of bank's staff in using the Internet channel is often incomplete. Your staff should provide answers to frequently asked questions (FAQ) about using the Internet channel to their customers. Incompetence of the staff can turn people to draw two conclusions:

1. We do it (Internet banking) because everyone does it.
2. We do it but we do not think it is important to us.

Either way, that is obviously not a good way to make your Internet channel popular.

Education process can be done through courses after the job or by stimulating staff to use Internet banking from home (you could participate in PC purchase or try to obtain discounts from local Internet Service Provider - ISP).

Permanent Marketing

We have a good solution for Internet banking, but number of online users is very low after initial setup; what is wrong? The answer is: We need a permanent marketing campaign!

Customers who were not ready for new service at the moment of initial introduction will be ready after few months. So the secret is in marketing cycles – to involve customers that became ready in the meanwhile. The key of success is enthusiasm, especially among the management.

How to do marketing? First of all, as we said, you should spread enthusiasm among staff. You can also use common media for advertising (for that you should hire some professional agency). You can also organize education about Internet technologies and new banking services among customers, and you can try to make some agreements with local ISPs and resellers of computer equipment.

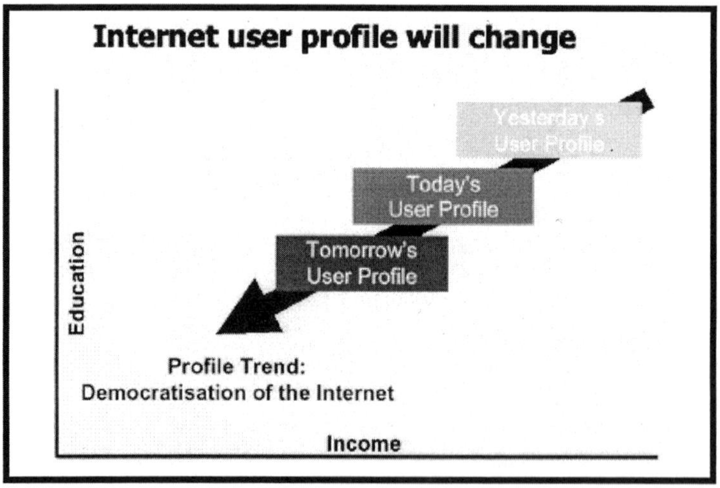

Figure 5.18 Internet users profile

Education of Customers

Studies show that 7% of bank users are technically advanced, while 25% is open to new banking services but they lack technical experience. As you can see on **Figure 5.18**, you can expect that number to rise in the future.

In order to attract more online customers, bank should organize courses for using computers and Internet; they should provide computer installations inside bank halls and rooms accessible to customers, and as we said before, to try to make agreements with local Internet Service Providers to give discounts for online bank customers. A good idea is, also, to organize periodical meetings where online customers can exchange information about Internet banking services and E-Business in general.

Monitoring Activity on Internet Channel

In order to react fast you should gather information about channel use. You should make different statistics such as number of visitors, number of transactions, which services are the most/least used, average time spent at our Web site by common user, etc.

Obtaining Information about Competition and Potential Customers

To be successful in any business (including Internet banking services) you constantly need information about competition such as what they offer and what are the complaints of their customers, in order to improve your own service. Also you need information about potential customers and investors. Among other ways for obtaining information, it is useful to monitor the Web and Web activity using search engines. We shall take a closer look on that subject later.

5.3.2 Internet Bank Demo

As an example of Internet bank channel, we shall present a small community bank – **The Bank of Northern Michigan (BNM).**

The Bank of Northern Michigan is a community bank from Petoskey, Michigan, USA. It is an independent, full service financial institution with more then 140 years of experience. It has a strong customer-bank relationship and is committed to new banking technologies. This bank is a member of FDIC (Federal Deposit Insurance Corporation). Their contact addresses are:

Web: www.bankofnorthernmichigan.com

Mail: talktous@bankofnorthermichigan.com

BNM Web site was created and is maintained by an ASP – the DiamondBullet Design.

BNM allows individuals the ability to view account balances, transfer funds, make loan payments and perform many other useful tasks. Individuals also can pay their bills through BNM's bill payment system. For businesses, BNM provides all services featured in their personal online banking product, and some more. Businesses can issue wire transfer instructions, transfer funds, and both pay down and draw on established lines of credit.

BNM uses Equifax as an Application Service Provider. It is visible on their login screen. In the process of signing in, you are automatically redirected to the following location:

www.efxibank.com/clkpcb/072414006/default1.asp

Customer session is established through 128-bit SSL connection, as indicated by the little yellow padlock in the system line of user's browser. The SSL connection is established between client browser and online bank ASP (Equifax).

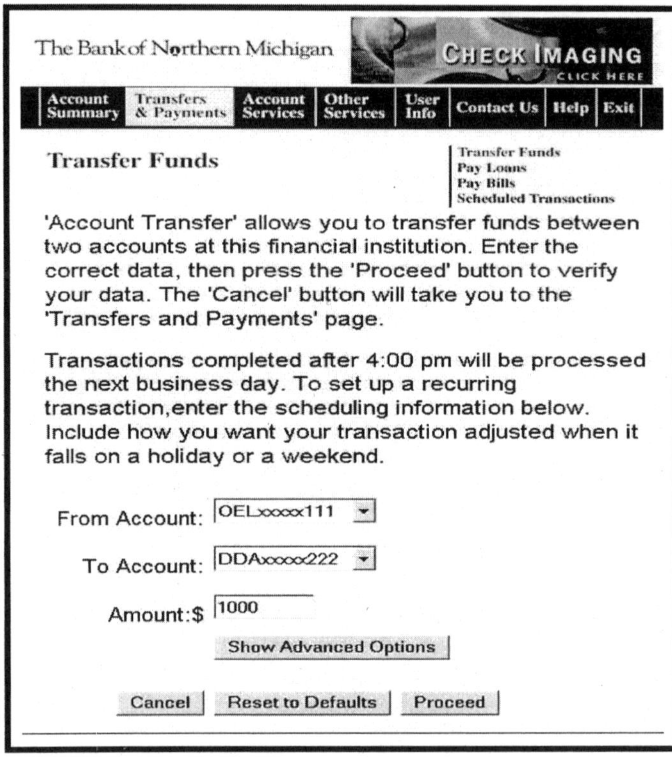

Figure 5.19 The Bank of Northern Michigan – Transfer Funds Screen

Customer session *is timed out* after 10 minutes of inactivity. Also, browser cache *is disabled* when working through a secure connection.

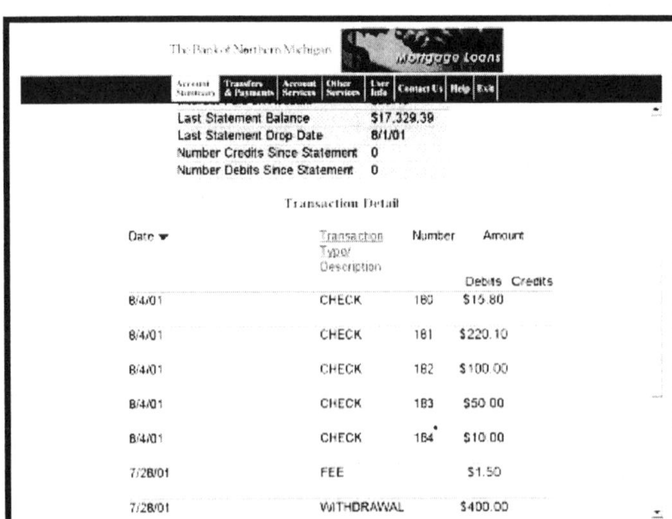

Figure 5.20 The Bank of Northern Michigan – Account Balance

On the **Figure 5.19**, you can see how transfer funds screen look like. A transfer funds option (for an individual user) allows you to transfer funds between two accounts in this financial institution. You are able to make ordinary transactions, as well to schedule recurring transactions.

And on the **Figure 5.20** is an example of an account balance report. The report provides all the necessary information, such as the last statement balance, the last statement drop date and detailed list of previous transactions.

Customers pay their bills through CheckFree. Online bank software redirects you automatically to www.checkfree.com.

As you can see, the Bank of Northern Michigan has well distributed services. The Web design is done by DiamondBullet Design; Web hosting is provided by a local ISP; and the Web administration is also covered by DiamondBullet Design. Core online banking services are trusted to Equifax and payment of bills and e-bills are provided by CheckFree.

5.3.3 Searching for Financial Information on the Web

This is a necessary step you need to take in order to be successful in e-Banking business. In this section, you will learn the importance of Web search in banking business, see what searching services are available on the Web and learn how general search engines work and how to search for financial data with focused crawlers. At the end, you will be given a few useful links to visit.

Huge amount of financial information is publicly available on the Internet. Among 660 largest companies form 22 countries (30 from each), 62% had some form of financial data available on their Web sites (IASC Report). Independent companies for market research also provide a lot of information; the most popular are DigiTRADE, EDGAR, Wall Street City.Com, Yahoo! Finance, etc. Among others, we can find information about:

- Quarterly and annual financial reports
- Financial history
- SEC fillings
- Stock quotas
- Press releases
- Information request forms
- Other shareholder information.

Internet banking market is very dynamic. As we mentioned earlier, in section 5.3.1.3, one part of successful Internet banking business is collecting information about potential customers and potential competitors. A vast amount of information can be acquired using search engines and monitoring interesting Web sites.

Searching Services on the Web

We can generally search the Web using three types of searching services: subject directories, search engines that use crawlers for collecting data, and meta-crawlers.

Within *Subject directories* links to Web sites are collected according to topics they treat. Those links are collected by humans who evaluate and sort them. This approach is useful when you are searching for some topic in general, but it is not effective when you're trying to find something specific. Good subject directories are Yahoo!, Lycos, LookSmart, Excite, etc.

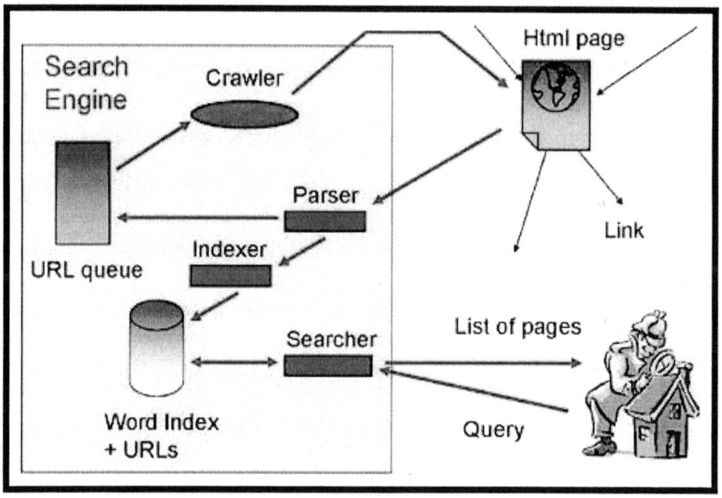

Figure 5.21 Search Engines – How Do They Work?

Search engines try to collect as many as possible pages from the Web and store them locally for later keyword search. Pages are collected by using crawlers (which are software components - software agents to be exact). Search engines are good for performing searches on specific query. The results pages produces by the search are sorted by relevancy (there are straightforward mathematical equations used for calculating the relevancy based on back link count, page rank, location metric, forward link count and similarity to a driving query – but that is beyond the scope of this chapter). The one problem with search engines is that the results can be out of date (this is called currency problem). The best search engines are Google, AltaVista, Fast, Northern Light, etc.

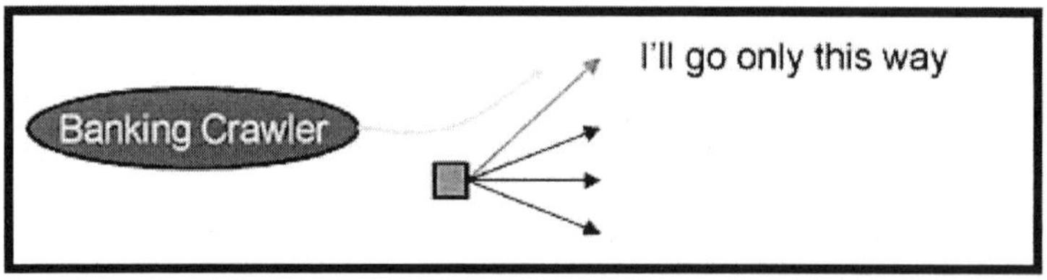

Figure 5.22 Focused Crawler – not all links are followed

Figure 5.21 shows the general method of operation of a typical search engine [SCU01]. When a new Html page is located (using a crawler), search engines runs it through a parser which analyses the contents of a page. All links leading out from the page are inserted in the URL queue (for later processing) and the rest of the contents are passed to an indexer, which retrieves (or extracts) keywords from that page, and place them in a database (called World index) together with the URL to that page. When a user makes a query to the search engine, it really communicates with a part called "searcher" which processes the query by consulting the World index. After that, the "searcher" sends back to the user a list of page hits.

Meta-crawlers utilize other search engines concurrently by sending user's request to them. This approach is good for queries about exotic topics, but the queries have to be simple because of different formats among search engines. Examples of meta-crawlers are MetaCrawler, Dogpile, HotBot, etc.

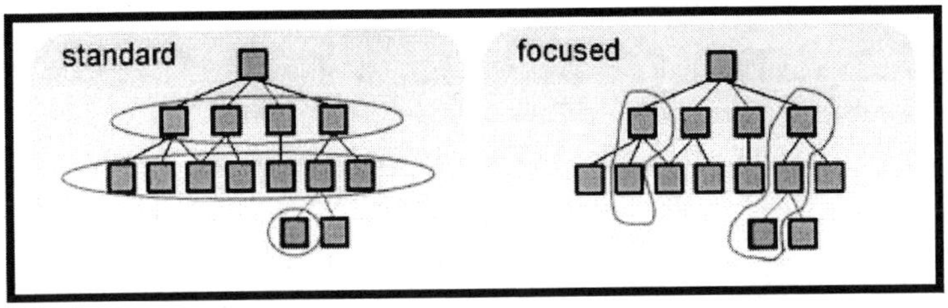

Comment: How focused crawlers can solve the currency problem (out-of-date page problem). Red square indicates the page with newest information that can slip by the standard crawler.

Figure 5.23 Focused Crawlers vs. Standard Crawlers.

Instead of ordinary crawlers, we can also use focused crawlers (**Figure 5.22**). Such crawlers visit *only* topic specific pages, thus eliminating the ones unworthy to our specific needs. The benefit of focused crawlers in search engines specialized in certain topic is that they also can eliminate the currency problem (**Figure 5.23**). The World index of some search engine, of course has limited capacity – that is why we are often forced to follow links only to certain depth. However, if there is a page with newer information buried rather deep into the structure of the Web location, our search engine may not locate it. Focused crawler optimizes the path; because we are now not following all the links, we are able to go deeper into the structure, thus locating the previously missed page.

Comparison of Search Services

Relatively recently (September 2001) PC World's staff conducted extensive comparison of search engines, subject directories and meta-crawlers [PCWorld01]. This article together with explanation of method of testing, as well as complete results can be found on the following address:

http://find.pcworld.com/11060

General-purpose search engines with the highest marks – the ones that provide the best service by all means are:

Google – www.google.com

Fast – www.allthweb.com

Yahoo! – www.yahoo.com

Lycos – www.lycos.com

Northern Light – www.northernlight.com

If you want to use some other, perhaps more specialized search engines, you can look at the following locations:

Search Engine Guide – www.searchengineguide.com

Argus Clearinghouse – www.clearinghouse.com

BeauCoup – www.beaucop.com

Search Engine Watch – www.searchenginewatch.com

There is even directory of directories of search engines:

SearchAbility – www.searchability.com

You can also try with the public databases not accessible to the search engines, such as Lycos Searchable Databases Directory:

http://dir.lycos.com/reference/searchable_databases

Useful financial-related links to visit

- Financial data meta-crawler: www.streeteye.com/cgi-bin/allseeingeye.cgi
- Finance specific directory search: www.moneysearch.com
- Excellent financial portal for investors: www.dailystocks.com
- One more excellent financial portal for investors: www.companysleuth.com

5.4 Conclusion

In this chapter devoted to e-Banking we covered many of its aspects. You have learned what an e-Bank is and what the benefits of the e-Banking are; you familiarized yourself with the structure of an e-Bank, learned how to implement your own Internet channel and how to afterwards search for financial information on the Web in order to improve your business. You have also learned what possible security problems can occur and how to fight those problems.

As a conclusion, we can say that every bank should implement its Internet channel, because of a reduced cost of transaction (see **Figure 5.2** in section 5.1.2) and global connectivity.

Also, small and mid sized banks could benefit using Application Service Providers for different kind of services (and choosing the good ASP is the most important step).

As a last thing in this chapter, we shall mention some common Internet myths [Rodriguez00]:

Myth 1: *Internet requires little upfront investment.* This is not true, because like everywhere else, you get what you pay for.

Myth 2: *The Internet will drive transactions from other channels.* The fact is that the channel behavior is additive (and like studies show, channel adoption has always been additive).

Myth 3: *Internet customers are inherently more profitable.* The fact is that the Internet customers' profitability is inconsistent.

Myth 4: *The Internet is borderless.* Well, this is partially true, but brand marketing and consumer behavior are generally local, so it is very important to keep those things in mind when planning any Internet business including e-Banking.

5.5 Problems

1. What are the benefits and what are the shortcomings of e-Banking?
2. Describe three main security problems in electronic communication.
3. Explain how Digital Signatures work.
4. What is the purpose of Digital Certificates and how do they work?
5. What is SSL and how does it work?
6. What is the difference between In-house and Out-of-house bank architecture?
7. Explain the difference between standard client-server architecture and n-tier architecture. Describe the Application Tier.
8. What is Application Service Provider? What are the advantages of using the ASPs, and what are the shortcomings?
9. Briefly describe the required tasks after initial introduction of a new channel.
10. Explain the general idea of search engines. What is the focused crawler?

References

[eTForecasts01]	www.eMarketer.com, April **2001**
[ABA99]	"IDC: Beyond 2000", American Banking Association, **1999**
[Jupiter00]	Jupiter Communications, www.jupiter.com, **2000**
[eStats99]	www.eStats.com, December **1999**
[Greenspam00]	Greenspam, A., "Structural change in the new economy", addresses to the National Governor's Association, **2000**
[FDIC01]	Federal Deposit Insurance Corporation, www.fdic.com, September **2001**
[Menezes97]	Menezes, A., "Handbook of Applied Cryptography", **1997**
[ITU01]	ITU-T, "Summary of ITU-T Recommendation X.509", www.itu.int, April **2001**
[Shostack95a]	Shostack, A., "An Overview of S-HTTP", **1995**
[Shostack95b]	Shostack, A., "An Overview of SSL", **1995**
[MSDN00]	Microsoft Developers Network, April **2000**
[Gerck00]	Gerck, E., "Overview of Certification Systems", **2000**
[Novel95]	Werner, F., "Novell's Complete Encyclopedia of Networking", **1995**
[Equifax01]	"CustomerLink Primer", www.equifax.com, Jun **2001**
[SCU01]	"The anatomy of the Google search engine", www7.scu.edu.au/programme/fullpapers/1921/com1921.htm, Jun **2001**
[PCWorld01]	PC World Magazine, IDG Press, September **2001**
[Rodriguez00]	Rodriguez, M.L., "European ECM momentum", San Jose State University, **2000**

E-Business and E-Challenges
V. Milutinović and F. Patricelli (Eds.)
IOS Press, 2002

CHAPTER 6
VIRTUAL MARKETPLACE ON THE INTERNET

Zaharije Radivojević, Živoslav Adamović and Veljko Milutinović

In this chapter, a short introduction is given on the subject of Virtual Marketplace. Structure and organization of Virtual-Marketplace are presented in the first five sections. At the end of this chapter Oracle Exchange is presented, as one of the most interesting tools for creating an e-Marketplace.

6.1 Introduction to Virtual Marketplace

The Internet has changed the face of the Earth more than any other technological innovation after the discovery of the electrical energy. For less then a decade, the Internet has essentially changed the World of business. Many new commercial activities, processes, and business models have been created, and many old ones have been forgotten. This is the story of one new model, the Virtual Marketplace, or as it is probably better known, e-Marketplace.

Online business trade in the U.S. has hypergrowth, setting the stage for B2B e-Commerce to hit \$2.7 trillion in 2004. During this enormous five-year growth spurt, historical operating norms will come under attack, as 53% of this Internet trade will flow through e-Marketplace." *Forrester Research*

As each marketplace, this one has its own lows and unpredictable future, but today it is the best way to do the business. While we are talking about marketplaces, we do not think about some grocery store; we think about something much bigger - about a real market, where people are negotiating, and fighting for their interests and their rights.

Each marketplace has its own laws, but some of these laws are the some on each marketplace. These are laws of business. Business is law, judge, jury, and executor.

E-Marketplace is considered as one of the most important features of business-to-business (B2B) electronic commerce and is expected to be a source of substantial efficiencies. On one side we have buyers with their needs and on the other side we have sellers with their items to sell; in the middle we have the marketplace. Marketplace stands there as some middleman whose job is to make everyone as pleased as it is possible. Marketplace can not make everyone happy, but it can reduce the number of discontent buyers, and can, according to Aberdeen Group [Aberdeen00, Sterling01], give opportunity to buyers to expect:

- Decrease of product costs from 5 to 15 percent.
- Decrease in process costs of about 70 percent.
- Decreasing of average process costs from \$107, when product is ordered manually, to \$30 if ordered electronically.
- Reduction of 50 to 70 percent in purchase requisition cycle time. This can be achieved if all sections of the processing order from initialization through fulfillment are done by using some electronic solution.

Opportunity for sellers is in increasing the number of Internet users and potential buyers. According to eTForecasts, the number of Internet users will rise by the end of the year 2005 to a level of almost 1.2 billion, of which 62% will be wireless users. This means that the number of potential buyers would increase also.

6.2 Structure of e-Marketplace

For the beginning of each successful business transaction it is necessary to have at least two sides, one fore buying, and one for selling, and that is enough. Sometimes it is also enough even for successful ending of the transaction, but not always. Today it is necessary to have at least one more side - the e-Marketplace. This new side has its own laws and connections and it is necessary to build some interface to both old sides, to the buyers and to the sellers. This interface is not complicated to use and usually consists of different browsers, applications, and some integration tools. The most complicated part of each marketplace is the central part connected with the exchange. The central part may be separated in four basic parts connected with different parts of the exchange. These four parts are:

Transaction Support

Content Management

Supply Chain Management

Value Added Service

At the very end, we have a link to other e-Marketplaces, (for more, see [I-faber00]). This link is an important part of each marketplace, because it connects this marketplace with the rest of the World. On the other e-Marketplaces, this link takes role of buyer or seller, depending of how it got there, as representative of buyer or seller side on the first marketplace. Existence of this link is important for maintaining the number of participants on the marketplace; from the users point of view, they never have to leave the marketplace they start with, and all their transactions would be finished successfully.

6.2.1 Transaction Support

This part of the marketplace is responsible for every transaction that can happen on the marketplace, not just financial transactions but also logistic transactions, and definition of new users of the system. Part of the Transaction Support connected with definition of new users and their insertion in system is called Marketplace Administrator; and there is part responsible for negotiation between participants in exchange. It is important to support multiple transaction model, because without that part there would be no dynamic pricing.

Marketplace Administrator

Job of the Marketplace Administrator is to define new users and their rights, new relations on the marketplace, and to monitor the system.

Users Definition. User registration is two-step process, in the first step is necessary to define new user, and in the second step is to give some privileges to user of the e-Marketplace. Defining new user is creating users profile. Some basic data are necessary for this operation, and is usually done on first login on the system. User profile can not be defined unless company, it represents, is already registered.

Authorization Management. This part is responsible for groups definition, profiling group members, and their level of privileges in the work on the marketplace. Each participant has its own privileges in work on the marketplace, these privileges concern buying, selling, leading the auction, and company administrating.

Relations and Contract Management. This part is responsible for defining relations between users, and their relation to business transactions.

Event Reporting. The Marketplace Administrator is responsible for monitoring the system, and for periodical notification of events. Events in the system are dynamically generated, so it is of great importance for all participants to receive fresh and reliable information. The Marketplace Administrators job is also to discover any disturbance in the system, to prevent it if possible, and to eliminate it.

Negotiations

Negotiations are the most interesting part of each exchange concerning participates in the exchange. During negotiations it is important to know are prices dynamically generated or not. Dynamically generated prices are of the greatest interest for each participant in the exchange, because they are the necessary support for evaluation of the prices.

Fixed Pricing

Fixed Pricing. Type of the relationship: one-one (one buyer, one seller). This way of pricing is probably the oldest pricing method. It was implemented even in the first e-Marketplaces ever made. Methodology of this pricing mechanism is simple, on one side we have sellers with their prices, and on the other side we have buyers with their needs; duty of the marketplace is simple, it only has to deliver prices to potential buyers. However, fulfillment of this simple goal is not so simple. Let us start from the beginning. First, we have sellers with their catalogs and prices. Problem with this is that catalogues are different; each seller has its specific sort of catalogues. Marketplace has to read all catalogues, to find all-important facts and to put them together in specific way in some Master Catalogue. This Master Catalogue is then forwarding to all interested buyers. The Master Catalogue is not fixed creation; contest of the catalogue is changing each time seller puts new product for selling, or when price is changed. These changes do not happen very often, so it is possible to observe this catalog as a static creation. This is just one sort of catalogues, public catalogue accessible to all. The other sort of catalogues is Private Catalogue, it is also a catalogue, but it is not accessible to all. This sort of catalogues is made for buyers especially marketed by sellers. Appearance of these catalogues is the same as appearance of the public Master Catalogues, but contents is different. When buyer wants to get some product, whose information are in the catalog, only thing it has to do is to find product in the catalogue and to order it.

Dynamic Pricing

This is possible the most significant part of the whole system; without this part there is no real marketplace, only fix pricing, which is not very attracting way for doing business for all users. Dynamic pricing is mechanism where price is dynamically changed during some period of time according to laws of economy. Dynamic pricing has three basic categories: Auctions, Reverse Auctions, and Exchange. These categories represent number of participants on each side, number of buyers and number of sellers.

Auctions. Type of the relationship: many-one (many buyers, one seller). This sort of pricing is good for sellers because their product is reaching better price this way, but it is not usable each time. It is usable only if product is rare, new, and unique. At the beginning of the auction the seller gives some upset price, after that potential buyers start their competition. Auction is finished when just one buyer is left, with the best price. Auctions are good for the primer quotation of new or rare products.

Pricing mechanism	Industry characteristic	Product characteristic	E-Marketplace responsibilities
Fixed pricing	Stable and predictable behavior of demand and supply	Brand names features No need for dynamic pricing (prices are too low)	Catalog publishing and multiple vendors data reorganization Multi-supplier product competition is provided
Negotiated price	Participants in the exchange are open for negotiation Differentiation in prices for the some items	Rare and unique products Negotiation is justified by high prices	Security and authorization services for protecting and enhancing communication channel for users Workflow tools
Auction	Products have different value for different buyers	Product has to be sold by a deadline Surplus item	Maintain liquidity by attracting large numbers of buyers for auctioning items
Exchange (double auction)	Unstable and unpredictable behavior of demand and supply	Commodity items	Maintain liquidity by attracting both buyers and sellers Neutrality to all participants

Comment: Participants in different categories have different types of pricing mechanism that leads to the goal.

Figure 6.2.A. Industry and product characteristics (source [IBM01])

Reverse Auctions. Type of the relationship: one-many (one buyer, many sellers). Reverse Auctions enable to buyers to get the best possible price for product(s) their want to buy. This sort of auctions is of grate interests for the large buyers (states, large companies, etc). At the beginning buyer sends to same number of sellers request for item it want to buy (Request For Quote - RFQ). After some period of time sellers starts with betting for the best price they are willing to give, but this time it is not the best price for the sellers but it is for the buyer. This sort of pricing gives opportunity to selling companies with lowest price to push through

Exchange. Type of the relationship: many-many. Exchange is the most sophisticated type of relationship between buyers and sellers. It is important for establishing real value of each product. Exchange is also called Double Auction, because we have many buyers and many sellers betting for the best price. Price of each item on the marketplace is dynamically generated according to laws of demand and supply.

In the Figure 6.2.A was shown how users could do pricing in the best way.

6.2.2 Content Management

This part of the e-Marketplace is responsible for management and maintenance of on-line catalogues and support.

Central part of each marketplace is database where marketplace data and exchange participants data where held. It is not easy to make the database if all items have different way of coding, and different format of recording. It is not enough to make database, it is important to make fast and reliable database with as much as it is possible useful and different functions. This is important for many reasons, because if data can not be find fast and in comprehensible way, it is the same as there are no data. Incomplete or inflexible data can make more damage than not having any data. Some of basic assignments of the Content Management are:

Data Acquisition and Categorization

Data Adaptation

Data Maintenance and Accession

Data Acquisition and Categorization. Data published by different participants in the exchange could and usually are made in different file types. This variety of different types, but not just different file types but also different protocols used by different creators makes it almost impossible to one to understand and to use them in fast and comprehensible way. The first step that has to be done is to separate all these data in few different catalogues. Some data might be putted in more then just one catalogue, this from the reason of fast finding and paralleling process of data acquisition. In many cases collected material has lot of redundancies. This would not be a problem if all documents encompassing redundant material would have the some contents. Data must be preserved at any price and in form suitable for users to use. It is important to accent that all users do not have the some right in viewing the data. Some users have just particular rights in dealing with data like reading complete data, reading just data fragments, writing data, deleting data, and data modification. On this level of the data preparation, it is important to say that data is still in the form not suitable for computer using, and for the presentation in uniform shape.

Data Adaptation. This is probably the greatest problem in data manipulation, because data from variety of forms had to be transformed into new form, specified by the system. New form made this way has to be suitable for all users, and easy to understand and easy for extension. Data from this stage had to be prepared for integration in many different areas so it is necessary to adopt some communication standards. Integration with buyers and sellers need to be supported using Application Programming Interface (APIs) or using eXtensible Markup Language (XML).

Data Maintenance and Accession. These are most used operations over database, so it is important to maximally readjust database, and data for these operations. For reducing access time and for increasing number of transaction it is important to use good indexing mechanism (ways for data arranging in database), and more flexible algorithms for data manipulation. In the last two steps we have reducing data redundancies but now we have increasing data redundancies. It is not the some thing; we are not at the beginning, because at the beginning we had redundancies caused by too many data, similar but not the same, but now all redundancies is made for reducing access time. That trade-off is necessary to be made for increasing performance. Database consistency will insure safe transactions and will increase safety of database.

6.2.3 Supply Chain Management

Organization of Supply Chain is complicate and it is biggest problem one e-Marketplace can encountered with. This is not just technical problem, it is more organization problem, but using new tools and technologies can much improve quality of business transaction. Connecting as possible more potential participants in the chain can improve quality of the business transactions. Each user should have many connections, but not too many, because it could felt confuse which one to use. These user connections should not be long; they should be as shorter as it is possible, but it is necessary to have as mush as it is possible connections between users. New tolls should increase level of automation along value chain. The automation is necessary part of the transactions, because dealing with problems just using free will and experience is not enough anymore, today each lost transaction or customer can mean the end of the firm. While dealing with this problem, it is necessary to take concern about these five aspects of supply chain:

Collaborative Supply Planning

Collaborative Demand Planning

Collaborative Inventory Visibility

Collaborative Order Promising

Collaborative Product Development

Collaborative Supply Planning is of the great importance for the suppliers, because it automatically checks and compare demands with product capacitates in order to find the best possible way for suppliers to sell their products. This means that program performs an auction, if possible, in order to find best price for the supplier and stops further acquisition of products that can not be sold in the short time.

Collaborative Demand Planning is connecting buyers and sellers in order to establish stabilize supplying of the marketplace. All this is done automatically using appropriate software. On usual marketplace humans do all this, but that is too slow.

Collaborative Inventory Visibility also concerns buyers and sellers in order to help to all to understand situation on the market. In this way, it is possible to increase transfer rate on the marketplace by producing just products that are requested on the marketplace. Software also predicts events that can increase transfer rate on the marketplace.

Collaborative Order Promising helps buyers to find products they need in short time by using available data. When supplier is found request is automatically transferred to the supplier. If there is more then one supplier, then request is automatically passed to all, and if necessarily, an auction is performed.

Collaborative Product Development is way for generating prototypes and production plans on the base of progress reports. This can increase the level of potential transactions by informing potential buyers of product capabilities and providing information about prototypes. Sometimes it is possible to predict propagation of the product development.

Many software tools have been made, but the most interesting are Software Agents. They are capable of finding potential solutions to the problems by exploring a marketplace. If there is no solution to the problem they are offering solution next to optimal, more of this in section 6.7.

6.2.4 Value Added Service

These services are main elements that define functional structure of each marketplace. Without these services marketplace would not be able to communicate and to cooperate with its users. These services can be classified in four categories:

Security and Authorization Services

Financial Services

Certification Services

Logistic services

All these services are of crucial interest for each marketplace, because they qualify and differentiate the marketplace. It is necessary to the marketplace to have some strong strategic friend in all groups connected with these services.

Security and Authorization Services

Any work at the Internet is potentially dangerous, because the Internet is public network and anyone can potentially see our messages, or can imitate someone else messages. During the exchange, it is of great importance for the marketplace to know who are actors and to eliminate potential intruders. Absolute security does not exist, but it is important to increase level of protection of all data, users and transactions as much as it is possible. It is important for the marketplace to monitor transactions and to notify all participants how and when to protect themselves, if it is not possible to do so automatically. It is important to guarantee safety, reliability and confidentiality for each participant in the exchange. This can be achieved by using secure protocols like HTTP-Secure connection. One of the mostly used protocols is SSL (Secure Socket Lear); it is still not standard by it probably will be. There are lots of more different protocols to be used, but these are mostly used.

Financial Services

Frequent usage and number of the financial transaction made this sort of transactions attractive for the implementation. Increasing number of transaction can increase the number of participants. These sorts of transaction include Payment and Collection Services. This sort of services would not have any sense without cooperating with the other services especially Security and Authorization Services.

Transaction Insurance. The e-Marketplace is responsible for insurance of transferred money, in this case, the marketplace has the roll of intermediate, and it guarantees successful result of the business transaction. This roll has its advantage, because money transferred from the buyers account would not go directly to the sellers account, it would go to the e-Marketplace account. There, money is in safe for the period of "money back guarantee" period. After the period is pasted, if everything were OK the money would be transferred to the sellers account, not all money, some money would be taken as transaction fee. This is probably the safest way to guarantee the correctness of the business transaction.

Financial Service, in true sense. This category includes on-line credit management services, as the most used sort of services. These services guarantee the extension of commercial loans and the management of on-line credit risk.

Support Services. This is an important category, because it is supporting two interesting aspects of the business - Law and Taxes. In this way it is possible to guarantee that all business transaction would be done according to the law, and that the system would be optimized for the fiscal burden.

Certification Services

For all participants in the exchange it is important to know if partners they are dealing are what they claim to be. It is important for the marketplace to have as much users as it is possible, but not all sorts of users. There has to be some sort of control and rating over the participants in the exchange. This sort of control service can be put in two categories: Qualification and Inspection.

Qualification. This sort of service can be understood as monitoring the commercial and the financial reliability of the participants in the exchange and usually is periodically performed. It is important to say that this is not only ranging of the sellers it is also ranging of the marketplaces.

Inspection. These sorts of services are important for ranging commercial products. Trough this it is possible to guarantee as mush as it is possible quality of products on the marketplace.

Logistic Services

This is probably the most critical category, because e-Marketplace itself is not able to satisfy all these service, and it important for the marketplace to become partner with lots of different sorts of operators specialized in logistic. Some of the services in this category are:

Safe Custody

Transportation Management

Carrier Contract Services

Transaction Services

Safe Custody. This sort of services is oriented on safeguard of goods that are the object of the transaction.

Transportation Management. With out this there is not fulfillment of the business transaction, because sometimes it is not sellers job to organize transportation. In that case someone has to organize transportation of the goods from the sellers to the buyers, buyers can, but it is not good for the marketplace not to organize this.

Carrier Contract Services. Carrier contract negotiations enable easy and simple way to negotiate terms and costs of the transportation on the base of the type of merchandise being transported, the urgency, possibility of damaging, etc. Through this it is possible to find the best way for transporting using experience attainment in the past.

Transaction Services. Services that will enable on-line transportation of commercial documentation connected with deals (orders, order confirmations, delivery notes, etc).

6.3 Types of Virtual Marketplaces

There are two basic categories in which we may put Virtual Marketplaces. These two categories are vertical and horizontal marketplace. Difference between them is number of the industry sectors they are involved with. When we say the number of industries we mean one or more then one.

Vertical Virtual Marketplaces are focused on providing goods and services for the specific industry sector, sometimes industry sub sectors, such as steel industry, plastic industry, chemical industry, electronic or similar ones. Operate as hubs for a specific business sector, offering a variety of products and services for sale, located on one or more of an industries value chain. Examples: e-steel, PlasticsNet, e-Chemicals, PaperExchange.

Horizontal Virtual Marketplaces are providing goods and services for multiple industries, such as procurement, project management, media buying. They are usually focused on reducing the inefficient of spot purchasing. Main way for making money in this type is attracting as it is possible more users. Examples: Intelisys, TradeFind.com, BidCom, Adauction MRO.com, EmployEase.com, etc.

6.4 Models of e-Marketplaces

There are four models of e-Marketplace: Buyer-Driven e-Marketplaces, Sell-Driven e-Marketplaces, Independent e-Marketplaces, and Technology Provider e-Marketplaces. For more information see [Russ01].

Buyer-Driven e-Marketplaces. Buyers in the similar areas of business usually establish this e-Marketplace model, in order to procure products from their suppliers via the Internet. Examples: Covisint, GlobalNetXchange.

Sell-Driven e-Marketplaces. A consortium of suppliers/sellers that are looking to sell products on-line via the Internet established this model of e-Marketplace. Examples: Global Healthcare Exchange and MetalSite

Independent e-Marketplaces. This is the basic model of the electronic marketplace, because main motive for establishing this model is revenue, without interfering in the product manufacturing or exploitation. Owners of the marketplace are usually independent organizations, whose main motivation is obtaining of revenues through operating the marketplace on behalf of buyers/sellers. Examples: Alibaba.com, BT Trading Places (www.bt.com/tradingplaces), eBay (www.ebay.com), Enron (enron.com), Tejari.com.

Technology Provider e-Marketplaces. This e-Marketplace model is subtype the of Independent e-Marketplace model and was established by an e-Marketplace technology provider instead of independent organizations. Difference between these two e-Marketplaces models is in motivation for organizing marketplace. The main motivation for the technology provider to set up e-Marketplace can be quite different to those of the company that are establishing an independent e-Marketplace, like testing communication software, database integrity or new search engines. Examples: SAP - mysap.com, Oracle - oracleexchange .com (Exchange.Oracle.com).

These all four e-Marketplace models have one common characteristic: bring together multiple buyers and suppliers through one exchange engine, the software solution that runs the e-Marketplace. That characteristic enables companies to sell and/or procure products using the exchange engine. These four models can be separated in the two categories B2B (business-to-business) and potential B2C (business-to-customer). All of the four models of e-Marketplaces are B2B, but buyer-driven e-Marketplaces only are pure business-to-business (B2B). The other three types are currently primarily B2B, but have the potential to be also B2C.

6.5 Benefits to e-Marketplace participants

The e-Marketplace gives great opportunity to succeed to all participants, because it connects lot of people in the exchange and makes it possible to communicate and to perform business transaction from any place in the World. Different sorts of participants have different sorts of aspirations but there is enough place in the World of business for everyone. Buyers and sellers have different aspirations, but there are even some differences between buyers and buyers, and sellers and sellers depending of 5are they owners of the marketplace or not.

Potential benefits to all participants of the marketplace are presented in Figure 6.5.A. As it was shoved in Figure 6.5.A the marketplace participants have different benefits depending on the marketplace model. Before chousing model of the marketplace, one has to think of potential benefits to all participants and for benefits for itself.

Control type	Benefits to Buyers	Benefits to Sellers
Buyer Controlled	Best prices is obtained by aggregating demand (from smaller buyers) Acting as purchasing agent Observing complementary products (across industries) that fulfill a buyer need in the single point of access	Opportunity for reaching a large number of buyers Low sales and marking costs Qualified sales leads
Seller Controlled	Possibility to access to the system on one access-point Observing complementary products from an industry Observing comparable/competitive products from multiple suppliers	Opportunity for reaching buyers for off-grade or surplus inventory Opportunity for smaller suppliers to consolidate supply for large buyers Acting as sales and marketing agent
Independent	Obtaining real time access to the global base of suppliers Buying goods and services at lower cost Opportunity for sharing product design in real time	Opportunity for access to new markets with no startup costs Reducing the cost of retaining existing customers Opportunity for gaining access to demand information

Comment: Orientation of the marketplace, for some participants, may not be appropriate, but with a good selection, everyone can find a marketplace for itself.

Figure 6.5.A Potential benefits to buyers and sellers (Sources [IBM00, Oracle00])

Someone would say that e-Marketplace made more problems to the participants than it made benefits. In some cases that is probably true, but those cases are probably sellers content with "Status Quo" on the market, with no intention for decreasing fees and for negotiating with competitors.

Benefits from e-Marketplace are many, and different for different sorts of participants see Figure 6.5.B. In Figure 6.5.C was shown what were common benefits to all buyers or to all sellers. Figure 6.5.C represents what are benefits to the participants form different industries and how much should they expect from e-Marketplace.

Operator Benefit	Applicability:	
	Customer facing	Supplier facing
Inventory reduction		+
Cost and time savings on transactions	+	+
Improves company visibility/presentations	+	+
Better information in real time		+
Product cost reduction	+	+
Cheaper and more responsive communications	+	+
Improved procurement control		+
Cost and time effectiveness through collaborative design and planning	+	+
Accelerated time to market	+	+
Efficient integration with SCM	+	+
Efficient integration with CRM	+	

Legend: SCM - Supply chain management
CRM - customer relationship management
+ - Operation supported with benefits

Figure 6.5.B Benefits for e-Marketplace operators (source [Russ01])

Industry	Estimated savings from business-to-business e-Commerce
Aerospace machining	11%
Chemicals	10%
Coal	2%
Communications	5-15%
Computing	11-21%
Electronic components	29-39%
Food ingredients	3-5%
Forest products	15-25%
Freight transport	15-20%
Health care	5%
Life sciences	12-19%
Machining (metals)	22%
Media and advertising	10-15%
Oil and gas	5-15%
Paper	10%
Steel	11%

Comment: Different industries have different potentials for success at the e-Marketplace. Estimated savings percentage is the greatest at industry of electronic components and at forest products; these two industries have noting in comment except potentials for increasing savings

Figure 6.5.C Possible B2B e-Commerce (e-Marketplace) operator savings by sector (source [Russ01])

6.6 Liquidity

One of the most serious problems, that e-Marketplace can meet with, is problem of maintaining liquidity. Sometimes is relatively easy to earn money at the beginning of life of the e-Marketplace. However, if marketplace owners do not have right strategy in the relationship with all participants in the exchange (buyers, sellers, and owners) marketplace could have very short life and at the end there could sty just an idea. As for maintenance of the marketplace idea is not enough, sometimes it can be very dangerous to have just an idea, we need to fond some good strategy for capturing idea and maintaining successful life of the marketplace. Life of each e-Marketplace is a dynamic function of time, interesting for evolution process. It is necessary to control each phase in life of the marketplace. If system is not able to reward each participant in the exchange properly in each phase, there is big opportunity for the system to fail; participants would simply leave. To achieve long life e-Marketplace must have system of dynamic accommodation for new changes, which can prevent, and neutralized any dynamic change in the system. The exchange is as good as liquidity lets it to be. Without enough business transactions there is not enough value, which is essential part of each transaction, and what is necessary to capture for good of all participants. Without captured value there is no reason for the life of an e-Marketplace.

To insure liquidity of system in the dynamic World there must be concerned three crucial aspects of the marketplace:

Pricing

Neutrality

Partnering

Just if grate concern is given to these three aspects there is hope for the e-Marketplace to have successful life. If in dealing with problems one always searching for new, still not proven ides, chance for him to succeed are minimal, but if it succeed price would be greater than standard one. In this part are going to be explained just proven methods whose understanding and right choosing lead to success.

6.6.1 Pricing

While choosing right pricing policy at e-Marketplace one must take concern of many different factors. Purely chosen pricing policy leads to one sort of customers, and that is usually not enough for successful life of an e-Marketplace, because any disturbance on the market will reduce the number of users. There should be taken in to consideration how chosen pricing mechanism is reflecting on real and market value of the money, how it makes for new participants in the exchange, and how it reflects on the marketplace neutrality. There should be taken in to consideration all factors of successful business in order to find right compromise that would help marketplace to live. There are many ways for pricing service, and some of them are shown in the Figure 6.6.A.

Percentage Transaction Fees. Percentage taken this way is usually varying from 0.5 to 15 %. Often this percentage depends of lots of factor, like average price, number of transactions, number of participants, etc.

REVENUE SOURCE	EXAMPLE
Percentage Transaction Fee	Ventro, one of the early independent e-marketplace charges a transaction fee of between 4 percent to 6 percent
Flat Transaction Fee	GM is charging a flat transaction fee through GMAC.
Subscription Fee	DeRemate.com charge US$25 fee per month through service called Myshop.
Referral Fee	Online Asset Exchange provides access to third party service providers with whom it has a revenue-sharing agreement.
Fee for Service	iNetProcure is based on an ongoing fee-for-service from the participating vendors, including basic and optional services.
Private Label Services	2Source offer private label services to interested marketplaces and private clients.
Advertising Revenue	PartsBase.com sells advertising on the site.
Related Premium Content	Farms.com provides, to users, periodic strategic research reports and commentaries on the leading agriculture commodities

Comment: All marketplaces start with some pricing technique but during the time all change pricing mechanism. In many cases they migrate to subscription or to commission based model.

Figure 6.6.A: e-Marketplace Pricing (sources [Chung01, CNET02, Commerce02, iNetProcure02, SCM02, and Venture02])

Flat Transaction Fee for Running the Auction. Running the auction, as frequently given task is charging separately. Fee may not be equal for everyone, what is usually, and can depend on number of different factors.

Subscription fee. This is probably the easiest way for paying the fee on the marketplace. At the beginning/the end of each period users are paying specific sum, which can be fix for all users, but it does not have to be.

Fee for Service. On the marketplace exists some price list and each user can chose what service is going, and when to use.

The best way for choosing what pricing mechanism is most appropriate for using of the marketplace one must understand behavior of all potential users of the marketplace and to generate some models, to analyze them and at the end to choose one, or more depending on results. Some marketplaces are offering few different ways for paying the fee, and uses can chose one way for paying. During the time, the marketplace can change paying mechanism, or to leave to participants to chose one.

6.6.2 Neutrality

During maintaining of the exchange, specific care must be given to neutrality in all transactions, because if any side in the transactions fills any disturbance or irregularity in any way it will leave. That is the worst thing that can happen to the marketplace - to lose ones confidence. There has to be strong confidentiality on the marketplace, and each transaction has to be properly treated. If just one of the participants in the exchange after made transaction felt betrayed, not as a winner it would leave the marketplace and would newer return, because its rights were not protected enough, and the marketplace would be real loser. If owners of the marketplace would like to increase number of buyers by pressuring sellers to reduce their price, sellers would leave very quickly. There would be lots of buyers but just a few sellers, and then there would be no one to generate enough products, and the profitable financial transactions, so profit would be low. Making pressure on sellers is not the only problem. More serious problem is reveling of private information. This is intolerable behavior and cannot be justify by any reason. That is the crime against integrity of person and is punishable by the law.

6.6.3 Partnering

For one e-Marketplace is of great interest to maintain stable connections with as possible more participants, because they bring profit to the marketplace, but that is not enough. Stable connections had to be made with potential participants and even with others. This does not include only partners connected with basic level of interests of the marketplace, but also partners connected with any potentially interesting area. That is necessary, because during run-time, many things might happen and system has to be prepared, fast, and concurrent. Every participant in the exchange has to be served as it possible sooner. Some of partners outside of primary area of the marketplace are shoved in [Chung01].

6.7 Software Agents

Concept of Software Agents is new concept that can help in many sectors of electronic business to increase productivity (for more information see [Moor99, Horvat99]). Basic idea of this concept is to eliminate presents of humans in performing business transactions as much as it is possible. Presents of the humans should be minimized as it is possible more, and the computer usage should be maximized, because human time is expensive, and humans could not do some things as fast as computers could. Humans should be present just in early phases of the business transaction and at the verification phase. Presents of the experience market analysis are no longer necessary because program does all that faster and cheaper. The beginning of the transaction is the first spot where human presents is necessary, but only if is performing some new model of transaction, to determine start parameters for starting transaction. When parameters (e.g. value, quality, time for delivery, manufacturer, etc) are inserted in the system presents of human is no longer necessary. This is job for the Software Agents and has to be done in the shortest possible time. Second spot where human present is necessary is at the end of transaction. Job for Software Agents is to find best possible solution that would fulfill mission specified by human if possible, if not possible then to find solution that is closest to parameters user gave. Software Agents are starting on the marketplace where are created. They are gong from one place to another until all parameters necessary for the transaction are put together. If Software Agent finds more then one selling place that fulfills conditions specified by buyer it could deliver requirement for buying to all of them. However, if not possible according to some algorithm, one or more sellers with closest offer would by informed or even non-of them would, but buyer would, and the list of closest solutions would be posted to the buyer to decide. Decision is always on the buyer to say is it going to buy or not.

Designing of an Agent is very complicated, because it consists of opposite requests, like: Agent has to be no ones and everyone's. Agent has to "think" on just one user but has to have view of all market. Second thing necessary for Agents is to "know" how to do dynamic pricing, how to perform auction and how to communicate with other Agents or even humans. Software Agents are not just "search engines", because sears is dynamically generated and search does not include one database, it includes more even searching databases on different marketplaces or communicating with humans and performing dynamic transactions. Agents had to know how to negotiate with other agent, and how to decide what solution is better.

It is possible to put them in three basic categories: Agent, Vendor, and Trader. We have one mote category; that is Commerce Object (object of the transaction they all are dealing with). Characteristics of these objects are shown in Figure 6.7.A.

Agent. When buyer wants to find product in what it is interested in it calls an Agent, gives all necessary information to the Agent and starts search. Then the Agent starts its journey thought the e-Marketplace in hope to find best solution for buyer, it pasts through supply chain searching for solution, comparing all necessary facts on the marketplace with instructions given by the buyer. If result is positive the buyer is informed, and if not it goes further to other marketplaces. After some period of time specified by the buyer, best solution would be given to the buyer. Solutions depend of algorithm for comparison given to the Agent. Here can be defined Quality of Services for services of searching and fulfillment of requests.

Vendor (seller) agent is special sort of agents that interacts with customer Agents, or real persons and starts transaction if possible. This sort of agent offers products or services to visiting agent or person. This includes: types of offering products or services, and unified interface of Commerce Object. Here can be defined two types of Quality of Services like for flexibility or "lazily bound" distributed configuration.

Marketplace Agents	
Agent	• Independent, executable object that moves through a dynamically changeable distributed processing environment (moves from one e-Marketplace to another). • All necessary information were stored in Commerce Object, (in XML statements or CLIPS/JESS rules, meta-data and control logic).
Vendor	• Independent process that offers products or services to visiting Agent or person. • This Agent includes all necessary attributes like: types of vendor offering product or service, product(s) or service(s) prices, and Quality Of Service attributes • Providing all necessary information of Commerce Object with unified interface.
`Trader	• Providing a set of enhanced naming directory services, (Yellow Pages), to the Agents. • Maintaining a list of active vendors, the merchandise or service types they offer, and other useful market information. • Add vector of Commerce Objects to the list.
Commerce Object	• Contains all necessary data about a particular product, service, vendor offer, customer offer, or transaction plus meta-data (travel history, locations, time spent at a Vendor). It is a wrapper for knowledge, usually in XML or CLIPS.

Legend: XML - (eXtensible Markup Language)

JESS - (Java Expert System Shell)

Comment: These all sorts of programs should improve quality of the work on e-Marketplace and should improve rate of each company. Quality of these programs is of the greatest importance, so great deal of time should be spent on their improvement.

Figure 6.7.A: Marketplace Agent Characteristics (source [Moor99])

Trader. This sort of the agents is providing a set of enhanced naming services, sometimes called Yellow Pages. Its intent is to allow to other sorts of agents to select a service provider based on description of financial and qualitative attributes of the services. This sort of the agent has other responsibilities like maintaining a list of active vendors, the merchandise or services types they offer, and some other information necessary for life of the marketplace.

Commerce Object. This is a description of structure of the object that is in use on the commercial marketplace and it should comprise all necessary information for uninterrupted performing of the transaction. Information, (in XML, CLIPS, etc), about each product, services, each vendor or customer offer, or transaction, or some meta-data are part of Commerce Object.

6.8 Problems of Virtual Marketplace

There are several problems with dealing with Virtual Marketplaces. These problems are products of many different causes. Some of these problems are purely technical, but some of them have their causes in economical or cultural differences between people. This problem may be put in five categories:

Design of the system. This is purely technical problem. It involves all parts of the systems design. In each part of the system destine System Designer has to think about all other parts, and about their interconnections. Problems made in this section have many impacts on the systems work. Answer is in using standard tools, without using exotic methods, which might not be supported by standard.

Trust, Confidence, Security. This is not just technical problem it is also social problem. Maintaining the trust of the marketplace participants, ensuring the appropriate access and authorization to services, and ensuring confidentiality of information and transactions is absolutely essential in the Virtual Marketplace. Solving this problem is not simple, because there are always some persons who would like to usurp other persons proprietary. It can be solve by using new methods of protection, periodic change of system protecting mechanism, and frequent monitoring of usage of the data.

Change in Virtual Marketplace. As each "live" system this one has its own dynamic, so changes are part of this system. Any change has to be predicted, because the system has to work under any conditions. If it is not possible to predict changes then the system has to accommodate to new relations on the marketplace, as it is possible sooner.

Voluntary participation. Each participant in the Virtual Marketplace is there on its own free will and can leave it any time. Main problem is how to satisfy all users of the marketplace, only satisfied user would like to continue using the marketplace, all other would like to leave. Solution to this is in offering lots of different services to users and guaranteeing level of services.

Users understanding. This is typically social problem. Participants in the exchange usually have different views of the situation on the marketplace, and it is important to bring together users with similar needs that fit in. Solution is in using better algorithms for connecting participants in the exchange.

6.9 The Oracle Exchange

This section is dedicated to one of the most interesting tools for creating e-Marketplace, to Oracle Exchange. The Oracle Exchange is based on the Oracles database system, the safest, and the fastest database. It is more then just a database; it is complete product that integrates all components necessary for one e-Marketplace. The Oracle Exchange is one of the key components of the Oracle e-Business suit; complete set of business applications that run entirely on the Internet. It enables to users to reduce costs across customer relationship management, finance, human resources, professional service automation, supply chain management, and project management functions. It is fully hosted e-Business service that can be distributed over the Internet as required by any e-Marketplace type. It does not concentrate on just financial transactions, it is concentrated on much wider area, this can be seen just from titles of its key components: Oracle Exchange Marketplace, Oracle Supply Chain Exchange, Oracle Transportation, and Oracle Product Development Exchange. In this section these references have been used [Oracel01a, Oracel01b, Oracel00, and Aberdeen00]. For users Oracle Exchange is simple and intuitive, no previous experience is necessary for using any parts of this software package. For becoming part of the exchange only necessary things are common Web browser and Internet access. For company or personal registration only necessary thing that has to be done is posting company profile, product, and preference information to specific directory. This has to be done for each user, and users should have different priorities, like right to perform auction or to buy something in company name. Ones reiterated there is no need for downloading specific software from the e-Marketplace. For participation in the exchange, registered user has only to login on the e-Marketplace and that is it!

Database provided by Oracle is highly scalable and secure, and it supports mission-critical, high-transaction volume, 24¥7 business environment. The Oracle Exchange supports multiple communication protocols, including Open Application Group's (OAG) open standards for XML (eXtensible Markup Language), EDI (Electronic Data Interchange), FTP (File Transfer Protocol), and e-mail. For better visual effects Oracle Exchange is using Java or DHTML (Dynamic Hypertext Markup Language) for dynamic generation of unique users interface.

Components of the Oracle Exchange will be presented in next few sections.

6.9.1 The Oracle Exchange Marketplace

This part of the Oracle Exchange presents some basic elements that are necessary for participation in the exchange. Without these elements no transaction is possible, and this elements present essence of each marketplace, some earlier models have only these components. These basic functions are: Registration and Profiling, Catalog Purchases, Buyer and Seller Auction and Catalog Management.

Registration and Profiling. Before starting any transaction at the marketplace each marketplace participant has to be defined and some roles and privileges, has to be given to each participant. Registration is simple and only just necessary information is required. Registration of firm is performing when the firs representative of firm starts its registration. The first registered person is Company Administrator and it has power to give roles to all other representatives of that firm. Roles that could be assigned are: Buyer, Limited View Buyer, Buyer / Sourcing Professional, Seller, Catalog Author, Account Manager and Comp.

Catalog Purchases. This is the oldest way for doing business on the Internet. Main idea of this is to store all necessary product information in some catalog(s) and to present them to the potential buyers. It is possible to achieve operational efficiencies by rationalizing and automating procurement functions. Information received from seller or manufacturer are published in the catalogs viewable to buyers and presented in a form suitable for interpretation. This can help buyers to receive precise, real-time information that can improve the quality and timeliness of purchasing decisions. Ones price and product characteristic are published buyers can make arrangements with sellers in order to achieve better price for goods and services. This way buyers can be marked by sellers and in the future only special catalogs would be presented to them. This sort of catalog is not accessibly to all, just to chosen ones.

Buyer and Seller Auction. This is the powerful weapon for all participants in the exchange, because if guarded well, it can obtain efficiently the best possible price for goods and services. Without this marketplace would not have its basis characteristic - Dynamic pricing. It is possible to perform real-time interaction between participants of the marketplace, potentially placed on the different parts of the Word and to increase potential benefits. Difference between these two types of auctions, Buyer and Seller Auction, is in number of participants on each side, one or more. Buyer (Reverse) Auction is relation between one buyer and more then one seller. This is request for quotation (RFQ). Seller (Forward) Auction is relationship between one seller and more then one seller. This sort of auctions is for rare and new products.

Catalog Management. This part is responsible for catalogue and it can be observed as part of the Catalog Purchases but because of its value context, it is put as separated part. Catalog Management can help to both buyers and sellers by offering efficient way for publishing and searching catalogs.

6.9.2 The Oracle Supply Chain Exchange

The Oracle Supply Chain Exchange is something new that can help to the marketplace to increase number of participants by reducing long chains between buyer and seller side. Main components that enable this are: Supply Planning, Demand Planning, Strategic Planning, Global Inventory Visibility, and Order Promising.

Supply Planning enables automatic comparison of demands and allocated capacities. If any discrepancy is noticed, auction (reverse) could be generated for filling capacity excess. Its easy- to-use interface enables becoming part of the supply planning process without the need for investing in new EDI (Electronic Data Interchange), ERP (Enterprise Resource Planning), or APS (Advanced Planning and Scheduling).

Demand Planning is part of Oracle Exchange that connects buyers and sellers in order to establish stabilize supplying of the market. This can be achieved by comparing distributors and buyers forecast with production forecasts. Any discrepancy can be quickly allocated and eliminated.

Strategic Planning magnifies responsibility to customer demand by enabling organization to publish and to the model multiple production-planning scenarios across the supply chain.

Global Inventory Visibility also connects buyers and sellers in order to help to all to understand situation on the market. In this way it is possible to increase transfer rate on the marketplace by producing just products that are requested on the marketplace. Software also predicts events in future that can increase transfer rate on the marketplace.

Order Promising helps buyers to find products they need in short time by using available data, when supplier is found request is automatically transferred to supplier. If there are more then one then request is automatically passed to all, and if necessarily auction is performed.

All of this can be done by using variety of formats for viewing, sending, and receiving data like: spreadsheets, e-mail, flat file, XML, etc.

6.9.3 The Oracle Transportation

Oracle Exchange is one of rare products that care about transportation of items from one place to another. This is something new, but it gives good results in reducing the price of the shipping and in minimizing time that is necessary for transportation. Oracle Transportation includes four components needed for safe, fast, and secure transportation: Transportation Sourcing, Transportation Execution, Transportation Service Catalog, and Transportation Communication.

Transportation Sourcing is service that can help to the companies that manufacture or distribute goods to create successful relationships with transportation providers. This sort of relationship can improve quality of transportation and can help in negotiations between transportation providers and transportation product users. This can be done by creating short-term and long-term transportation service contracts. When this kind of services is needed, companies that manufacture or distribute goods can find best available solution. If buyer needs long-term requirements RFQ's (Request For Quote) can be created or for short-term and spot shipment auction can be performed.

Transportation Execution is the main part of the Oracle Transportation and it centralizes execution of the transportation services. Companies that need to have their product transported can capture transportation contract details, upload shipment, and submit tenders, track shipment, and record booking on simply way. In this way all necessary information can be loaded, processed, and distributed to all participants in the transportation transaction.

Transportation Service Catalog is special sort of storage catalogs that can help to all participants in the transportation transaction to present their services or their needs. Safe platform for transportation providers to publish their service offerings is implemented in this package.

Transportation Communication provides a central hub for the logistic transactions information. In this way, it is possible to increase number of messages sent from-to participants in the exchange. This exchange data are using many forms including XML, EDI, or e-mail.

6.9.4 The Oracle Product Development Exchange

Oracle Product Development is part of Oracle Exchange that provides an environment for collaborative product design and development across the supply chain. It includes these functions: Item Information Management, Project Collaboration, Document Management, People Management, Change Management, Issue Management, and Product Development Intelligence.

6.10 Conclusion

Existence of e-Marketplaces nowadays is absolutely necessary, because the World has changed drastically in the last few years, and customers have changed to - noting is the some any more. Days when buyers were lazy enough not to be informed are the past. Today everyone has access to the Internet and everyone would rather lose moment of its time, than to lose some money on unnecessary costs (like paining someone to work small jobs for him/her). The concept of the e-Marketplace is new, but it is well accepted by many especially buyers and small sellers without a well-known name; however, some businesses do not like this concept. These are some large selling companies. These companies like to have rich customers with no time to lose on exploring the marketplace and with no interest for changing partner in the relationship. Number of the e-Marketplaces will grow in the future, but not endlessly. In one moment, balance between companies would be made and all e-Marketplaces would have opportunity to exist.

REFERENCES

[Aberdeen00] Aberdeen Group, "The e-Business Marketplace: The Future of Competition," Executive White paper, (www.aberdeen.com), Aberdeen Group, One Boston Place Boston, Massacusetts 02108 USA, **April 2000.**

[Chung01] Chung, A., Long, B., Ephraim, A., Oliver, K., Heckmann, P., Schwarting, D., Laseter, T., von der Decken, T., "The e-Marketplace Revolution: Creating and Capturing the Value in B2B e-Commerce," Viewpoint of the BOOZ-ALLEN&HAMILTON, (www. boozallen. nl/content/ publications/5D_Viewpoints.asp), USA, **November 2001.**

[CNET02] CNET Networks, Inc. (http://techupdate.zdnet.com/techupdate/stories/main/ 0,14179,2607353,00.html), **February 2002.**

[Commerce02] Commerce One Operations, Inc. , (http://www.commerceone.com/news/releases/gm.html), **February 2002.**

[Horvat99] Horvat, D., Milutinovic, V., "A Survey of Mobile Agents and Java Mobile Agents Toolkits," (http://galeb.etf.bg.ac.yu/~vm/tutorial/internet/ business/ebi2/ebi4.html), Internal Report, University of Belgrade, Belgrade, Serbia, Yugoslavia, **January 1999.**

[IBM00] IBM, "Creating a successful business-to-business e-marketplace," White paper, (www-4.ibm.com/software/webservers/commerce/ gsw1754f.pdf) IBM Global Services, Route 100 Somers, NY 10589 U.S.A, **November 2001.**

[I-faber00] "Project: I-faber," UniCredito Italiano, (http://www.ifaber.com/en/ marketplaces), Italy, **November 2001**.

[iNetProcure02] iNetProcure, (http://www.inetprocure.com/maincontent/aboutus/ m_about_inet.htm), iNetProcure Inc.100 Jersey Avenue Suite B201 MailBox B-10 New Brunswick, NJ 08901, **February 2002.**

[Moor99] Moor, D., Greengrass, E., Sud, J., "Agents in the Virtual Marketplace," (home.att.net/~dana.moore/pubs/Component99/ AgentVMarkt.PDF) **October 2001.**

[Oracel01a] Oracle, "ORACLE SUPPLY CHAIN EXCHANGE version 6.1," Data sheet, (www.opacle.com) Oracle Corporation, **November 2001.**

[Oracle01b] Oracle, "ORACLE SUPPLY TRANSPORTATION version 6.2," Data sheet, (www.oracle.com), Oracle Corporation, **November 2001.**

[Oracle00] Oracle, "ORACLE EXCHANGE MARKETPLACE version 5.0-5/1/2000," Data sheet, (www.miraculum.co.za/exchange%20data%20sheet.pdf), Oracle Corporation, **October 2001.**

[Russ01] Russ Nathen, "E-marketplace: new challenges for enterprise policy, competition and standardization," Workshop report, (http:// europa.eu.int/comm/ enterprise/ict/e-marketplaces/workshop_final_report.pdf), Brussels **23-24 April 2001.**

[SCM02] The SCM Digest, (http://www.scmdigest.com/SCMDigest/SCM Digest72.html), **February 2002.**

[Sterling01] Sterling Commerce," E-Marketplace Liquidity: Bridging existing EDI communities with the Global Trading Web," White paper, Sterling Commerce Inc, (www.sterlingcommerce.com/solutions/products/ebi/wp/pdfimages/emarket/EMktLiquidWhit_04-12.pdf), **November 2001.**

[Venture02] Venture Capital Newsletter, (www.latinvalley.com/VCNewsletter/VC%20newsletter%20-%20August%2001.pdf), **February 2002.**

E-Business and E-Challenges
V. Milutinović and F. Patricelli (Eds.)
IOS Press, 2002

CHAPTER 7 E-MARKETING ON THE INTERNET

Darko Milutinović, Petar Kočović and Veljko Milutinović

Today everything goes to the e-... side. Before we start with discussion we will give some basic concepts of e-everything.
E-Commerce uses the **Internet** simply as means of conducting **sales transactions,** while **e-Business leverages** new and existing technologies to **interact, transact,** and **collaborate** with members of the organization's **value chain** (see also [Zikmund99]).

E-Marketing as a Part of e-Business

The main reason for successful employing of e-Marketing is growing of E-Business since 1994. Figure 7.1 shows this boom.

So what makes the business different?

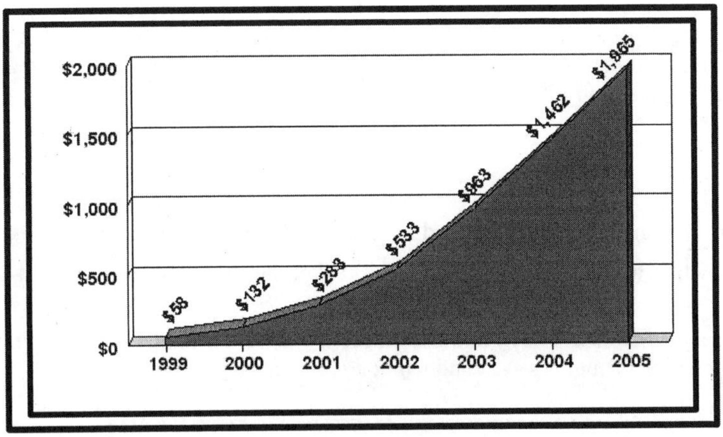

Comment: **(US$ Billions)**

Figure 7.1 E-Business Revenue Projections 1999 to 2005

First order differences:

- Automation
- Transaction costs
- Access

- Process scope and visibility
- Data richness
- Market capitalization
- Globalization
- Personalization
- Separation
- Elimination of boundaries

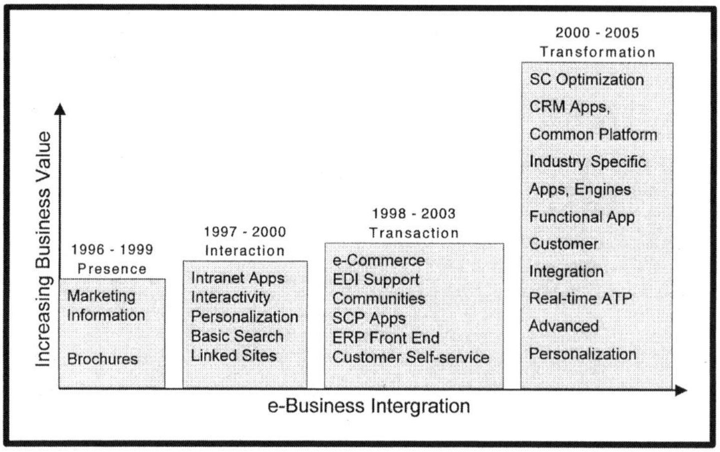

Figure 7.2 **E-Business Integration**

Impacts:

- New business models
- Outsourcing decisions
- 24 x 7 operations
- Corporate boundaries/alliances
- Valuations
- Legislation trailing business change
- Customer segments of one
- Information and product allowed to follow different paths/economics

It is obvious that e-Business move beyond Web presence toward business transformations.

Business-to-business (B2B) and exchanges are about exchange of information between organizations for the purpose of conducting commerce.

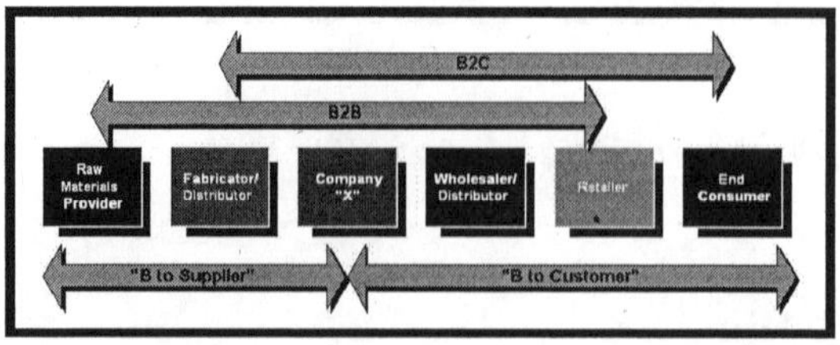

Figure 7.3 "B2B" and "B2C" are focused on transactions at various points among the value chain

Business-to-consumer (B2C) represents transactions between businesses and consumers where currency and/or information is exchanged for goods and services.

"B2B" and "B2C" are focused on transactions at various points among the value chain. Another approach is "B to Supplier" and "B to Customer" (Figure 7.3).

Collaboration is sharing information and collaborating on decisions within or between stakeholders.

Internal processes are optimized/streamlined using Internet technologies.

We can focus on the following internal processes in enterprise:

- Production
- Collaboration
- Sales
- Marketing (e-Marketing)
- Service
- e-Learning

Digital marketing is utilizing Internet technologies to advertise and increase brand awareness. We can introduce the following issues:

- Customer relationship management
- e-Selling
- e-Marketing
- e-Servicing

E-Business enables extended enterprise concept.

Global Information Systems and the Internet

A customized communications network gives Texas Instruments (TI) the ability to communicate with and control all its branches around the world from its headquarters in Dallas, Texas.

Texas Instruments works constantly to maintain its competitive advantage in an ever-changing semiconductor market. Leadership in the marketplace is difficult in an industry which experiences such rapid change and incredible technological advances. Semiconductor manufacturers are constantly struggling to make profit on products which have continuity shortened life-cycles.

One of the ways TI has been able to survive in such a volatile market is by networking its global operations. TI's decision over 20 years ago was to develop a new information system called single-immage network, with manufacturing and marketing facilities all over the world.

With the help of the single-imae network It is 76.000 employees are able to communicate with over 50.000 workstations to obtain information from other employees or to access any of TI's 20 data centers around the world. This system transmits over 250.000 messages and documents daily. The network has streamlined communications from the production operation to the order processing department and marketing, identify when orders will be shipping, print order lists, and provide shipping instructions to remote plants.

Global information systems - The well-being of a multinational corporation-indeed, the health of any business organization that plans to prosper in the twenty-first century-will depend on information about the world economy and global competition. Contemporary marketplaces require timely and accurate information from around the globe to maintain comparative advantages.

A global information system is an organized collection of computer hardware, software, data and personnel designed to capture, store, update, manipulate, analyze and immediately display information about worldwide business activities.

Data versus information - Marketing managers must distinguish between data and information. Data are simply facts or recorded measures of certain phenomena; information is a body of facts in a format suitable to support decision making or define the relationship between two pieces of data.

The characteristics of valuable information - Not all information is valuable to decision makers. Marketing information is useful if it helps a marketing manager make a decision. Information can be evaluated using four characteristics: relevance, quality, timelines and completeness.

Relevance - Information is relevant if it suits the needs of the marketer. Relevant information applies to the situation if it clarifies the questions the decision maker faces.

Quality - High-quality information is accurate, valid and reliable. High-quality data present a good picture of reality. Information quality depends on the degree to which the information represent the true situation.

Timelines - Marketing is a dynamic field in which out-of-date information can lead to poor decisions. Marketing information must be timely, that is, provided at the right time.

Computerized information systems can record events and dispense relevant information soon after a transaction takes place.

Completeness - Information completeness means having the right quantity of information. Marketing managers must have sufficient information about all aspects of their decisions.

Decision support systems - A marketing decision support system is a computer-based system thet helps decision makers confront problems through direct interaction with databases and analytical software programs. The purpose of a decision support system is to store data and transform them into organized information that is easily accessible to marketing managers.

A decision supports system requires databases and software.

Databases and data Warehousing - Because most companies compile and store many different databases, they often develop data warehousing system. Data warehousing is the term managers of information technology use to refer to the process that allows important data collected from day-to-day computer systems to be stored and organized into separate systems designed for simplified access.

The role of the Internet - It is estimated that 10 million computers and 100 million users are linked across the internet. The number of users doubles annually, making it the fastest-growing communications medium in history. Many people believe the Internet is the prototype of a new communications infrastructure that will be as widespread and influential as the international telephone network, satellite television and the postal system.

Computer communication and messages discovery are two central functions of the Internet. Exchanging e-mails on daily base is way for communication within individuals.

The domain is typically a company name, an institutional name or an organizational name associated with the host computer. Com, edu and gov indices the domain as commercial, educational or governmental. The introductory page, or opening screen, is called the home page because it provides basic information about the purpose of the document along with a meny of selections, or links, that lead toother screens with more specific information. Thus, each page can have connections, or hyperlinks, toother pages, which way be on any computer connected to the Internet.

Imagine that you can build your business in a place where everyone could see it and access it, from all around the world, at their convenience. And imagine that the construction process could be completed in just a few weeks, at a reasonable cost. Better yet, suppose you could quickly learn what each customer wants most from your company and respond personally. In that way, you could improve customer relationships and increase loyalty.

Today, the Internet can make that vision possible and it can create a universal point of connection between people, businesses and organizations. The Internet was invented by scientists. Then the Web came along with its ability to deliver content to everyone's desktop in a universally comprehensible format which made it an ideal way of publishing and delivering your company information. New value is found in each design tweak - sound, video, animations, etc. Nowadays, simply having a Web site is not enough. It should be more than just a place for company's stationery. It is about time the Internet finally discovered the world's second oldest profession - marketing.

Marketing a product online is extremely different from marketing it offline - but there are a few similarities. Offline has commercials - online has Web sites. Offline has an office - online has a Web site and an e-mail address. Offline has newspapers - online has e-zines. This list is endless. But the differences are important. Online, people cannot see you, and they cannot touch the product. You have to attract them, make them trust you and present the product in such a way that they feel like they have it in their hands.

Billions of dollars are being spent online each year. This number will of course continue to increase every year. People are making money and You can be part of all that - all you need to know is how to do it! First, you have to realize that business online is done very differently than it is offline. People do not just arrive at your Web site, take what they want, pay you and leave. It does not happen that fast online. People have to find out that you exist - this is the part where the marketing comes in. You have to make them believe what you say and describe the product in such a way that they feel like they are holding it in their hands - but that is not really marketing in the online world. Marketing is where you get them to come to your site to check out the product in the first place, or make them ask for more information. That is e-Marketing.

7.1 What is E-Marketing?

E-Marketing is a general term for a wide array of activities conducted over the Internet. Some of them include:

Web site building and promotion - Web site is the most important element of company's Web presence so it should be carefully built and promoted.

Customer communications - Without communication with customers a company cannot find out their wishes and suggestions and cannot count on having a successful online advertising campaign.

E-Mail marketing - This is one of the most popular e-Marketing options because it is cheap and available to everyone and it is also a lot easier than Web site creation.

Newsgroup advertising - This is forgotten but in some cases very useful e-Marketing option which can enhance your online advertising campaign.

(All these e-Marketing options will be explained in details later.)

E-Marketing is NOT only creating a Web site. It also focuses on communication online using customer directed dialogue. In this way you can easily find out what your customers want most from your company and respond to them personally, increasing customer relationships and loyalty and making it easier for them to do business with you.

In short, we define e-Marketing as all the things company has to do to find, attract and keep customers (see also [Cisco2000]).

7.2 Why E-Marketing?

In this section we'll present you some quick reasons why a company should have a Web presence. You are probably familiar with all of them but we will give them for the online advertising beginners.

Internet access is now available virtually anywhere - This means that you have a potential to reach more customers, you can introduce new products and services quickly and you can easily collaborate with your suppliers and partners.

Internet standards enable users from all over the world to plug into the Web - The potential customers can use the Web regardless of the computer type they use and regardless of the communication service they use. The cost is negligible and the world of information is instantly within reach.

All businesses can compete - Businesses of all sizes and in all industries can effectively compete over the Internet hoping to have a successful online advertising campaign.

7.3 E-Marketing Options

This section will cover some aspects of using the three most important e-Marketing options. Advanced techniques will be discussed in the "E-Marketing Options (Advanced Approach)" section.

Three major e-Marketing options include:

- Web site building and promotion
- Banner advertising
- E-mail marketing

They will be explained in details in the following sections.

7.3.1 Web Site Building and Promotion

In this section we'll give you some very important tips for building and advertising effective Web sites (see also [Enlow99] and [Worsley2000]).

Since your Web site is the only thing your customers can judge you by, you have to build it very carefully. It must show your confidence and demonstrate your competence, professionalism and personality.

To illustrate the potential errors of an ineffective Web site, let's imagine a real store in one of the city's streets.

From the street you can see a sign on the front of the store that simply says "Store". You follow its path - but you cannot find the door! After pushing on different sections of the wall, you finally find a hidden door that opens up and lets you in. Inside, it is pretty dark and hard to see except for a few bright neon lights and a lot of random flashing lights that hurt your eyes. When you eyes adjust, you discover a lot of products randomly organized on shelves, but you cannot read their descriptions because they are written in an orange text on a bright pink background. Even when you are able to read them, there is not enough information to interest you in buying anything. When you finally find something worth buying, you cannot find a salesperson or a cash register. After more painful search, you find a sign telling you to mail a check and in three weeks after your check clears the product will be mailed to you. But you wanted to buy the product today!

How long do you think a store like this would last? Not long. But the problem is that there are thousands of Web sites just like this store all over the Web, taking up valuable space, clogging up the search engines and making it harder for the legitimate offers to be found.

Let us now see what we have learned from this store example. We have learned what we have to do to avoid the dreadful mistakes presented in the store example.

1) Let your intro page be simple - It should consist only of your logo and a couple of lines of some useful information. Since your competition is just a button-click away, do not make your customers wait for some stupid logo to display that doesn't provide any useful information.

2) Make sure that all links are clearly marked - This is true especially for the links that lead to your ordering page because that's the most important page of your whole Web site.

3) Put a link to your home page and to your ordering page on every page - In this way you will make it easy for your customers to navigate through your site and to find the ordering page. It is insane to make them hard to find this page!

4) Lose the stupid animations - They are distracting your customers and make it hard to actually read what you are offering. Imagine a basketball player who is making a free throw. Why do you think the fans of the opposing team are weaving their hands behind the basket? Of course, to distract him. The same goes for the unnecessary animations on your Web site. Do not distract your customers from your goal - selling them your product.

5) Lose the funky backgrounds - The truth is: black text on the white background is easiest to read so you should use this combination on all your Web site pages. If you insist on using some other backgrounds, find some acceptable combination and try to use it on the left-hand side of your Web pages (that's the place where navigation tools are stored).

6) Organize your products so that they make sense - According to e-Marketing experts, the best way is to advertise your strongest product and to offer links to your other products. If you have to advertise more products, organize them in a logical manner and do not confuse your customers with too many choices.

7) Make it easy to order - Put a link to your ordering page on every page of your site. Provide as many ways to order as possible and be reassuring as possible. Since your ultimate goal is to make customers buy your product, do not make them search for your ordering page and let them provide only the necessary ordering information.

8) Do not make it easy for the visitors to leave your site - If you're going to permit outside advertising using banners, do not put them on pages where the visitors are in the middle of activity (like placing the order or asking you a question about the product)

9) Guarantee prompt delivery - No one wants to wait for anything. Offer to send products within 24 hours of receiving an order and do not wait for checks to clear. The quicker you can promise to put the product into the customer's hands, the more likely they will buy it.

10) Think twice about sites you link to - Your potential customers judge you on everything because it is all they have. Therefore, only provide links to Web sites you would be proud to be associated with.

Your Internet efforts do not end with the perfect Web site. When you create your new Web site you have to promote it so the potential customers can find out about it. If no one knows you exist, the customers won't come to visit. Here are some online basics to get your site noticed and keep it visible.

You have two options. You can hire a **submission service** that will do the entire job for you (this is a good option if you are a beginner or if you do not have time to do the job yourself) **or you can do the Web site promotion yourself** (much better option recommended by most e-Marketing experts). In order to do that you will need the help of:

Web Directories - These are indexes to various places on the Web, listed alphabetically, by region, or by subject. The most effective sites list by subject or by category. Since you want the most people to see your site, it is very important to carefully choose the category for your site. We strongly recommend that you be totally familiar with each directory service and how it works before you submit your site. This will help you choose the best category for your site and might mean the difference between 10 hits/day and 100 hits/day. The most popular Web directories are Yahoo (www.yahoo.com) and Infoseek (www.infoseek.com).

Search Engines - Web search engines are quickly becoming the most popular way to find sites on the Web. Users just type in what they are looking for, and the search engine lists all the sites that it thinks you might be interested in. There are a lot of important techniques to incorporate on your site before you list it (these techniques will be explained later). The most important Search engines are Google (www.google.com) and AltaVista (www.altavista.com).

Newsgroups - The place in the Usenet community where you must announce your new Web site is comp.infosystems.www.announce (this is a moderated newsgroup). Please read the charter before posting because it will save you time.

Specialized Newsletters - These are newsletters sent out to a mailing list (also archived on the Web). You can announce anything about the net here because all postings are moderated. The most popular specialized newsletters are Net-Happenings and Net Surfer Digest.

7.3.2 Banner Advertising

One very successful technique of getting people to your site is the use of banner advertising. Banners can be seen on many Web pages. You can buy banner space or you can exchange banners. You can also host banners and you can create them. Here are some quick tips for creating great looking banner ads (see also [Dean99]).

1) Always use the words "Click Here" or "Enter" - You may think that these words are overused but tests have proved that these words can increase the effectiveness of a banner by 20-30% without changing anything else. They inspire the readers to click on the ad if the headline of the banner interests them.

2) Animate your banners - An animated banner will increase your banner ads effectiveness by 30-40%. The key in using animation in your banner is keeping it small. The reason you do not want big pictures or images that look like live video in your banners is the fact the banner will load too slowly. The visitors just do not like that.

3) Create quick loading banners - The potential customers do not want to wait for the banners to display because they will lose interest. Keep most banners under 10-12 KB. This will be very difficult to accomplish when you are using animated banners but you have to do that. The way to do this is to keep the banners simple with only one or two movements and to decrease the number of colors. You need a nicely designed high quality banner that loads quickly.

4) Use an interesting headline - Good looking banner is not enough if do not have a catchy headline that will attract your potential customers. A good technique to use is to keep the same headline on your banner ad that you have on your entry page.

5) The best word to use is "FREE" - This doesn't mean to put this word without any other text. Tell your potential customers what exactly they will be getting for free. Using this word will make your response rate increase dramatically.

6) Use blue underlined text - When Internet users see blue underlined text, they know it is a link leading to another page on the Web. In this way, you will achieve a higher click through ratio.

7) Use your Web site address or your logo - Do not focus your banner on your logo or your Web site address, but do include them. Your main preoccupation should be the headline but including these elements will help you produce a branding effect on people's minds.

8) Use trick banners - Trick banners look like something in Windows that people are used to click on. A number of effective banners use what looks like a Windows slider and you can create trick banners that look like buttons, checkboxes or drop-down menus. These tricks will bring curiosity in people.

9) Change banner ads frequently - According to research, most banner ads start losing effectiveness third time a person has seen them. If they haven't clicked on them by then, they probably never will. Therefore, change your banner ads frequently and your customers won't be bored.

7.3.3 E-Mail Marketing

Not so long ago, e-mail marketing meant placing an ad in a newsletter and waiting for the traffic. It is not the case anymore.

E-mail can be used in every step of the online advertising process, from driving traffic and building brands, to customer service and marketing special offers. Almost every commercial or e-commerce site on the Web collect e-mail addresses and send out newsletters.

The reason for that is simple - e-mail is Internet's killer application. There are enough e-mailboxes in the world for everybody. According to eMarketer, there were 3.4 trillion e-mail messages sent in the world. Another reason: e-mail is dirt cheap. E-mail is an extremely cost-effective, high-response-rate option, which can acquire and retain customers, sell and promote products, drive loyalty and reinforce branding efforts. Internet marketing is estimated to be 60-65% cheaper than traditional advertising (Source: *Yankee Group*). Cost-per-piece comparison: $0.01-0.25 for e-mail, $1-2 for snail mail (Source: *Jupiter Communications*). The average number of commercial e-mail messages that US online consumers receive per year will increase from 40 in 1999 to more than 1,600 in 2005. One of the biggest challenges that businesses face in e-mail marketing is growing their internal e-mail contact database effectively. Companies must realize that they have to leverage all available channels (Web, phone and retail) to capture e-mail collection efforts into all points of contact with consumers aggressively, both online and offline. Jupiter's research revealed that 65 percent of companies are spending between 1 and 5 percent of their marketing budgets on e-mail marketing.

Consumable products	50%
Personal interests	45%
Computer & electronics	43%
Fashion & style	43%
Collectibles & hobbies	41%
Toys, games & entertainment	38%
Investments	38%
Office supplies	37%
Travel & entertainment	32%

Comment: **According to ActiveMedia Research**

Figure 7.4 Types of sites that send marketing e-mail

E-mail marketing can be **untargeted** and **targeted**.

Untargeted e-mail marketing usually comes down to sending too many e-mail messages to a lot of people who do not like that. That is called unsolicited bulk emailing and it is not a smart way to do e-mail marketing. Therefore, you should avoid this type of marketing because it generates spam and your potential customers will probably hate you for that.

Targeted e-mail marketing means sending your e-mail to recipients that have approved of it. Of course, the cornerstones of such e-mail marketing program have to be permission and privacy. If you want to see high response rates, if you want to develop long-term loyalty, if you want to be seen as a business with integrity and future, you have to follow the highest permission and privacy standards. Successful e-mail campaigns are based on trust, and if you do not honor permission and privacy, you're not even standing at the starting line when the whistle is blown and the race begins. Targeted e-mail marketing comes in these forms:

Opt-in marketing - You can rent e-mail lists of people who have approved receiving e-mail about certain topics. This is not the cheapest form of targeted e-mail marketing, but it works. On average, you will have to spend about 10-15 cents per address. The companies that rent addresses even do the mailing for you. The most popular companies that offer "opt-in" e-mail marketing are Postmasterdirect (www.postmasterdirect.com), Bulletmail (www.bulletmail.com) and Htmail (www.htmail.com).

E-zine advertising - This is a low budget technique which enables you to advertise your product in other companies' newsletters or online magazines. Compared with the high costs of other advertising techniques, e-zine advertising is a bargain. Many large companies are just starting to realize this and are entering into this exciting new advertising medium. Of all the e-mail marketing methods available, e-zine advertising could be the most effective.

Newsletter publishing - One step better than advertising in e-zines is actually publishing your own newsletter. In this way, your customers and prospects will constantly be "in touch" and your newsletter can keep them informed about new products and services as you make them available. Unlike traditional newsletters, there are no printing or postage costs. Since your own cost is zero, you can offer free subscriptions, ensuring a steady flow of new potential customers.

While creating your own newsletters, keep in mind these tips: send them daily/weekly/monthly, set up an autoresponder to send to those who send you unwanted messages, respond to all e-mail messages regarding your service and site immediately (sites lose visitors/customers when they do not respond in an efficient amount of time) and add a signature to the bottom of all your outgoing e-mails.

When we were talking about untargeted e-mail marketing, we mentioned that this kind of marketing generated **SPAM** (see also [Alch2001]). What is spam exactly? Imagine this situation: you're coming home and you're playing your answering machine in order to listen to the recorded messages. Instead of some meaningful messages, you find dozens of messages offering "amazing" products that fill up your machine. Sometimes you receive a vast number of these unwanted messages and you cannot hear the really important ones. What's worse, you get billed for all of them! Of course, you wouldn't like to be in this kind of a situation. The same goes for the e-mail messages. Never blast them to unsuspecting people or addresses. That is called the spam! Although there is no law that will prevent you from sending unwanted messages repeatedly, you must know that your potential customers will most likely hate you for that and they'll never want to buy anything from you. Another analogy that is often used while explaining the reasons why spam is bad is this one: yes, you have the right to walk the street and say whatever you like, but you do not have the right to stick your head in someone's house at 3 am and shout through a bullhorn.

If you're wondering where the term "spam" came from, here is the answer. It came from a Monty Python sketch in which the characters were in a restaurant which mainly sold Spam. Items on the menu included things like "Spam, Spam, eggs, ham, and Spam". Whenever the waitress recited the menu, a group of Vikings in the corner would sing with her, repeating the word "Spam" over and over again, drowning out everything else.

While talking about spam, another question arises. How can you protect yourself from spam? If the truth is to be told, we must say that you cannot completely protect yourself from spam. But we can give you some tips which can help you lower the number of the unwanted messages you receive.

The most present sort of junk e-mail is commercial advertising. The senders of these messages feel that junk e-mail is not objectionable and that the recipients will just delete it if they do not want it. To stop the commercial junk e-mail you have to show its senders the error of their behavior. When you receive this kind of unwanted messages, **reply to them with a message telling you're not at all amused**. Do not use profanity and do not mention the sender's parents in the rude way even if you're tempted to do so. Just sound like a serious potential customer who doesn't want to be bothered with unwanted messages. However, this is often impossible because the spam message senders hide their return addresses (they use dummy return addresses). If this is the case, the real address is probably hidden within the body of the message. This assumes that if you are not interested in buying the product, you won't read the whole message and find the real address. Therefore, if your reply gets undelivered, check the whole message for the real address.

If you receive unwanted message referencing a Web page, you can find the real address of the server owner and direct your comments to him/her. This can be very effective tool for decreasing the number of the unwanted messages you receive. Although the spam message sender can ignore your replies, the domain owner from which the message originated most probably will not do the same thing. Most domain owners do not want their domains to be used for sending spam. Therefore, instead of sending the reply to the spam message sender, **send it to the postmaster or the system administrator** (if you want to know how to find out the address of the system administrator, check the "Catching Spam Senders" section) who will eventually find and punish the sender of the unwanted messages.

There are companies whose business is generating spam. They collect e-mail addresses for "clients" who pay them a lot of money. Complaining to these companies rarely works - they even think they have the right to spam! But these spam generators can be shut very easily using **filtering systems in e-mail clients** like Outlook Express or Eudora. You can create filters which will automatically reply to the unwanted messages or block them.

However, although these mentioned ways are very effective, from time to time you will encounter someone who needs more convincing. In that case, if all the above ways do not help, **only a threat will do**. You can send him/her a message threatening that you would sign him/her to 1000 mailing lists to demonstrate what it is like to receive unwanted e-mail messages.

7.4 E-Marketing Options (Advanced Approach)

In this section you will be introduced to some advanced e-Marketing techniques. You will learn how your Web site can get top search engine positioning, you will find out about the Web site extras (additional possibilities that will make your site even more interesting to the potential customers), you'll be introduced to site tracking and usability testing, and at last we will give you some tips for proper newsletter writing.

7.4.1 Getting Noticed by Search Engines

There is a myth among Web site managers that simply submitting your Web site to hundreds of search engines will increase traffic to your site. Another myth is that simply inserting META tags in your Web pages will also increase your traffic. These are just not true. You must use **search engine positioning**. This is the most affordable choice. Here are some statistics to prove it: over 95% of Web users find what they are looking for by visiting the top 6 search engines. Everybody knows that even a few good positions on even one or two important keywords or phrases can drive thousands of visitors to a Web site per day. According to research, people hardly ever go past the top 30 search results. The top 10 results receive 78% more traffic than those in position 11 to 30. The top 30 results get over 90% of the search traffic. This fact explains why some sites do so well and others so disappointingly and why it is such an advantage to be ranked highly.

	1999 (%)	2000 (%)
Search Engine	67	81
Link from another site	39	59
Viral Marketing	28	56
Television	16	48
Guessed URL address	22	41
On-line Advertising	10	20
Radio	6	19
Direct Mail	5	10

Comment: According to June 2000 Forrester Research

Figure 7.5 How users find sites?

Now that you are ready to promote your newly created Web site, the first thing you will want to do is to register your site with the search engines. You can pay someone else to do it for you, but if you are on a limited budget or you want to do it yourself (which is a much better option than hiring someone) go for it. You can easily do this yourself. The process doesn't have to be time-consuming. It is not much different than placing the ads on the Internet. If you are set up for it, you can do it fast and efficiently. Although there are Web sites where you can automatically submit your site to many search engines at once like Add Me (www.adme.com), Register It (www.registerit.com) and SubmitShack (www.submitshack.com), the best option is to do the job yourself by going to each search engine site individually. Why? Because every search engine has its own algorithm for ranking Web sites. Here are some tips for positioning your Web site at the top of search engine results.

Avoid or minimize frames - Frames are multiple Web pages that form one bigger Web page. If you're using frames you have probably heard that it is difficult to get high visibility on search engines. This is true because most search engines get confused when they encounter frames (they just do not know in which frame to look for the keywords, phrases and META tags). However, in some cases you can easily solve this problem. Use the <NOFRAMES></NOFRAMES> tags and put your main keywords between them. Since most browsers support frames, most of your visitors won't see this. For the few that still use older browsers, you can offer a professional look by using the complete sentences instead of keywords and phrases.

```
<IMG WIDTH=120 HEIGHT=60 SRC="btn.gif"
ALT="Text with important keywords">
```

Figure 7.6 Using keywords in image ALT tag

Avoid splash pages - Splash pages are entry pages consisting only of a company's logo that should be clicked in order to get to the next page. They do not have keywords and META tags and therefore search engines cannot rank your Web site. This is of course not what you want and you should avoid creating these pages.

Use keywords in image ALT tag - When using graphics, always use the ALT tag along with the important keywords (Figure 7.6). Some search engines index this tag in the search results (AltaVista, Infoseek, Lycos and Excite).

Always use META tags - Before you list your site, be sure to include HTML "META tags" at the top of your page. These tags are not seen in the completed page, but search engines use them and list your page according to the information you have supplied in them. Writing effective META tags will help the placement of your site in the search engines. Mastering these tags isn't as hard as a beginner might think. It is important to include them in every page on your site because it helps the search engine to index your site properly. It also helps visitors to find your site. However, META tags can get very complicated. They can be used to identify the author of the page, what HTML specifications the page follows, the keywords and description of the page, and the refresh parameter, which can be used to cause the page to reload itself or to load a different page. In this section, we will discuss only the most important META tags.

Many HTML editors have META tag creators, which are very handy for beginners. But if you are an experienced user do not waste your money on them because it is always better to create your own META tags. They go between <HEAD></HEAD> tags in your document and they should be typed on a single line, without the brakes (Figure 7.7).

```
<HEAD>
        <META NAME="Description" Content="Page description">
        <META NAME="Keywords" Content="Keywords, ... ">
        <TITLE>Document title</TITLE>
</HEAD>
```

Figure 7.7 Using META tags properly

While writing META tags, you have to pay special attention to writing proper keywords and descriptions.

The keywords must be less than 1000 characters because that's the maximum search engines use. But that doesn't mean that if you use 999 characters all the search engines will include all of your keywords. For example, Infoseek only uses up to 744 characters while Alta Vista uses less than 500.

Do not repeat any keyword more than three times. The search engines consider this spamming. If they catch you doing this, they won't index your site at all. Some search engines are case sensitive. If you're concerned with this, you will have to contact each search engine to find out. And that takes time. It is better to either use all caps or all lower case.

Description must be less than 150 characters. This is what the search engines display when they index your site. It should be something that "hooks" the viewer and makes them want to see more. Use a few of your very important keywords in your description and avoid using commas.

Do not rush while creating META tags. Take time to examine all the keyword combinations. Some search engines even give you a hint as to what keywords to use. When you type in a keyword, it will come up with your results and give you a choice of words to add to your search that might help narrow it all down. Why are we talking so much about the keywords? Because they are the key - and they need to be targeted. But you need to target the direct market, as well as the indirect market. Good trick is to use common misspellings in your keywords. Not everyone who is using the search engines has a dictionary handy. You should also use plurals in your keywords whenever possible (for example, if you use the word "tools", searches for both "tool" and "tools" will produce your listing).

Once your keywords are optimized, you will need to work a little on your site's title. This goes between <TITLE></TITLE> tags of your HTML document. When the document is viewed in a Web browser, the title appears in the top bar of the browser window. The title of your page is seen as keywords in most search engines. You should use two or three most important keywords in the title. It is also best to begin your title with a number, or with one of the first few letters of the alphabet.

Use doorway pages - Doorway pages, also known as entry or bridge pages are Web pages designed specifically to rank highly on the unique ranking algorithms of each search engine. The two best things about using these pages is that they cost far less than other promotional tools such as banner ads and they work better when properly designed. As it is almost always the case with the e-Marketing options, you can create doorway pages yourself or have someone do it for you.

If you decide to do it yourself, be prepared to invest a considerable amount of time because beating the search engine algorithms is not an easy matter! You should also be prepared to make a number of doorway pages - for each keyword that you want to be positioned well. You should target 10 to 50 keywords and keyword phrases. Usually, a page that ranks well on one engine may not rank well on other engines. There are a lot of good sources that now tell you exactly what search engines are looking for in a page that will rank highly (one of the best sources is SearchEngineWatch.com).

The hard part is actually creating the doorway pages. First, you have to realize that ranking criteria varies from search engine to search engine. Most of them evaluate your pages on all these criteria:

Keyword prominence - How early in a page a keyword appears?

Keyword frequency - Number of times the keyword appears. Be careful not to simply repeat the keyword because grammatical structure and keyword weight also play important role.

Site popularity - A few search engines consider how popular is your site when ranking.

Keyword "weight" - This is the ratio of keywords to all other keywords. Each search engine has a threshold. If your page crosses it, the search engine labels it as spam and ignores it.

Keyword proximity - How close together the keywords are to each other (especially when the searched item is a phrase)?

Keyword placement - These are the locations where an engine will look for the keyword (i.e. in the body, title, META tags, etc.)

Grammatical structure - Some engines consider grammar in their calculations. They do this to prevent spammers.

Synonyms - Some search engines look for words similar in meaning to the keyword.

As you can see, the ranking criteria are dynamic, using complex algorithms. An important criterion to look deeper is the keyword placement. Here are some of the most important places where engines look for keywords:

- Keywords in <TITLE> tag
- Keywords in the <META NAME="Description"> tag
- Keywords in the <META NAME="Keyword"> tag
- Keywords in <H1> and other headline tags
- Keywords in the <AHREF="URL address"></A> tag
- Keywords in the body copy
- Keywords in ALT tags
- Keywords in <!— comments> comments tags
- Keywords in the <INPUT TYPE="Hidden" NAME="Hidden" VALUE="list of keywords"> hidden type tag
- Keywords contained in the site address (i.e. www.keyword.com)

To fully cover the process of figuring out the parameters of each search engine algorithm is beyond the scope of this chapter. This process demands a lot of efforts. But to conclude, there are several ways to create doorway pages, depending on the resources at your disposal.

7.4.2 Web Site Extras

This section will present you some of the additional possibilities to enhance your Web site and make it even more interesting for your potential customers. Adding a few extras to your site can give it what is called "stickiness" - the way of keeping your visitors at your site longer. Some are affiliate programs; others are added forms of entertainment. Just remember that simple is better - do not overload your site with a bunch of extras and lose your content and purpose in the process. Here are some of the most popular Web site extras:

Internet personals - Many people are meeting other people through the Internet so the personals have become a lucrative business. There are some programs which offer Webmasters the opportunity to have their own personals program for free. These are usually commission-based affiliate programs that give the Webmaster 20% of the earned money.

Chat rooms - Chat rooms are the hottest places to visit, especially for newbies (new Internet users). Again, there are a lot of companies which offer java-based chat rooms for free or you can choose from different plans ranging from $50/year up to $300/year. The entire process of setting up takes only a few minutes. Also, the script for the chat room is executing on your page which means you can place your advertisement.

Guestbooks - Guestbooks enable visitors to tell you what they think about your Web site. It is a handy way to get to know your visitors and listen to their suggestions. One of the most popular guestbooks is Guest World which offers you the ability to download the information to get your site's statistics.

Message boards - These are the places where people can post messages and respond to already posted ones. A lot of companies offer free message boards which give the owner the option of moderating which posts are accepted or denied.

Web polls - Web polls enable you to be interactive with your visitors and obtain information at the same time. Your Polls company offers a free poll page which you can update as often as you wish.

Sweepstakes & contests - Creating excitement on your site and building your mailing database makes this e-Marketing strategy very useful. Using this strategy, you will bring people to your site that would normally never have found you. If you want to reach your target audience, have a prize that only they would be interested in.

Postcards & classifieds - Allow your visitors to be interactive with others and to market themselves with your postcards and classified services.

Industry & headline news - Get free or paid headlines to your site to keep the site fresh and your visitors up to date with the latest events.

Although we have already said it, we'll repeat again: do not use all of these extras on your site at the same time or you will lose content and purpose. Always research which features and programs are the best for your site and your site's visitors.

7.4.3 Site Tracking

Site tracking is a very important part of e-Marketing. Learning who is visiting your site, where visitors are coming from, what keywords get them there, and what are their computer settings will become very important information used to help create or re-create your e-Marketing plan and site's design (see also [Miller99]).

Site tracking can be done in two ways: using the **software** (service) or using the **feedback on site and service**. As always, you'll get the best results if you combine these two methods.

You should find the software or service that will best meet your site's needs. The software/service should include (but not limited to) the following information:

Browsers - Software should tell you what browsers your visitors are using to view your site. Sites should be created to be readable in Microsoft Explorer, Netscape Navigator and, if able, in Opera (which is becoming very popular) and AOL's browser. Creating a site to be viewed only in one browser will cut out visitors and this is not in your best interest.

Resolution - Find out what resolution your visitors are using. If you create your site with your computer set at 1024 x 768 pixels and your visitors have their computers set at 800 x 600 pixels or vice-versa, your site may appear to them to be distorted.

Referring sites - Find out which sites have you linked and which ones are sending you the most visitors. Those are the places you should consider placing your banner.

Referring search engines - You do not just want to know which search engines are sending you the most visitors, but you also want to know which keywords are being used most to find you. For the search engines that are not referring you, find out how to get your site higher on their results.

Referring e-mails - Find out if your mailing lists, sponsorships and/or e-mails are paying off. If not, consider rethinking your strategy.

It is best to monitor site tracking on a weekly basis.

Getting feedback from your visitors is vital to learning how effective your site is. The two recommended methods are site feedback forms/e-mails and market surveys.

Feedback forms/e-mails - Using this method, visitors can fill in the information as they browse your site and you can send e-mails to members of your mailing list with questions of their opinions.

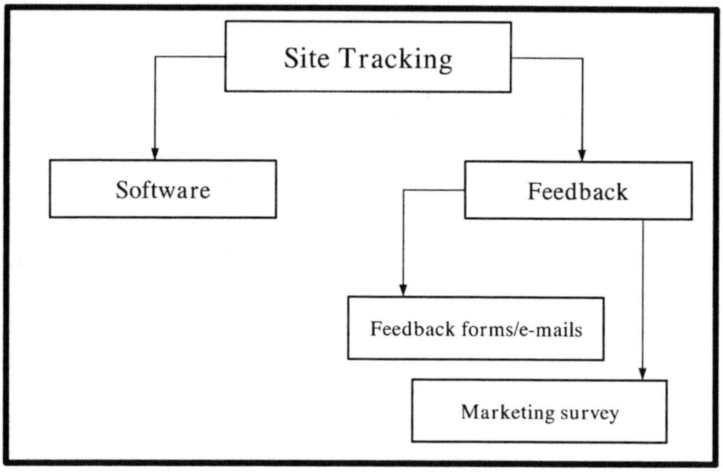

Figure 7.8 Site tracking options

Market survey - Market survey should be done before and during the marketing of your site. If you choose a reputable online marketing company, you will have more accurate results. They have an established list of Internet surfers who will receive cash and prizes for their time. When you get the results, decide if you're going to make changes to the site or to your current plan before you start marketing.

7.4.4 Usability Testing

Web development is almost always done under the deadline threat. For that reason, few years ago, usability testing was recognized as an advantageous but unnecessary step in site development. Now, usability testing is a necessary (if not integral) part of Web site development. Consider these three simple truths:

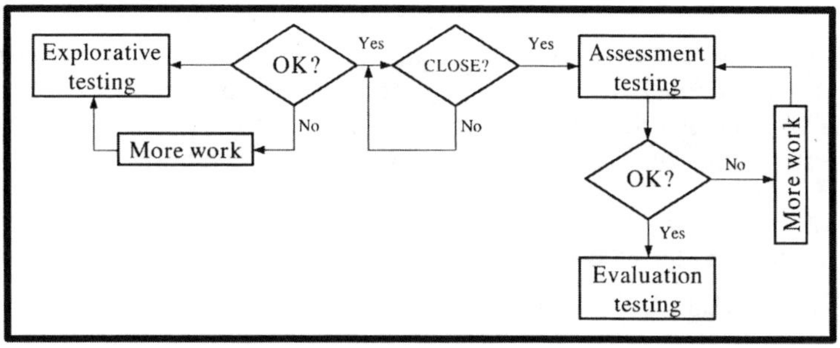

Figure 7.9 Usability testing flow

1. If customers find your site difficult to use, they will get frustrated and leave.
2. It is not a good thing if customers leave your site.
3. If you do not test your site with actual customers before launch, you cannot be sure that customers won't leave your site.

There are many ways to get feedback from customers about the usability of a site. However, what is most commonly referred to as usability testing are one-on-one interviews with customers that explore their opinions about a site.

Here is how usability testing generally works. A moderator sits down with a participant representing a customer or a potential customer. The moderator shows the participant a version of the Web site in development and the participant tries to accomplish some tasks. Then he gives feedback on the process, telling the moderator what he likes and dislikes about the site and what frustrations he experienced while using the site. This information is used to revise the site in the development.

Usability testing comes in lots of forms and can occur at different points in the Web site development process. These are the three most important forms of usability testing:

Explorative testing - This testing gathers input from participants in the early stages of site development. Using the experience and opinions of participants, development team can decide the appropriate direction for the site's look and feel, navigation and functionality.

Assessment testing - This testing occurs when the site is close to launch. In this phase, you can get feedback on issues that might present huge problems for users but are relatively simple to fix.

Evaluation testing - This kind of testing can be useful to evaluate the success of a site after the launch. Web site can be compared to competitors and the results can be used to evaluate the success of the entire project.

7.4.5 Newsletter Writing Tips

Even if you are just an average Internet user, you probably receive a lot of e-newsletters each week. The trouble is most of them are just an attempt to disguise spam or raw advertising messages as valuable information.

On the other hand, buried within these messages is the real thing - an e-newsletter that you can actually look forward to receiving each month. It could be in a flashy HTML format or maybe it is just a simple, text-based e-mail full of valuable information. Whatever format it uses, it is important to notice that people do read e-newsletters if you make them worth reading.

But there is a dilemma. HTML or plain text? There are pros and cons for each. Text newsletters are still the best option if you are on a tight budget. What about the HTML newsletters? On one hand, they look more professional, but on the other hand, they are instantly recognized as not being personalized e-mail so there is a chance they won't get read. The newsletter format should be determined by the message you want to achieve from the newsletter.

Here are some tips for writing effective newsletters:

- Include a "What's Inside" section
- Create interesting headlines
- Include a list of past newsletters at the bottom
- Your lead article should be housed completely within the e-mail so people can view at least one article without clicking through the site
- Include special offers, surveys and contents
- Include links to interesting resource sites
- Do not use it solely for promoting special offers or selling stuff! You will chase away most of your potential customers that way.

7.5 Forgotten Techniques: Newsgroup Advertising

When we are talking about promoting an e-Business, there are many other techniques of the online world that can also help to effectively bring traffic to your Web site - and some are often ignored by most marketers. One of them is newsgroup advertising. The Usenet is a worldwide distributed system of online discussion groups, called "newsgroups". They have names that are classified hierarchically by subject and each newsgroup is dedicated to a particular theme. Newsgroups are also great places to put your messages. Newsgroups can be moderated (your posts are filtered by moderator who usually do not allow advertising messages) or non-moderated commercial newsgroups (exist for sole purpose of advertising).

Usenet appeared in 1980 as a UNIX network linking sites which needed to talk about UNIX system configuration. Message traffic started out at a few messages per week, but the system was so useful that traffic quickly boomed and Usenet almost immediately expanded to include other subjects.

In the beginning, Usenet was largely confined to educational institutions (universities and colleges) and to research companies and other commercial enterprises with UNIX machines on-site. It has now grown to include millions of users at commercial sites and at companies around the world involved in every sort of business.

However, many of the today's Usenet customs have their origins in the days when Usenet was very small. One such custom is the tradition and belief that it is rude to advertise for profit in moderated newsgroups. To help you understand this let's imagine a meeting at your workplace. At this meeting, people are discussing a certain issue. In the middle of the discussion, someone walks into the room, reads an advertisement for a local restaurant and leaves without waiting for a comment. Now imagine if this happened each time you have a meeting. Similarly, it is very difficult to keep moderated Usenet newsgroups interesting and useful when people deluge them with advertisements (see also [ICS99]).

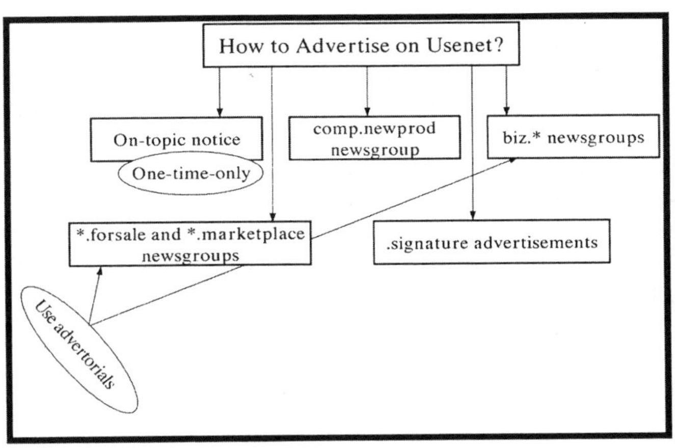

Figure 7.10 How to advertise on Usenet

There are acceptable ways to advertise in the Usenet newsgroups. Here, we will present you some of the most important ways.

The on-topic notice - A notice is not an advertisement. It is a brief mention of the product with information about how interested persons can find out more. If you have a product or a message that is specifically related to a particular Usenet newsgroup, it is usually all right to post one (and only one) notice about it. One way to tell if a post is appropriate is to look at a newsgroup's charter - a formal declaration of what is on topic and what is not which is generated at the time the group was created (if it is created in so-called Big 7 hierarchies:

comp.*, soc.*, rec.*, talk.*, misc.*, news.*, sci.* and humanities.*). Other groups have charters as well, but not all of them.

However, on-topic notices are not always welcome - the increase of the number of inappropriate advertisements has resulted that all ads (and even the on-topic notices posted to appropriate newsgroups) are not welcome. Therefore, you should follow any local restrictions a given newsgroup's readers have place on advertising.

***.forsale and *.marketplace newsgroups** - There are many newsgroups directly involved in advertising. You can generally spot them by the words "forsale" and "marketplace" in their names. It is considered rude, though, to crosspost a notice about your product to every forsale newsgroup. You should post your notice only to your local forsale newsgroup, if it exists.

comp.newprod - If you work for a computer company which is releasing a new product and you want to tell about it to the computing community, you can post a notice to this moderated newsgroup. The moderator requires submissions to be informative so the people can use this newsgroup as a reliable source of information.

biz.* - The hierarchy of these newsgroups exists mainly for announcement from companies of new products, fixes and enhancements, posting of demo software, etc. There are a few dozen biz.* newsgroups. Some of them are used regularly and some are not functional. If you think your site belongs to one of these newsgroups, you can find out more about the hierarchy by asking in biz.config, biz.general and biz.misc.

.signature advertisements - A .signature is a small file that is automatically appended to any Usenet messages you post (regardless of the content). Weather or not you can create and use it depends on the sort of the system you use to access Usenet newsgroups. While writing .signature file, you must consider some basic rules.

If your using .signature file while posting to moderated newsgroups, it is considered bad manners to put more than four lines of information. Also, do not put advertisements in your .signature file. On the other hand, if you're posting to non-moderated commercial newsgroups, your .signature file should not be limited to your identification. It should also include descriptive information about your product, special and free offers, your physical address and so on.

A final note: when you're posting to commercial newsgroups (like *.forsale, *.marketplace and biz.*) try to use advertorials instead of blatant advertisements. Since your ad will be among a lot of other ads, advertorials are a great way to attract the attention of newsgroup readers. If you make your ad to look like an educational tool instead of a promotional message, your ad will have better chances to be seen.

Now when you know how to properly advertise in the Usenet newsgroups, let us remind you how not to do it. Unfortunately, there are just about as many inappropriate ways to advertise on Usenet as there are appropriate ones. While advertising your product in the Usenet newsgroups, you should not do the following:

Post off-topic messages in unrelated newsgroups - Each message you post to Usenet, regardless of its content, should only be posted to related newsgroups. Try to look the situation from the point of view of the person who reads unwanted messages. If you'd resent someone posting an ad for "their" product to "your" favorite newsgroup, why would you post an ad for "your" product to thousands of other people's favorite newsgroups?

Spam - Spamming is defined as posting identical or nearly identical messages to a lot of newsgroups, one right after the other (we have already explained some aspects of spamming in the "E-Mail Marketing" section). But spam can be dangerous. People who have spammed lost their accounts, they have been mail bombed, had people call up and yell at them in the middle of the night, had people sign them up for thousands of unwanted magazine subscriptions, etc. Spamming is very unwelcome on the Usenet.

Send unsolicited junk e-mail - Another often-practiced and often-punished scheme is to send e-mail messages to thousands of strangers whose addresses you found in various Usenet newsgroups. This is a really bad idea. Most sites will cancel your account if you do this.

'Mail-merge' ads - Some advertisers started posting their ads to dozens of newsgroups while varying a line or two to make it look sufficiently different to avoid being cancelled by the spam cancellers. Spam that makes an effort to relate to each newsgroup it is posted to is still spam, and will be erased.

7.6 Psychology & E-Marketing

The successful advertiser must understand psychology. He must know that certain effects lead to certain reactions, and use that knowledge to increase results and avoid mistakes. Effective advertising is based on knowledge of a human nature. You are dealing with the same people who have the same desires they have always had. The principles pf psychology are everlasting. You will never need to unlearn what you learn about them.

The first principle of advertising: your prospects are inherently selfish. The visitors will ask only one question: "What's in it for me?" This is the first question you have to answer with your Web site. It has to tell and show your visitors what's in it for them. What would they get out of ordering from your site that isn't available anywhere else?

Below we present four aspects of the human nature which you can and should use throughout your Internet advertising (see [Dean99] and [Hopkins99]).

Curiosity - Curiosity can be a powerful motivation. It is one of the strongest human incentives. People are afraid to miss out on something. You can take advantage of this factor of human nature by providing some of the results which were achieved with the help of your product, but not actually revealing the way to do it. In this way you will pull on the curiosity of the readers and cause them to order.

Extravagance - People want absolutely the best, but they want to feel like they got it at a bargain price. Nobody wants to feel that he paid a lot of money for anything. Therefore, you need to give your potential customers an impressive product at a bargain price. In most cases, that simply comes down to explaining the exact process it took to create the product. Even if all of your competitor's go through the same process you do, it will still be effective for you to be the first who will tell the story to your customers. This is called preemptive advertising. Any other company will end up looking as a copycat. When customers understand the value involved in your product, they will be glad to purchase it at such a bargain price.

Fear of failure and of making the wrong decision - This is the biggest obstacle that advertisers have to overcome if they want to sell their product. People are afraid they are going to make a bad decision in buying your product. They are afraid you are going to rip them off and not give them the product they are expecting. People have been lied to before when it comes to advertising, so they look at your ads wondering if you are any different.

There are two ways to overcome this resistance. The first one is to present and add credibility to your ads. Credibility is made through your "proof" and through testimonials which you provide (it is almost impossible to build the credibility without testimonials). The second one is to give a risk free guarantee. Let your potential customers know that they can return the product for any reason.

An even better method of overcoming the customers' resistance is to allow them to try out the product for free and have them pay for it at the end of the trial period. Would you rather buy from the person who gives you the car to try for a week and allows you to pay later, or from the person who requires up-front payment?

Exclusivity - People like to get a "special" deal made just for them. They like to be told that they are special and they like to have their names mentioned. They like to have their names engraved on the objects they purchase. According to research, an offer limited to a certain class of people is far more effective than a general offer. For instance, an offer limited to executives. People who are entitled to any seeming advantage will do everything not to lose that advantage.

7.7 E-Marketing Options (Revisited)

This section will try to convince you that banner ads are really effective although they are being constantly attacked and it will also show you how to catch spam senders, that is their upstream providers (companies that sell them Internet time).

7.7.1 In Defense of the Banner

For years, the banner ads have been under attack. They are a target for criticism of all online advertising. Ever since it has become fashionable in the media to humiliate Internet business and online advertising in particular, the banner ads started to signify a medium without impact. Is that really so? According to researches, critics are wrong. Let's see why the most common arguments against banner are just not true (see [Graham99]).

Attack: Low click-through rates prove that banners do not work.

Defense: First, the advertising volume has increased so much that if the early click-through rates were sustained, users wouldn't be doing anything *but* clicking on ads. Second, banners have powerful branding effect that is independent of click-through rate.

Attack: The Internet is not an evocative medium.

Defense: This is true - banners are not TV or radio commercials. But clear, simple messages can be memorable and they can make an impact on consumers.

Attack: People do not see banner ads.

Defense: This argument usually comes from the highly subjective assertion "I do not look at banners". The evidence, however, contradicts those views. According to researches, 45 percent of subjects looked directly at banner ads when reading the news online, and they focused on the banners for an average of about a second.

Attack: People on the Internet are goal-oriented.

Defense: The proponents of efficient online experience often make the argument that users have specific goals and anything getting in their way is useless and inappropriate. Therefore, they argue, online advertising is ignored. But people driving down the highway are goal-oriented, too. That doesn't mean that billboard advertising doesn't work. Good online advertising integrates into the user experience and offers relevant information just as any other form of advertising.

Attack: I do not remember banner ads.

Defense: Can you remember the radio commercials you heard this morning? Probably not. Advertising has a subtle effect. It is meant to trigger a response at the right time (which is usually the point of purchase). It is not meant to stay in your mind all day long.

Attack: Banner ads are never relevant.

Defense: People rightfully complain when they are fooled by "tricky" banners. We need to invest in making online advertising better, but this is not a reason to throw the baby out of the bathwater.

7.7.2 Catching Spam Message Senders

The attempts of spammers (people who send spam messages) to hide at the Internet can be stopped by finding out where their mail comes from. Although you most probably will not get the actual e-mail address to contact the spammer himself, you will find an address of his/hers upstream provider (the company which sells Internet access) which is (if you think better) more useful option - most providers will not tolerate getting lots of e-mail messages about the poor behavior of their customers (and they will, hopefully, punish them).

If you're using any version of Windows, you have a handy utility called TraceRoute. You just give it a domain name or an IP address and it will walk the Internet from your server to the server you have specified, showing you all the "hops" (computers) along the way. The last hop is the domain or the IP address of the spam source and the next to last hop will be the domain of the upstream provider (see [Alch2001]).

```
C:>TRACERT yahoo.com

Tracing route to yahoo.com [204.71.177.35]
over a maximum of 30 hops:

1 151 ms 161 ms 162 ms iah14.barrie.connex.net [209.212.39.193]
2 164 ms 159 ms 163 ms bcicor1-100bt-e1.barrie.connex.net [205.189.200.35]
3 270 ms 327 ms 234 ms spc-tor-7-Serial3-1.Sprint-Canada.Net [207.107.244.213]
4 261 ms 260 ms * core-spc-tor-2-POS2-0-0.sprint-canada.net [204.50.128.13]
5 * 180 ms 179 ms sl-gw21-pen-1-1-0-T3.sprintlink.net [144.228.178.5]
6 177 ms 189 ms 195 ms sl-bb10-pen-5-2.sprintlink.net [144.232.5.133]
7 231 ms 245 ms 233 ms sl-bb22-stk-6-0.sprintlink.net [144.232.8.178]
8 230 ms 232 ms 259 ms sl-bb21-stk-9-0.sprintlink.net [144.232.4.105]
9 258 ms 234 ms 244 ms sl-bb21-stk-0-3.sprintlink.net [144.232.4.82]
10 291 ms 287 ms 320 ms isi-border2-hssi4-0-0-T3.sprintlink.net [144.228.147.10]
11 325 ms 294 ms 326 ms fe4-0.cr1.SNV.globalcenter.net [206.251.7.42]
12 288 ms 266 ms 307 ms pos0-0.wr1.SNV.globalcenter.net [206.251.0.106]
13 305 ms 305 ms 262 ms pos1-0-OC12.wr1.NUQ.globalcenter.net [206.251.0.73]
14 310 ms 320 ms 306 ms pos5-0.cr1.NUQ.globalcenter.net [206.251.0.121]
15 310 ms 295 ms 311 ms yahoo.com [204.71.177.35]

Trace complete.
```

Figure 7.11 TraceRoute at work

If you do not have a Windows system, or you just do not like DOS programs, you can use TraceRoute online at the following URL address: http://cities.lk.net/traceroute.htm.

Let's see how TraceRoute works. In the example (Figure 7.11) we looked for the path to yahoo.com (which is, of course, not a spam generator). If you wished to get in touch with the upstream provider for yahoo.com, you could send e-mail to root@globalcenter.net. Unlike return addresses, the route a message takes over the Internet cannot be faked by a spam generator.

Some spam generators like to express their URL addresses as strange looking numbers, such as http://4291330012. This address looks strange because it doesn't seem to be a domain or an IP address. In fact, these long numbers are IP addresses - they are just written in a way that make them hard to work with. You can break this single-number address into the four components of a conventional IP address. Here's how to do that (we'll do some math now):

Divide the single-number address by 2^{24} and take the part of the result on the left side of the decimal point ($4{,}291{,}330{,}012 \div 2^{24} = 255.78320$). This is the first of the four numbers of the conventional IP address.

- Now you need to find the remaining part of the single-number address after the first IP address value has been removed (4,291,330,012 - 255 $\times$ 2^{24} = **13,139,932**)
- Divide the first remainder by 2^{16} and again take the part on the left side of the decimal point (13,139,932 $\div$ 2^{16} = **200**.49945). This is the second number in the IP address.
- Find the second remainder: 13,139,932 - 200 $\times$ 2^{16} = **32,732**.
- Divide the second remainder by 2^8 to find the third IP number: 32,732 $\div$ 2^8 =**127**.85938.
- Finally, calculate the third remainder: 32,732 - 127 $\times$ 2^8 = **220**. This is the fourth part of the IP address.

As you can see, the address http://4291330012 was easily translated into the conventional IP address http://255.200.127.220. After you have found this address, you can use it in TraceRoute to find the upstream provider for the spam source.

7.8 How to Avoid Online Ad Failure

A lot of bad advertising is present out there. Many campaigns are failures. It is too bad because a few simple guidelines could increase the chance of success. Online advertising is more art than science. But online advertisers should keep in mind some guidelines (several based on research) when planning a campaign (see [Graham99]). Some of things to avoid are these:

Cluttered ads - Banner has a limited space. All too often, advertisers try to do too much in one space. The result is a mess through which no messages get across at all. Marketing experts suggest that limiting the number of visual and text elements within ads can make them more effective from a branding perspective.

Ads that make you wait - Most people do not log on the Internet to look at advertising. In most cases, your potential customers will spare only a glance at your ad. Because of that, strategies that have a build-up approach to their messages usually do not work that well. For animated ads, important information, such as the company logo, should be omnipresent.

Invisible ads - If you're buying a fixed placement or sponsorship on a niche-site, you might be getting more of a niche than you bargained for. More often than you might think, advertisers place ads or their own content in places that get very light traffic. It is because no one wants to click through to a special content area that the advertiser has created. All in all, money is wasted.

Ads that won't leave you alone - Branding increases with frequency so you should make sure that your potential customers see your ads more than once. But do not push it, especially with pop-ups. Branding effectiveness stops at a frequency of about seven. Beyond that, you are making angry those who are sick of your ads. Pop-ups and other intrusive ads should limit the number of their appearance.

Tricky ads - These are the ads that disguise themselves as something else (like a pop-up ad that disguises itself as an error message). A whole category of these so-called tricky ads preys on the inexperience of some Internet users to get cheap clicks.

7.9 E-Marketing Statistics

This section will present you some statistical information in order to show you that e-Marketing is a serous business which can bring a great deal of money if the online advertising campaign is properly conducted using the tips and advice given in this chapter.

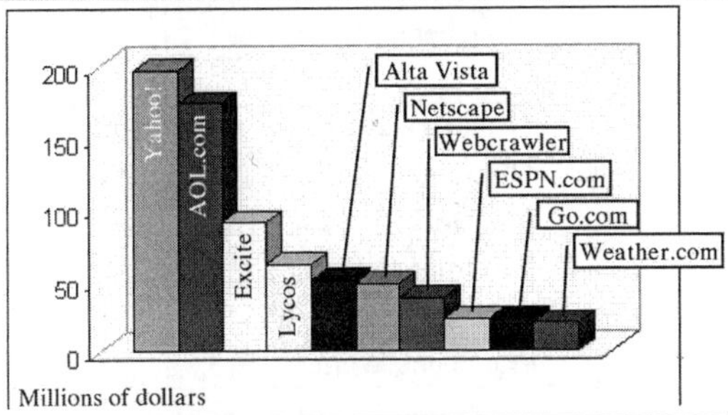

Figure 7.12 Top online revenue by site

Rank	On-line Techniques	Rating (%)	Use (%)
1	Traditional Advertising	58	69
2	Links	47	76
3	Search Engine Positioning	37	73
4	On-line Advertising	34	56
5	Public Relations	28	64
6	Packaging	26	53
7	E-Mail	22	55
8	Direct Mail	14	34
9	Incentives	8	22
10	Sweepstakes	7	21

Figure 7.13 What tactics are most used by Brand Advertisers

Rank	On-line Techniques	Rating (%)	Use (%)
1	Traditional Advertising	58	69
2	Links	47	76
3	Search Engine Positioning	37	73
4	On-line Advertising	34	56
5	Public Relations	28	64
6	Packaging	26	53
7	E-Mail	22	55
8	Direct Mail	14	34
9	Incentives	8	22
10	Sweepstakes	7	21

Figure 7.14 What tactics are most used by Direct Marketers

General Motors	$25.4
eBay	$24.3
Amazon.com Inc.	$16.2
Classmates Online	$15.1
J.P. Morgan Chase	$14.9
Barnes & Noble	$14.3
Verisign Inc.	$13.7
AOL Time Warner	$13.3
Providian Corp.	$12.7
Bank One Corp.	$11.1

Comments: Millions of dollars

Figure 7.15 Top online spenders by company

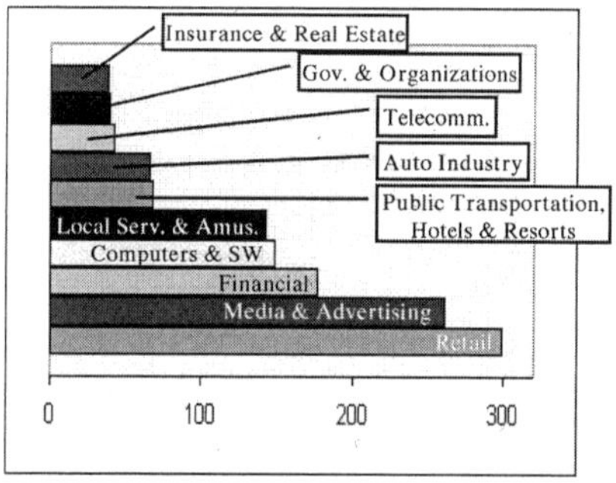

Figure 7.16 Top online spending by industry

Rank	Advertiser	Impressions (000,000)	Reach (%)
1	Microsoft	1,842	49.5
2	TRUSTe	1,597	31.4
3	Yahoo!	1,125	37.9
4	eBay	821	30.3
5	Amazon	701	51.7
6	Barnes & Noble	700	48.7
7	ClassMates	692	46.1
8	AOL	679	38.7
9	Providian	662	41.0
10	Netscape	649	31.1

Comments: At home Internet users

Figure 7.17 Top 10 Web advertisers (June 2001)

Rank	Advertiser	Impressions (000,000)	Reach (%)
1	Microsoft	1,509	63.4
2	TRUSTe	1,263	49.2
3	Yahoo!	628	50.6
4	Netscape	615	43.7
5	eBay	593	37.3
6	Amazon	487	47.7
7	Orbitz LLC	467	40.4
8	Barnes & Noble	467	4.6
9	Providian	432	60.0
10	ClassMates	411	53.1

Comments: At work Internet users

Figure 7.18 Top 10 Web advertisers (June 2001)

7.10 Common Mistakes

In this section we will introduce you to some common mistakes which many Internet businesses are making over and over again. Each of these mistakes can easily cost your business a lot of money. A number of Internet businesses have no chance of success because a couple of those problems are central part of their campaign. If your business is built on a weak foundation, there is no way it will be able to produce maximum profit.

You have a short-sighted vision - You do not have a long term plan for your business? Some marketers have a multiple years plan. You must know the lifetime value of a customer. It is a lot easier to sell a product to an existing customer than to a new one. You have to build the relationships with your current customers because they are very important for your business. However, in the same time, you have to find new products that meet other needs and wants of your customers. You cannot do that if you do not have a long term vision.

You are not willing to think outside the box - Most Internet advertisers see only two types of advertising - free (free classifieds, free links, newsgroups, etc.) and paid (offline advertising, banner ads, and paid links). Did you think about finding people in your businesses to sell your products or services to their customers and splitting the profits? Press releases can quickly get traffic to your site if you have a product that people want or need. Maybe you should set up your own affiliate program? This is the quickest and easiest way to expand the sales of the product. Let other people start selling for you.

You like the wrong product very much - According to research, this is one of the main reasons for failure. It is all right that you like your product very much, but you have to give it up if it isn't what market wants. Every day the world market is changing and you have to be changing too. How to find out whether your product is what your customers want? Start asking questions to your Web site visitors or e-zine readers. Ask them what they want. Statistics show that only one out of every seven products is a winner. Be prepared to change your product if your market wants something different.

You do not have a special Web position - If you have no answer to the following questions, then you do not have a corresponding Web position needed to succeed in e-Marketing. What makes your site different from the others? Why should the potential customers visit your site instead of some others? Why should they buy your product instead of the competition's product? What can you do to improve it? Visit the competition. Think what it is that you do better.

You have not researched your market enough - If you do not know why people buy from you, how can you target them correctly or write a successful sales letter? Do you know what your market wants? Have you ever asked your customers why they bought your product in the first place? Have you spent time in newsgroups and mailing lists to find out what problems people might be having? Concept is very important. A poor concept could never be made profitable.

You are not dealing with people as individuals - Automating the sales process is OK, but there still comes the time when you have to deal with people as individuals. Do not talk to everyone. People are not just numbers. Your customers are live individuals who have wants, needs and desires. Deal with them that way. Be willing to help.

You give up too soon - This almost goes without saying, but a lot of Internet advertisers give up too soon. They make some of the mentioned mistakes, lose a little money and then give up thinking that the Internet just doesn't work. Before you give up, try to change your Web site or your ads a little - you can be surprised with the results.

7.11 Example of E-Marketing Plan

This section will present you an example of an e-Marketing plan for a singer who has just released his first CD and who wants to become a start in the music industry. The objective of this e-Marketing plan is to utilize the Internet to its fullest potential to increase the amount of memberships in the fan club and Web site visitors.

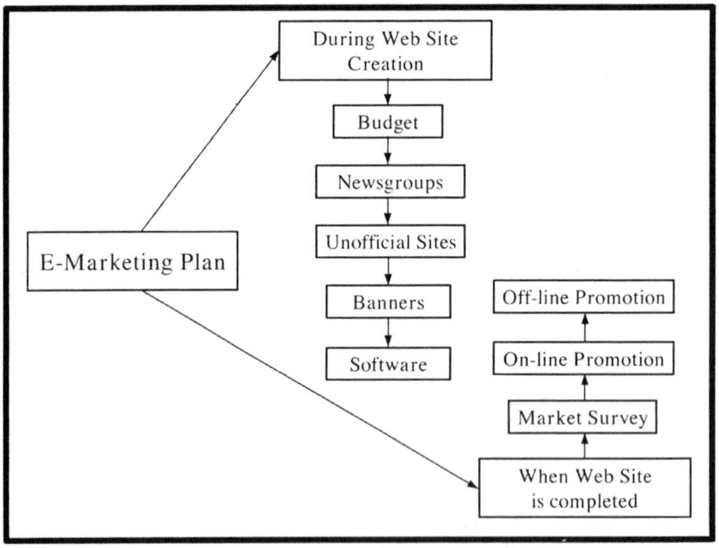

Figure 7.19 E-Marketing plan

Before the e-Marketing plan can be developed, research must give you the basic guidelines: for whom you are designing your product ore service (this is called market segmentation) and exactly what that product ore service should mean to those in the marketplace (this is called market positioning).

E-marketing plan is divided in two phases. The first one include the steps you have to take during Web site creation (along with the already mentioned tips and advice on how to create effective Web sites) and the second phase include the actions you have to do when the Web site is completed (relatively speaking since a Web site is never completed but always growing). Here are the parts of the first phase of e-Marketing plan:

Budget - The budget should include, but shall not be limited to, the following:

- Cost of submission software
- Cost of site tracking
- Cost of different banners on industry related sites and mailing lists for industry related mailers
- Cost of offline advertising (magazines, newspapers, brochures, etc.)
- Market Research Survey

Newsgroups - Utilizing newsgroups can be tricky but very lucrative. Newsgroups should be used according to the following plan:

1. Verify if there is an existing newsgroup with the singer's name.
   - If there is, on a daily basis:
     - Hang out and read the posts
     - Post to the group
   - If not:
     - Get the new newsgroup started
     - Do the same as above: start posting as a fan
2. Advertise the newsgroup everywhere on the Internet.
3. Go to other music related newsgroups and see if the singer is mentioned and if not add some posts. The objective is to keep his name alive in the newsgroups until the site is finished.

Unofficial sites - These sites have visitors that you may not have currently. Use them in the following way:

- Go through all unofficial sites to verify accurate information for the singer.
- E-mail corrections to the sites that have inaccurate data (leave the spiteful sites alone unless you choose to send a legal e-mail).

Banners - Use the tips presented in the "Banner Advertising" section to create effective banner ads. Do not forget to change them frequently.

Software - Purchase submission software which will save you time once the site is completed. Also, get the site tracking software which will be useful in determining where to place the most advertisements, who your visitors are, etc. (see the "Site Tracking" section).

The following are the parts of the second phase of the e-Marketing plan:

Market survey - Before the site is ready for marketing at full force, it is good to have a market research survey done. You should consider hiring one of the Internet marketing research companies - they have a database of Web surfers that can conduct a one day to one week survey. An online feedback from the singer's site should be added to allow the visitors to offer comments and suggestions. Finally, when you have all the results, decide weather you're going to make any changes.

Online promotion - Use the tips presented in the "Web Site Building and Advertising" section to successfully promote singer's Web site.

Offline promotion - While conducting offline promotion you should take the following steps:

- Print 'Check us on the Web' pamphlets to send out with response to fan letters.
- Add the singer's Web site address to all stationery.
- Place advertisements or send press releases to industry related magazines and newspapers.

Read all Internet magazines to see what industry sites are mentioned. These sites are going to increase traffic drastically and will prove to be great places to put up advertisements banners.

7.12 Problems

1. Create a personal Web page using just a simple HTML editor.
2. Create a personal Web site using an advanced Web design tool (e.g. Microsoft Front Page).
3. Think of some more reasons why companies should have a Web presence.
4. Imagine a product you would like to advertise online and create a Web site for this product according to the tips presented in the chapter.
5. Find a Web site promotion service on the Internet to promote your newly created Web site. Then do the same job yourself according to the tips presented in the chapter.
6. Create a couple of banner ads for your product and try to put them on other companies' Web pages.
7. Organize an e-mail marketing campaign for your product and try to avoid spamming.
8. Enhance your product's Web site to get high visibility on the most popular search engines by adding META tags and creating doorway pages.
9. Find a site tracking software and use it to obtain information about the visitors of your site and their computer settings.
10. Try to find the source of the unwanted messages you probably receive using the TraceRoute utility.

REFERENCES

[Cisco2000] The Easy Guide to E-Marketing, Cisco Systems Inc., **2000**

[Alch2001] Death to Spam, Alchemy Mindworks Inc., **2001**

[Graham99] Graham, J., In Defense of the Banner, Avoiding Online Ad Failure, **1999**

[Dean99] Dean, T., Tips For Designing Killer Banner Ads, Applying Psychology to Internet Marketing, 7 Internet Marketing Mistakes Which Are Destroying Your Business, **1999**

[Enlow99] Enlow, M., Creating a successful Website - Tips From the 'Master Webmaster', **1999**

[Miller99] Miller, E., Marketing plan, Site Tracking, **1999**

[Hopkins99] Hopkins, C., Scientific Advertising (Chapter 6 - Psychology), **1999**

[ICS99] Advertising on Usenet: How to do it, How not to do it, ICS, **1999**

[Zikmund99] Zikmund G. William: Essentials of Marketing Research, Dryden Press, **1999**

[Worsley2000] Worsley Tim: Building a Website, Dorling and Kindersley, **2000**

[Shimp2000] Shimp A. Terence: Advertising Promotion, Dryden Press, **2000**

E-Business and E-Challenges
V. Milutinović and F. Patricelli (Eds.)
IOS Press, 2002

CHAPTER 8
E-GOVERNMENT

Jasmina Pilipovic, Miodrag Ivkovic, Dragan Domazet and Veljko Milutinović

Digital technologies are fundamentally transforming our economy and society, and have potentials for transforming the Government. Advances in technology are changing the way governments do businesses with citizens. Today's progressive governments are introducing electronic methods for delivering services (such as renewing driver's licenses and vehicle registrations), commonly referred to as *e-Government.* In this chapter you will see what is e-Government, exactly, what kind of services it can provide, what kind of technical support it requires, and how can one Government move from traditional way of doing businesses, to a well improved and effective manner of dealing with citizens.

8.1 Introduction

E-Government is the transformation of internal and external business processes toward customer-centricity based upon service delivery opportunities offered by new communications technologies (such as Web based technologies) to better fulfill the purposes of private entities to provide efficiency and effectiveness as well as profitability [NECC2000].

It is connecting Citizens, Suppliers, Employees, and other agencies securely using a) the technologies of the Internet, b) the standards of the Internet, c) the public Internet, and d) private intranets.

This kind of government is based upon three W-s: *whenever, whatever, wherever.*

In other words, this means that citizens are able to address the Government whenever they need to, for whatever purpose possible, and from where ever they are. Such a Government is working 24 hours a day, 7 days a week, 366 days per year! More than that, it is integrating all informational systems and subsystems of government in all levels [Vaskovic22].

One goal of an e-Government initiative is to provide a site on the Internet's World Wide Web where citizens can access government services at a reduced cost, regardless of which agency actually provides the service (as shown in Figure 1.1). To be successful, the site should be designed from the citizen's point of view, making services easy to locate and use.

There are following categories of e-Government users:

- G - Government,
- E - Employees,
- B - Business, and
- C - Citizen.

The Government is using e-Government for interoperability among agencies, as well as for the communication between its employees. It is focusing on managing digital records and documents and their preparation for the Web usage.

Employees are using government intranets as important communicational tool. They receive the information they need, and have possibilities for receiving instructions, advertising, improving their education etc. The price for this kind of internal system for distributing information is significantly lower when using Web based technology, and its efficiency is hard to compete.

Business partners and companies have the opportunity to improve their efficiency as well, thanks to online services. Information gathering, ordering, purchasing, advertising are just few examples of applications of interest.

And in the end, services available for citizens: issuing permits, licenses, and certificates, various payments and transactions, communication with authorities and many others that will follow with further development.

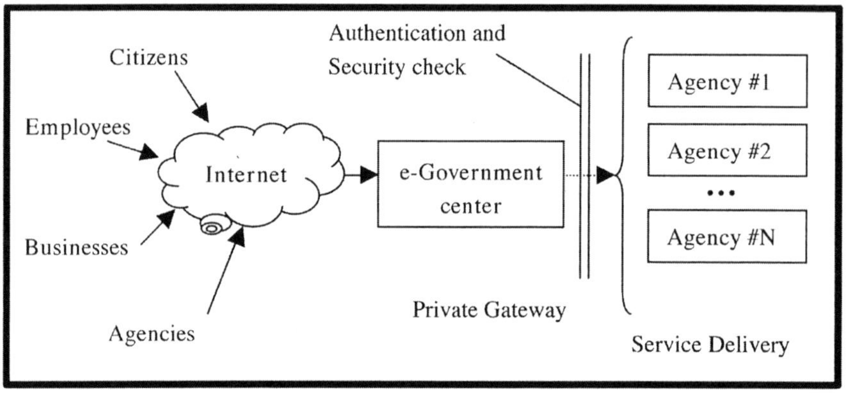

Legend: e-Government - a site on the Internet's WWW

Comment: Citizens can access government services at a reduced cost, regardless of which agency actually provides the service.

Figure 1.1: e-Government center

Now that we have determined what the users of e-Government are we shall focus on the benefits that digital transactions can offer. It is more than obvious that due to reduced time and effort investments we get the efficiency and comfort that have not existed so far. Starting of this initiative is asking for a lot of investments, but still cost savings in conducting everyday transactions are very likely to make up for them in a very short time. e-Government is now, as we said before, operable for 24 hours a day, and therefore we have a permanent contact with all of agencies.

Every government is collecting a large amount of information on their citizens, companies, properties, etc. For each one of these issues there is a single database developed, with all of the information included. Once a single informational system is developed, and a single database as well, these information pieces will be reorganized and we shall get reduced redundancy as an outcome.

Therefore, the convenience that electronic services entail to the client, and their cost-effectiveness to the supplier, inevitably make the Internet a very attractive channel for service provision. Governments have been slower than the private sector in realizing the potential of the medium, but are now embarking on the widespread use of Internet-based service delivery and the dissemination of information, of which it is a precious resource.

8.2 Technical Aspects

Creating e-Government involves a major change in the way governments do businesses with citizens and partners. The key challenges are not technological but cultural. It is not an IT issue, but an economic, structural adjustment, and business strategy issue. The experience of others shows that the main enablers and barriers to the delivery of e-Government are not technical or even legislative. They are cultural and social. Enablers include strong political leadership, commitment to funding, an enabling regulatory environment, and the integration of technology across government to achieve economies of scale and provide commonality of service and interface to citizens.

However, what we shall focus on will not cover these issues. Instead, we shall try to set our minds to designing and developing of e-Government architecture, and leave the cultural and social issues to more qualified authors.

The complexity of e-Government architecture will be presented with a model (as shown in Figure 2.1) consisting of several segments: a) sub-infrastructures, b) legal and political constrain, c) standards and protocols of networking, and d) applications [Ivkovic98].

What we can learn from this model is: e-Government is not just a set of well-designed applications, but a serious strategic issue. To realize the benefits that can be achieved through e-Government, governments must be willing to change their traditional structures and business processes.

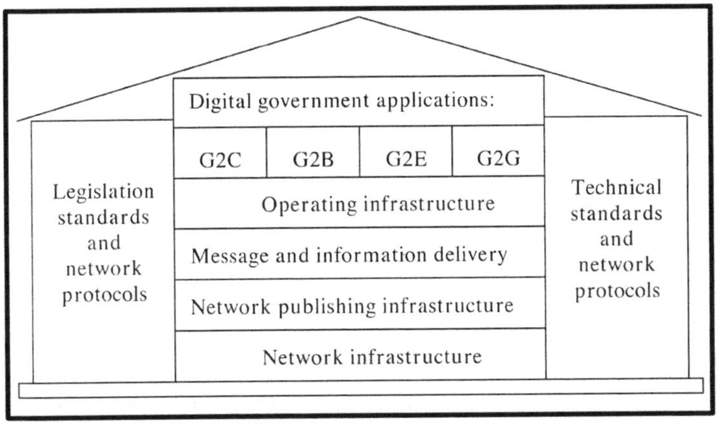

Legend: G2C – Government to Citizen
G2B – Government to Business
G2E – Government to Employees
G2G – Government to Government

Comment: Creating e-Government is more then just a technical issue. It implies legislative issues as well, and setting up the protocols and standards of net working.

Figure 2.1: e-Government infrastructure

These changes may be accomplished through legislation to reorganize the traditional government model, modification of existing statutory and regulatory requirements, and through strong IT leadership and policy. Once the leadership, technology, and policies are in place, the final piece of the initiative lies with the human resources supporting e-Government. The competency of the individuals developing, implementing, and supporting technology is crucial for the effectiveness and efficiency that can be achieved through e-Government.

8.2.1 Network Infrastructure

When we are talking about network infrastructure we refer to the physical network. It is the very basis of complete infrastructure of e-Government. The combination of the government's internal IT infrastructure and the external public infrastructures make up the combined infrastructure. This new infrastructure will be as important for enabling government processes in the future as the traditional physical infrastructure of roads etc. has been in the past. For example, if there are multiple wide area networks (WANs) in place in government, spanning different geographic locations, departments, Ministries, and functional groupings, then they are requiring different support staff who understands the details of the network standards, resulting in a huge overhead cost.

Multiple complex networks make it extremely difficult for different parts of the public service to understand the government's total relationship with each citizen or customer. A strategy of customer-centric services is not achievable with a disparate infrastructure in place. A common infrastructure must be based on agreed-upon standards across multiple government organizations with a central coordination function.

In order to achieve appropriate communicational connection, we have to improve our networks and move towards new communication technologies. Plane old telephone service is no longer providing suitable speeds and security levels. More and more, countries are focusing on cables due to the fact that they are already wide spread. In combination with satellite and wireless technology we get a single informational superhighway that is located in a center of a virtual geography. Therefore, e-Government is not just about access to the Internet; it also includes services delivered by telephone, digital TV, and kiosks [Boylee2000]. However, around the world a growing gap between those who are able to access and use ICTs, and those who cannot, is being identified. Referred to as the *digital divide,* it has many dimensions, including those between young and old, between city and country, and between different ethnic and socio-economic groups.

To conclude this story, IT infrastructure refers to the systems and network hardware and software that supports applications. IT infrastructure includes servers, hubs, routers, switches, cabling, desktop, lap and handheld devices.

8.2.2 Network Publishing

Internet is giving us an opportunity to exist in a *digital world.* We have the ability to present text, images, video, and audio contents. These days, many identify Internet with WWW, which is just one of the Internet services. With the need to present information on the Internet came up the idea of a well developed concept of hypertext, and the turning point was the introduction of the language called HTML, the protocol for sharing of hypertext information (included in TCP/IP), and the system program called Browser (for viewing of hypertext information coded in HTML). Programs written in HTML encompass both the local and the remote information, in the way that is compatible with popular browsing programs. Browsers are not the only tools used to view and operate documents on WWW. Other tools for electronic publishing on WWW are a) the variety of authoring tools, b) all kinds of filters, c) the variety of script languages, and d) all kinds of tools for indexing and indexing-based search [Milutinovic2001].

Coding in HTML is possible but not recommended, instead, special tools for efficient creation and maintenance of HTML documents, are suggested. The most convenient tools are of the WYSIWYG type (What You See Is What You Get). However, for more sophisticated design usage of HLL (High Level Language), such as Java is recommended. Java is an object oriented HLL like C++. It is portable, distributed, multi-threaded, architecture independent, and interpretable.

The concept of WWW is based on the classical client/server architecture. The essence of the operation is illustrated in Figure 2.2. The document is stored at the WWW server site. The

WWW server is actually a program that responds to HTTP (Hypertext Transfer Protocol) requests. On the other side, the user/viewer of the document is located at the client site.

The way it is described so far, WWW implies static contents, and is basically a one-way interface. In the case of static WWW contents, the amount of interaction between a WWW client and a WWW server is limited. Also pages have to be edited, compiled, and linked manually.

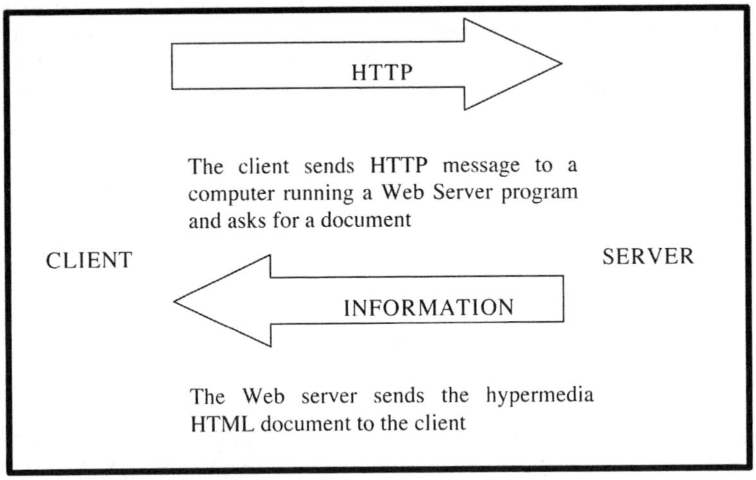

Legend: HTML – Hypertext markup language

HTTP – Hypertext transfer protocol

WWW – World Wide Web

Comment: Note that the client runs a WWW browser program that initiates the HTTP request, and the WWW server responds by sending the information that is stored at the prespecified location.

Figure 2.2: Basic client/server architecture

In the case of dynamic WWW contents, interaction between a WWW client and a WWW server is maximal, and pages (or parts there-of) get generated/modified on the fly (when a WWW client requests a page from a WWW server). Dynamic WWW contents are ideal for online transactions such as shopping.

8.2.3 Message and Information Delivery

Since we have already explained the amount of information accessible on the Internet, it is more then obvious that we need some kind of algorithms that will improve Internet search. There are two basic approaches to Internet search: a) indexing based search and b) links-based search [Milutinovic2001].

Examples of indexing-based search engines are Altavista and similar, and examples of links-based search engines are Spiders and similar. The indexing-based search approach is widespread and well known. Since information can not be found unless it is indexed first, and it can not be done instantaneously it has a serious drawback. Therefore, links-based search methods are recommended for the so-called *mission critical* businesses.

Now that we have found the information we need, we have to worry about delivering it. Data that we send or receive can be both structured and unstructured. Unstructured data is being delivered by e-mails, e-faxes, SMS, etc. Structured data refers to some fill-up forms and documents for submitting. This kind of delivery is automatic.

Due to lacks of physical network, delivered information could include errors as well. Therefore, we have to take care of error and control handling. This kind of services are included in protocols of networking, such as IP with checksums and control bits, and a special protocol called Internet Control Message Protocol ICMP is developed for error and control handling, when it comes to routing and delivering. Beside this, frames from higher levels, such as TCP and UDP include controls for the contents of messages (data), also based on checksums.

8.2.4 Operating Infrastructure

The Internet has given us the possibility to conduct various online transactions. In order to do so, we have to procure the safety and the means for it. Now, we shall define some terms relying on this issue [NECCC2000].

Privacy – Privacy means the assurance that the information provided for a specific transaction will not be used for purposes not authorized by the provider. The question is: How do I know what you are going to do with my data?

Security – Security supposes to be protection from intended and unintended breaches that would result in the loss or dissemination of data. The question is: How do I know that no one will alter, or erase data that I provide?

Authentication – Authentication should give us the assurance of the identity of parties to a transaction. The question is: How do I know this web site is actually the agency that it purports to be?

Confidentiality – Confidentiality is the assurance that no one is able to eavesdrop on the transaction in progress. The question is: How do I know no one is listening (in on my transaction)?

Integrity – Integrity is the assurance that the data received is the exact data that was sent. The question is: How do I know that no one has changed the data sent to me?

Non repudiation – Non repudiation is the assurance that no one can take place in an action and deny it. The question is: How do I know that parties in a transaction will take the responsibility for it?

Access control – In order to achieve safe transactions we have to define strict access limitations. The question is: How do I know who will have access to the information I provide?

Once we have taken care of security issues, we have to provide the means for purchasing, and conducting any kind of monetary transaction over the Internet.

The most widely used way of purchasing over the Internet is Credit Card, and it will be dominant for at least the next few years.

Electronic Cash is informational equivalent of physical bank notes and coins. Electronic Cash can offer such benefits as anonymity of the buyer and global acceptance.

8.2.5 Digital Government Applications

Digital government applications are the very subject of this paperwork. Therefore we shall describe what they are about in briefly, and return to this issue later. There are several classes of applications [Vaskovic22], and the most important are:

- G2C – Government to Citizen,
- C2G – Citizen to Government,
- G2B – Government to Business,
- B2G – Business to Government,
- G2E – Government to Employees,
- G2G – Government to Government.

This categorization is based on the fact that in each transaction we can distinguish at least two parties involved. Therefore, G2C applications are online services and Digital Democracy, where the Government is working for citizens. The opposite of that are C2G applications, meaning communication between citizens and the authorities. G2B applications are for supplying, information gathering and services for business associates of government, and B2G refers to communication again. G2E is developed for government employees and their education, instructions, advertising, and 'chat rooms'. And the last, but not the least, G2G refers to communication with other governments and for communication within one government.

Government has the responsibility for gathering and processing data correctly, and its intranet is a basic communicational, informational, and organizational tool for managing digital documentation.

8.2.6 Legislative and Official Politics

In order to develop a successful e-Government it is necessary, but not sufficient, to follow the next few steps [Boyle2000]:

- Widespread adoption of digital technologies,
- An appropriate legal framework,
- An integrated technical infrastructure,
- Robust data protection, and
- Political leadership and commitment.

In order to keep pace with the new era of global communication and efficiently provide citizens with services they require, an effective legal framework is needed [NECC2000]. What also could be required is some form of legislative revisions, as current laws, rules, and regulations may not recognize the legality of electronic documents and processes. For example, legislation should ensure the following: electronic authorizations, contracts and signatures have the same legal effect as those on paper. In short, to adapt to the electronic environment, governments need to establish a legal framework that treats electronic processes and traditional processes equally.

Now we shall list some of the major risks in conducting digital government affairs that should be both legally sanctioned and, if possible, overcome with software and hardware solutions [Drakulic2001]:

- Exterior attacks on sites, national and global infrastructure, informational systems, data delivery – hackers activities are becoming one of the greatest frets, as much as terrorist attacks by individuals, groups, or foreign governments;
- Attacks and misusage "from inside" – a protest, or in a process of elections;
- Electronic espionage and sabotage – satellite or cyber espionage, or destruction of installations, data, software;
- E-War,

- Endangering rights and freedoms of citizens – obstruction of freedom of information, access privileges, or privacy;
- Corruption and organized crime,
- Economical and financial frauds,
- Intellectual property protection ,
- Monopolization in managing government affairs.

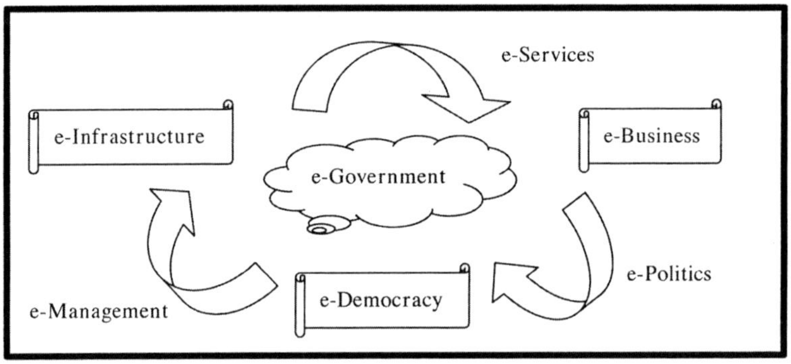

Legend: E-infrastructure – the realization of e-Government
E-business – the associates of e-Government
E-democracy – communication between government and citizens
E-politics – state politics considering e-Government
E-services – digital services offered by e-Government
E-management – authorities for managing e-Government

Comment: This figure explains how designers, users, authorities, and managers work together in developing of e-Government and setting goals for it.

Resolving of these problems has taken several separate ways:

1) delivering of laws and regulations that cover all of these issues, or at least most of them;

2) delivering of particular law for each issue;

3) adjusting the existing laws.

Experiences of other governments show that making new regulations rather then just rewriting the existing ones is bringing more results.

Figure 2.3: e-Government framework

8.2.7 Technical Standards and Protocols

Common standards and policies to ensure data integrity, efficient data communication and effective return on capital investment are key to e-Government. The adoption of common Internet system policies and standards is critical to providing the common 'view', which is a pre-requisite of cost-effective e-Government. These standards and policies should be [NZGISPS2000]:

- Based on Open Standards, wherever possible,
- Supportive of contestable supply from multiple vendors,

- Intended to deliver interconnection between products from diverse vendors,
- Able to support a very scaleable infrastructure.

Infrastructure components must support transactions across multiple Government agencies in a secure, reliable, and cost-effective manner. Current standards suggested by IETF (The Internet Engineering Task Force) that are relevant to e-Government are:

- TCP/IP as the network protocol
- SMTP and IMAP for mail transport
- LDAP for Directory services
- HTTP for delivery of client transactions and information.

Agencies participating in e-Government should continually monitor the development and implementation of emerging standards. However until such standards receive widespread support in the community and are supported by multiple vendors they should not replace any existing standards.

8.3 Digital Government Applications

There are literally hundreds of applications that could be developed to allow businesses, citizens, and other governments to interact with the Government digitally. In order to get a clear picture on what these applications are about, we shall divide them into four major categories [Vaskovic22]:

- Information gathering,
- Interactive service delivery,
- Online supplying,
- Digital democracy.

Each of these categories will be presented with a listing of applications included, some examples from various countries and with a list of problems that follow the implementation of such applications.

8.3.1 Information Gathering

Among all of services and applications developed so far this is the one most widely used and the one that has been available for quite some time. Information gathering is already existing, without introduction of e-Government. But what still needs to be done is to organize all available information, make them visible and easy to access. Citizens could have an insight on various types of information, such as:

- Government services, agencies, and employees;
- Event calendars, statistics, news;
- Flight and train schedules;
- Useful links.

All of us have sometimes been in the situation to be desperate to get some piece of paper, urgently. What happens, quite often, is that one can not say who has the jurisdiction to provide him with the document in question, what documents does one need to prepare in order to apply for the document in question, and in the end where is the office he should go to? More then that, ones you get to the 'face of the place' the adventure is just beginning: long lines, lunch brakes, and time our as same as your own. Therefore, one of the most important applications is gathering information on government services, agencies, employees, event calendars, statistics, news. What follows is just an extension of 'informational' comfort. Information on flight and train schedules, as well as weather conditions, delays and similar are more than useful in a modern world with frequent travels. In the end, many useful links not mentioned so far could be provided, such as encyclopaedias, museums, theaters, health centers etc.

Comment: An example of site in Australia with useful links and information on government

Figure 3.1: Australia.gov

What are the problems that we are facing when it comes to information gathering? Some of them will follow [PPI2000]:

- Need for standardized information tagging system;
- Need to expand the amount of accessible information;
- Need for developing "expert systems" to access information;
- Need to make the web the first place to put information, not the last.

Some of these problems are already being faced, and some solutions have already seen the light of the day. Most of these problems refer to the problem of information dissemination. Databases are widespread, and need to be integrated so that each piece of information is accessible. Expert systems can be of help when it comes to seeking for some kind of professional information, especially if one is not competent enough.

8.3.2 Interactive Service Delivery

When we started this paperwork we indicated some major benefits from e-Government, and one of them was comfort. This is the place where we shall come back to this advantage of digital transactions. In every state the largest expands in conducting government affairs are those in every day's work. If we could transfer some of these transactions into homes, offices, companies, etc., we would achieve better efficiency, as well as serious cost savings. What appears at first site is that this would result in loss of job positions, but the fact is that new way for conducting business will not abolish traditional ways, it will only help improving them. Beside this, new technologies are also opening new job positions. What is also important is that once we move towards interactive service delivery what we shall get is automatic data gathering and clear insight in statistics. Some of services that could be delivered digitally (and already are in some states) are [PPI2000]:

- Issuing permits and licenses, as well as renewing them;
- Businesses and individuals could file tax returns directly, at no cost;
- Paying tickets, bills, memberships, etc.;
- Companies could file environmental compliance forms online (and other forms of compliance);
- Individuals could apply for visas, social security benefits, job positions, etc. online.

And now, let us see some of the problems concerning interactive services [PPI2000]:

- Need to expand and standardize the number of applications for online forms;
- Whenever possible use web based technology;
- Online forms should use shared information about the submitter;
- Integrate forms;
- Focus on intergovernmental solutions.

All of these problems are similar to the ones we faced before. Expanding and standardizing applications, as well as integrating forms, is something that could apply to any Internet application. What I would like to emphasis, is focusing on intergovernmental solutions. This means that applications have to be interoperable with other government solutions, forms have to be standardized and integrated as well. Governments need to cooperate with other governments, with other agencies and institutions, and with private sector as well. Therefore, for example, assigning certificate bodies (in charge of assigning certificates) is one of the responsibilities that government is in charge of.

In the following text we have included the figure that shows us the delivery of some services in Canada and United Kingdom (Figure 3.2).

8.3.3 Online Supplying

The third category of digital applications focuses on online supplying. There are number of items that citizens and companies could purchase online, some of them already available. Thanks to Internet purchasing we can move to the center of virtual geography, meaning that suppliers do not have limited market. More than that vendors are offering contestable goods, and companies can bid on what is offered. Also, government has the possibility for digital tenders, when in need for some equipment. What needs to be explained further is that governments and distributors can take action in improved collaboration on scheduling, prices, and just-in-time replenishment of supplies.

What are the problems that we are facing? We need to: develop new monetary system, or to simply improve the existing one; insure that authentication and other security issues are guaranteed; improve advertising and publishing over the Internet; and in the end we need international laws and legal regulations to follow these transactions. Beside all of these problems, Internet shopping and purchasing already exists in private sector. There are many Internet shops all over the Internet, and these experiences will serve us well in designing sites for supplying.

In the following text we have included the figure with an example of online supplying in Canada (Figure 3.3).

8.3.4 Digital Democracy

Digital democracy is designed for communication between citizens and authorities. Information gathering, previously mentioned, covered information on government employees and activities. Digital democracy is moving towards more interactive communication. Citizens can have access to memorandums, reports and plans, but also address authorities personally, and inform them on their opinion, suggestions and take initiative in developments. What is more interesting, a complete e-Government site includes 'chat rooms', specially designed for discussions between citizens on various topics considering the operability of their government and similar issues. This way, governments get the information on the nation's reaction to important issues, and fresh ideas in solving problems. The traditional way through questionnaires takes more time and effort, but still should not be substituted but combined with new means.

Another aspect of digital democracy is communication between employees. Sometimes time for making decisions is limited and it is not possible to organize meetings. In that case, modern intranet in the use of government can be an appropriate 'meeting place'.

In the following text we have included the figure that shows how the Government of United Kingdom is dealing with digital democracy (Figure 3.4).

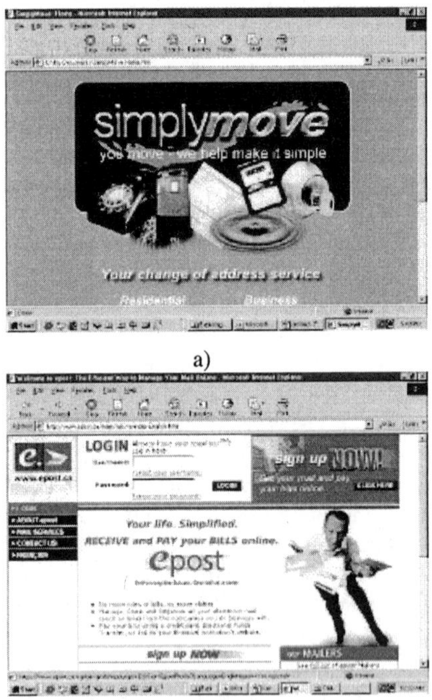

a)

b)

Legend: epost – An agency in Canada for paying bills online Simplymove – An agency in U.K. for change of address service

Comment: Some examples are given for online services, both of which are easy to access and available from official government site.

Figure 3.2: Interactive service delivery

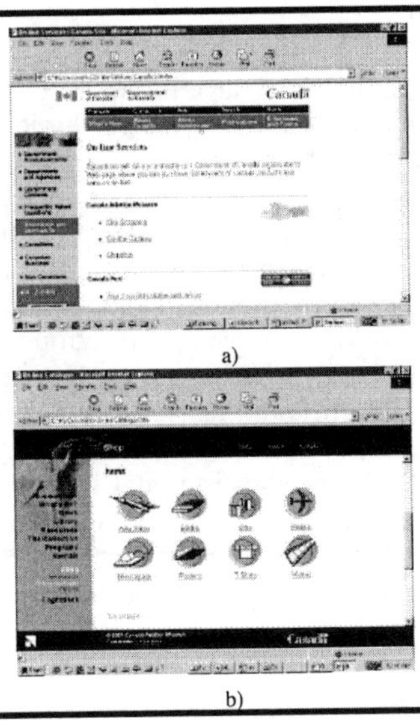

a)

b)

Legend: a) Official government site in Canada

b) Internet shop and its catalogue for ordering of goods.

Comment: In this site one can see a complete list of goods or move to next site for ordering, which is clearly marked.

Figure 3.3: Online catalogue

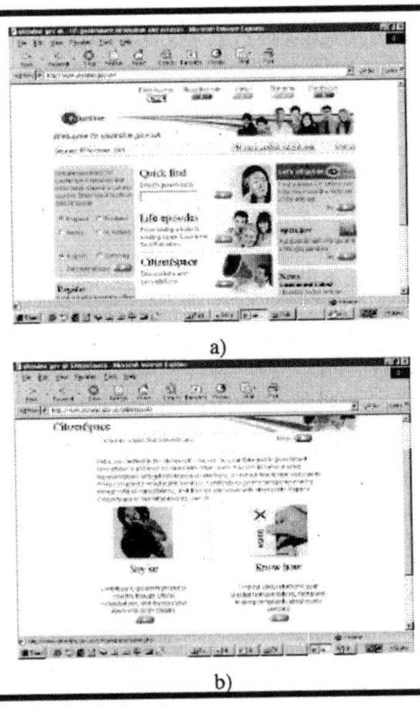

a)

b)

Legend: a) Official government site in U. K.

b) Citizen Space, an example of *digital democracy* site

Comment: Citizens of United Kingdom can access a so-called "Citizen Space" site through official government site. It has two segments: 1) *Say so*, for entering the chat room, and 2) *Know how* for information on elections and making complaints on public services.

Figure 3.4: Digital Democracy

8.4 Experience In The Field

Most of the countries are still in the early stage in the shift to the concept government online, and therefore it is highly unlikely that there is a "recipe" for its successful development and implementation. There is a whole set of variables that stands against simple transfer of ideas – cultural, political, legal, and others. But there is at least one connecting point for all leading industrial environments. The use of Internet is increasing each year (Figure 4.1, 4.2, and 4.3 show some charts that will support this statement). As we have already mentioned, e-Government relays not only on Internet delivery, but telephone, digital TV, and kiosk delivery as well. In the US, almost all of government efforts to implement electronic service delivery are Internet-focused, with minimal use of kiosks. In other countries, Netherlands and Finland for example, telephone is recognized as a useful mean for delivery. Interactive Voice Response and call centers are also widely used, especially in UK and Australia. An important tool for getting electronic service delivery into low-income households is digital TV and it is recognized in UK.

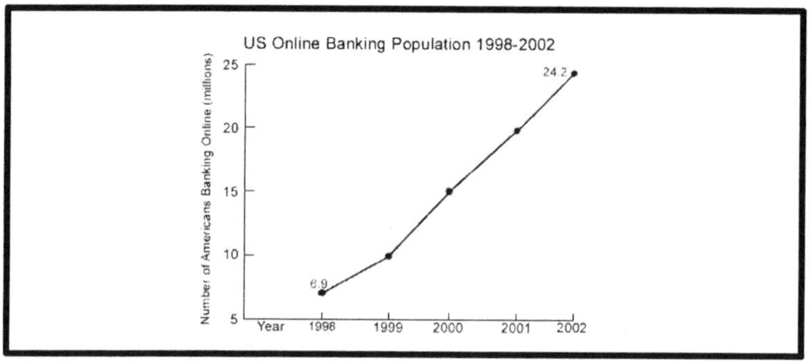

Comment: High increase of online banking population in US can be related to e-Government services.

Source: [NUA2001]

Figure 4.1: Online Banking in US

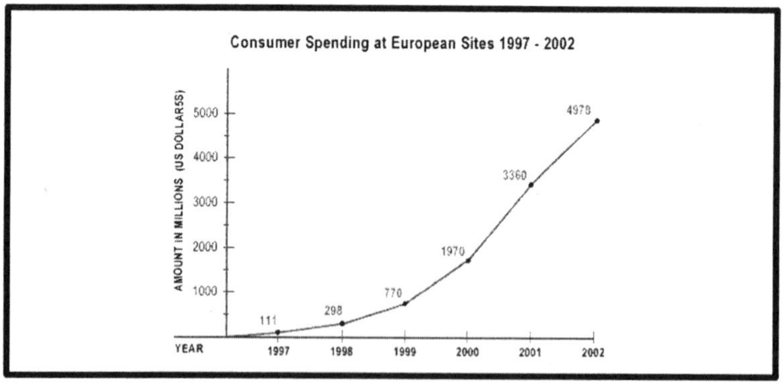

Comment: By the end of the year 2002 it is expected that consumer spending will come to the amount of almost 5 billions of US dollars, and currently it is estimated to the amount of 3,5 billions.

Source: [NUA2001]

Figure 4.2: Consumer Spending in EU

The number of citizens who have bank accounts also has an impact on the ability of the state for introducing electronic payment system. For example, in Australia, Finland, and Netherlands most citizens have bank accounts, an on the opposite of that in the UK and US we get a different picture.

Another important issue is the use of identification cards (ID). Some countries prefer using electronic ID card that enables the holder to do business with both private sector and government agencies (Finland, for example). On the other hand, some countries are adopting a different approach and users may have a variety of digital certificates for different purposes.

In terms of the legal framework, European and US approach differs significantly. EU Directive sees data protection mandatory in all sectors, and in the US private sector is currently covered by a set of self-regulatory schemes.

Comment: Figure shows that the growth of online spending in UK is even higher than the one in US.

Source: [NUA2001]

Figure 4.3: Online Spending in UK

8.4.1 New Zealand

The government in New Zealand released a vision statement for e-Government in New Zealand on September the 28th, in 1999. This vision was built upon the work of the Chief Executives' Group on Information Management and Technology and the State Services Commission (SSC) [Boyle2000]. Here we shall list some of the objectives from that statement. By the year 2005:

- It is expected that people and businesses should be able to electronically register with central government what ever they need to (e.g. births, deaths, marriages).
- By the same year people should be able to transact all their dealings with IRD online, as well as other government-related businesses.
- All government forms should be available online, as well as all services suitable for full or partial electronic delivery. A single point of access for government information and services should be delivered.
- Enabling people to have their say in the policy-making process.
- The health intranet should enable authorized medical professionals to securely access records of a person's health information.

- All necessary technologies, laws, and policies should be in everyday use by government, businesses, and citizens.
- *Landonline* should enable subscribers to electronically post transactions from their office and receive documentation.
- Recording change of address (and other personal information) should be provided.

In addition to this action plan, we shall now list critical issues currently identified by the CE Working Group in New Zealand:

- **Leadership** – cabinet leadership, agency involvement, chief executives;
- **Strategy;**
- **Ensuring a focus on citizens** – a strong emphasis upon improving services, citizen access to technology and skills, and engaging people in government;
- **Avoiding the digital divide;**
- **Governance** – strong coordination, facilitation, resources, and guidance;
- **Integration** – acceptance by all agencies participating in e-Government is required;
- **Resourcing ;**
- **Reskilling government** – education and training must be done;
- **The need for communication** – a commitment to effective communication with and consultation of citizens is required.

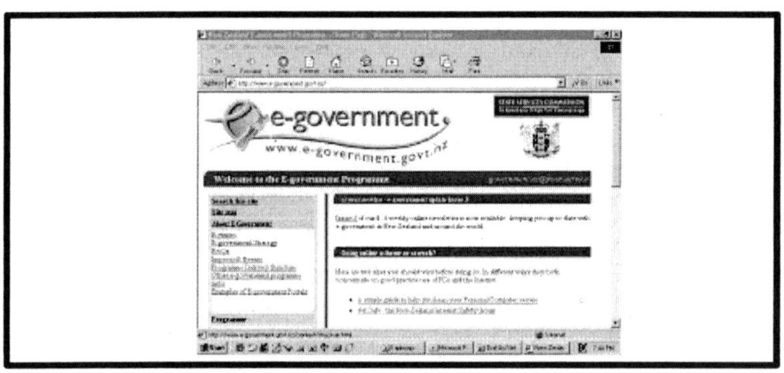

Comment: Official government site for New Zealand.

Address: www.e-government.govt.nz.

Figure 4.4: New Zealand

8.4.2 United States

Although the US is one of the most technologically advanced countries, due to its fragmentation problem this advantage does not stand for e-Government. Integration across federal services or between states and federal government is rather week, initiatives are still at the informational stage and transactional systems are rare (with the exception of the IRS). National Partnership for Reinventing Government (NPR) came up with a two-year strategy for moving toward e-Government in late 1998. NPR has been largely non-funded and sees a role for greater private sector investments [Boyle2000].

Major barrier to e-Government is lack of reliable authentication services – paper ID card does not exist (driver's license serves that purpose), and unique identifier is Social Security number. Digital divide is also one of the major barriers. Digital TV and lowering computer prices is one of the ways to bring ESD into low-income households, but still the degree of skill, comfort and familiarity with the technology is sharply uneven. More than that, it is said that so called "racial ravine" and rural areas are the latest concern in the US. Beside all of this Internet access via PC is still seen as the primary delivery platform for e-Government, since mobile phone usage is lower in the US than in Europe. In the end it seems that people who would most benefit from improved services and who deal most with government, are the same ones who have difficulties to access it electronically.

We shall now focus on e-Government initiative in the state of New York. Office for technology was established in 1997 and charged with coordinating New York State's technology resources. It has six standing subcommittees that include: Business Applications, Local Government, Procurement, Best Practices, Network Infrastructure, and Geographic Information Systems. Its major projects include:

- **Establishing a statewide IP network -** connecting state and local government agencies with voice, data and video services, and offering common applications, based on interagency and intergovernmental cooperation;
- **Implementing a comprehensive plan** – strategic investments in technology, executive training, management development, and technical training;
- **Restructuring the state's data centers** – in conjunction with the Office of General Services;
- **"Best Practices" sessions** – for administrative applications;
- **Statewide legislation;**
- **Cooperation with local governments** – to ensure their involvement and to make them equal partners with state agencies;
- **Reviewing all purchases of technology -** to ensure consistency and insight in state agency activities;
- **Participating in projects** – major technology projects that serve as pilots for future efforts.

Following figure will present official US government site. It is important to notice that search on this site can apply both to federal level and to state level.

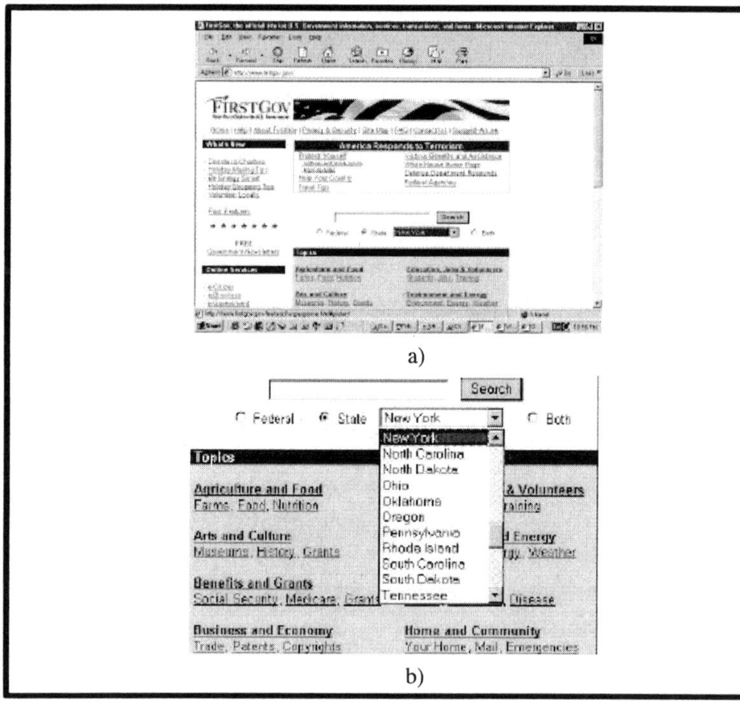

Legend: FirstGov – official US government site

Comment: The site shown in Figure a) could apply to federal or state level, what depends on selected box, as shown in Figure b).

Address: www.firstgov.gov.

Figure 4.5: The United States

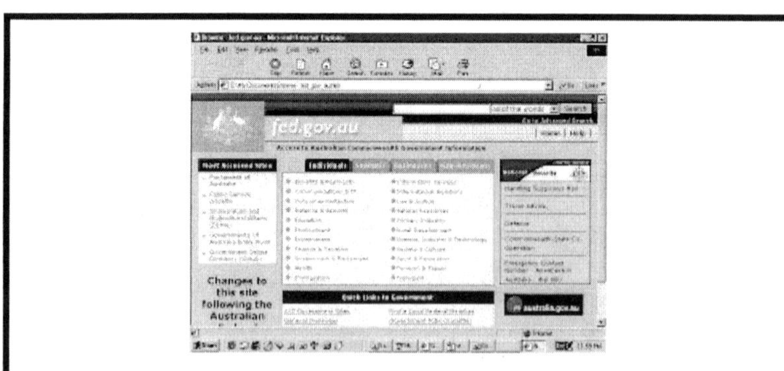

Comment: Federal government of Australia.

Address: www.fed.gov.au.

Figure 4.6: Australia

8.4.3 Australia

Public sector management reforms in Australia have followed the same path as the ones in Canada, UK, and New Zealand. Most e-Government initiatives cover market-type mechanisms and privatization. Federal initiative was to deliver all Commonwealth services electronically via the Internet by 2001 [Boyle2000].

In 1999, over 18% of all households had home Internet access (79% of that in major cities), and still made Australia one of the most wired countries in the world. Remote and rural areas are not even within the local phone calls of an Internet Service Provider. In the same year there were about seven million mobile phones.

One of the first e-Government programs was Multimedia Victoria (MMV) in Victoria, of course, with initial strategy document in 1995. The need for kiosk project was identified, as well as the need for system that could support multiple agencies and delivery channels. Therefore the government is also derived into channels: business, land, health channel, etc.

It was estimated that setting up an application costs between A$100k and A$200k and service providers are charged 80 cents to $2 per transaction. The problem with charging government departments to use the system results in charging service providers, and these costs are translated to citizens – an obvious drawback! Another problem is with the legacy system. All of this results in the fact that states are further advanced in their deployment of ESD than the federal government. Still, Australia can draw on real examples of ESD with many impressive achievements.

8.4.4 United Kingdom

In 1999, UK published its White Paper: Modernizing Government. Key themes of this work are [Boyle2000]:

- **Electronic Procurement** – making 90% of low-value government procurement electronic by April 2001;
- **Government Business Processes** – equivalence to written and digital documents;
- **Service and Information Delivery** – 25% by 2001, 50% by 2005, and 100% by 2008;

Beside the ambitiousness of the UK, use of the Internet is not as high as in Scandinavia, the US, or Australia. The tax system is very complicated, and there is no single, integrated national database to be used to roll out ESD. To help drive change the government has appointed an e-Envoy and e-Minister. The digital divide issue was resolved with opening of e-libraries and placing computers in schools and neighborhoods.

Another problem is that there are number of statutes in the UK that prevent data gathered for one purpose to be used for another, and the access to the data is seriously limited. Therefore services that only need parts of data must be developed. Beside this, due to parallel systems in operation, cost implications of e-Government have not been fully realized, and it will take some time to realize cost savings.

8.4.5 Ontario, Canada

In 1998, an Information & Information Strategy was released, as a plan to invest in common infrastructure, set needed corporate policies, standards, and governance structure. It establishes a strong corporate information and IT organization, with a Chief Information Officer on the head of it. Its duties are to manage the corporate plan and budget, develop corporate policies and standards, design and manage the architecture, and manage infrastructure services [Boyle2000].

Before establishing of this strategy, the Ontario government had too many IT systems with poor evidence of integration among agencies and weak links to the broader public sector. Used technology was incompatible and variety of networks made it difficult to implement systems across government. New technology was the enabler for equipping the province to deliver public service in an integrated manner, and to establish linkages between federal and provincial government. This consistency was to be achieved across several key areas: common infrastructure, policies, standards, governance, organization, and accountability. The idea was to introduce 'cluster delivery' instead of delivery to

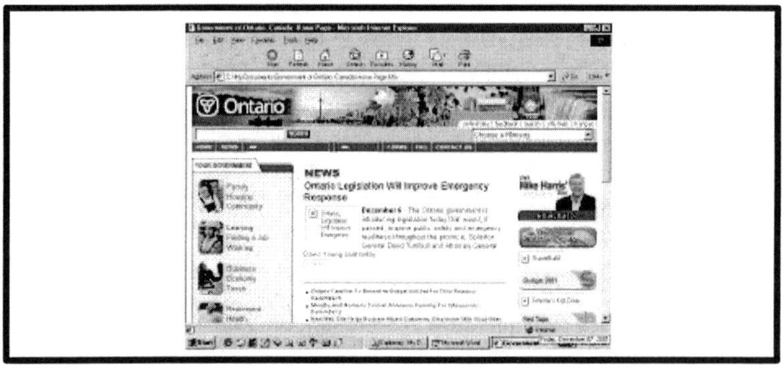

Comment: Official Ontario government site.

Address: www.gov.on.ca.

Figure 4.7: Ontario, Canada

individual agencies. A business cluster is defined as a set of government programs and services with common themes, designed for similar purposes and can be supported efficiently with common or similar support. Seven of these IT clusters were introduced: resource/land; economics/business; human services; justices; community services; transportation; and finance.

Each IT cluster has a responsibility to develop a cluster IT plan and manage the cluster's information and IT resources. Other responsibilities are managing the corporate framework architecture, information and IT products, as well as development of business-specific applications and relations with business program vendors.

To conclude, Ontario Information & Information Technology Strategy focuses on aligning IT planning and business strategy across government, with respect to broad stake holder interests, but the stress is put on the design from the perspective of the consumer, rather than government.

8.5 Strategy Planning

Planning of e-Government is characterized with complexity and deep impact on society. As we have seen from experience in various jurisdictions, given in previous chapter, it takes a completely different approach comparing to traditional business planning. We shall first focus on establishing a sustainable project and then move to other strategic issues.

8.5.1 Elements of a Business Case

Developing a business case for the implementation of an e-commerce project or any type of information systems project includes many elements to consider. Beside the differences between the private and public sectors, agencies within the federal government are facing the same issues and challenges that private firms must deal with in case of developing and launching a new project [UM2000].

Identification of Sustainable Projects

For deciding on new projects we can use either a top-down or bottom-up approach. Once a project idea has grown, there are several steps that may be used at this stage either to develop a project further or to reject it. Once several potential ideas have been brought forth, it is necessary to evaluate each one, with respect to budgetary limitations, agency resources and the potential for the project to fulfill an agency's mission. What must be considered at this stage are the intended benefits and beneficiaries, scope, duration and technological requirements.

Value Chain Analysis

A critical step in estimating the importance and reflections of a potential e-commerce project involves analyzing what value a project can add to the current operations of an agency and what are the cost savings that project can introduce. There are three different levels for conducting the value chain analysis: the micro level, the general level, and the macro level.

The micro level involves just one agency, or a bureau within an agency, that must consider how a project will reduce costs or add value at any one of the steps outlined above

The general level covers a number of agencies with a cross-functional scope and its goal is to realize synergies that may be gained from combining and sharing resources.

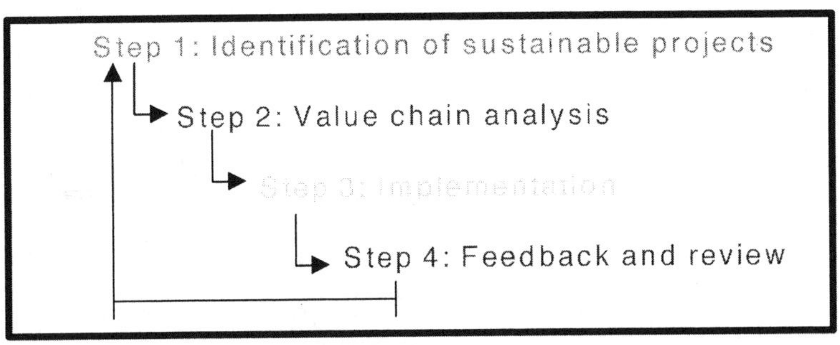

Comment: This diagram illustrates some recommended steps in the development of a business case for government e-commerce initiatives.

Source: [UM2000]

Figure 5.1: Business Case Steps

The macro level covers the entire federal government, and a given project must have a far-reaching purpose and function, in order to provide a number of benefits for all stakeholders, as well as the various different areas of the Federal government. Another type of activity that can potentially affect conducting business among many different agencies is procurement at this level (how private contractors interact with the range of agencies that they serve).

Implementation

E-commerce projects within the private sector differ in many ways from those within the public sector. Previous experience shows that many corporations have rushed into *web world* with little regard for cost, duration, scope or overall purpose. Due to competitive forces many private companies have implemented e-commerce web systems without using a gradual, strategic approach. Fortunately, federal governments do not have to compete in these types of competitive markets and planning and implementing e-commerce projects can be followed with a great deal of thought by using a methodical and strategic approach. A project that has been identified, selected and analyzed can be implemented in a variety of ways and should be divided into discrete phases with clear and firm deadlines. Within each phase, it should be broken up into manageable stages of development, what could involve securing resources, installing new software or systems or similar. Phases of a project should be long enough so that there is sufficient time to complete all the steps necessary for implementation, and also need to be short enough to ensure quality and consistency of management.

One of the most critical factors in the implementation stage refers to the market and the characteristics of the customer base of a potential project. Project developers must ask themselves about changes in the intended market, future use of the project, user competency in on-line services, and security issues. During the examination of the market for a project customers should be categorized based on how quickly and readily they adapt to and use innovative technological systems as: innovators, early adopters, early majority, late majority, and laggards.

Feedback and Review of Success or Failure

It is critical to know whether or not:

- A project has met the goals that were outlined in its original plan,
- Costs and revenues were accurately forecasted,
- The project should continue in its current or any form.

Case Dimension	Description
Idea Generation	the source and impetus for a new project
Customer and Market Research	an evaluation of the intended potential users and beneficiaries of a project
Technology Development	an analysis of the technological resources necessary to build and service a new project
Risk	uncontrollable factors that may jeopardize implementation or customer adoption of a project
Approval Process	the level of authority within the government required for project initiation
Success Measures	tools used to assess whether or not a project has met its intended goals

Comment: It is necessary to evaluate a project based on a number of different issues. This table includes a list of topics that pertains to public e-commerce projects.

Source: [UM2000]

Figure 5.2: E-commerce projects evaluation

Some of the tools that can be used at this stage to evaluate and benchmark projects are: financial payback measure, percent increase in customer adoption, percent decrease in labor and other expenses, customer satisfaction, acceptance, experience and positive public awareness. Finally, once a project has reached the stage of review after several years of operation, it is necessary to determine whether the project is still aligned with the goals of the agency that developed it in the first place.

8.5.2 Planning of E-Government

In order to emphasis the importance of strategic planning in this area, it is necessary to understand the needs of "digital society". They can be categorized as follows: a) economical growth (support for industry and existing economy scene with politics, laws, etc.); b) politics in telecommunication (encouraging *fast* technologies); c) education (citizens need to be educated in order to be able to use new technologies); and d) government services (as example for others).

Now we shall define some planning issues important for successful development [YUINFO2001]:

- **Motivation** – it is important to inform citizens of all activities, spending and results. Usually it is done through following pieces of information: same services and lower prices, more services for same price, and improved services;
- **Budget** – e-Government asks for high investments before it starts introducing cost savings (research, development, implementation, maintaining, exploitation);
- **Result measuring** – user's satisfaction, rate of acceptance, transaction duration, error handling, reliability rate, etc.;
- **Development competency** – realistic evaluation of competency in handling requested software projects;
- **Contract and project managing** – need for good mangers and appropriate leadership;
- **Best practice** – in order to achieve good results in short time it is important to use standard and reliable components;
- **Relationship managing** – it is necessary to include following services: telephone service for technical support, help on the Web, FAQ services, processes for various analysis (for navigation improvement, for example);
- **Technology** – defining of secure architecture is the first step: application architecture, data structure, and infrastructure architecture.

Planning of e-Government can be divided into three major steps:

1. **Executive appointment**, one body or person that is held in charge of handling the project;
2. **E-Government vision**, defining clear and prospect vision of all services;
3. **Global plan definition**, divided into following stages: Stage I - Strategy (what should be done) Stage II - Competency (what could be done) Stage III - Implementation (what will be done).

Strategy planning should start with a meeting of all executives, leaders of the project, and technical experts. Before setting up of this meeting, following materials are to be prepared: business strategy summary, good practice strategy, and current trends and current stage evaluation. During this meeting issues and reports, such as: business targets report, e-Government vision, e-Government targets, project candidates, project priority criteria, priority criteria evaluation, and alternative resources, should be discussed and resolved. This meeting should end with clear and mature idea of the project and bring following outcomes: classification of chosen subprojects (G2C, G2B, G2E, and G2G); project priority list, subproject dependencies and interoperability, timing schedules, and alternative resources selection.

Competency planning can be divided into government and users competency. In order to define these competencies we must make certain questionnaires.

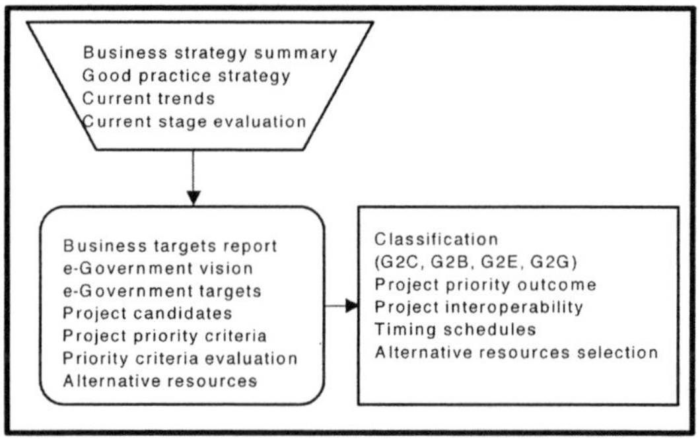

Comment: Strategy planning starts with a meeting of e-Government authorities, based on previous research (input block), with important subject discussions (block in the middle), and its purpose is to define future projects and operations (output block).

Figure 5.3: Strategy planning of e-Government

These questionnaires should provide answers such as: is there a need for eye-to-eye contact among users, what are the cultural and language limitations, what are the possibilities for handicapped users, what is the average economical status, what are the geographical limitations (if any), and is there a need and desire for education among citizens. When it comes to government competency we should define:

- **Leader's competency -** understanding and involvement;
- **Legal readiness;**
- **Handling with digital records;**
- **Privacy and security** – of system and transactions;
- **Central authority** (CIO – Chief Information Officer) both for strategic and for technical issues.

Implementation planning is based upon defining approach and priorities for global e-Government project and for subprojects. After certain approach is adopted and priorities are established we can move to evaluations and schedules. Steps of implementation planning are given in the Figure 5.4.

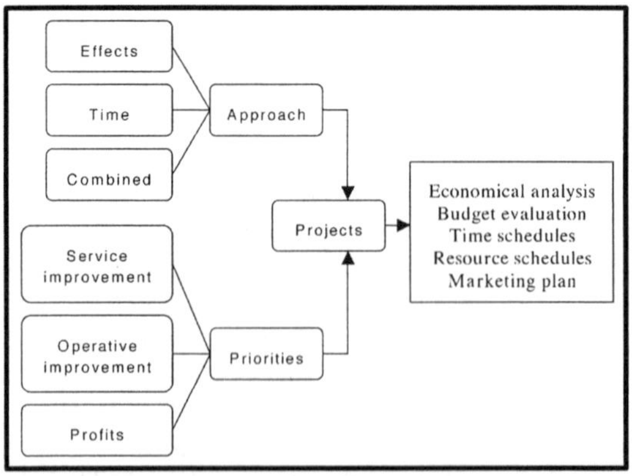

Comment: In order to achieve a good implementation plan, first step is to be defining approach (meaning fast or efficient development), second step is defining priorities, and third step is project approval, selection, and evaluation.

Figure 5.4: Implemention Planning

8.6 Summary

In order to improve internal and external business processes, and bring them closer to customer-centricity, modern governments are introducing e-Government, based upon service delivery opportunities offered by new communications technologies.

Major changes in government organization, legislative regulations, technical support, and cultural and social behaviors are needed in order to make e-Government a reality. The key challenges are not technological but cultural. These changes may be accomplished through legislation to reorganize the traditional government model, modification of existing statutory and regulatory requirements, and through strong IT leadership and policy.

Therefore, the architecture of e-Government can be divided into several segments: network infrastructure, network publishing, message and information delivery, operating infrastructure, legal and political constrain, standards and protocols of networking, and applications. Network infrastructure refers to the physical network and network publishing to languages and tools for Web designing and programming. Message and information delivery applies to delivery of structured and unstructured data, which brings us to security issues that are covered within operating infrastructure. Legal regulations are given within legal and political constrains, and the standards and protocols already in use with Internet services, are also taken as a serious limitation of liberty in designing and implementation. In the end, applications are divided into interactive service delivery, information gathering, digital democracy, and supplying. This categorization is based on the type of service. On the other hand, from the government point of view, it can also be divide as G2G (Government to Government), G2B (Government to Business), G2E (Government to Employees), and G2C (Government to Citizen).

Most of the countries are still in the early stage in the shift to government online, and therefore it is highly unlikely that there is an "recipe" for its successful development and implementation. Planning of e-Government can be divided into three major steps: executive appointment, e-Government vision, and global plan definition (consisting of competency evaluation, strategy definition, and implementation planning).

8.7 Problems

1. Try to design a web form that contains the following controls: a) name (Text box); b) address (Text box); c) age (Text box); d) Mr. / Mrs. / Miss (Radio button group); and e) reset and submit buttons. Enhance the form so that the user can not submit the form if some of the fields is left empty or contains a non-valid value. Provide a message in these cases.
2. Try to develop a servlet that accepts the submitted page from previous exercise, and returns a page with a reply to the user. Enhance the servlet so that it inserts a new record into the database table of the users with the submitted data.
3. After setting up your own Web sight try searching for it using some index-based search engine. Measure how long it will take until your Web sight is visible.
4. Make the same search with some links-based search engine and compare the results.
5. Find out about the services your Government is offering to you online and see if you can order a birth certificate or similar document. Now try to get the same paper directly from your town hole and compare the time spent on each of these tasks.
6. Try sending a message to a non-existing address and see if your Internet provider will inform you of mistake and how long it will take him to respond.
7. Think of an algorithm for encrypting and decrypting together with your friend, and then send him an encrypted message. See if he will be able to decrypt it.

8. Now ask your friend to send you an message encrypted with the same algorithm, but with a key that is not known to you. See if you will be able to decrypt the message.
9. Think of a service not yet provided by your e-Government, that would be of use to citizens, and send an e-mail to authorities in your town.
10. Try setting up your own e-Business with minimal investments. See if you will be able to refund your investment. Did you follow our instructions in choosing and developing your project?

REFERENCES

[NECCC2000] Critical Business Issues In the Transformation to Electronic Government, National Electronic Commerce Coordinating Council (NECCC), December, **2000**

[Milutinovic2001] Milutinovic, V., Infrastructure for E-Business on the Internet, **2001**

[Vaskovic22] Vasković V., E-Government, published in "Internet ogledalo", issue 22

[Boyle2000] Boyle B., Electronic Government for New Zealand: Managing the Transition, May **2000**

[NZGISPS2000] New Zealand Government Information Systems Policies and Standards, November, **2000**

[YUINFO2001] Konjovic Z., Ivkovic M., Stratesko planiranje uvodjenja E-vlade, V strucno naucni skup, YUINFO, Belgrade, **2001**

[Ivkovic98] Ivkovic M., Radenkovic B., Internet i savremeno poslovanje, **1998**

[Drakulic2001] Drakulic M., Drakulic R., Pravni aspekti elektronskog poslovanja i elektronske vlade, INESS, Soko Banja, **2001**

[UM2000] Developing a Business Case for Electronic Commerce Project Selection, Robert H. Smith School of Business, University of Maryland, December, **2000**

[PPI2000] Atkinson, R., Ulevich, J., Digital Government: The Next Step to Reengineering the Federal Government, Progressive Policy Institute, Technology and New Economy Project, March, **2000**

[NUA2001] Nua Internet Surveys, www.nua.com, December, **2001**

E-Business and E-Challenges
V. Milutinović and F. Patricelli (Eds.)
IOS Press, 2002

CHAPTER 9
AD HOC NETWORKS AND THE MOBILE BUSINESS ON THE INTERNET

Nikola Milanovic, Djordje Trifunovic and Veljko Milutinović

In the last decade of the 20th century, one of the hottest topics in computing and communications has been the wireless technology. It has attracted many users, and has undergone numerous transformations. The next step in evolution of wireless communication are Ad Hoc* networks, which do not require any other network infrastructure beside the already existing mobile nodes. In this chapter we will cover basic ideas of Ad Hoc networking, compare Ad Hoc networks with classic wireless networks, explain some routing protocols, briefly comment on some security issues, give a short example of one possible realization of Ad Hoc network, and at the end, try to go even further that the pure Ad Hoc networking – towards the wireless Internet and the existing software and hardware support.

9.1. Mobile Networks

In this brief introduction, we will try to explain what the Ad Hoc networks really are, and how they relate to the existing wireless networks (for example, GSM).

Ad Hoc networks have the ability to establish connection and communication without any predefined network infrastructure (routers, base stations, and optical fibers) except the mobile nodes themselves. How is this possible? First of all, every mobile node acts as a switch during the communication. Therefore, message is effectively transmitted over idle nodes. Let's stop here for a moment, and consider the following situation.

Suppose we have to transmit a message from one office building to another. We have several solutions. First, we could use the existing wired networks and protocols. However, the existing networks are overloaded, and furthermore, we want to ensure mobility. Then, our second choice is to use the existing wired infrastructure and to spread a grid of base stations (like GSM). Thus, we would provide mobility, but this is very expensive solution, because of the need to install base stations. Also, maintenance of networks such as this is very costly. Our third choice could be to presume that many other electronic devices around us have the same ability of wireless communication. This is fairly reasonable assumption in most urban areas, and we certainly do not have office districts in desert! Then, we could transfer message from one mobile node to another, from source until it reaches destination. It is obvious that every mobile node in this architecture must have routing capabilities, that is, every mobile node must be able to make a decision what to do with message destined for some other node.

Comment: The message hops from one node to another. Every node acts as a switch and has routing capabilities.

Figure 1.1: Basic Ad Hoc network architecture.

The benefits of this approach are:

- easy installation and upgrade
- modest requirements for existing infrastructure
- low cost and maintenance
- great flexibility

It can be said that Ad Hoc networks present a new step in the evolution of wireless communications. In order to understand them better, we will briefly look at the existing wireless solutions.

In classic wireless network infrastructure we can distinguish between several actors: mobile (wireless) nodes, mobility support routers (base stations) and fixed nodes. This situation is presented on figure 1.2. We can se how a cell is formed. The range of mobility support router defines a cell. Mobile nodes 1 and 2 are in range, while mobile node 3 is out of range, thus is unreachable, even if it is in range of mobile node 2, for example.

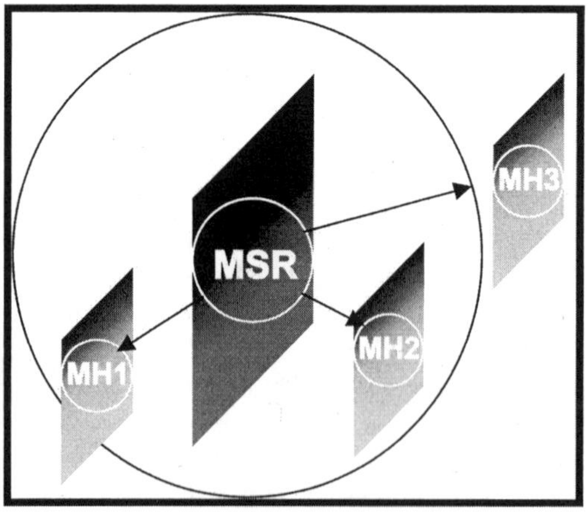

Comment: Each mobility support router covers the area limited by its range; this range is referred to as a cell. Mobile hosts can communicate with the mobility support router only.

Figure 1.2: Cellular communication

We can say that mobility support routers are bridges between wired (or fixed) network and mobile hosts. No direct communication between mobile nodes is allowed – mobility support router mediates everything.

In figure 1.3, we have an example of typical network topology. We can see the fixed (or wired) part of the network (consisting of fixed hosts FH1, FH2, FH3 and FH4), then there is mobility support router (MSR), and two mobile hosts (MH1 and MH2).

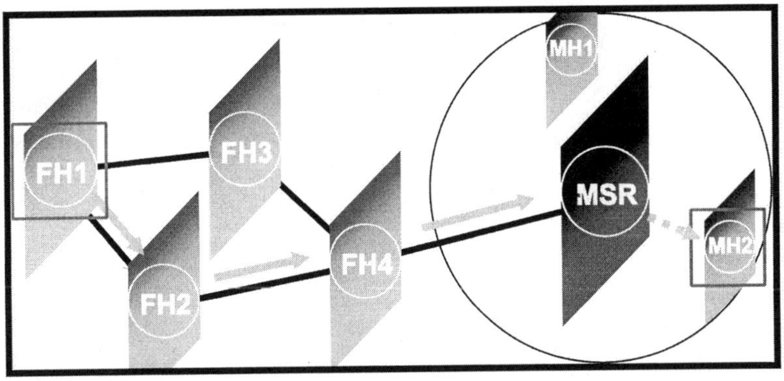

Comment: FH1 is source, and MH2 is destination. Network communication is divided into two parts: Over the fixed and over the wireless part of the network.

Figure 1.3: Classic mobile network topology

We can see that network communication is divided into two parts:

- fixed part – message is transferred over fixed (wired) part of the network, and it eventually reaches mobility support router;
- wireless part – mobility support router broadcasts message to all mobile nodes in its cell.

In this way, the mobility is hidden. Fixed host does not know it is addressing a mobile host. For fixed host 1, address of mobile host 2 is just another network address. Because of this, routing protocols designed for this kind of wireless networks are called **indirect protocols**.

What are the limitations of existing wireless networks? The basic problem is this – this communication we described is **one hop** communication. That means that in every connection, there is always only one wireless hop, between mobility support router and destination mobile node. Even if two mobile nodes from the same cell wish to communicate with each other, they must use mediation of mobility support router. So, even if we have high gain antennas on our mobile nodes, we are limited by the range and processing power of mobility support router. Then, sometimes it is necessary to establish connection even if network infrastructure is damaged (wars, floods, fires) or non-existent. In such situations, classical wireless networks are helpless.

The basic idea of Ad Hoc networking was already stated: to establish connection without the preexisting network infrastructure. Let's take a closer look at the meaning of this. The following figure describes nature of Ad Hoc communication:

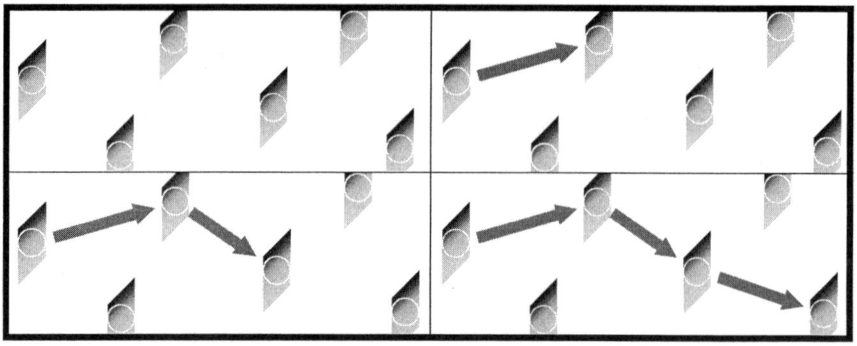

Comment: The message is propagating through the network using intermediate nodes as switches. Therefore, each node must have routing capabilities.

Figure 1.4: Ad Hoc communication

What else can be noted here? First, mobile hosts can communicate on much greater distances that covered by their ranges. This is possible thanks to the presence of other mobile hosts than can be reached by the source host, and that are willing (or free) to retransmit the packet further. Thus, propagating from one mobile host to another, the packet reaches its destination.

Then, we call this a **multihop** communication, because there are many wireless hops in one connection. Remember that in classic wireless architecture there is only one wireless hop per connection.

9.2. Routing protocols in Ad Hoc Networks

The basic problem in Ad Hoc network realization is the efficient routing protocol. How can the message find the right way? By now it should be obvious that every mobile node must have routing capabilities. However, the question remains: which routing protocol is suitable to use?

Fixed computer networks use route advertising. Routers periodically broadcast routing information to each other, thus keeping everybody's routing tables updated. Can the same mechanism be applied here? Of course it can. The obvious benefit would be that route to every mobile node would be known at any given time. However, there is one big problem. If we adopt route advertising, we are wasting precious bandwidth and battery power even if there are no changes in network topology. Therefore, a new class of routing protocols is being developed, called **on-demand** routing protocols. The basic idea is that route advertising is done only when needed, that is, on demand. Furthermore, if there is no routing information, the process of **route discovery** is initiated.

In this section, we will briefly describe three algorithms for on-demand Ad Hoc routing:

- Dynamic Source Routing (DSR)
- Ad-hoc On-demand Distance Vector (AODV)
- Temporally Oriented Routing Algorithm (TORA).

9.2.1. Dynamic Source Routing

The first algorithm that will be considered here is Dynamic Source Routing [IETF2001b]. This algorithm is based on the concept of source routing. That means that sender always provides a sequence of addresses through which the message must travel. These addresses are stored in the route cache, which every node maintains for itself. You can imagine these caches as routing tables.

The main benefit of this approach is that there are no periodical broadcasts of routing tables. Instead, route is determined dynamically, and only when needed. When mobile node wants to send a message to other mobile node, and it does not have a valid entry for that node in route cache, the process of route discovery is initiated. The source node sends a **route request** packet, which propagates through the network, collecting addresses of all nodes it passes through. You can see this process on figure 2.1.

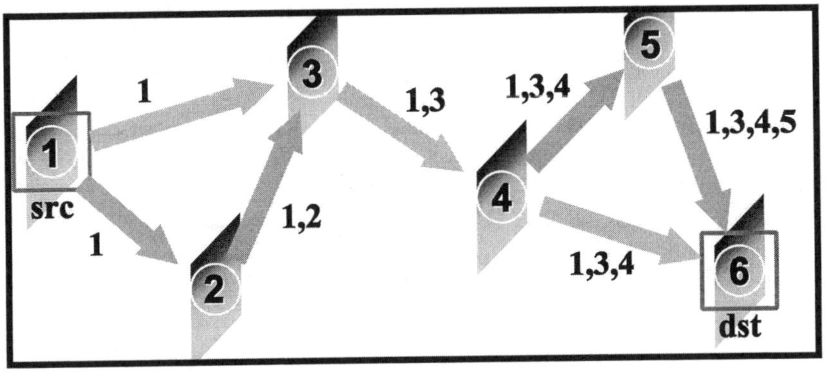

Comment: Route request packet propagates through the network, collecting the addresses of all visited nodes. Upon reaching the destination node, route request will contain the entire route from source to destination node.

Figure 2.1: Dynamic Source Routing

After this has been acomplished, destination node must inform the source node about new-discovered route. It does so by sending a **route reply** packet, as shown on figure 2.2.

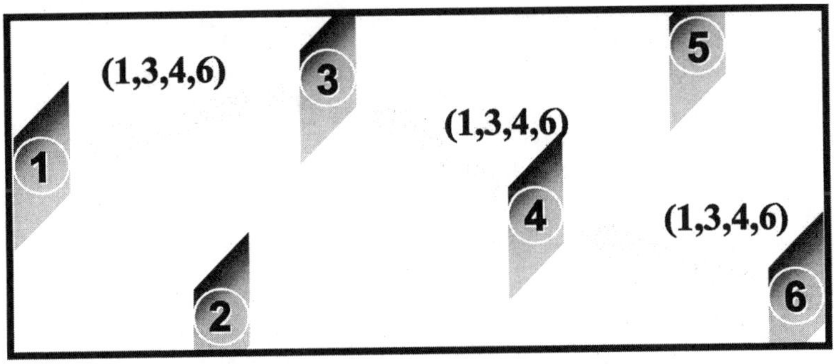

Comment: Node 6 must inform node 1 about the valid route, and it is done using the route reply message.

Figure 2.2: Route reply

Benefits of this routing algorithm are that is it very easy to implement, it can work with asymmetric links, there are no periodical broadcasts, so bandwidth and power are conserved. Also, there is no overhead where there are no changes in the network topology.

However, there is a large bandwidth overhead when the network is large. Then route request packets start to grow, and soon reach the unacceptable size. This causes potentially huge route reply packets. Also, since whole route must be sent along with the message, routing information can become bigger that the message itself. There is also a problem of scalability, because mentioned problems limit the network diameter.

9.2.2. Ad Hoc On Demand Distance Vector Routing

The second routing algorithm is called Ad Hoc On-Demand Distance Vector routing [IETF2001a]. It works in the very similar manner to DSR. There are no route broadcasts; instead route request packets are sent to discover unknown routes. But, there is one big difference. There is no route cache in route request packet. Instead, only the next hop is recorded.

When intermediate node receives route request packet form its neighbor node (n1), it can safely update its routing table, because it knows that it can reach source node via node n1. The same applies for route reply packet forwarding. When intermediate node receives route reply packet from its neighboring node n2, it can update routing table to destination node via node n2. This process is shown on figures 2.3 and 2.4.

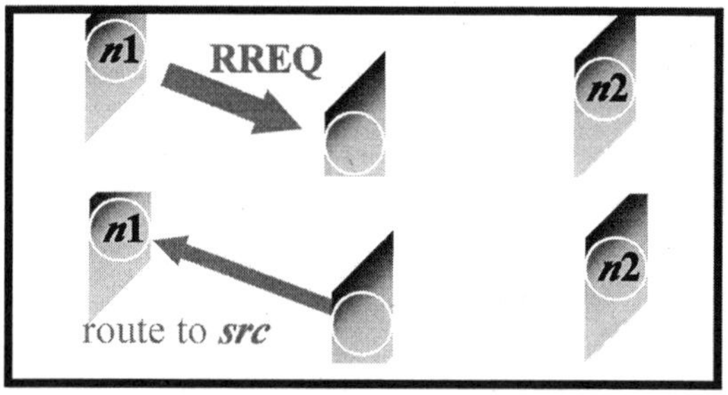

Comment: When receiving RREQ from source host via some intermediate host, the current host updates its routing table with route toward that source host.

Figure 2.3: Adding inverse route to source

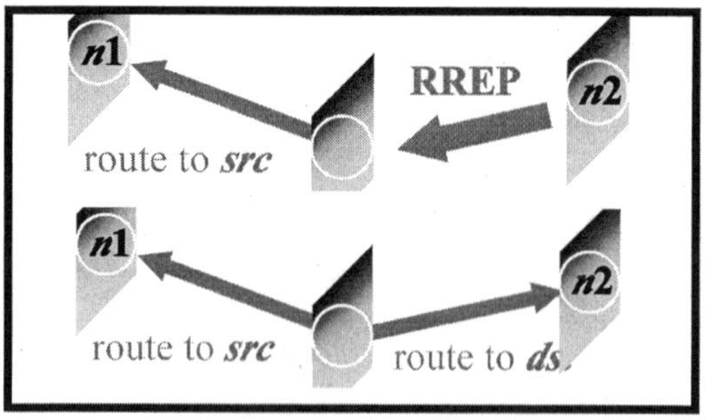

Comment: When receiving RREP from destination host via some intermediate host, the current host updates its routing table with route toward that destination host.

Figure 2.4: Adding inverse route to destination

One of the main benefits of this algorithm is that network topology is updated at all nodes through which the route request and route reply messages pass, and not only at source and destination nodes. Each host through which these messages pass will update its routing table to source and destination nodes.

Instead of keeping the whole route, hosts keep only the next hop, that is, the address of neighbor to which it should transfer packets for the required destination.

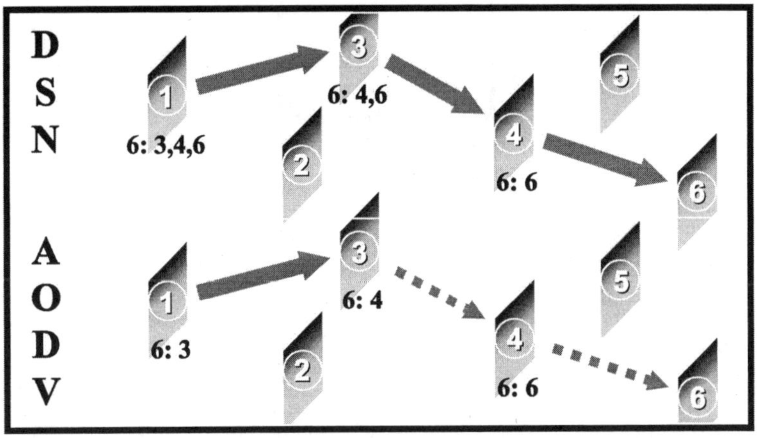

Comment: The main difference is that DSR maintains the whole route record, while ADOV remembers only the next hop.

Figure 2.5: Comparison of DSR and AODV approaches to routing

How are the changes of network topology managed? The mechanism used is sequence numbering. With each route, several sequence numbers are associated. These sequence numbers are stored in routing tables, and then sent with each route request and route reply. If any discrepancy is found between sequence numbers in route request/route reply packets and intermediate routing tables, appropriate action is taken.

Some advantages of AODV over DSR include smaller bandwidth overhead, because the control messages are smaller. Then, only two messages are needed for routing, instead of whole route. This improves scalability.

The most important drawback of this approach is that it works with symmetric links only.

9.2.3. Temporally Oriented Routing Algorithm

The third routing algorithm examined here is Temporally Oriented Routing Algorithm - TORA [IETF2001c].

The basic idea is to define a network topology using a directed acyclic graph (DAG). Hosts are represented as nodes with directed links. Direction of a link is realized by assigning a height to every node. The link is always directed from node with greater height to node with lower height.

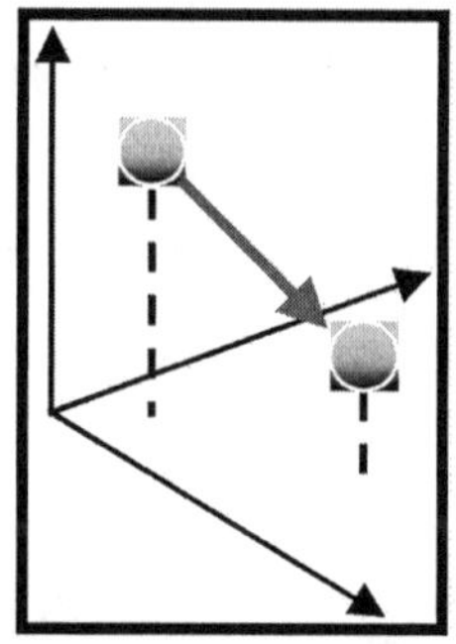

Comment: Each node is assigned a height. The link is always directed from the node with a greater height to the node with a lover height.

Figure 2.6: Directed Acyclic Graph

Destination node should have minimal height in the graph. Other nodes are assigned greater and greater heights, as their distance from destination node grows. Then, packets may be sent only from "higher" to "lower" nodes, that is, only via downstream links.

DAG is formed when source node does not have any downstream links. It sends query packet (equivalent to route request) which propagates through the network and marks nodes that can be used for transport as "interested" nodes. Then, after reaching some node that has downstream links, update packet (equivalent of route reply) is generated, assigning appropriate heights to "interested" nodes. The process is shown on figure 2.7.

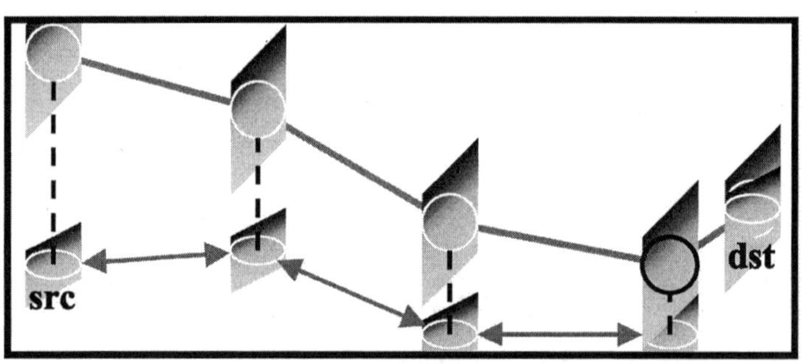

Comment: The downstream path is formed from the source node to the destination node.

Figure 2.7: DAG forming

The most important drawback of this approach is that, in order for this solution to work, there must be an external timing mechanism (for example GPS), needed for synchronization. This makes the implementation very expensive.

9.3. Security in Ad Hoc Networks

As in any computer network, main attributes of security in Ad Hoc networks are: availability, confidentiality, integrity, authentication and non-repudiation. We won't be going through them here in detail, because their meaning is essentially the same as in any other network.

However, use of wireless links renders an Ad Hoc network susceptible to link attacks ranging from passive eavesdropping to active impersonation, message replay, and message distortion. We should not only consider malicious attacks from outside a network, but also take into account the attacks launched from within the network by compromised nodes. To achieve high survivability, Ad Hoc networks should have a distributed architecture with no central entities. Introducing any central entity into our security solution could lead to significant vulnerability: that is, if this centralized entity is compromised, then the entire network is subverted.

There are two sources of threats to routing protocols: external attackers and compromised nodes. By injecting erroneous routing information, replaying old routing information, or distorting routing information, an attacker could successfully partition a network or introduce excessive traffic load into the network by causing retransmission and inefficient routing. To defend against this kind of threats, nodes can protect routing information in the same way they protect data traffic, for example through the use of cryptographic schemes such as digital signature.

The second and also more severe kind of threat comes from compromised nodes, which might advertise incorrect routing information to other nodes. In order to combat this threat, the principle of distributed trust can be used. Instead of designating one central entity for digital signature or other cryptographic operations, this function is distributed over many nodes. Then, if for example, k out of n nodes perform this function correctly we accept the message, otherwise we reject it as invalid.

9.4. Wireless Sensor Ad Hoc Network

In this section, we will describe a new application of mobile communications – a wireless, sensor, multihop Ad Hoc network for data acquisition and remote administration. This project was realized at the School of Electrical Engineering in Belgrade, during the course of IEEE Computer Society International Design Competition.

The goal of this project was to create a complete hardware/software specification for replacing and/or upgrading the existing wire systems for data acquisition and process control.

You can see the system overview on the figure 4.1. We will briefly describe each component of the system before proceeding on to the detail analysis.

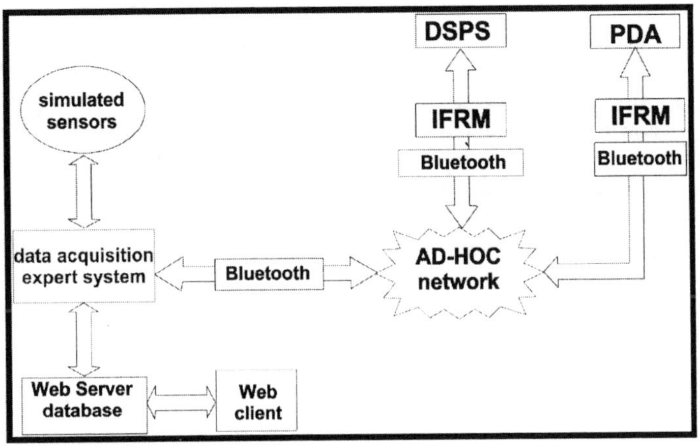

Comment: Essential parts of the system are: Ad Hoc network (routing protocol), Interface and Routing Module, Personal Digital Assistant, Data Acquisition and Expert System Software.

Figure 4.1: System overview

Multihop Ad Hoc sensor network and IFRM: The basic idea of an Ad Hoc network is establishing communication without a predefined network infrastructure. In other words, routing is dynamic, and data packets are hopping through other nodes that act as switches.

The role of the network subsystem is to provide a communication between other components of the system (server, DSPS, PDA...). In order to be scalable and flexible, network was designed as a multihop Ad Hoc wireless network, which means that nodes perform routing of packets.

The appropriate routing protocol was designed and optimized for execution on a microcontroller with very limited resources. In order to enable integration of the existing data acquisition devices into the system, interface to the Bluetooth module was designed to give such devices an illusion that they are in direct cable connection with the server.

Personal digital assistant: The role of the PDA is to inform the person in charge about status of the process he/she is monitoring. Also, PDA enables a person to send commands to remote parts of the system. Communication with the rest of the system is realized through the interface that is universal for each component that has an access to Ad Hoc network.

Digital Signal Processing System (DSPS): A device with TI DSP chip for digital motor control and signal processing was designed as an example of sensor that can be connected to this system. The basic role of this device is gathering of information from different peripheral devices, real time processing of gathered data and transfer of processed data to the server (through IFRM and Ad Hoc network), where the monitoring and additional processing are available.

Data acquisition and the expert system: Software for data acquisition and expert system for decision making reside on the server. If any irregularity is discovered, expert system tries to solve the problem by sending control commands to the part of the system that caused the problem. If the system is unable to fix the problem, person in charge is informed. If no response is received, a backup messaging system is activated. Every activity of the system is also logged in a database.

Database: All relevant activities of the system are recorded in a database: received sensor data, discovered irregularities and emergencies. Database is accessible from the Internet. The idea is to provide remote diagnostics and administration, beside plain recording of data, when the expert on site is unable to solve the problem on his own.

The basic advantage of this idea is that it offers universal and open platform, which can be implemented in any environment with small adjustments. For example, using this low cost kit, it is possible to upgrade factory sensor infrastructure. The existing wire sensors can be easily incorporated into the network, while it is possible to add any number of wireless sensors for each production process that is being monitored. Engineer in charge would be equipped with a PDA, which shortens the response time for any anomaly discovered.

The main problem that we face when trying to realize such a system is providing critical data transmission rate and stable ad-hoc network. The first problem was solved using the Bluetooth modules, which ensure fast enough transmission. The question of stability was addressed with careful design and implementation of the Ad Hoc routing protocol. Testing and detail simulations, the results of which will be presented in this chapter, showed that this protocol, with realized hardware and software infrastructure, is capable of operating in extreme load conditions, which is a prerequisite for eventual industrial exploitation.

You are welcomed to download complete project report from the following URL: http://galeb.etf.bg.ac.yu/~mnikola/belgrade.pdf.

9.5. Wireless Internet

The possibilities of use of Ad Hoc networks, as they were described, can be: **specific wireless applications** and/or **wireless Internet**

Specific wireless applications are of the type described in previous section: wireless sensor networks. Using the developed infrastructure, numerous wireless products can be developed, from industry to home and entertainment applications. Here are a few examples: hospital data acquisition system, wireless traffic control system, urban wireless services, house of the future, wireless guide for the blind people

The wireless Internet has yet failed to come and fulfill its potentials, partly due to the lack of standards, and partly due to the lack of technology. In order to understand what are the problems of the wireless Internet, let's first consider how the classic Internet works. The main thing is the protocol layering, which can bee seen in figure 5.1.

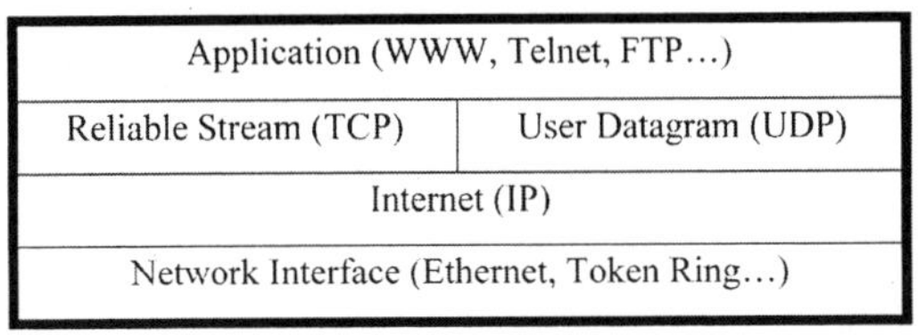

Comment: By having an unreliable IP protocol above the network interface, the Internet is able to encapsulate all data in IP packets before sending them over any existing network infrastructure. The network hardware does not have intimate knowledge of data in IP packets, it only knows that the type of information is IP packet.

Figure 5.1: Conceptual layering of the Internet protocols

What can we do to make the Internet wireless? There are two solutions: introduce wireless protocols in the network interface protocol layer or modify IP addressing scheme

If we adopt the first approach, the idea is to design Ad Hoc routing protocol that would be able to encapsulate IP packets, and transfer them over Ad Hoc wireless networks as ordinary data.

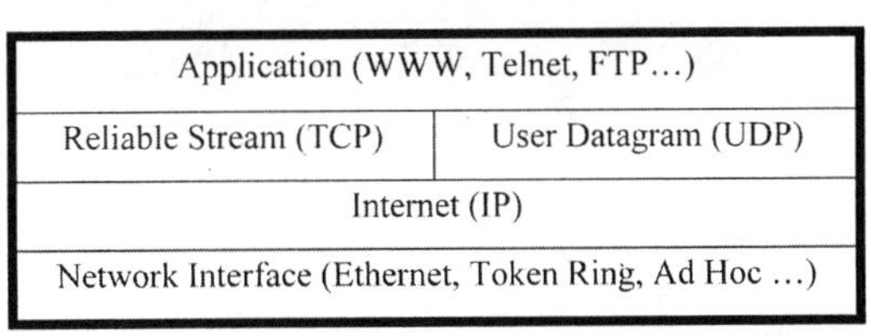

Figure 5.2: Extending Network Interface layer with Ad Hoc routing protocol

The second choice is to modify existing IP addressing scheme, as in figure 5.3, so we can explicitly support mobile devices.

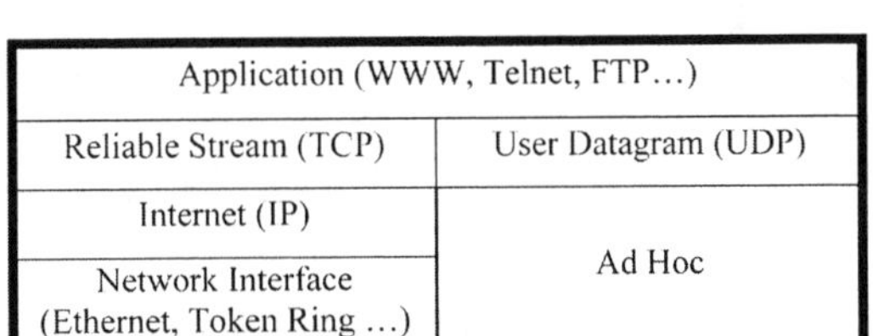

Figure 5.3: Introducing Ad Hoc routing at both layers: Network Interface and the Internet layer.

Now, the existing IP addressing scheme should be modified. Why is this important? We cannot serve the same content to high-end server and mobile phone. Facilitating us in this job is the new Microsoft .NET technology and ASP.NET Mobile controls. We'll briefly comment on them, in the last section of this chapter.

9.6. ASP.NET Mobile Controls

Mobile Controls are the building blocks for developing mobile applications. Mobile Controls are similar to the HTML Button control and Grid control in Visual Basic. Mobile Controls simplify application development by providing the capabilities that the programmer needs.

Let's see an example of a ASP.NET page which displays "Hello, World!", using mobile controls [Wireless2002] :

```
<%@ Page Inherits="System.Mobile.UI.MobilePage">
<%@ Register TagPrefix="Mobile" Namespace="System.Mobile.UI">
<Mobile:Form runat="server">
<Mobile:Label runat="server">Hello, World!</Mobile:Label>
</Mobile:Form>
```

If we compile and run the above code on the Alcatel mobile phone, we will get the following result:

Figure 6.1: WML Output

And if we compile and run the same code in Pocket IE, we will get this:

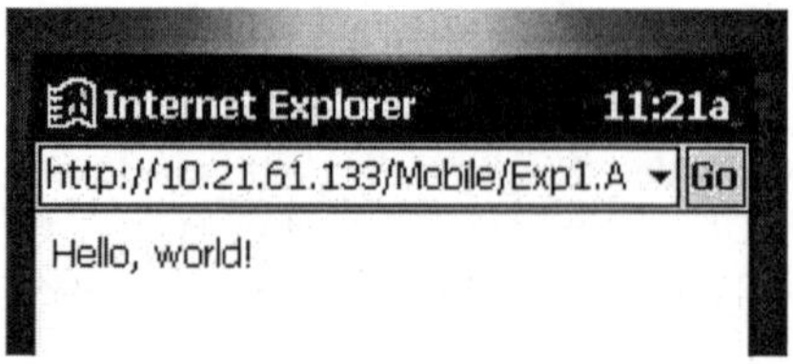

Figure 6.2: HTML Output

So, ASP.NET mobile controls generated WML code for mobile phone, and HTML code for Pocket IE. Mobile controls have the capability of detecting the browser and spooling the content they support. This gives us the capability to "develop once and serve any mobile device". And that is just what we need for the wireless Internet, isn't it?

9.7. Conclusion

In this chapter we tried to introduce the basics of Ad Hoc networking, as it can well prove to be a foundation for future mobile and wireless e-commerce applications. So, we covered the following topics:

- Existing wireless architecture
- Basic Ad Hoc routing protocols
- Security issues in Ad Hoc networks
- Wireless Ad Hoc sensor networks
- Wireless Internet
- ASP.NET Mobile Controls

No matter whether it will be Ad Hoc networks or cellular communication like GSM, whether it will be Bluetooth or Wireless LAN, this way or another, the wireless Internet is coming of age and we must be ready for it.

9.8. Problems

1. Name two types of Ad Hoc networks, and then explain the basic idea behind Ad Hoc networking.
2. Explain advantages of Ad Hoc networks compared with classic wireless networks.
3. Define on-demand routing protocols, and give at least three differences between on demand routing protocols and classic routing protocols. What are the benefits and downsides of on-demand routing protocols?
4. What is the basic idea of source routing? Why it is not feasible to use this protocol in networks with many nodes?
5. Explain Ad Hoc On Demand Distance Vector Routing algorithm. How is sequence numbering used to reflect the dynamic topology changes?
6. What are the advantages of Temporally Oriented Routing Algorithm compared to DSR and AODV? Why TORA needs external timing system?
7. Explain briefly five attributes of security. In which way is the security management different for Ad Hoc networks compared to the classic networks?
8. Comment the downsides of presented project for wireless Ad Hoc sensor network. What improvements of described environment would you propose?
9. Give general comment of how the Ad Hoc networks and the wireless Internet are related.
10. What is the main goal of ASP.NET Mobile Controls?

REFERENCES:

[BTSig2001] Bluetooth Core Specification v1.1, Bluetooth SIG, **2001**

[Miller2001] Miller,B.A, Bisdikian,C., "Bluetooth Revealed", Prentice Hall, **2001**

[IETF2001a] IETF, Manet Group, "Ad Hoc On Demand Distance Vector (AODV) Routing", **2001**

[IETF2001b] IETF, Manet Group, "The Dynamic Source Routing Protocol for Mobile Ad Hoc Networks", **2001**

[IETF2001c] IETF, Manet Group, "Temporally-Ordered Routing Algorithm (TO-RA) Version 1 Functional Specification", **2001**

[IETF2001d] IETF, Manet Group, "Landmark Routing Protocol (LANMAR) for Large Scale Ad Hoc Networks", **2001**

[Velasevic96] Velašević,D., Bojić, D., "Zbirka zadataka iz ekspertskih sistema", Elektrotehnički Fakultet, Beorad, **1996**

[Leinecker2000] R. Leinecker,R., Archer,T., "Visual C++ 6 Biblija", Mikroknjiga, Beograd, **2000**

[Microsoft2001] Microsoft Corporation, "Microsoft Developer Network Library"

[Popovic99] Dr Miodrag V Popović, "Digitalna obrada signala", Nauka, Beograd, **1999**

[Bakken2001] Stig Saether Bakken et al., "PHP Manual", **2001**

[Wireless2002] http://www.wirelessdevnet.com/

E-Business and E-Challenges
V. Milutinović and F. Patricelli (Eds.)
IOS Press, 2002

CHAPTER 10
INTERNET AUTOMATION

Goran Timotic and Veljko Milutinović

10.1 Introduction

In the last ten years the Internet has become available in almost every house and every office. In the last few years it has become available in many exotic places. Via the Internet you can now access your toaster or the 37th light on the left side of your street.

10.1.1 Why the Internet for Automation?

In the first place, Internet or intranets are everywhere. All you need to access the Internet is a computer, a phone line, and an ISP (Internet Service Provider). There are no borders, no time zones and no working hours. These facts allow great possibilities for anything you want to do remotely.

The second important characteristic of the Internet is that it is open and available. Anyone, anywhere can access the Internet quickly and inexpensively on wide range of hardware. From mainframe computers over desktop PCs to mobile phones. Mobile phones, which support the WAP (Wireless Access Protocol) protocol, are nothing else but small computers with Internet access. You are bound by your mobile phone screen size, the low speed connection, but it really works.

The Internet certainly represents an opportunity to add significant functionality to products such as vehicles, wireless devices, telecom equipment and consumer electronics, but it also exposes these products to security threats from competitors and hackers. Certain level of security is achieved, but similarly to other aspects of life, there is nothing totally secure. There are firewalls, whose main role is to detect suspicious connections and to disallow them. Nevertheless, if an unauthorized break-in succeeds, data encryption is the way to improve security, because even with the most powerful computers it is difficult to decode original data.

And finally, the most important characteristic from the aspect of Internet Automation. Only software needed on user's computer is a Java-ready browser. This means no additional costs for user, because almost every browser on the computer software market is Java-ready.

10.1.2 Usage

The first idea was probably to control specific devices at distant locations. For example, you are in your office, your workday is over and it takes you 30 minutes to drive home. Before you start you connect via the Internet to your home's air conditioning system and turn it on.

You arrive home and it is like a paradise. In addition, you can control any device that is adapted for distant control, like refrigerators, microwaves, etc. That was the example of home automation system.

Some companies have already been selling home automation systems, which include systems for home automation, home security and home management

Home automation systems include home appliances that can be accessed via the Internet, that is to say "Internet appliances".

Home security systems include fire detection and burglar alarm system.

Home management is the most interesting part of home automation systems. Imagine that, while you are at work, your refrigerator makes a list of needed food, contacts your supplier, reminds you to go to your supplier store, and on your way back from work, you just go there and get your supplies.

Building Automation has the same base and the purpose as Home Automation. To maximize the comfort of the inhabitants while minimizing energy costs. To make lighting controls, ventilation, air conditioning and security systems play together.

The same principle is used in factories. There are robot arms, CNC machines, and you want to control them remotely. You link them to the local network, that network links them to the Internet, and now you are available to control entire production process. Of course, you can also connect a single device to the Internet and control it remotely. How? This book will help you to find out.

10.1.3 Conclusion

Thanks to the Internet and the market explosion of new technologies, embedded systems are becoming smarter and more network-friendly every day.

Today's embedded systems are capable of controlling microwave oven, but tomorrow's systems might be capable of downloading recipes via the Internet or alert repair companies of product malfunction.

Remember, Internet-connected devices are not always more intelligent than stand-alone devices. In most cases, connectivity only means more intelligent device management.

10.2 Home Automation

Statistic analyzes say that for every PC shipped, about 30 toasters, watches and pagers with microprocessors inside also hit the shelves. Also, the average middle-class family home has 35 to 50 devices that contain certain type of microprocessors, even though much simpler than ones used for PC.

Predictions say that by 2003, 400 million Internet appliances will be in use, and that by 2010, all home PCs will be replaced by embedded system-based devices. In this scenario, most home offices would probably use one or more separate Internet appliances, which will either be industry-specialized or will converge many technologies (phone, fax, Internet, and TV) into one device. For more details, the interested reader is referred to [Huang98].

10.2.1 What is Home Automation?

In its most simple form Home Automation is the ability to control Lighting and Household

Appliances remotely. Almost everyone already has a limited amount of Home Automation. When was the last time you got out of your chair to change channels on the TV Set? Probably when you couldn't find the remote control!

All you have to do now is to proceed. Wouldn't it be great if with the press of a button you could turn off the main light and dim your table lamps from the comfort of your favourite armchair?

10.2.2 Typical Home Automation System

A typical home automation system consists of a house server, which is the core of the system, and devices connected to that server. You just connect to the house server via the Internet and you can control any device attached to that house server. You can adjust temperature in your house, turn on garden sprinklers or pull the blinds down. You will find much more about it further in this book.

To bring your house on the Internet you can use any of the known ways of connecting to the Internet (dial-up, leased line, ADSL, etc.). As it was already said, you are allowed to access your home automation system using desktop PC, hand held devices, mobile phones and generally speaking, using any device capable of accessing the Internet and supporting web browsers.

10.2.3 Home Networking

In order to use Internet appliances we have to link them to the Internet. Actually, we have to network the house.

There are two basic categories of communication backbones for home networks: wired and wireless.

Under the wired network category, you can network your house using ethernet, phone lines, coaxial cable or using AC power lines (standard household wiring).

Wireless platforms basically use radio frequency electromagnetic transmission as networking media. Currently, there are several standards and working groups focused on wireless networking technology (radio frequency [RF]). These include the IEEE 802.11, HomeRF, Bluetooth, and standard wireless access protocol (SWAP). Wireless-based transport element technology can be used to distribute multiple types of information within the home. Some examples use a discrete controller device, some a PC as a controller device, and others no controller device at all (i.e., peer to peer). Wireless RF transmission is probably the best choice for home networking because of its flexibility, mobility, and ability to network without wired connections.

In the Figure 2.1 you can see a comparison of different home-networking technologies.

	Ethernet	Cable	Phoneline	Powerline	Wireless RF
Data Rate (Mpbs)	10/100	100/800	1-2/10	<1-2	1-10
New Wire?	Yes	Yes	No	No	No
Security	Medium	Medium	Medium	Low	High
Noise/Interference	Low	Low	Medium	High	Medium
HWInstall cost	Low/medium	High	Low	Medium	High
Standards	IEEE	IEEE	HPNA, etc	X10, CEBus	Bluetooth

Figure 2.1 A comparison of different home networking technologies and platforms [Huang98].

You can see that all of them dispose with different capabilities in the sense of data transfer rate. The biggest data transfer rate can be achieved with coaxial cable, while the others are significantly slower. It is not too important for home networking, because big data transfer rate are not needed for home appliances, but that is not case in factory environments, where we have to take care about that.

Some of those technologies, such as the Ethernet and coaxial cable, require building of new infrastructure, while others such as phone-line and power-line technologies use existing infrastructure in the house.

Security varies from platform to platform, same as influence of noise and interference.

You may notice that installing costs depend on whether the platform requires building of new infrastructure or the existing infrastructure can be used.

Next few sections are dedicated to different home networking technologies and to their specifics.

10.2.3.1 Wired – Ethernet

The Ethernet, is based on the IEEE 802.3 standard. It uses twisted Copper-pair or coaxial

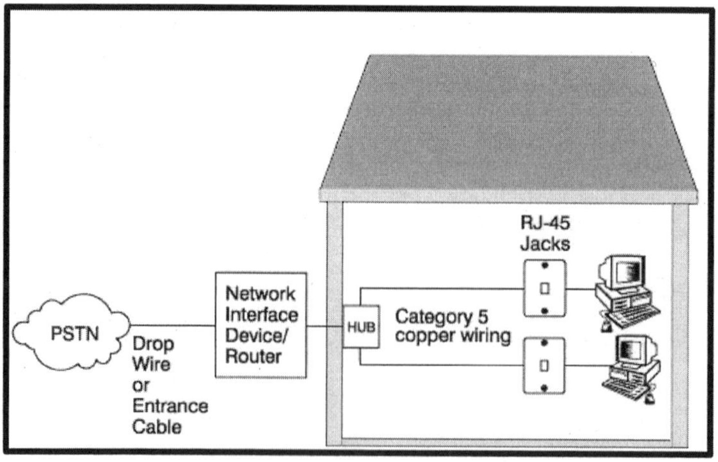

Legend: PSTN - Public Switched Telephone Network.

Figure 2.2 Typical topology of an Ethernet home networking system [Huang98].

wires. Data transport is bi-directional and highly reliable. It is interoperable between different manufacturers. Therefore, the Ethernet is widely used among businesses as the standard choice of networking office PCs and peripherals. However, they require the use of bulky CAT 5 cabling with RJ-45 Ethernet jacket, and typically expensive to install, particularly in the home environment, but that is the price that must be paid for the quoted benefits. The typical topology of those systems is demonstrated in Figure 2.2.

10.2.3.2 Wired – Phone Line

The phone-line based technology uses the existing phone wiring found in every home today. However, selection of signal characteristics for data transport over this medium is critical to resist interference from other shared devices, such as answering and faxing machines, modems, telephones, and data transport devices like ISDN and DSL equipment that uses the line simultaneously. The typical topology of these systems is demonstrated in Figure 2.3.

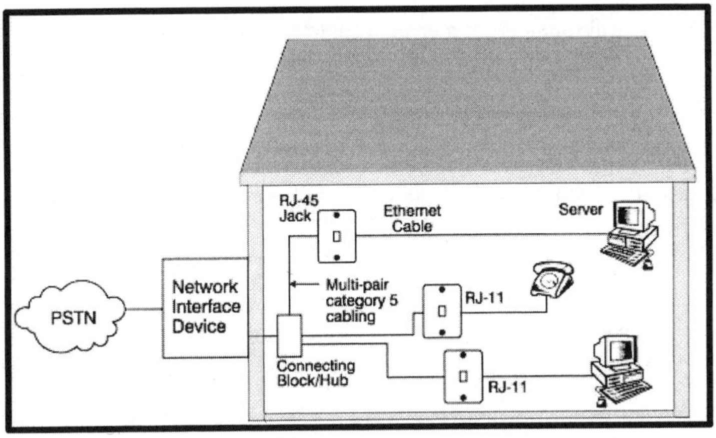

Legend: PSTN - Public Switched Telephone Network.

Figure 2.3 Typical topology of a phone line home networking system [Huang98].

10.2.3.3 Wired – Coaxial TV Cable

The same type of cable used for cable TV transmission is used for coaxial cable home networking systems. A coaxial TV cable has long-distance capability and it is a reliable medium for data transport. It is bi-directional and uses wires such as CAT 5 and RG-6 coaxial cables. Such a system requires a combination of coaxial cable and twisted pair to allow PC to PC communication. Currently, there is no system allows PC to PC communication using only coaxial cable. A major problem for distributing data through the home is termination, since those cables are often terminated near TVs and there is no cable in each room as phone lines and power-lines.

Lastly, such a system requires pre-planning with homeowners, builders, or developers, because the system is limited to network access by well-placed jack locations. Any post-installation for additional access locations has very limited success and flexibility without surface wiring and jack installation, and most importantly, presents considerable additional expense for homeowners. The typical topology of those systems is demonstrated in Figure 2.4.

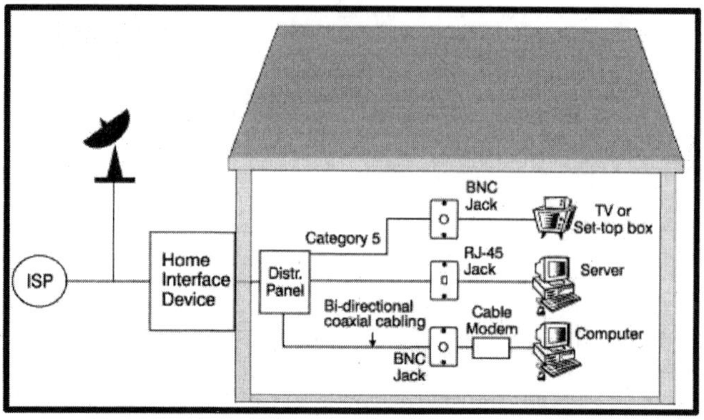

Legend: ISP - Internet Service Provider.

Figure 2.4 Typical topology of a coaxial cable home networking system [Huang98].

10.2.3.4 Wired – AC Power Lines

Alternative current (AC) power lines are readily available as network transport conduit throughout a home, even more than phone lines, because building codes in the U.S. and Europe specify a power outlet at every few meters. The advantage of this route into and through the home is that there is an installed base to some degree, since most of the home-automation schemes have used the power line to link appliances and electronic devices to some central control point. For example, they are used as transport facilities to send and receive discrete frequency-based control, monitoring, and communications messages to home smart devices that manage lighting (e.g., turn-off, turn-on and dim) and environment systems. However, such systems transport signals at a very low data rate - few achieve much more that. In recent years, they have been used as voice-communication media for telephone extensions, computer-modem access and intercom devices through standard electric outlets. But still, for any application requiring higher data rates this can be challenges. The typical topology of those systems is demonstrated in Figure 2.5.

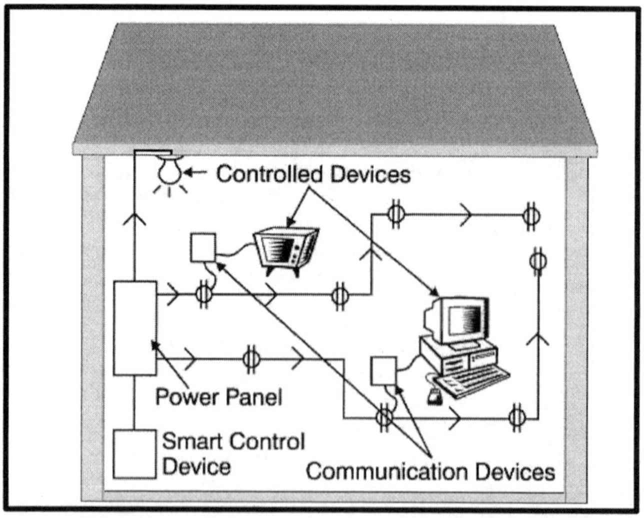

Figure 2.5 Typical topology of a power line home networking system [Huang98].

10.2.3.5 Wireless - The PC–Centric

Some software and hardware suppliers provide home-networking solutions via a wireless LAN. They use the home's PC as the central control element. Figure 2.6 reflects a wireless home LAN configuration in which one PC acts as a master to the network. It provides network addressing and routing between the home and the Internet.

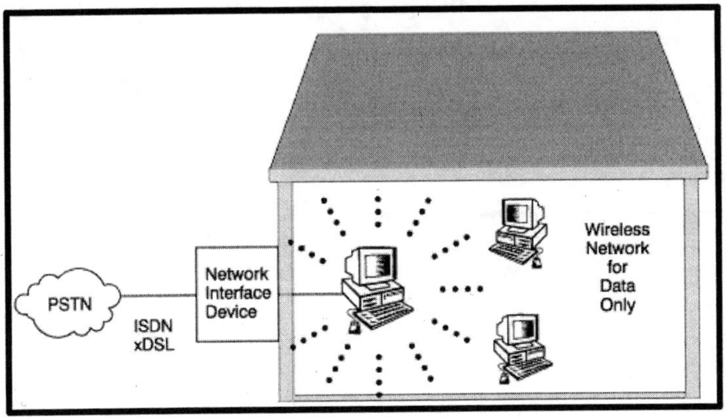

Legend: ISDN – Integrated Services Digital Network
DSL – Digital Subscriber Line

Figure 2.6 Typical topology of a PC centric home networking system [Huang98].

Home network built around a master PC implies that the PC will always be on and available for communications. It also implies that no other software or hardware application running on the PC can interfere with its ability to perform its communications tasks.

10.2.3.6 The Controller-Based

Figure 2.7 demonstrates the use of one integrated home-network system available on the market today.

In this scenario, the microprocessor-based digital switch acts as the communications server, addressing and routing voice data traffic throughout the home. It also sends the home network–transport element through a powerful on-board RF transceiver. The transceiver is based on patented digital spread-spectrum technology and has an effective reach of several hundred meters from the home.

The controller shown in Figure 2.7 supplies a robust home network for voice and data with high bandwidth capacity. It is the bridge between the transport network element serving the home from the customer-selected service provider and the wireless home network. Networked devices require no wires or fixed wired jacks. This system also offers several hundred meters of accessibility within and outside the home. There are no relocation restrictions.

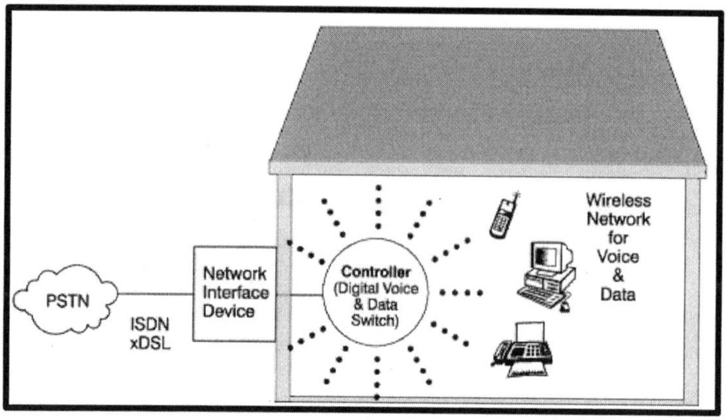

Legend: ISDN – Integrated Services Digital Network
DSL – Digital Subscriber Line

Figure 2.7 Typical topology of a controller-based home networking system [Huang98].

10.2.3.7 Wireless – Transmission Radios

Wireless RF platform basically uses radio frequency (300-900 MHz UHF, 2.4 GHz, and 5 GHz) electromagnetic transmission as the networking media. Most of wireless RF home networking systems employ spread-spectrum technology, which offers high bandwidth capacity and is used widely in the military because of its security and reliability. Two types of spread-spectrum radios are in practical use today. One is so-called "frequency-hopping spread-spectrum" or FHSS, a narrow-band carrier with changing patterns of transmission that are recognized by both receivers and transmitters. When the two devices are in synch, they produce one logical communications channel. The other is the "direct-sequence spread-spectrum" or DSSS radio, which produces bit patterns called chips or chipping codes with its reliability relying on the length of the chipping code or on how many bits of data it carries. Because particular error-correction codes (ECC) are built into radio, it is not necessary to retransmit data, even though detected with recoverable errors, thus greatly improving performance.

10.2.4 HES

The *Home Electronic System* (HES) is a standard under development by a formal Working Group sanctioned by the ISO (International Organization for Standardization) and the IEC (International Electrotechnical Commission) of Geneva, Switzerland. For more details, the interested reader is referred to [Wacks98].

Primary goal of HES is to specify hardware and software so that a manufacturer might offer one version of a product that could operate on a variety of home automation networks. To accomplish this, the Working Group is specifying the following components for HES:

- Universal Interface: An interface module to be incorporated into an appliance for communicating over a variety of home automation networks.
- Command Language: A language for appliance-to-appliance communications independent of which network carries the messages.
- HomeGate: A residential gateway to link home control networks with external service provider networks.

The HES Working Group is also chartered to investigate applications of networks for command, control, and communications in commercial and mixed-use buildings. Mixed-use buildings may be apartment houses with retail shops and offices, as is common in Europe.

10.2.5 X-10

In this section, we will bring some basic information about X-10, which is most commonly used standard for home networking. With regard to the fact that the X-10 uses power lines for networking, we will discuss benefits and downsides of this approach. For more details, the interested reader is referred to [Cooper98].

10.2.5.1 What is X-10?

X-10 is a communications protocol for remote control of electrical devices. It is designed for communications between X-10 transmitters and X-10 receivers, which communicate on standard household wiring. Just plug transmitters and receivers into standard electrical outlets and the system is operative.

10.2.5.2 Transmitters

The simplest X10 transmitter is a small control box with buttons. The buttons select which unit is to be controlled, and which control function is to be sent to the selected units (e.g. "turn on", "all units off", etc). There are also clock timer transmitters, which can be programmed to send X-10 commands at certain times. Some of these can be programmed with buttons on the timer; some must be connected to a computer to select the times. There are other special purpose transmitters that send certain X-10 commands at sunup or sundown, upon detecting movement, or as commanded by tones over a telephone.

10.2.5.3 Receivers

The simplest X10 receiver is a small module with an electrical plug (to connect to a standard wall outlet), an electrical outlet (to provide controlled power to the device it's controlling) and two dials (to set the unit ID code) on it. An appliance module has relay inside which switches power to its outlet on or off in response to X-10 commands directed to it. A lamp module is similar, but has a triac instead of a relay and will respond to dimming commands as well as on or off commands. Other receivers can be wired into wall outlets or into lamp fixtures. Note that the standard wall switch is a receiver, not a transmitter; it does not transmit X-10 commands, and only takes action when it receives the appropriate X-10 command or local button-push.

10.2.5.4 Functioning

The functioning principle is simple. Transmitter sends commands such as "turn on", "turn off" or "dim" preceded by the identification unit to be controlled. Receiver units listen for messages and react upon identification of its ID. Receivers ignore commands not addressed to them.

X-10 specifies 256 different addresses, so you can control 256 different devices. In effect, you can control much more than 256, by setting some of them to the same IDs. When set on the same ID, multiple devices are controlled in parallel, and react to the single message.

Naturally, there are several ways to connect your computer to X-10. The easiest way of giving your computer some control over X-10 modules is via the CP290 Home Control Interface. This is a small box that connects to a standard RS-232 serial port and has its own internal battery backed up by seven-day clock. It is sold with software to work with a PC, Mac, Apple, or Commodore 64/128, and comes with the appropriate serial cable (the CP290 box itself is the same for all). Once you set up to 128 events (on, off, dim) using your computer, you can turn off the computer and the box will transmit scheduled X-10 commands on a daily or weekly schedule. The CP290 also has an "immediate" mode to send X-10 commands from the computer to X-10 receivers.

There are also other X-10 modules to interface computers directly to the power line to send and/or receive X-10 commands. One of them is the TW523, which is able to send and receive commands.

The TW523 is a low level two-way interface to the power line. It contains a PIC controller to decode incoming signals and store them for transmission to the host computer. It's essentially a 120KHz modulator and demodulator, with just enough smarts to recognize a valid X-10 command code. The computer interfaces to the TW523 through an RJ-11 modular phone jack.

10.2.5.5 Why Use the Power Line for Home Networking?

In the first place, there is no need to make new infrastructure. Every house has power lines. Standard electrical outlets are located every 3m in most homes.

Because its ubiquity and high number of access points, cost advantages over phone lines are significant.

The low silicon cost of power line modems and their peripheral circuitry gives the power line strong cost advantages over Radio Frequency Networking.

10.2.5.6 Technical Power Line Communications Problems

The power line is an extremely hostile communications medium. Electrical appliances introduce a variety of interference onto the power line, including noise, pulses, spikes, and Continuous Wave (CW) interference. As a communication media the power line introduces several major engineering problems, as detailed below:

- **Phase coupling:** American homes have two phase coupling, and European homes have three phase coupling. Since network users do not care in which electrical phase their device is plugged, cross phase power line networking must be guaranteed by the robustness of the power line modem. The problem of cross-phase communications is solved using high frequency signals, which are coupled between electrical wires.
- **Frequency response:** each electrical device that is connected to the power line has a different effect, and every house differs in number of used electric devices and the power line infrastructure, thus causing a random frequency response that varies frequently. In order to overcome these problems, we use spread spectrum technique, which uses differential modulation (DCSK).

10.2.5.7 What Applications Can Be Run Over the Power Line?

The residential power line can be used to network all tethered electrical devices. Applications include:

- Shared Internet Access through Power Line extensions of CABLE, xDSL, and POTS modems.
- File Sharing in Multiple PC Homes
- Remote Peripherals: Printers, Scanners, Fax, especially when these peripherals are connected through the USB port
- IP Telephony from 'Fat Pipe': Extensions of IP and other forms of Cable modem telephony from set-top boxes to telephones around the house.
- Power Line Audio Systems: Remote deployment of speakers playing PC based music
- Ethernet Power Line Networking Modules
- Home Automation

10.2.6 The Future of Home Networking

The home is the center of a convergence of competing technologies, architectures, and suppliers. Each of them has a unique set of advantages and solutions. Systems are being researched, developed, and deployed to manage, monitor, and control the following list of functions:

- Data and voice communication electronic entertainment devices
- Service appliances that prepare food
- Service appliances that maintain the home appearance
- Systems and devices that maintain the in-home environment
- Devices that keep the home secure from intrusion or damage from internal and external man-made or natural events

A home-network system provider must develop a system with all mentioned capabilities, to make it successful. A central controller of that system must be capable of capturing home-network events and of reacting.

The market, or, more precisely, homeowner's need for flexibility and mobility, dictates that the home network transport medium of the future will be wireless. It means that the high cost and inconvenience of wire-based installations will be avoided.

In addition, consumers will require a system that manages everything within the home, including voice, data, and appliances. Wireless technology will provide necessary convenience, simplicity, and long-term cost savings.

10.3 The Internet Home

The presentation that follows is based on the reference [Cisco01]. The Internet Home is a partnership between Cisco Systems and the Laing Homes construction company. They have designed home for a hypothetical couple with three children, and the have equipped it with all needed appliances that are, naturally, controlled via the Internet. This house has been set up to showcase technologies that are already available and will become a norm in the new millenium. From the exterior, it is normal house, as you can see in Figure 3.2, but the interion is another story.

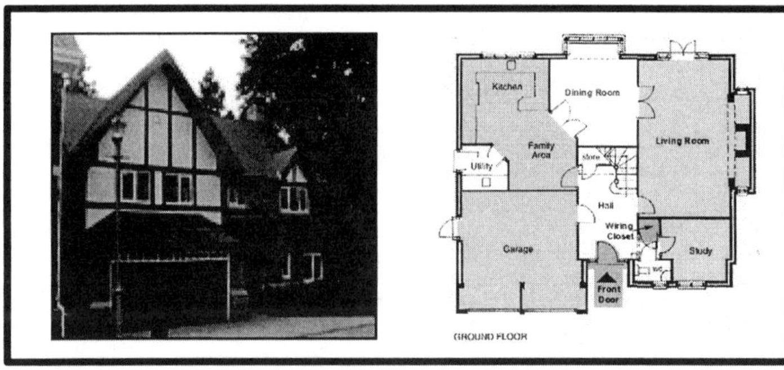

Figure 3.1 The Internet Home and its floor plan [Cisco01].

The Internet Home is equipped with Hometronic system. Hometronic is Honeywell's wireless home comfort technology. Its function is to control all of the heating, plus some of the lighting, small appliances and garden sprinklers. System contains a number of intelligent modules that communicate with Hometronic Manager module.

The house is equipped with a dozen of Hometronic devices. Some of them will be presented in the following text.

The core of the system is the Hometronic Manager (HCM 200). HCM 200, as you can see in Figure 3.2, is interactive central unit for time and energy control. It is capable of monitoring up to 16 consumption measuring devices, and of controlling up to 16 temperature zones as well as of controlling up to 32 modules for light.

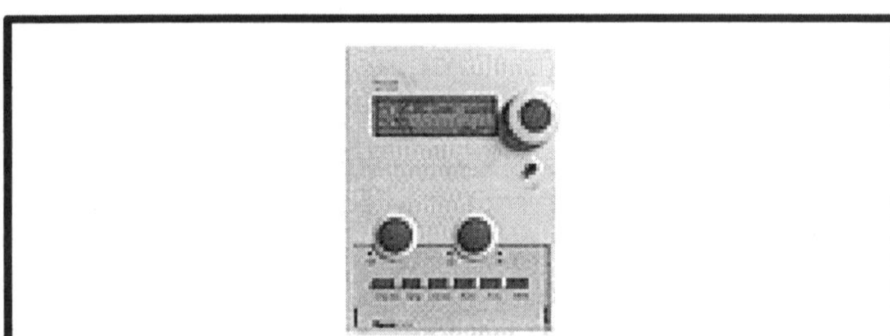

Figure 3.2 HCM 200 – The Hometronic Manager [Cisco01].

Hometronic radiator controller with battery-operated servomotor is used for continuous control of the room temperature. Figure 3.3a

Hometronic Room Module, which monitors the current room temperature and sets desired temperature. Figure 3.3b

Hometronic Light Module, which control indoors and outdoors light sources. Figure 3.3c

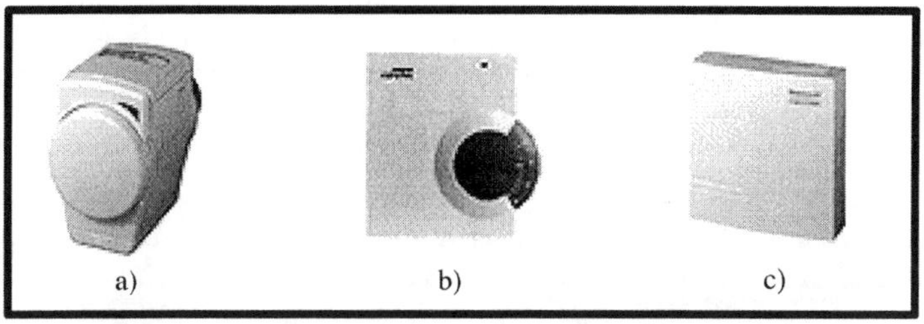

Figure 3.3 a) Hometronic Radiator Controller [Cisco01]
b) Hometronic Room Module [Cisco01]
c) Hometronic Light Module [Cisco01]

Hometronic Brightness Sensor is a very interesting part of this system. It monitors the brightness of the sun and transmits the values to the Hometronic Manager. Why is that so important? Let's assume that in your conservatory there are some sensitive plants, whoch don't like too much sunlight. Blinds are pulled down automatically upon Brightness Sensor signals. Figure 3.4a.

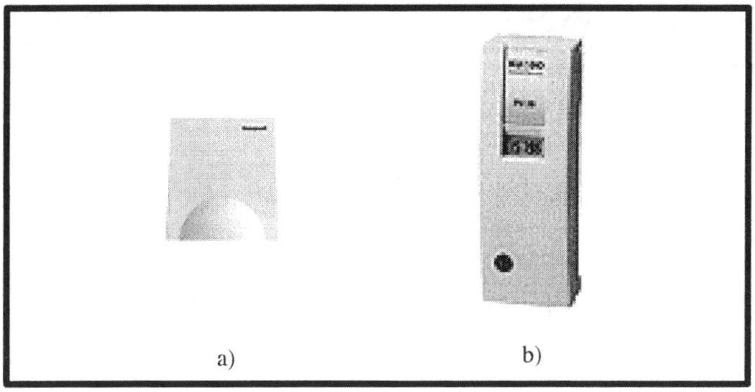

Figure 3.4 a) Hometronic Brightness Sensor [Cisco01]
b) Consumption Data Monitoring Device [Cisco01]

The last device that is presented is Consumption data monitoring device, which monitors the consumption of the heat, water, and gas and transmits values to the Hometronic Manager. Figure 3.4b.

You can adjust your lighting inside the house using a PC, a web-pad or the Internet. The same counts for heating. Generally, all devices connected to any of the mentioned Hometronic devices could be controlled using a PC, a web-pad or via the Internet.

Now, something more about the software for the control of those devices. A company named Perception in close co-operation with Honeywell, Polaris and Axis has developed an interface for remote control and monitoring of the Internet Home.

The software could be set up on many different profiles, depending on your habits, needs, etc. There are several usual profiles, such as evening, waking up, party, etc.

Using profiles you can have the temperature in each room suit its use at particular time of the day. The rooms you do not use at that time remain at a lower temperature, saving energy and your money. For example, in the morning, before you go to work, you do not use living room and there is no need to warm it up.

Certainly, security is one of the most important aspects of these systems. In this system, security is controlled through the interface. You input your access code, and you can arm or disarm your house or different areas of the house. You dispose with web cameras, which you can use to check who is standing at your front door, wherever you are in the world. In this system you can use four cameras, so besides front door camera, there are other three to use in other areas of the house.

There are four basic interface's looks. In Figure 3.5 you may see one of them.

Figure 3.1 Classic interface look and feel [Cisco01].

In the top left corner of the interface is the control of alarm system. You must input access code in order to control alarm system of the home. You are able to arm or disarm the whole house or certain areas of the house.

In the bottom left corner are camera views and in the middle is overview of the status of the whole house.

The right side of the interface is for the control of heating and lighting as well as for setting profiles.

10.4 Industrial Automation

As we have already said, the same principle that is used in home automation, is also used in factory automation. The factory environment is more inhospitable than home environment, in the first place in the sense of networking (noise, interference, etc.), but all experience from home automation may be used for making a system for remote control of factories using the Internet.

10.4.1 The Motives

There are many reasons to control factories remotely. In the first place, a manager or owner is not enforced to be present at all times in the factory. Via the Internet, wherever you are in the world, you can check the production process status, or how many employees are currently on their workplaces.

Do not forget difficult working conditions. Imagine that you are an owner of a plant that produces compact disc mediums. A production process needs sand and the best location you have is somewhere in the deserts of Africa. You need to minimize a number of workers, because you have to reduce accommodation and water expenses. The most suitable system to use is remote control via the Internet, because all the management and control personnel can be placed hundreds of kilometers away.

The same goes for factories that use toxic materials in their production process. There is no reason to expose workers to risk, when they are able to carry on the job from safe distance.

Finally, from the owners' point of view, cheaper labor means bigger profit, thus it is reasonable to locate factories in the parts of this planet where labor is cheaper. Naturally, owners do not want to move away, and now they may use the Internet to control their factories.

10.4.2 The Principle

A typical Internet automation system looks as the system in the Figure 4.1. On the left side of the picture is a client, connected through the Internet Service Provider to factory server (in the middle of the picture). The factory server is the core of the factory side of the system. It receives commands and queries from the client, forwards them to the local network and returns back to the client requested data from the machines or the management back to the client.

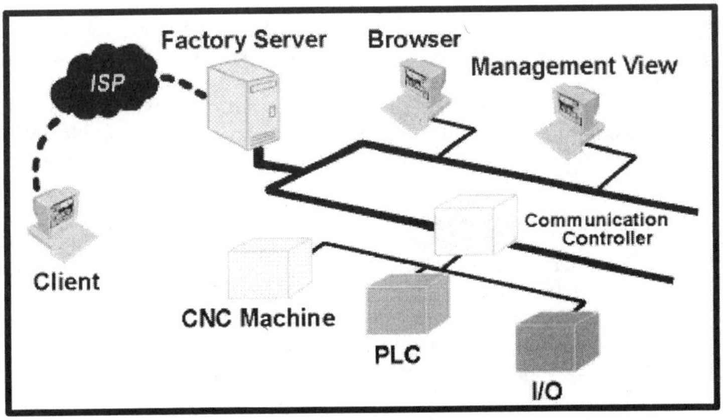

Legend: **CNC** - Computer Numerically Controlled
PLC – Programmable Logical Controller

Figure 4.1 Typical industrial automation system.

10.4.3 Network Enabling Industrial Automation

Many Industrial Automation networks started with simple RS-232 and RS-485 serial connections. Over the years, manufacturers enhanced their designs by developing their own media, protocols and hardware to meet the industry's reliability, topology, and determinism requirements.

This mixture of media, protocols and hardware plays a major role in today's installations. Their evolution has created problems of interoperability. As a result, the integration of networks and information today is often very complex and expensive.

Unlike information networks, industrial control networks place a greater burden on the designers of system components. An industrial control network requires fast and guaranteed (deterministic) throughput to effectively control machines and manufacturing processes. Additionally, some industrial environments require a greater level of performance due to the elevated levels of noise and contaminants common to those installations.

As the popularity of 100 Mb (Fast) Ethernet increases and component costs decrease, the use of Ethernet for control applications becomes increasingly attractive.

However, there are significant hurdles to overcome when using Ethernet in industrial environments. These can be grouped into two categories: Performance and Materials.

From a performance perspective, cables designed for higher-speed communications don't always translate into higher data rates in industrial environments. Due to operating conditions, it's more important to optimize the entire communications channel to yield the maximum possible throughput.

When choosing Materials, office-quality Ethernet products may not be suitable for use in some of the harsher industrial environments. In some instances, cable connector and component construction may need to be modified or optimized for use in some of the more extreme applications.

Additionally, many network and component designs may not be adequate for the high noise levels common to these environments.

10.5 Implementation

There are two basic approaches to build the system. Naturally, an investor may combine different approaches in order to obtain the best solution possible.

The simplest way is to buy some of "ready-to-use solutions", which are offered by several companies. Their solutions include all needed hardware, software and technical support. The companies selling those systems are responsible for installing and maintenance, as well as for training of customers' employees.

What do we get with "ready-to-use solutions"? Firstly, a relatively short time span between planning and implementation. This may be very useful when we need short time-to-market for our product, when we want to beat the competition.

With regard to the fact that "ready-to-use solutions" are complete systems and that they are tested, we may say that they are reliable.

Also, a very important fact is that companies, which make those systems, provide technical support for their customers. When the things go wrong, it is very important.

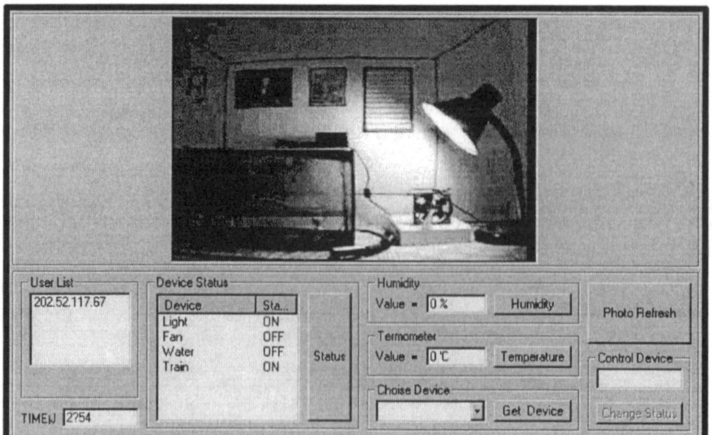

Figure 5.1 An interface of system for remote monitoring and remote control of temperature and humidity using ActiveX

Naturally, this way has several downsides. One of them is that such system is never a hundred percent customizable. Either the system does not do everything we want, or some resources are unused.

The second approach is "do it yourself". You may buy the hardware and develop the software by yourself. You can develop the hardware and buy the software, or develop it all by yourself. Which way you will choose depends on your capabilities for developing hardware and software, the money and the time you dispose of, and many more factors. Most of the factors will be discussed in this book.

The first advantage of "do it yourself" approach is that the system is a hundred percent customizable and adaptable. Obviously, this is true only if the system is well designed and made.

Those systems usually have good price/quality ratio. This is not true in all cases. First of all, if we need one or two remotely controlled devices, it is not worth it. In that case the first approach is better choice. If a lot of devices need to be controlled, the second way is better, and the price/quality ratio becomes better.

As you all know, development of new software and especially new hardware is a way full of misses, bugs and errors. Development time may exceed the time allocated to the project. The same thing is with your budget.

There is one more crossroad - whether to base controlled system on PCs or to base controlled system on embedded systems.

If is remote system based on a PC platform, we have easy purchase of software and hardware versus unused resources and an expensive solution.

On the other hand, in the case of embedded system based platform, we get the system that completely fits the purpose, naturally, if it is well designed and made. The operation of that system is reliable, the size is smaller and the price per unit is lower.

The development may take a long time, but that is the price that must be paid for the quoted benefits.

10.5.1 Microcontrollers

Most appliances don't need powerful processors, such as Intel's Pentium II or Pentium III to do their work. Often, relatively slow processors satisfy the requirements.

Intel has been the first manufacturer that made a small on-chip processor, with I/O capabilities. Highly integrated chipsets include all or most parts needed for the controller. The most important thing is that microcontrollers drastically reduce design cost.

In Figure 5.1 you may see that the market require several billions of microcontroller units per year, and demand keeps growing.

Figure 5.2 shows how much the microcontroller market is worth and Figure 5.3 shows some popular microcontrollers and their producers.

	'95	'96	'97	'98	'99	'00
4-bit	1100	1100	1096	1064	1025	970
8-bit	1803	2123	2374	2556	2681	2700
16-bit	157	227	313	419	501	585

Figure 5.1 Worldwide microcontroller shipments (in billions) [Esacademy00].

	'95	'96	'97	'98	'99	'00
4-bit	1826	1849	1881	1856	1816	1757
8-bit	5634	6553	7529	8423	9219	9715
16-bit	1170	1628	2191	2969	3678	4405

Figure 5.2 Worldwide microcontroller shipments (in millions of dollars) [Esacademy00].

Big part of the microcontroller market is occupied with PIC microcontrollers by MicroChip. The company's focus is on products that meet the needs of the embedded control market. Different families of its microcontrollers contains additional features such as A/D converter, LCD Driver, Analogue Comparator, etc. It gives you great possibilities for fast time to market, and it allows you to easily serialize the product. Of course, there is less risk, since the same device is used for development as well as for production.

PIC micro devices are grouped in several families by the size of the instruction word. The three current families are Base-Line (12-bit), Mid-Range (14-bit) and High-End (16-bit).

For more details, the interested reader is referred to [MicroChip01].

Producer	Microcontroller (or microcontroller family)
Intel	8048, 8051, 80186, 80188, 80386 EX
Motorola	MC14500, 68HC05, 68HC11, 683xx
MicroChip	PIC Families
National Semiconductor	COP400 Family, COP800 Family, HPC Family, Project Piranha
Texas Instruments	TMS370
Zilog	Z8
Hitachi	HD64180

Figure 5.3 Popular microcontrollers and their producers

PIC micro devices are grouped in several families by the size of the instruction word. The three current families are Base-Line (12-bit), Mid-Range (14-bit) and High-End (16-bit).

10.6 Embedded Internet

An idea. Integrate embedded systems and the Internet and you get Embedded Internet.

A key to development of embedded Internet and to development of embedded connectivity is the infrastructure. Most workplaces have Ethernet networks to plug devices into. In homes, power lines and phone line media are available. You no longer need to provide end-to-end path between devices and a control server; you can just hook the device into infrastructure. In environments lacking an infrastructure, wireless technology can solve most problems. You can now access connectivity for embedded devices with little additional costs.

10.6.1 Definitions

Firstly, we will bring some definitions that are required for thorough understanding of Embedded Internet.

10.6.1.1 Client

Let us start from the definition of an ordinary client. A Client is a logical entity that initiates a request for data or a request for an action. It is dependent upon presence of associated server to perform requests. A Client may refer to client software, client hardware or combination used to implement logical client. It is designed to communicate with servers using the Hypertext Transfer Protocol (HTTP).

10.6.1.2 Server

A Server is complementary logical entity to a client. It listens for client data requests and services those requests. Server may refer to server software, server hardware, or combination used to implement logical server. It is also designed to communicate with clients using HTTP.

10.6.1.3 HTTP

Hypertext Transfer Protocol (HTTP) is a data communication protocol that specifies how client and server communicate, and define handshaking that takes place between a client and a server.

10.6.1.4 HTML

Hypertext Markup Language is human-readable file syntax designed to convey hypertext documents across networks.

10.6.1.5 Browser

Lastly, browser definition. A browser is HTTP client software program, which interacts with HTTP server to access and display documents.

10.6.2 Functioning principle

Figure 6.1 shows how it works. Practically, we are connected directly to the device. Now, we will consider a typical HTML/HTTP transaction scenario. User, more precisely HTTP

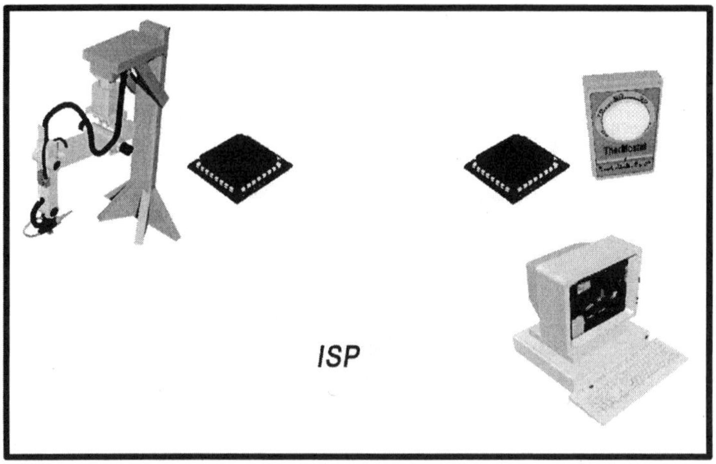

Figure 6.1 Functioning principle of an Embedded Internet System

Client, submits request to HTTP Server, through the browser and the Internet. Transaction block diagram is presented in Figure 6.2.

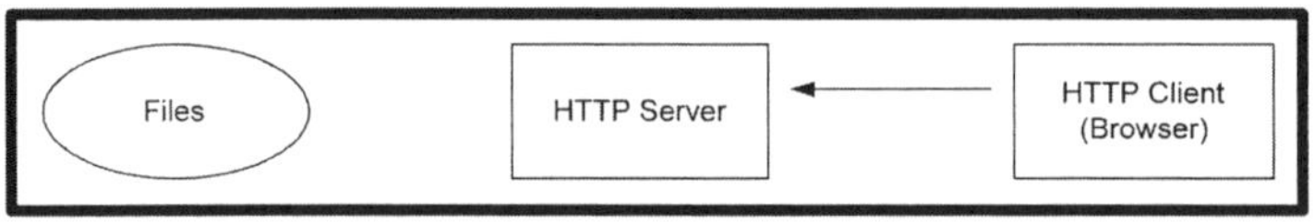

Comment: User submits request (through browser) to HTTP server

Figure 6.2 Typical HTTP/HTML transaction scenario.

HTTP Server accepts request and challenges for user name and password. Of course, this is user identification transaction scenario and it is optional. Figure 6.3.

Then user responds with correct user name and password, and it is showed in Figure 6.4.

Now server fetches requested data file from disk. You may see it in Figure 6.5.

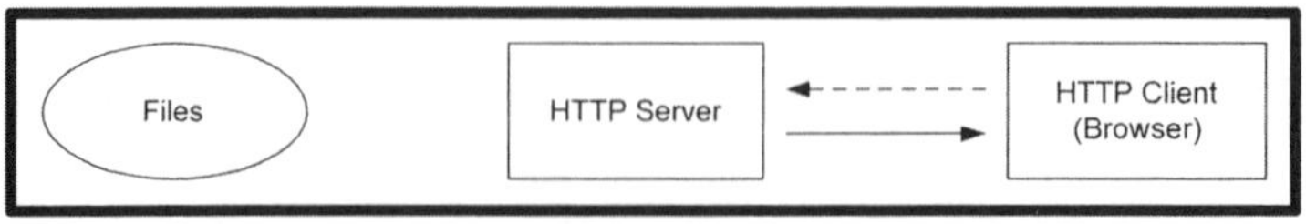

Comment: Server challenges client for username/password

Figure 6.3 Typical HTTP/HTML transaction scenario.

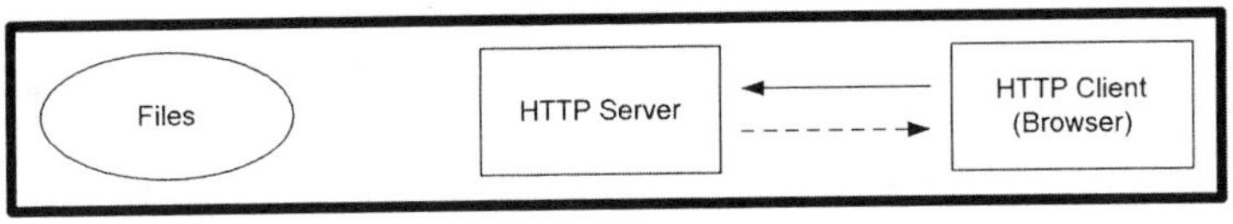

Comment: User responds with valid username/password

Figure 6.4 Typical HTTP/HTML transaction scenario.

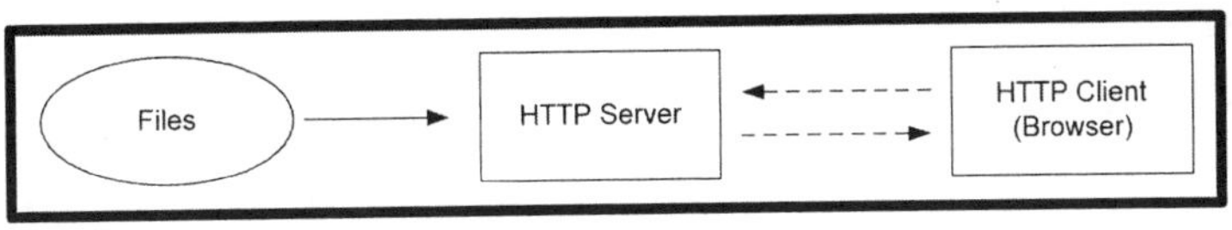

Comment: Server fetches requested data file from disk (or internal memory)

Figure 6.5 Typical HTTP/HTML transaction scenario.

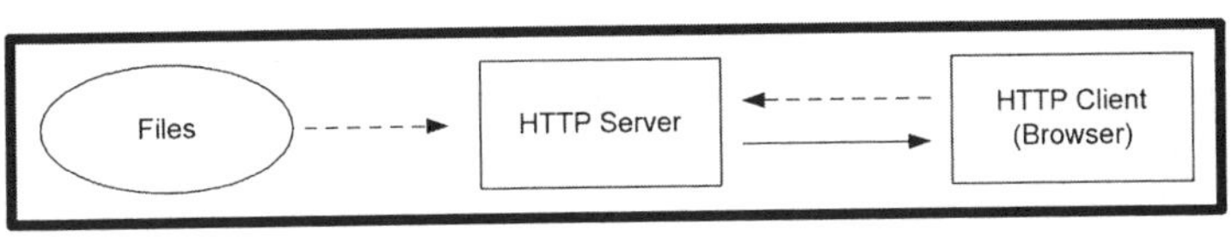

Comment: Requested data file transmitted to client computer where it is displayed by browser software.

Figure 6.6 Typical HTTP/HTML transaction scenario.

At last the server transmits it to client computer where it is displayed by browser software.

What are web servers? Firstly, web servers are usually general purpose workstations. It is often high-end hardware designed for server applications, using non real-time operating systems. Server programs are large and complex, but it is designed to be run on PC's and other general-purpose workstations under Unix, Windows or some other operating system. Nevertheless, web browsers and their basic functions are identical across big range of hardware and operating systems. That fact allows great flexibility and portability. Of course, different browsers give different capabilities. Some of them are more, and some are less advanced.

What modifications need to be done in order to get an embedded real-time environment? Firstly, in the field of hardware. Server hardware isn't general purpose workstation than an embedded processor. Naturally, we have to make a leap from general purpose operating system to a real-time operating system. Server software is no longer usual server software but a real-time embedded software. We have to add interface to real-time command and control software subsystem in order to control hardware sensors, actuators and other complex devices in real-time. An important fact is that client environment remains unchanged, because real-time performances are not needed for browsing. All of these facts leverage existing browsers and GUI tools.

Figure 6.7 shows resulting configuration of an embedded real-time environment. On the right side there is a user, in the middle is embedded processor that encapsulates an HTTP embedded web server and real-time command and control. That embedded processor fetches data files from file storage medium (hard disk or something else), and controls devices attached to it.

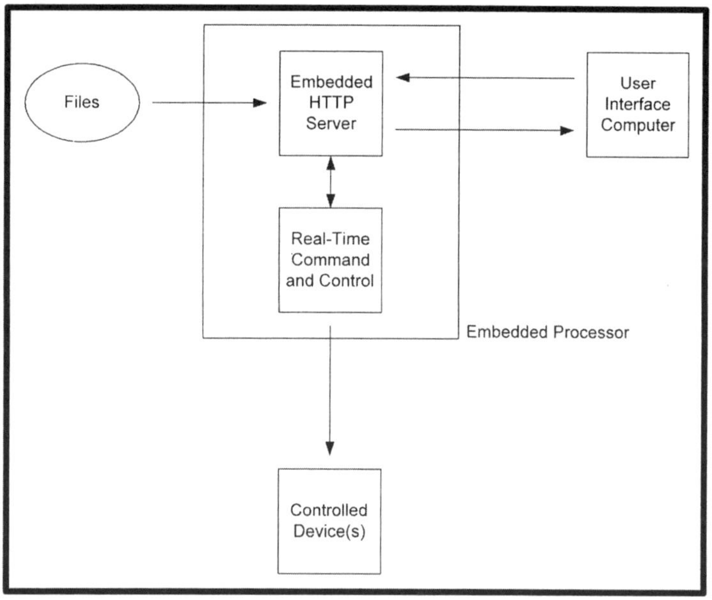

Figure 6.7 Embedded real-time environment resulting configuration.

10.6.3 What conclusion have we made so far?

For embedded Internet we do not need ordinary microcontrollers. We require some additional features such as TCP/IP protocol stack and an embedded HTTP server. The function of a TCP/IP protocol stack is to provide communication with the rest of the world. The HTTP server contains HTML or XML or Java web pages that are served to any client that supports a web browser.

From the end user's point of view this way of remote control is very appropriate. Web browsers are widespread and almost everybody is familiar with them. It also means lower training costs for employers.

Maintenance costs are probably one of the most important factors, when we choose between several technologies. In the case of microcontroller implementation of an automation system, maintenance is low cost and simpler. All software is in the networked microcontroller. Code in any networked desktop can be updated from any browser, of course, with the appropriate secure shell.

10.6.4 Browser

The web browser has become the universal GUI. The browser is platform independent. It is easy to use and easy to understand. The staff needs minimal training. The browser itself formats and presents the data. Various types of pages can be served to the client (HTML, XML, ASP, PHP, Java, and Java Script.)

There are two types of browser pages: Informational pages and Dynamic pages. Informational pages present static data to the browser. This type is mostly used to provide help or display some static data.

Dynamic pages are pages that accept input from the operator and provide feedback on the status of an embedded system.

Figure 6.8 An example of dynamic web page.

10.6.5 TCP/IP

TCP/IP is a set of protocols developed to allow cooperating computers to share resources across a network. It is widely deployed standard, which lets you to connect and control devices and communicate with software on almost every operating system and over most transport media. TCP/IP was developed by a community of researchers centered around the ARPAnet.

As we have already said, TCP/IP is a family of protocols. A few provide "low-level" functions needed for many applications. These include IP, TCP, and UDP (These will be described in more detail later.) Others are protocols for doing specific tasks, e.g. transferring files between computers, sending mail, or finding out who is logged in on another computer. The most important "traditional" TCP/IP services are:

- FTP - File Transfer Protocol allows user on any computer to get files from another computer, or to send files to another computer. Security is handled by requiring the user to specify a user name and password for the other computer.
- TELNET - The network terminal allows a user to log in on any other computer on the network.
- SMTP – Simple Mail Transfer Protocol. This allows you to send messages to users on other computers.

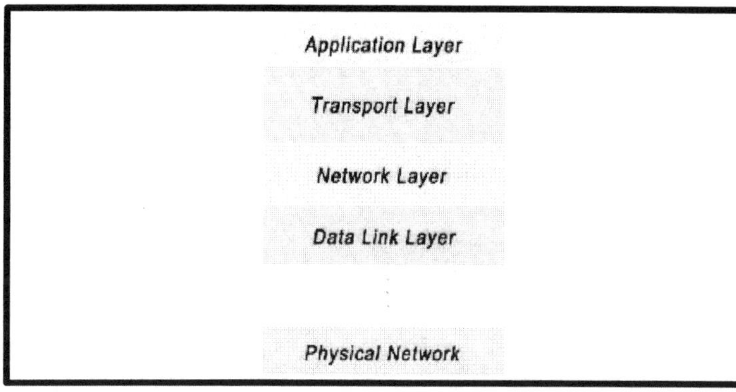

Figure 6.9 Layers of OSI (Open System Interconnection) model.

TCP/IP works over several layers of OSI (Open System Interconnection) model. Those layers are showed in Figure 6.9.

10.6.5.1 Application layer

The first layer is the Application Layer, and the Application Layer is user-system point of interaction. The point of interaction with an embedded Internet system is the browser.

10.6.5.2 Transport layer

The second layer is the Transport Layer. It manages the flow of data between two hosts. The flow may be operated by one of two transport protocols, TCP or UDP.

TCP is a connection oriented, reliable, byte stream service. TCP is where all error protection and flow control is carried out.

TCP requires all data to be acknowledged. There is no need to acknowledge each segment individually. TCP uses a pointer scheme where the receiver acknowledges the position of the index or pointer on last reliable block of data received. Each segment thus carries a block of data plus an index pointer into an imaginary array of bytes, that is, where the data block belongs in the array.

TCP also guarantees in-order arrival of data at the application layer, and the node receiving the data restores the order.

UDP in contrast, has an optional checksum, no in-order guarantee, and no retransmission, although an application itself can simulate these functions. UDP is useful when you have a reliable transmission media, such as LAN, and you don't want the complexity or overhead of TCP. However, software implementations can require a lot more memory comparing to low-end processors. For example, a 40 Kbytes stack may seem small until you try to squeeze it onto a 64Kbytes processor.

10.6.5.3 Network Layer

On the Network Layer we have the Internet Protocol (IP). The job of IP is to get data block to its destination. Its main contributions are addressing, routing and fragmentation.

Each IP packet (better known as datagram) has a header and a payload component. The most important items of information carried within the IP header are the source and destination IP address. In effect, the Internet Protocol encapsulates the TCP packet and adds the datagram's source and destination to the message.

IP datagrams are independent of each other and contain no in built error protection or recovery. TCP takes care about that.

IP allows datagrams to be chopped i.e. fragmented into shorter sections of the right size for transmission and, vice versa, short sections packet into single, longer datagrams.

Therefore, each IP datagram contains exact information about the position and size of their payload within this imaginary buffer. This allows for fragmented datagrams to be received out of sequence. A receiver accumulates datagrams until they all neatly fit into contiguous block. It follows that fragmented IP datagrams are not completely independent of each other. This will introduce a time element in any system. A receiver for example, has to consider when to give up waiting for missing out of order packets, and dump any previously stored.

Fragmented datagrams cause problems with small embedded systems. In theory, a receiver needs to allocate a 64KB buffer for every first out of sequence datagram received. This means one buffer for every different open socket being serviced. This is impractical for small RAM limited systems. One practical solution is to disallow or ignore fragmented IP datagrams. This way not is much of a problem if transactions involved are small, par example for a small data logger. However, there may be problems for systems dealing with log streams of block-encoded data such as voice or video. Fragmentation is not much of a problem with TCP as TCP can be engineered to use small segments to start with.

10.6.5.4 Data Link Layer

Finally the Data Link Layer routes the data across the network. An example is Ethernet.

10.6.6 TCP/IP protocol stack

If you want to network enable your embedded system or generally speaking, your application, you will need to decide to go for the ready-made route (ready-to-use solutions), for example, buy cards, modules or components, or roll your own. Naturally, it depends on how complex your application is.

There are several ways to implement the TCP/IP protocol stack in your embedded system.

10.6.6.1 Solution #1 - Pseudo TCP/IP

The best known method for implementing a TCP/IP protocol stack on a lower performance processors is a special, unique microcontroller and a dedicated gateway computer used to connect controllers to the Internet/Intranet. In this case it is not a full-fledged TCP/IP implementation, because a gateway is used between the microcontrollers and the Internet, and the communication between the gateway and the low-performance nodes is done by proprietary protocol. The "gateway" method allows a large number of small microcontroller units to communicate with typically embedded PC that acts as gateway onto a larger traditional Ethernet network or in fact the Internet itself. As an example, in a building security system, all the entry keypads may be connected to a central PC via a proprietary serial communication link. This PC then interfaces to the Internet via a dial-up link or a leased line. In this case embedded microcontrollers, strictly speaking, do not run TCP/IP, but the overall effect is similar.

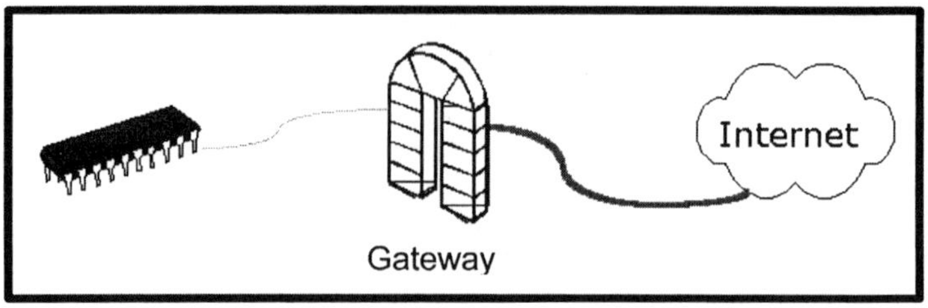

Figure 6.10 A pseudo TCP/IP protocol stack [Microcontroller01].

This approach arose because, traditionally, TCP/IP protocol stacks were too large to run on microcontrollers with only 32K of ROM and a few hundred bytes of RAM, hence the need to put the heavyweight software in a larger machine like an embedded PC. However, for applications where the embedded units are very small devices with just a few KB of ROM, the gateway approach will remain the only solution.

An advantage of this approach is that for some applications, such as home networks, several protocols may be in use. For example, nodes on a home network might use TCP/IP; power-line protocols, such as X10; phone-line protocols, and wireless protocols, such as e.g. Bluetooth. A gateway would serve as a bridge between all of the protocols.

Finally, even with a fully embedded TCP/IP, you still need system management and security features that might be best left to a gateway. By pulling some of the networking load into a gateway, you can implement either a proxy or a less-than-complete TCP/IP stack and reduce the processor performance required at each node. For example, a gateway could implement one firewall for several nodes instead of a firewall for each node. Gateways are advantageous in many applications. However, for some devices, such as toys and cameras, users will want to directly connect to their home LANs or ISPs, and anything short of a full TCP/IP won't do.

In Figure 6.10 we have so-called pseudo TCP/IP that can be used in simple networks. This is a combination of a small TCP/IP stack implemented on microcontroller and gateway, which do rest of the job.

The disadvantage of this system is that it deviates from industrial standards on several points. Communication between the gateway computer and the nodes (electronic devices) uses a proprietary protocol, whereas the gateway runs closed-end software, developed by a single manufacturer for connecting the device to the network.

Another handicap is that manufacturers incorporate special protocols for microcontroller-gateway communication, and it may bring about a significant delay. Protocol must be implemented within the microcontroller of the target system. Certain types of processors are supported by the given manufacturer, others are not. Protocol implementation code can take up precious - and usually not expandable - memory area in microcontrollers with limited (1-8 KBytes) program memory. According to specifications, this may be up to 1 KByte, inevitably resulting in limitations of functions executable in the remaining memory area.

10.6.6.2 Solution #2 – Separate Components

The second solution is to purchase a TCP/IP stack as a separate software component and to run TCP/IP protocol stack actually on the microcontroller. In this case your engineers write most of application code and integrate the components.

Once an embedded controller can use TCP/IP then it is a relatively simple matter to add additional features such as embedded web servers, FTP, e-mail, and the other familiar Internet facilities.

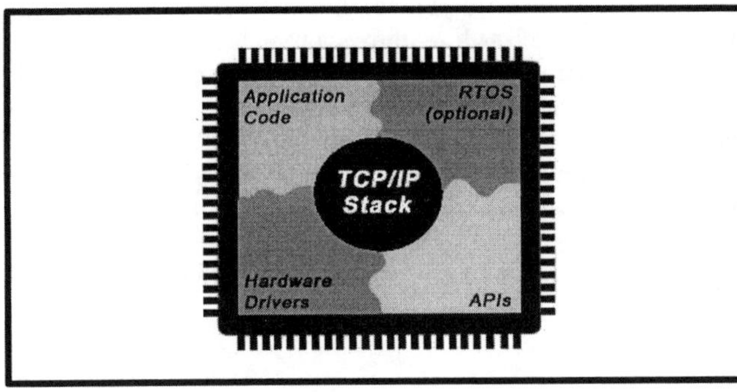

Figure 6.11 Separate component solution [Microcontroller01].

This is the highest integrated solution possible. In this case the microcontroller is a single point of software maintenance, and you get the best of breed of all components.

A big disadvantage of this approach is that this method requires a lot of engineering work. The design engineers must insure interoperability between all components. That requires redirection of application engineering reseources to networking. In this case time-to-market may be impacted due to the learning curve. At last, vendor claims and support must be verified.

10.6.6.3 Solution #3 — Integrated Networking

The third approach is "all in one solution" — networking software and hardware in one standard product.

It is unsurprising to find vendors that have implemented the TCP/IP stack in hardware. Many devices, such as credit card machines, vending machines, and meters, which connect to the Internet use processors lacking the ability to implement TCP/IP.

This is a typical "ready-to-use solution". The integration is already done and the microcontroller is a single point of software maintenance. This solution can be the fastest time to market, but we might not get the best of breed between all components.

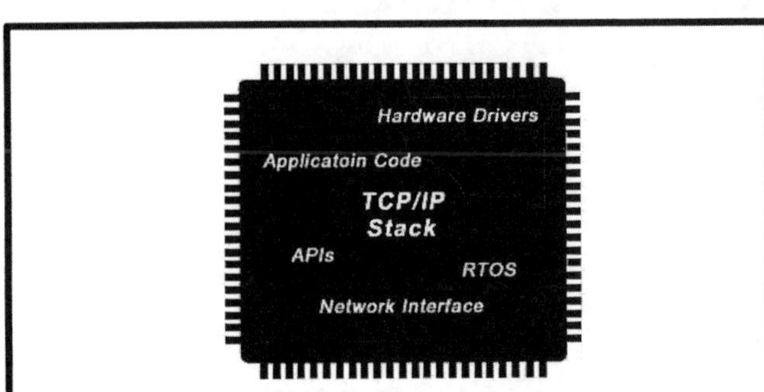

Figure 6.12 Integrated networking solution [Microcontroller01].

10.6.6.4 How to make a decision?

Deciding whether to go with hardware or software, full stack or proxy, requires a thorough understanding of how your device will connect to the Internet, what kind of information it needs to pass and receive, how easily you can integrate the software or chip into your design, and whether adding the stack will require a complete redesign of your product. For applications riding a bit tight on memory or MIPS, using a proxy protocol with a gateway or implementing the TCP/IP stack as hardware is probably the way to go. Simple applications, such as an Internet enabled meter, does not require a full TCP/IP stack to manage a few bytes of data that it exchanges with a control server. The gateway takes care of the task of converting the proxy protocol into proper TCP/IP and back again

For applications with powerful processors supporting connectivity is a matter of adding a software stack and network interface.

10.6.7 RTOS

The most pressing demand made on designers of embedded systems today is faster time to market.

Commercial, multitasking, real-time operating systems (RTOS) accelerate the system development. They provide designers with reliable software base upon which embedded applications can be built.

Ideally, an RTOS provides a robust set of system services and a flexible task scheduling system. At the same time, it is not allowed to require excessive memory. Moreover, an RTOS should be efficient and easily configurable, and to also offer feature-rich development environment.

Embedded systems, especially in industrial automation, require real-time deterministic response. Therefore, minimizing latencies with external interrupts, kernel services and task switching are mandatory.

Very important thing to remember when choosing an RTOS is to think long term. Learning to use a specific RTOS and develop applications requires a significant investment in time and resources. The investment, however, can pay off over and over for designers who use the same environment of future products.

Faster and faster processors will continue to emerge. Consequently, RTOS portability is very useful.

10.6.8 Examples

In this unit, several products from the embedded hardware and software market will be presented.

10.6.8.1 TCP/IP protocol stack by CMX

The presentation that follows is based on the reference [CMX01].

CMX MircoNet is a TCP/IP networking stack for 8-bit and 16-bit microcontrollers produced by CMX. This protocol stack can operate stand-alone or in conjunction with a Real Time Operating System.

CMX MicroNet provides support for TCP, PPP, UDP, SLIP, IP, and HTTP. With this stack, connectivity is supported by Dial Up or direct connection. CMX is planning to release some additional features, like FTP, TFTP, POP3 and SMTP.

Depending on configuration, the memory requirement is only 1,984 bytes in the simplest mode (Core, UDP), and 11,197 bytes kilobytes for the configuration that contains the Core, TCP/IP, PPP, the Modem, the HTTP Web Server and the Virtual File.

10.6.8.2 TCP/IP Development Kit

The presentation that follows is based on the reference [Rabbitsemiconductor01].

Rabbit Semiconductors makes a TCP/IP Development Kit, which contains all you need to develop microcontroller-based applications that network via Ethernet and use the Internet protocols.

This Development Kit contains a TCP/IP development board with the Rabbit 8-bit microprocessor and a complete software development environment.

Key benefits of the Rabbit 2000 TCP/IP Development Kit are:

- Ethernet ready - port to an Ethernet chipset is done for the Rabbit 2000 chip
- Cost-effective - no run-time royalties
- Simplified development - a complete Dynamic C software package (with integrated editor, compiler and debugger) is provided
- Sample demo programs, including HTTP web server and SMTP mail client, provide an advanced starting point for development
- Full hardware reference schematics help reduce development efforts
- Full TCP/IP source

10.6.8.3 NodEm Development Kit

The presentation that follows is based on the reference [Yipee01].

Kit contents:

- NodEm Development Board (with Yipee Cricket Module inserted on the board)
- Yipee Cricket Module (28 pins, PIC16F877 microcontroller, and Cirrus Logic Crystal LAN CS8900A Ethernet controller)
- Yipee Cricket Adapter (28 to 40 pins)
- Ethernet patch cable
- RS-232 patch cable
- Power supply
- CD-ROM with firmware, software, and documentation
- Quick Start Guide

Elements	Core IEF		Turbo IEF	
	RAM*	ROM*	RAM*	ROM**
Remote Setup	0	70	0	70
Ethernet	3	264	3	264
ARP	20	230	20	230
TCP	50	1108	50	1108
UDP	33	435	33	435
IP	74	336	74	336
ICMP	0	93	0	93
TCP Socket Interface	4	155	4	155
UDP Socket Interface	5	83	5	83
Device Manager	-	-	0	265
Active Interface	-	-	2	546
TCP Input Buffer	-	-	28	0
TCP Output Buffer	-	-	28	0
Glue Code***	53	839	53	848
TOTAL	182	3613	182	4422

Figure 6.13 Elements of NodEm Development Kit [Yipee01].

10.6.8.4 The CAD-UL and US Software Solution

The presentation that follows is based on the reference [USSW01].

The CAD-UL-US Software compatible development tools include:

- SuperTask! RTOS-a royalty-free, small-footprint, multitasking operating system based on the real-time kernel, Multitask!™. ROMable and reentrant, SuperTask! provides more than 70 system calls.
- USNET Web Server - an embedded HTTP server that supports HTML, Java applets, and dynamic page generation on client and server sides.
- USNET TCP/IP Protocol Suite - a processor- and RTOS-independent TCP/IP protocol stack, designed for use with real-time embedded applications. USNET is also royalty-free.
- CAD-UL XDB SuperTask! - a high-level language debugger specifically optimized for SuperTask!, XDB for SuperTask! is available as a ROM Monitor solution and optionally interfaces to the industry's most popular in-circuit emulators
- CAD-UL C/C++ Compiler System - a highly optimized compiler system that includes a compiler, linker/graphical linker, and C++ class and ANSI C libraries all tightly interfaced to the Workbench integrated development environment.

10.7 Conclusion

The Internet Automation is not future, the Internet Automation is the present. It is reality, which function is to help us to live easier and more comfortable. Those systems make our lives less stressfull liberating us thinking of "everything". In the same time, those systems save our time, save energy saving our money. All the facts mentioned are the reasons of the growing popularity of the Internet Automation systems. As after the rain mushrooms grow, after the Internet become available in some place, the next step is to use the Internet to automate that place.

10.8 Problems

1. Try to find as many as possible home appliances that could be accessed via the Internet.
2. In your opinion, what is the most useful Internet enabled appliance?
3. Make a calculation for home wiring using different systems (e.g. power lines or bluetooth).
4. Find several home automation systems on the market and compare their characteristics (e.g. number of different devices, user interface, accessibility, security features, price).
5. Devise several applications of Internet automation in factories. What products could be produced using only Internet automation systems, without presence of human being.
6. Using your personal computer and web camera, make small surveillance system that is accessible via the Internet.
7. Make a microcontroller-based device for controlling a motor. Later, that device can be used to control for example blinds in your home.
8. Adding TCP/IP stack or using gateway approach, provide Internet connection to the microcontroller-based device. Make a user interface for controlling the motor via the Internet.
9. Try to make a study about benefits and downsides of using different approaches to add TCP/IP stack to a microcontroller.
10. Make a comparison of characteristics of TCP/IP protocol stacks that can be bought on the market.

References

[Cisco01] The Internet Home, (http://www.cisco.com/warp/public/3/uk/ihome), **April 1999.**

[CMX01] CMX MicroNet, (http://www.cmx.com), **June 2001.**

[Cooper98] Cooper, H., "X-10 FAQ,", (http://www.nomad.ee/micros/x10faq.html), **April, 2001.**

[Esacademy00] Worldwide microcontroller shipments http://www.esacademy.com/automation/faq/primer/3.htm), **January 1998.**

[Huang98] Huang, H., "Home Networking - An Emerging Market of Telecommunication,", (http://oden.csom.umn.edu/idsc6452/Papers/HHuan/HHuang%20 Final.htm), **December 1998.**

[MicroChip01] MicroChip, (http://www.microchip.com), **June 2001.**

[Microcontroller01] TCP/IP Development Kit, (http://www.microcontroller.com), **June 2001.**

[Rabbit01] TCP/IP Development Kit, (http://www.rabbitsemiconductor.com), **June 2001.**

[USSW01] US Software Solution, (http://www.ussw.com), **June 2001.**

[Wacks98] Wacks, K., "HTINews Article,", **(http://**www.hometoys.com/htinews/apr98/articles/wacks/wacks.ht m), **April 1998.**

[Yipee01] NodeEm Development Kit, (http://www.yipeeinc.com), **June 2001.**

E-Business and E-Challenges
V. Milutinović and F. Patricelli (Eds.)
IOS Press, 2002

Chapter 11
Technology Transfer on the Internet

Aleksandra Popovic and Veljko Milutinović

11.1. Technology Progress Factors

The money was invented about 2000.B.C. by Phoenicians. According to today's economy experts the invention was a turning point for mankind. In the following centuries technology was advancing with the highest rate ever. Remains of technological accomplishments from that ages can be seen today.

The importance of money is that it links those with "goods" and those with "needs" in order to satisfy both sides and enable ideas to became reality.

What will be the next event that will induce technology progress acceleration? According to Robert Mundell, Nobel Laureate in Economy, the event is founding of the united world currency. He proved his theory by imaginary merging of three the most strongest currencies in the world: American Dollar, EURO, and Yen. The mission of new currency will be to globalize the market and to bridge geographical and political barriers. Market globalization will lead to faster, more efficient, and more productive flow of ideas, products, and patents.

It is obvious that money is compulsory factor for fruitful investments. Let us consider what information should investor and inventor have in order to produce an unique technology and contribute to technology progress. Information about trends in significant scientific areas must be provided for inventor to keep track with other scientist and follow their accomplishments. Also, information about available technologies must be accessible and thus prevent "multiplication" of inventions. On the other hand, investor must be able to access or collect information about customer needs in order to find out which technology can be commercialized and can produce in financial return.

The Internet is said to be the only true well of information. Nowadays over 400 million people worldwide is connected to the Internet and the number is growing rapidly. The Internet breaks geographical barriers and brings investor and inventor just one mouse click away of each other and desirable technology.

11.2. What is an Intellectual Property (IP)?

11.2.1. Introduction

Intellectual Property, or IP, allows people to protect their ideas and invention in same manner as physical property. Intellectual Property refers to creations of the mind: inventions, literary and artistic works, and symbols, names, images, and designs used for commercial purposes. Intellectual Property is protected with number of regional and international laws. In most cases, inventor must register his invention with some official IP institution in order to obtain IP right. In some cases IP right is recognized even if it is not registered and published. [1]

Each country has laws to protect IP. The main reason for protecting IP is to give inventor legal moral and economic rights for his patent. In those cases, the IP can be presented in public, without possibility losing rights and ownership over invention. Thus, anybody has right to obtain information about invention, and nobody has right to use that information without explicit permission given by IP owner. This concept gives support to technology progress, by supporting information flow within the society. These right doesn't apply to physical products, that was built using new invention, but to invention itself.

11.2.2. Classification of IP

Criteria for IP classification is type of protected property.

11.2.1.1. Industrial property

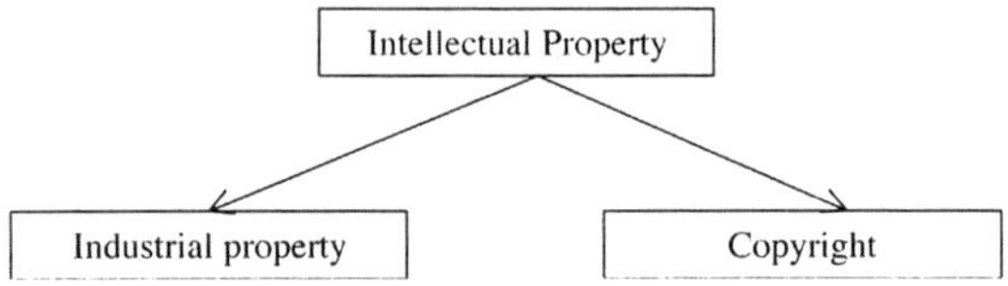

Figure 1: Classification of IP

Industrial property implies property that is used in industry production, such as patents, trade marks, design, etc. In simplified terms industrial invention is a solution to a technical problem, and it is used in industry production. Industry design is full description of industry product, including aesthetic appearance, functionality, design technology, and other issues concerning the product. All this issues can be protected as IP. Usage of it is restrained by international laws and laws of specific country. Laws concerning industrial property are not so restrictive, as in e.g. copyright, in order to avoid monopolization of some industry area, and to support further improvement of such inventions. For example, many patent agencies worldwide, do not allow lifetime protection to patent, but limit it to e.g. fifteen years.
Figure 2 shows types of Intellectual Property.

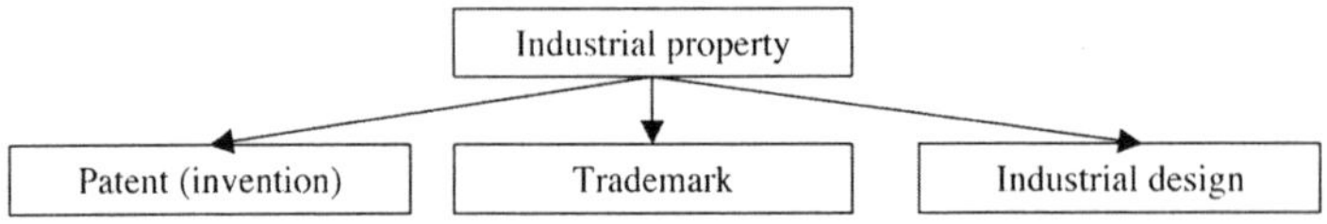

Figure 2: Industrial property types

11.2.2.1.1. What is a patent?

A patent is an exclusive right granted for an invention, which is a product or a process that provides a new way of doing something, or offers a new technical solution to a problem. [5] In simplified terms, patent is new and improved products and processes that are capable of industrial application. Patent is usually improvement in existing technology, and very rarely description of existing technology. [2]

Invention that can be recognized as patent must be applicable in "real life". Also, it must show innovation in existing technology or new technology. Some countries have restraint about what inventions can be patent protected. For example, most countries do not allow patent protection of inventions that are of most importance for society, such as medical treatment methods, and all invention in medical sciences. The reason is to make this invention available for all people, without restraints based on financial, religious, race, or any other qualification. No product can be patent protected. This means that only product design technology can be protected, and not the product itself.

Patents provide incentives to individuals by offering them recognition for their creativity and material reward for their marketable inventions. These incentives encourage innovation, which assures that the quality of human life is continuously enhanced.

A patent provides protection for the invention to the owner of the patent. The protection is granted for a limited period, e.g. 15 years.

Patent protection means that the invention can not be commercially used, sold, or distributed without approvement from patent owner. Patent owner has rights to send patent or to license it. It means that patent owner can approve usage of patent to other party. This agreement must be legally settled and it is called *license*. Second option is sell patent to other party. This means that patent owner waives ownership of patent and transfer it to other party.

When patent is prosecuted, the patent description is public domain and can be viewed by anybody. After expiration of patent, it becomes public domain, and owner has no rights about it. Expiration is generally after 20 years.

In order to apply for the patent, invention owner must provide following information: technical field, invention background, and invention description. Description contains scientific foundations of invention, visual description, such as design plans and diagrams.

The patent is granted by official patent agency, such as national patent office of regional patent office, e.g. European Patent Office. International law about patents - Patent Cooperation Treaty (PCT), administrated by WIPO (See section), describes the rights of owner of patent prosecuted at patent offices worldwide.

11.2.2.1.2. What is a trademark?

Trademark is the sign that can distinguish products and services of one trader from another. Trademark is a kind of Intellectual Property. The sign includes various representations of products or companies, such as company logo, product name, slogans, and sounds. If trademark is protected, other party can not use any of protected representation. The idea behind the trademark is to make some products or services easily recognized by users, and thus improve marketing of such products/services. Once developed through advertising, marketing, trade shows, and other means, trademarks become one of the most valuable assets of company. Customers identify the firm with the trademark. [3]

11.2.2.1.3. What is an industrial design?

An industrial design is aesthetic segment of a product. It refers to shape, configuration, lines, patterns, and color of given object. The main characteristic of an industrial design that distinguish it from other IPs is that it must be judged by eye. In simplified terms, design is visual representation of an object. The industry design owner has no rights concerning technical design of product or any other issue other than aesthetic view.

Design must be new and not recognized yet in order to obtain protection. Unique design helps in marketing the product and helps consumers to distinguish the product from other of some or similar functionality. In most countries industrial design protection expires, similar as patent, after 15 or 20 years.

Besides industrial design protection, visual representation of something can be protected as work of art using copyright laws (See section). In many countries this two protection exclude each other. This means that if design is protected as industry design it can not be protected under copyright law, and vice-versa.

International application is defined by Hague Agreement Concerning the International Deposit of Industrial Designs, administrated by WIPO (See section).

11.2.2.2. Copyright

Copyright is describing the rights of original creator of literal or atristic work. The kinds of works covered by copyright include: literary works such as novels, poems, plays, reference works, newspapers and computer programs; databases; films, musical compositions, and choreography; artistic works such as paintings, drawings, photographs and sculpture; architecture; and advertisements, maps and technical drawings.

Copyright laws protect only expression and not contents of work. Thus if someone wants to protect his ideas, for example published in a book, it is not enough to copyright the book. It is necessary, also, to protect the idea in some other protection method.

The copyright owner has right to forbid following usage of his work: reproduction, broadcasting, public performance, translation, adoption, or recording. Illegally produced goods are called "pirates".

Copyright itself does not depend on official procedures. A created work is considered protected by copyright as soon as it exists []. However, copyright can be registrated at national copyright offices worldwide. World Intellectual Property Organization (WIPO) does not provide it's user copyright registration program.

International law that describes copyright is "Berne Convention for the Protection of Literary and Artistic Works", that does not require any registration. [4]

11.2.3. World Intellectual Property Organization - WIPO

WIPO was founded as United Nations (UN) organization in 1967 with headchair in Geneva, Switzerland. The "Convention of Establishing World Intellectual Property Organization" is signed by UN member States in Stockholm in 1967. and came into power in 1970. Although WIPO is part of UN, it is holly independed entity. [6]

Intellectual Property rights are limited territorially. For example, patent granted by national patent office is valid only in that country. The idea of WIPO is to make IP rights global and applicable in any country that is member of the organization. Also, approaches and procedures in national intellectual property offices were getting more similar in the last decades. The idea is to make laws that are acceptable for all member countries, and thus make registration process easier for all IP owners. In past years governments made number of treaties, concerning IP. WIPO is administrating this treaties.

11.3. What is Technology Transfer?

11.3.1. Introduction

The first car safety bag was invented in 1955., and presented few months later, in the film in which the inventor claimed that in following years every car in US will have such protection. Air bag came into mass production forty years later. Why such good invention didn't reach it's users before? It didn't go through process of Technology Transfer. Technology Transfer is process of moving inventions from hand of inventor to final users. In other words it is process of shifting Intellectual Property rights from researches to for-profit sector for purposes of commercialization. It is important to emphasize that the object of Technology Transfer is **Intellectual Property**. The goals of Technology Transfer is moving of research results from laboratory into practice. It is important to notice that Technology Transfer is process that leads to the commercialization of inventions, ideas, and patents. This implies that Technology Transfer is not successful until the final product reaches hands of end users. Technology Transfer includes both moving technology from inventor to market and broad acceptance of technology by consumers [Johnson, 1997]. The second part of Technology Transfer process is sometimes called "diffusion of the invention".

Figure 3 shows the concept of Technology Transfer. The model includes technological activity and diffusion of invention.

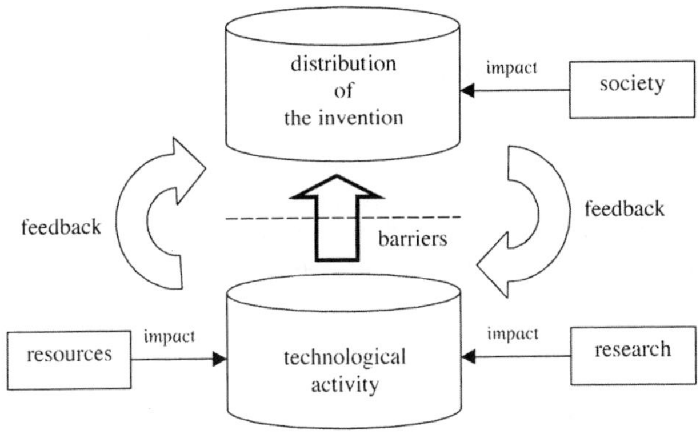

Figure 3: The concept of Technology Transfer

Technological activity includes all activities in process of producing new technology. First step is observing the market and tracking customers needs. This means that inventor must be aware of social context within he works, in order to make an invention that will be useful and thus easy to commercialize. This step is not necessary just in the beginning of process, but also during the development of invention. It is usual, e.g. in designing computer software, to design first version, than to wait for feedback from users, and to redesign existing software, concerning customers needs. Sometimes, customer develops it's need after using first versions of technology. Inventions that were good, but not balanced with society needs, didn't become widely used, and thus failed in the process of Technology Transfer. Technological activity includes knowledge, as prerequisite for successful technology design. Thinking process is involved, in order to realize scientific and marketing aspects of new technology. Finally, it is impossible to create new product without involving physical means, e.g. laboratory instruments. The result of technological activity is a new technology or improvement of existing one, e.g. in areas of physical, biological, chemical, and informational technologies.

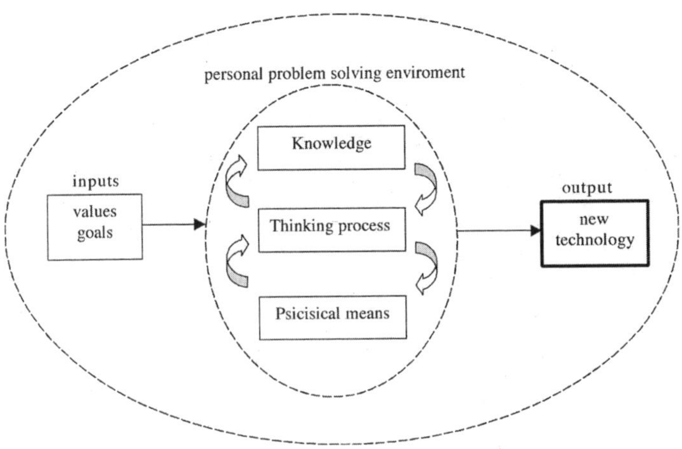

Figure 4: Technological activity

While technological activity is based on work of scientists in area of technology diffusion of invention fully resides in hands of marketing. Diffusion depends on customers needs and the way how technology is presented in public. Sometimes, the process of commercialization goes well, but the society does not accept product widely, so the financial aspect of process in not satisfied. This is considered as failed Technology Transfer.

11.3.2. Technology Transfer process

At the Figure 5 can be seen three departments that are significant for Technology Transfer: science and technology, marketing, and finance. Notice that those three departments are not obligatory within one institution. First step is defining the invention and it is done by science & technology. Marketing is responsible to investigate feasibility of project in terms of financial needs and financial possibility.

Financial department approves seed capital, provided from the Technology Transfer funds. Next step for science and technology is to translate invention from idea to reality, using the capital obtained from the financial department.

After the successful translation, business plan is constructed. For further development of product, T2 funds must by expanded in order to finalize the project. In final steps product must be commercialized, market must be prepared for new product and efficiently captured.

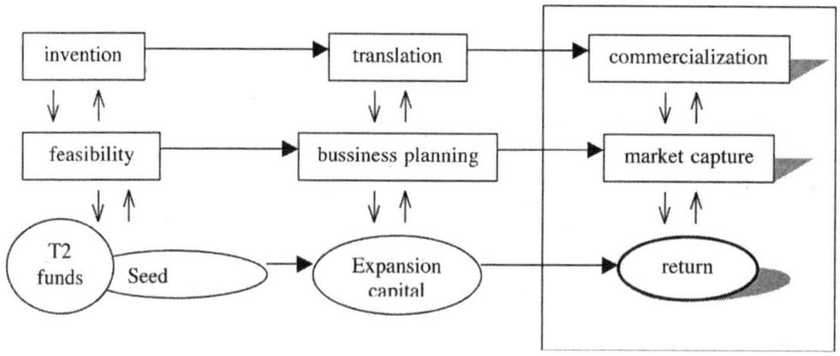

Figure 5: Technology Transfer process

The result of the whole process is return of invested capital, so the inventor and investor are both satisfied.

As seen before Technology Transfer is the way of matching technology and business together. Investors and inventors are involved in the process, in which they exchange Intellectual Property and financial capital, in order to produce new technology and financial return.

11.3.3. Technology Transfer Models

Many models of Technology Transfer exist in the literature.

Tenkasi discusses four predominate models of Technology Transfer: the appropriability model, the dissemination model, the knowledge utilization model, and the contextual collaboration model (Tenkasi & Mohrman, 1995).

The **appropriability model** follows the belief that good technologies sell themselves. Based on this model, purposive attempts to transfer technologies are believed to be unnecessary. When the developer of the technology makes it available through common communication channels (e.g., television, newspapers, technical reports, journals, conference presentations), interested potential users will adopt the technology without further effort on the part of the developer.

The **dissemination model** takes the view that transfer is best accomplished when experts transfer specialized knowledge to a willing receptor. This model suggests that the technology flows from the initial source to the end user much like water flows through a pipe as long as restrictions are kept to a minimum.

The **knowledge utilization** model focuses on strategies that put knowledge to effective use in the recipient's setting. While this model has gained acceptance in recent years, it still suffers from a linear bias (as do the first two models) that the process of transfer moves in one direction from the developer to the end user.

The **contextual collaboration** model is more of a diffusion model, building on the constructivist notion that knowledge cannot be simply transmitted, but must be subjectively constructed by the receiver through contextual adaptation. If innovations are to be transferred successfully, both the knowledge and the technology being transferred must be contextually adapted. This model goes beyond the other models that view transfer as information transmission or communication by implying that successful transfer requires learning on the part of both parties and the need to recognize the perspective of others.

Another set of Technology Transfer models has been proposed by Ruttan and Hayami (1973). Their model distinguishes three phases of international Technology Transfer: material transfer, design transfer, and capacity transfer. Material transfer is characterized by the simple transfer of new materials or equipment such as machinery, seeds, tools, and the techniques associated with the use of the materials. In this case, adaptation of the technology to the local conditions is not a direct concern. Design transfer is accomplished through the transfer of designs such as blueprints and tooling specifications so the receiver can use the new technology on site. Capacity transfer is the most comprehensive of the three, and involves the transfer of knowledge, which provides the end user with the capability to design and manufacture a new technology on their own. This type of transfer serves to expand and build upon a technology base while at the same time providing for learning and development of the receiver. Licensing agreements and franchises are two practical examples of this form of transfer.

11.3.4. Technology Transfer Steps

Technology Transfer is obviously complex process involving number of experts in variety areas of technology and economy. Simplified steps of the process are: Disclosing the invention, Patenting, Marketing the technology, Negotiating and licensing, and Managing the license.

11.3.4.1. Disclosing the Invention

Disclosing the invention is highly important step in process of Technology Transfer. It must be good timed. Sometimes scientist disclose their invention before it is complete and ready for commercialization. Such bad timing usually produce in not realized ideas. Also, premature disclosed invention is very difficult to sell and advertise.

It is extremely important, before disclosure, to define few explicit usage of the invention, so potential business partner can understand it. This step is mostly task of technology and science department.

11.3.4.2 Patenting

After disclosing the invention it must be decided whether it needs to be patent protected. The decision depends whether the technology is unique and new, or something similar already exist. If decision is to patent protect the technology fist step needed to be done is applying for patent at patent office. After prosecuting the patent and defining application, patent is ready for launching. . For purposes of patenting, the invention must be usable in understandable way. If not, patent office will not grant patent. Usability of invention is key factor in deciding whether to apply for patent.

11.3.4.3 Marketing

Marketing is done by marketing department, as seen before. If this step is done successfully, it results in market capture, so technology can be sold to potential partners.

Steps for marketing the technology are:

- Select licensing strategy
- Contact potential licensees
- Provide non-confidential information
- Ask for confidentiality agreement
- Provide confidential information

In selecting licensing technology, it must be decided if the invention will be sold as "know how" or it will be joint venture between inventor and investor. For contacting potential licensees the most important tools is the Internet.

11.3.4.4. Negotiating and Licensing

After contacting potential licensees, next step is negotiations and licensing. Phases in the step are:

- Make a term proposal
- Negotiate license agreement
- Construct the agreement
- Execute the agreement

11.3.4.5. Managing the License

After successful agreement execution license must be monitored, in order to track down whether the licensee has violate the agreement. Also, infringement from third parties must be monitored and litigated, when needed.

11.3.5. Technology Transfer Strategies

While the discussion of the nature of technological activity, the characteristics of technology, and the societal barriers that support or hamper Transfer provides a conceptual understanding of Technology Transfer, concrete strategies are needed to facilitate successful Technology Transfers. Facilitating a smooth transition from the owners of the current technology to the end users of the new technology requires a strategic plan. It is too often assumed that innovations can be transferred simply, as if by magic, to the user. In practice the transfer process is much more difficult. When successful, the transfer process could take anywhere from a few days or weeks to several centuries. Still, some transfer efforts are never successful and languish in a sort of Technology Transfer purgatory.

The chances of successful transfer are enhanced by understanding the Technology Transfer process and by developing strategies that can enhance the prospects of successful Transfer. The following lists identify many of the important strategies for successful transfer that emerge from the concepts discussed in the literature. While incomplete, these strategies highlight the complexity of issues that need to be addressed when supporting a Technology Transfer process.

These strategies are categorized according to technological readiness questions, design considerations, and end user needs.

11.3.5.1. Technological Readiness Questions

These questions provide the basis for an initial overview or Ôscan' of a user environment Answers to these questions help assess whether a user environment is prepared to embrace and develop the knowledge needed to successfully adopt a new technology.
Who will be using the technology?
What is their current level of technology?
Who are the stakeholders? the decision-makers? the influential people?
Do the end users have the education needed to adopt the technology?
Will training be needed?
What are the available financial resources? Will they be sufficient to sustain the technology?
Will the current infrastructure support the technology and its expected growth?
What other aspects might affect by this transfer?
Is the full benefit of the technology limited by other bottlenecks in the system?

11.3.5.2. Design Considerations

These design considerations build on the concepts of the appropriateness of technology and emphasize factors important in achieving more than a material transfer of technology. Design the technology and infrastructure so that it can grow with the user. Develop and adapt technology so that it is appropriate for the culture, and intermediate is the society's needs dictate. Present demonstration programs to assure small-scale success.

Keep the end user in the loop during the design process to assure that needs are being me Document technology procedures (in terms the user can understand) so that the user has as much information as needed to operate the technology independently. Provide research and/or training support to facilitate the transfer of knowledge. Maintain a systems view. Recognize that the technology is not independent, but affects other parts of the system.

11.3.5.3. End User Considerations

Central to the models of Technology Transfer is the role of user needs and wants in the technological development process. The issues described below build on the importance of the user in the design process and extend this consideration of users to the Technology Transfer process. Evaluate end user's needs and available resources. Consider how large a system the user will be able to staff and maintain. Identify influential people, stakeholders, and decision-makers. The power of the change agent may dictate a technology's success or failure. Facilitate communication among those involved, and foster a cooperative relationship. Treat the end user's values and culture with respect. Develop technology solutions that are fitting for that environment. Do not impose status and education on the receiving culture. Maintain two-sided innovative dialogue and establish communication channels.

11.3.5.4. Technology Transfer Glossary of Terms

Assignee: An assignee is the person or company to whom the patentee has given rights to the invention.

Claims: Claims are the effective part of a patent. They are numbered paragraphs that give a precise description of the invention and list all essential features.

Copyright: Copyright is protection for the expression of an idea.

Design Patent: Design patents are granted on the appearance of something.

"A patent is a contract between society and inventors. In the interest of spurring innovation society agrees to protect an inventor's control over an invention ...A patent protects the implementation of an invention's underlying idea." [5]

Industrial property: Industrial property implies property that is used in industry production, such as patents, trade marks, design, etc. In simplified terms industrial invention is a solution to a technical problem, and it is used in industry production.

Intellectual Property (IP): Intellectual Property refers to creations of the mind: inventions, literary and artistic works, and symbols, names, images, and designs used for commercial purposes.

Invention: The production of something new; a discovery; a finding. [5]

License: Authority, leave, permission; consent or permission granted by authority. [5]

In Technology Transfer – permission granted by IP owner to use invention given to other party.

Licensor: The person who sells rights to use IP.

Licensee: The person who buys rights to use a IP.

Patent: A patent is an exclusive right granted for an invention, which is a product or a process that provides a new way of doing something, or offers a new technical solution to a problem.

Patentee: A patentee is the person who is named as the inventor of a patent.

Trademark: Trademark is protection on slogans, logos, or product names. The primary function of trademark is to indicate the origin of goods and to distinguish them from those sold or manufactured by others

Technology Transfer: In other words it is process of shifting Intellectual Property rights from researches to for-profit sector for purposes of commercialization

Utility Patent: Utility patents are what most people think of as an invention; for example, a machine or process.

11.4. Problems of Technology Transfer

As seen before, Technology Transfer is extremely important for non-profit organizations and also for successful companies, who want to invest in scientific projects. On the other hand, the Technology Transfer process is complicated and also overloaded with problems. Some problem groups are listed below:

- Complexity
- Social problems
- Personal problems
- Geographical problems
- Legal problems
- Cultural problems

Complexity of the process is huge, as seen in previous chapters. This problems can be handled with Technology Transfer companies (See chapter), that provide service for it's users in area of Technology Transfer.

Social problems. Technology is transferred within a social system. The social environment decides if the innovation will be transferred and diffused. Good technology itself finds the way to reach users. Society forms the opinion about some product. Positive opinion about the product spreads fast, negative one even faster. The major number of new technologies is first presented and published in scientific newspaper. Whether some paper will be presented or not, is decided by editorial board, so the society has it's role in deciding whether the scientific work will be published.

Personal problems. Technology Transfer depends on personal profiles and their impact on each other, of following participants in process: inventors, managers, and final users. The problem with inventors is that they sometimes don't want to pay intention to market and consider customers needs as legitimate impact to their work. The result is technology that does not interest anyone. Also, the needs of inventors, that are small group within society and users that are major group, is not same, and even not similar. Problems with managers is that sometime they don't understand the importance of invention and thus some good inventions, never came into market. Also, there is the problem of communication between inventors and managers.

Antagonism between these two groups is subject of jokes. Finally, the main personal problem concerns users. One of the toughest tasks in Technology Transfer is investigating the market. First step is to find out what part of population will use new technology. After that, it is important to find out how to advertise new technology, in order to be widely accepted. This issues include psychological evaluation of potential customers, as well as social environment research. These problems are strongly connected with social issues and must be together considered.

Geographical problems. Geographical problems include problems of distance between inventor, investor, and potential users. It is known that inventions made in regions with lots of available investors, from profit organizations or government, has more opportunity to commercialize and thus reach users. On the other hand, inventors in regions that do not provide support for them, does not have opportunity to transfer and diffuse their inventions. That is one of the main reason why some advanced technologies did not reach final users. Geographical problems can be solved by using the Internet. Thus, distance is not measured by miles or kilometers, but by bits per second.

Legal problems. Legal problems include problems with legal settlement of Technology Transfer process, as well as political barriers that obstruct transfer. The number of laws concerning Technology Transfer were brought during the 70s and 80s, in US, Europe, and Asia. Also, the laws concerning Intellectual Property issues were extremely important for regulation of Technology Transfer. The idea is to protect someone's Intellectual Property, but also to allow the owner to sell it's technology or to license it. Legal problems were solved in 80s, but in past few years new problems came to scene. Internet-based Technology Transfer companies provide services in transfer and diffusion of invention. The problem is in on-line contracts, and their legal regulation. Also, it is not regulated whether a company must check the technology offered by their inventor-client before offering it to other clients. Because of these problems, many Internet-based companies offer technology that is suspicious for their functionality or even ownership. These problems must be solved, in order to move Technology Transfer to the Internet. Political barriers are problems generated by governments. Fortunately, after the fall of the iron curtain, these problems are surpassed.

Cultural problems. Cultural barriers also play a key role in Technology Transfer. In many cases, the culture in which a technology is designed is different from that where it is ultimately used. Thus, it is important for designers to communicate with and understand the receiving culture. This communication will help assure a solution that is appropriate for the culture and acceptable to social norms and values. Baranson (1963) stressed that designers should consider he characteristics of the labor force and the resources available in the receiving country. In developing countries, equipment should be small-scale, rugged, and require minimal training for successful operation. These features should not be limiting, however, as the technology should have the potential to expand as a country's needs and resources expand. He explains that "little attention has been paid to accommodating technological design to cultural traits; instead emphasis has been placed upon adjusting societies to machines". As systems become more automated, those in charge of technology tend to believe that more computer power will make their processes more efficient. In pulling manufacturing and design toward automation, the tendency is to give as much power as possible to the machine and leave the remaining job tasks to the worker. This automation philosophy discounts the knowledge and intuitive capabilities of workers and pushes them to resent the technology. A better approach is to design systems around the workers, which offers the workers a change from mechanistic job tasks to higher-level tasks.

11.5. Solutions

Before foundation of modern communications, it was extremely difficult to find potential partners, to communicate with each other, and to reach agreement. First revolutionary invention that helped people to find each other and to communicate is Bulletin Board Service (BBS). BBS used to be favorite way for matching people together. It was also used as a bulletin for selling and buying products, at business BBSs. Also, a number of Technology Transfer BBSs helped scientists to advertise their inventions.

It works as real Bulletin Board. Users are posting their messages, so everyone can see them. Another user can reply to these message, and thus messages are nested. BBS was very useful in early ages of computer communications, but it also had plenty disadvantages, that stopped it from becoming main tool for Technology Transfer. Main disadvantage is that BBS is not searchable. User can only go through messages in order to find advertisement for some interesting technology. It is impossible to search for invention by using keywords. Also, BBS is not settled legally. Nowadays it is used only for a small business.

11.5.1. Advanced Internet Solutions

Advanced Internet solutions are using advantages of the Internet, as source of information and tool for communication.

Also, the goal of these solutions is to surpass some problems that occur while using it. As Internet solutions we chose to present three:

- Internet search engines
- Genetic search
- Obelix – Customer-satisfactory system

11.5.2. Internet Search Engines

Internet search engines are used to search among Internet web sites. It indexes all web pages and stores information into database. Engine extracts keywords from user supplied documents and consults database to find adequate documents in which given keyword appear with greatest frequency. Internet search engines are used at Technology Transfer web sites in order to find the most suitable technologies for the user. Internet search engines suffer from huge databases and poor performance.

11.5.3. Genetic Algorithm

11.5.3.1. Introduction

Genetic Algorithm (GA) is intelligent search method. GA introduces the principles of evolution and genetics into search among possible solutions to given problem. The idea is to simulate the process in natural systems and thus reach the best solution. The concept is to follow the principles of survival of the fittest. Thus, the optimal solutions survive, and the worst ones die, during the algorithm flow. GA, also, resides on genetic principles of mutation, crossover, and reproduction operators. The main argument for introducing the genetics is to produce superior offspring, using above mentioned operators. [7], [8], [9]

GA is used when the search space is relatively large and cannot be traversed efficiently by classical search method, like indexing explained before. This is mostly case with problems whose solution requires evaluation of many apparently unrelated variables.

GA can be used for search among Internet documents, but also for search for technologies at Technology Transfer web sites.

11.5.3.2. Algorithmic Phases

The algorithms consists of following phases:

1. Generate an initial population.
2. Compute fitness for each individual in current population.
3. Compute fitness function for all genomes
4. Generate the next population, by selecting the individuals from previous population, in order to produce offspring via operators.

5. Repeat step 2 until a satisfactory solution is obtained.

First step is to initialize the population. The population is set of possible solutions. Every member of population is called individual or genome. Genomes is evaluated by unique function – fitness function.

In second step the algorithm enters a cycle where fitness of all genomes are evaluated, the genomes with fitness below the treshold are rejected, and the individuals for mating pool are selected, using the reproduction operators.

Next step is to perform crossover and mutation operators. Crossover is operator that combines good genetic material from two parents and thus produce "child". Mutation introduces randomness into population. The new offspring is inserted into population. Thus a new generation is obtained and algorithm continues from beginning.

The algorithm stops when stopping criteria is met.

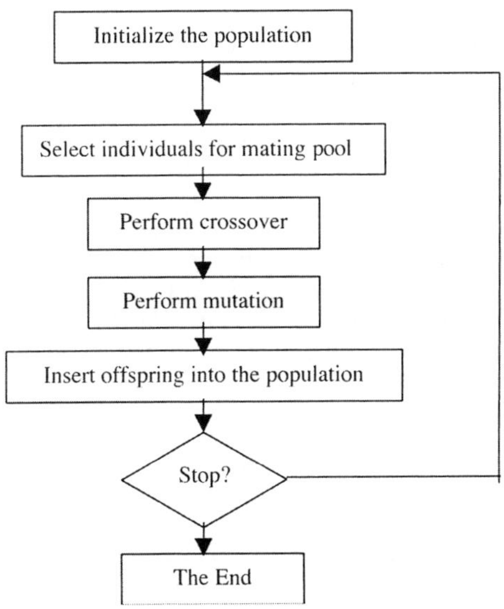

Figure 6: Genetic Algorithm

11.5.3.3. Design Steps

In order to design successful GA, following steps must be done:

- Define a search space
- Define fitness function
- Define reproduction, crossover, and mutation operators
- Define stopping criteria.

The first step in construction of GA is to define search space. The search space, or initial population, is set of randomly or heuristically chosen solutions, that will be used for producing next population. It is highly important to select a form of genome, as a data structure. The representation of genome is essential for successful implementation of GA.

The genomes must be simple enough to be stored and occupate less memory, but also detailed enough to be suitable for implementing operators, such as crossover, mutation, and reproduction.

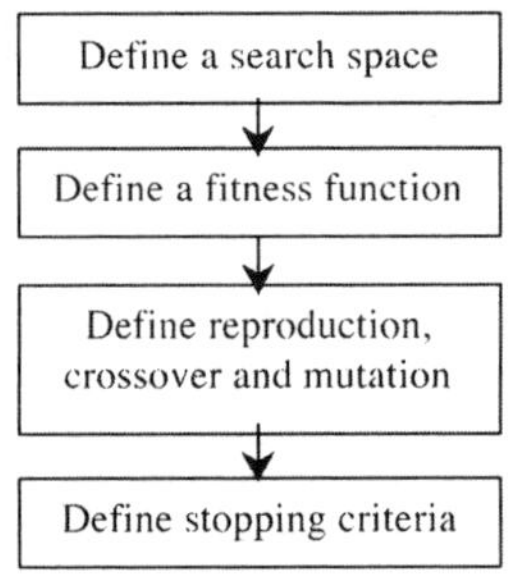

Figure 7: Design steps for GA

The second step is to define fitness function as an evaluation function. The task of fitness function is to determine what solutions are better that others. The idea is to associate each genome with a number that show how fit it is. When next population is generated, the genomes that are worst that others, e.g. their fitness number is smaller, are rejected, and the good genomes, e.g. with bigger fitness number, are inserted into new population. Different types of problems require different fitness function. In this book, is shown one way to evaluate the fitness Jackard's score.

The second step is to define fitness function as an evaluation function. The task of fitness function is to determine what solutions are better that others. The idea is to associate each genome with a number that show how fit it is. When next population is generated, the genomes that are worst that others, e.g. their fitness number is smaller, are rejected, and the good genomes, e.g. with bigger fitness number, are inserted into new population. Different types of problems require different fitness function. In this book, is shown one way to evaluate the fitness Jackard's score.

The third step is to define genetic operators: crossover, mutation, and reproduction.

Crossover is operator that combines good genetic material from two parents and thus produces offspring. Crossover is performed over two genomes that obtain high fitness function. It is expected that crossover between two good solutions can produce in better child. It is implemented as crossover in nature, with random exchanging genetic material between two DNA array or in case of GA two arrays that represent solution or genome.

Mutation introduces randomness into population, and thus spreads population and inserts new offspring. The genome changes itself due to mutation. However, mutation must be controlled, because unlimited mutation can lead to enormous growth of search space with negligible number of good solutions. Such algorithm would be slow and unpredictable.

Reproduction can be generalized. For example, the individuals for mating pool can be picked using fitness.

The fourth step is to define stopping criteria. There are two approaches to GA stopping. The first is to stop when previously defined number of solutions, whose fitness is above treshold, is reached. This solution is fast, but doesn't produce the best solutions. The second approach is to stop when improvement average fitness between two generations is below the predefined treshold. The second option is better, but it can be to slow and even enter indefinite loop.

After successful finishing all this steps, the genetic algorithm is ready to execute.

11.5.3.4. How to use GA for Internet Search?

GA can be used for intelligent search among Internet documents. Basic idea of Internet search is to construct intelligent agent, that uses user supplied documents, and find ones most similar to given. The agent can be designed using the Genetic Algorithm. The agent performs following steps:

- Process a set of URLs given by user
- Selects all links from the input set
- Evaluates fitness function for all URLs
- Performs crossover, mutation, and reproduction operators
- Repeats step 2 until a satisfactory solution is obtained

It is obvious that this five steps are the same as in GA. The intelligent Internet agent is just special kind of Genetic Algorithm. The main idea is to use URLs as individuals or genomes. The first generation is set of user supplied documents and all links from them. In order to evaluate fitness function for each genome, keywords from all documents must be extracted to compute fitness. Crossover, mutation, and reproduction operators obtain same task as in GA, but receive special implementation.

In order to implement GA for Internet search, the following problems must be solved:

- How to represent genomes?
- How to define the crossover and mutation operators?
- How to define fitness function?
- How to generate next generation?

In the following chapters, some widely used solutions are given.

11.5.3.4.1. How to represent genomes?

As said before all genomes are URLs. The idea is to represent each genome as array, that can be easily manipulated. The first approach is natural and assumes that contents of given URL is connected with it's string representation. The second solution is to present URL as array of strings.

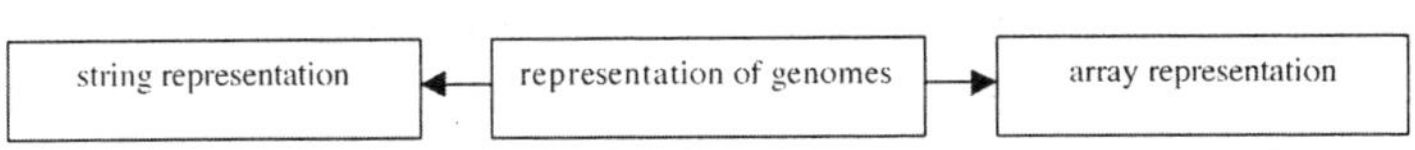

Figure 8: Methods for representing a genome

11.5.3.4.1.1. String representation

This solution is the simplest one, because it uses already existing representation of URL, as a string. The main problem with this solution is that the operators are highly complicated to define, since the genome consist of only one gene. Thus, crossover and mutation must be define as exchange or random change of one letter, and produce in number of offspring that don't exist, and if exist, is not connected, in any way, to given problem. This operators will lead to divergent algorithm with small chances to result in good solutions. Randomness will be to big, and thus search space will be huge, and number of good matches small. Those are the reasons not to recommend string representation for complicated problems and large search spáce.

http://galeb.etf.bg.ac.yu/~vm/tutorials/tutorial.html	EOS

Figure 9: Example for string representation

11.5.3.4.1.2.String array representation

The second solution is to represent URL as array of strings with actual meaning. At the Figure 10 can be seen the representation of the same URL as in Figure 9, but in array representation. It is important to emphasize that each string has its meaning. For example, the first string shows what protocol is used (ftp or http). In Internet search, documents are valid if they start with http. Next string represents server address (www, galeb, etc.). The most important part of address is one that gives the path from the server root to a particular document. For example, /~vm/tutorial/tutorial.html, Figure 10.

The advantage of this solution is obvious. Each genome, in this approach, has more that one genes (strings). The crossover operator is defined as exchange of strings between two genomes. Mutation is defined as random change of one string – gene.

http	galeb	etf	bg	ac	yu	~vm	tutorials	tutorial	html

Figure 10: Example from array representation

11.5.3.4.2. How to define crossover?

Crossover is defined as operator that combines genetic material from parent in order to produce superior offspring. The principle of natural crossover is to amplify good genes and surpress bad ones. In the following paragraphs, few solutions are given.

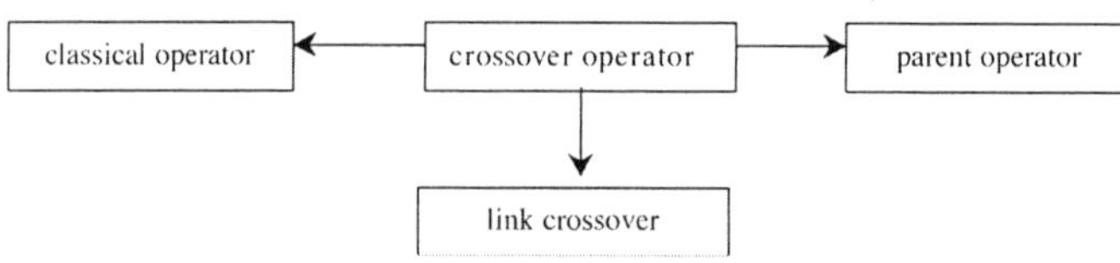

Figure 11: Types of crossover operators

11.5.3.4.2.1. How to define crossover operator?

Classical crossover is explained in paragraph II.1.2.String array representation. It combines two parent's string arrays and thus produce offspring. The idea is to exchange single strings – arrays. This approach is the simplest, but often produce in large number of non-existing URLs.

Parent crossover is realized by picking up parents from the mating pool and choosing a number of their links as offspring, without any evaluation. This method is extremely simply but may produce number of children that are not connected to user's interests.

Link crossover is the best crossover method, concerning fitness of offspring. Links from parents are evaluated and the fittest ones are picked for next generation. There is two evaluating methods in link crossover:

- overlapping links
- link pre-evaluating

In the first solution, the links that are the same for both parents are picked. It is supposed that the offspring links are connected to both web pages, and thus to user's interests.

In the second solution, the links are evaluated before, and those that are fittest are chosen. The problem with this solution is about time, since there can be number of links that must be evaluated, so the performance of algorithm is not good enough.

There are two types of crossover degree:

- limited
- unlimited

The idea of unlimited crossover is to allow indefinite number of offspring after the crossover.

In limited crossover, the number of children is limited, and thus avoided fast growth of population.

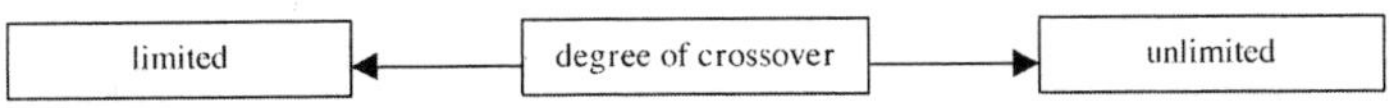

Figure 12: Degrees of crossver

11.5.3.4.3. How to define mutation?

Mutation introduces randomness into population, and thus spreads population and inserts new offspring.

There are three types of mutation operators:

- generational mutation
- selective mutation

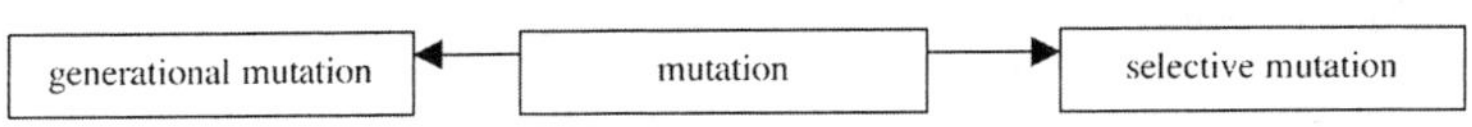

Figure 13: Types of mutation

Generational mutation is performed by generating random URLs. It is easy to implement, but has no significance, since produces not good solutions.

Selective mutation uses existing URLs for producing offspring. It can be:

- dB oriented
- Semantic

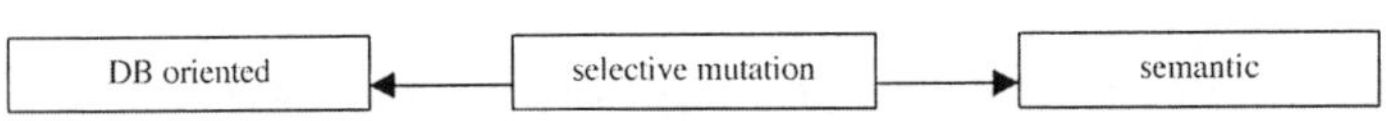

Figure 14: Types of selective mutation

For dB oriented mutation, dB of URLs must be obtained. Few of URLs from dB are chosen as offspring for next generation. First approach is to randomly pick up URLs from unsorted dB, and thus introduce randomness. This method is not promising, and very rarely produce good offspring. With the growth of dB, the probability that children will be similar to parents rapidly drops off.

The second, better approach is to pick up individuals from previously sorted dB, so the offspring is topic-similar to user's interests. The problem with this method is updating dB and deciding the topic of given URL.

Semantic mutation uses logical reasoning in implementing mutation. There are three types of it:

- spatial locality mutation
- temporal locality mutation

- type locality mutation

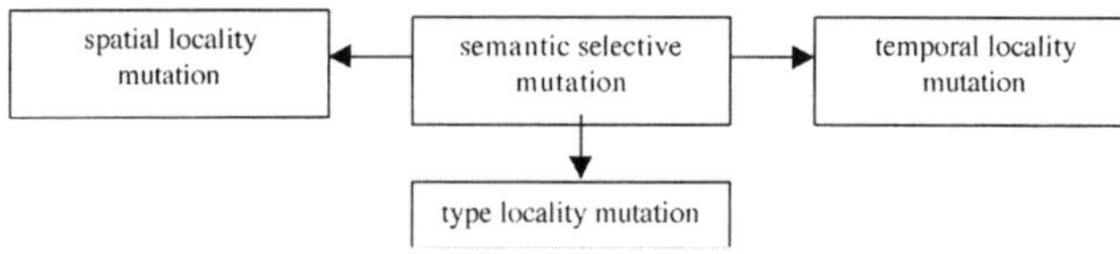

Figure 15: Types of semantic selective muatation

Spatial locality mutation resides on presumption that if some document has high fitness, there can be find similar document on the same server or local network. One approach is to pick random set of documents from the given server or to evaluate all URLs, which is time consuming, but more promising.

Temporal locality mutation resides on presumption that documents that are frequently used, are potentially good, so they are chosen as offspring. Genetic algorithm scores them on how frequently they appear in the set.

Type locality mutation is based on a type of the site the input documents are located on. If it is, foe example an .edu site, than it is strong possibility that some other .edu site will have similar contents.

The last two solutions are dealing with DBs, but since they use logic reasoning, they are not typically dB solutions.

11.5.3.4.4. How to define fitness function?

Evaluating genomes, using the fitness function, is highly important, since it decides what solutions are good and what are bad. At the Figure 16 can be seen, three possible solutions.

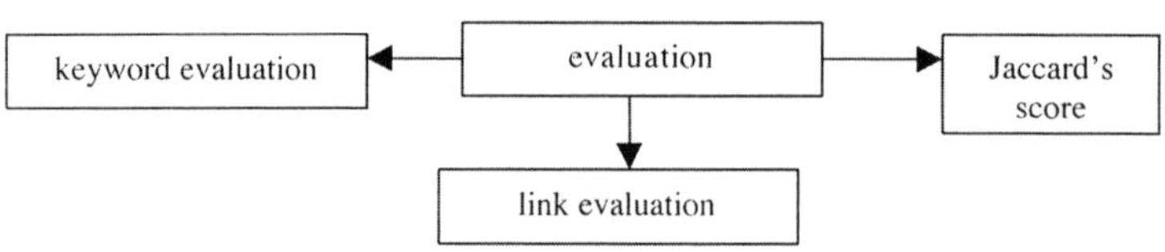

Figure 16: Evaluation types

In this solution, frequency of occurrence of given keywords is counted. The genetic algorithm add these numbers. For example, the one appearance of keyword can count as one, two appearances as three... Also, there can be special evaluation if keyword is in title or hyperlink of given page. This method can produce good enough solutions. Documents can be evaluated according to the number of links that belong to the set of links of input documents. This narrows the search space but can produce good results in most cases and is easily implemented.

11.5.3.4.5. How to generate the next generation?

There are two methods for producing the next generation:

- Interactive generation
- Post-generation.

Interactive generation picks good solutions from each generation and inserts them to results set. This method allows user to observe solutions before entire algorithm is performed. It is also possible to add new keywords or documents during the algorithm execution.

Post-generation uses the last generation to produce result. Thus, all genomes from last generation are inserted into result set. This solution is better, concerning the overall fitness of result set. However, user cannot modify search conditions before the end of algorithm execution.

11.5.3.5. System for GA Internet search designed by Electronic Business on the internet (EBI) group, Faculty for Electrical Engineering, University of Belgrade

11.5.3.5.1. Introduction

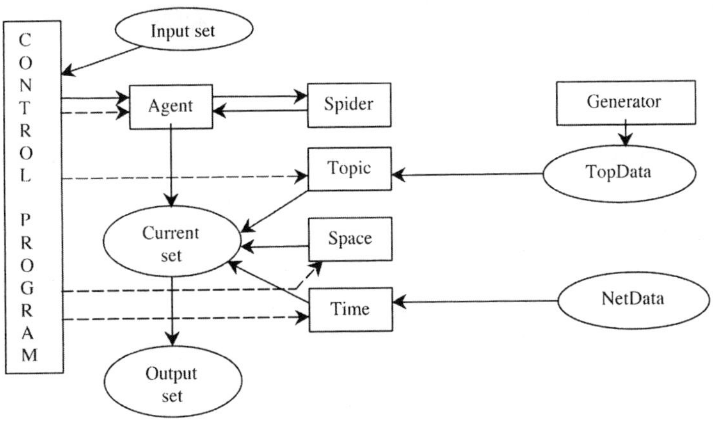

Figure 17: System architecture

For purposes of genetic Internet search system, the set of software packages was developed.

11.5.3.5.2. Architecture of the system

The entire system consists of following parts:

11.5.3.5.2.1. Spider

Spider is software packages that picks up Internet documents from user supplied input with depth specified by user. Spider's task is to produce the first generation, as explained before. The fetched documents are stored on local hard disk with same structure as on the original location.

Spider takes one URL, fetches all links, and documents they contain with predefined depth. This is done for all URLs supplied by user. Spider is used in each iteration of algorithm, when generation, crossover, and mutation is performed.

11.5.3.5.2.2. Agent

Agent as an input a set of URLs, and calls Spider, for every one of them, with depth 1. It then, performs extraction of keywords from each document, and stores it in local hard disk.

11.5.3.5.2.3. Generator

Generator generates a set of URLs from given keywords, using some conventional search engine. It takes as input the desired topic, calls Yahoo search engine and submits a query looking for all documents covering the specific topic. Generator stores URL and topic of given web page in database called TopData.

11.5.3.5.2.4. Topic

Topic performs mutation. It uses TopData DB in order to insert random URLs from database into current set.

11.5.3.5.2.5. Space

Space takes as input the current set from the Agent application and injects into it those URLs from the database NetData that appeared with the greatest frequency in the output set of previous searches. [1].

11.5.3.5.2.6. Time

Time takes set of URLs from Agent and inserts ones with greatest frequency into database NetData. The NetData DB contains of three fields: URL, topic, and count number. The DB is updated in each algorithm iteration.

NetData updating flowchart:

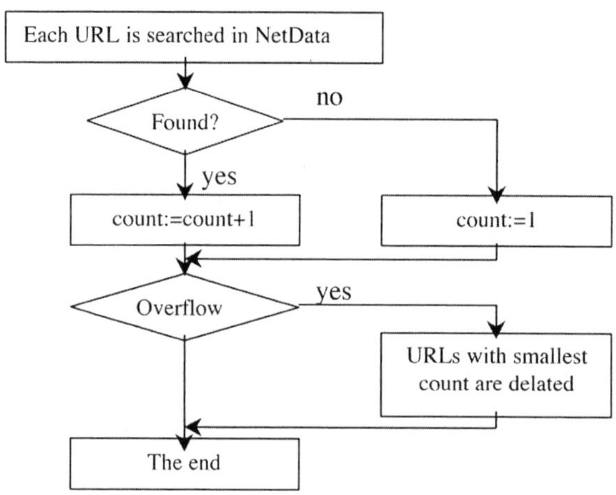

Figure 18: Flow chart of NetData updating

11.5.3.6. How to use GA to search among technologies at Technology Transfer web sites?

As for Internet search, genetic algorithm can be used for search among available technologies at Technology Transfer web sites. The idea is to perform GA anytime user wishes to find technologies matching given criteria.

Representation of technologies can be similar as representation of URLs, as described before. Both string and array of string representation can be used. as in Figures 19 and 20.

Ad-hoc mobile network platform	EOS

Figure 19: String representation

Figures 19 and 20 show how title is used to form full representation of technology.

Ad-hoc	mobile	network	platform	EOS

Figure 20: Array representation

The second issue concerning the technology search is crossover operator. This operator can be defined as classical crossover, as explained before. The idea is to mix two arrays from parents and thus produce the highly connected to contents of document this method is good enough. Comparing to URLs, technology titles are much easier to use and operate with.

The third issue is mutation. All mutation methods can be used to introduce randomness into the population. Since technology databases are much smaller then Internet ones, the DB oriented solutions are efficient and fast.

As a fitness function, indexing method can be used. All documents are indexed into DB by keywords and the appearance of given keywords are computed. For, example one occurrence of keyword may count as one, two occurrences as two, etc. The occurrence of keyword in title may count as ten.

For reproduction operator the widely used types of generalized operators can be used. Some of them are explained before.

The problem with technology search is less complex then one with Internet search. The major reason is that technology DBs, even at the highly developed sites, are much smallest, and thus easy to maintain, use, and update. Second reason is the lack of links to other documents so the search space is narrower. Finally, the documents are smaller, so the evaluation is faster.

11.6. Technology Transfer Web Sites

Nowadays, there are many Technology Transfer web sites, that offer services for investors and inventors.

11.6.1. Classification of Technology Transfer Web Sites

Criteria for classification is for whom is web site designed, and who uses it.

Historically speaking, the first web sites are academic Technology Transfer sites. At this sites universities, institutes, and other non-profit organizations are offering their invention for commercialization. This web sites are also used by investors, who can find interesting technology to invest in. Second class are web sites for specific areas of science.

Web sites specialized for sellers are web sites with huge database of technology want advertisements. There are just few of such web sites. The major number of Technology Transfer web sites are specialized for buyers. Each buyer has access to database of patents ready for commercialization. The most comprehensive companies are those who offer their services both to buyers and sellers. In further paragraphs, it will be explained how to use three, in our opinion, the best Technology Transfer companies.

11.6.2. Delphion.com Intellectual Property Network

11.6.2.1. Introduction

Dolphin can be accessed at web page http://www.delphion.com/. It is formed in May, 2000. By IBM and ICG (Internet Capital Group). Delphion is wholly independent, stand alone entity. Before Delphion ,IBM owned extremely successful .com company IP Network, since 1997.

It is made in response to the growing needs of individuals, organizations, and governments for more efficient methods of exploring Intellectual Property (IP). For the past eight years, IBM has been granted more patents than any other company in the world

In 2000, IBM's IP line of business generated over $1.5 billion in revenue, with a profit margin in excess of 90%.

11.6.2.2. Basic Characteristics of Delphion

First and possible the most important attribute of a internet-based Technology Transfer company is searchability of it's database. You will notice, that all three web sites have excellent searchablity. Those who does not have such characteristics are not worth of mentioning.

The size of IP database is, in our opinion, the greatest among a number visited web sites. At Delphion are listed all patents prosecuted at US, EEC, and Japan. Therefore, Delphion does not provide service of anonymous technology listing. Delphion does not require exclusivity for their clients, which means that the user can be client of a other Technology Transfer companies and list same products there.

Charging is $75-$150 per moth, depending what package you wish to subscribe.

Besides monthly fee, all users pay special services per use. Unfortunately, Delphion does not provide negotiating and contract support. In fact at Delphion one can search for potential partner, obtain information about him, and nothing else.

11.6.2.3. Registration and Services

To became a member of Delphion and review all of its services, first step is registration. But, before starting it one have to decide what subscription he wants. This is important decision, because different packages allow different services. By determining type of registration one determines how he will use Delphion.

There are three types of subscription:

1. One-day-pass: It is one day trial of all Delphion services, price is $29. This type is unique among T2 companies. Other companies also may have trial period, mostly without all services. One cannot register twice for a trial.
2. Group and corporate subscription: It is for large companies and corporation. Unlimited number of users can be subscribed to an one account.
3. Standard Subscription is for a single user:

After deciding to register as Group or Standard user, one needs to choose subscription package.

There are also three subscription packages:

1. Basic – for casual user, free of charge
2. Premier – for frequent user, charging is $75 per month
3. Unlimited – for business professionals, charging is $150 per month

If one is interested in some patent, he has opportunity to save it in his on-line personal folder of unlimited size in order to review it later. Also, one can download complete information about desired patented technology in .pdf format, for in-depth analyses. Each download is priced $3.00. Delphion allows only 5 downloads per day.

If client of Premier package has a question to ask or problem to solve he has opportunity to use customer support service, which responds to request in 24 hours.

Delphion Unlimited package provides all services of Premier, and some more:

1. Unlimited .pdf download.
2. Unlimited use of text clustering
3. As in Premier package, user has customer support, but this time much faster, within 6 hours.
4. Delphion assures his Unlimited clients with security shell connection, without fear of industry espionage.

Basic package user has opportunity to use this services:
1. Quick search and patent number search, only for US biblio
2. PDF downloads on pay-per-use basis
3. Registration and billing support

11.6.2.4. Delphion Conclusion

US06055562 04/25/2000 Dynamic mobile agents

Legend: L – marker to show that patent is licensable
US06055562 – number of patent
04/25/2000 – date of patent prosecution
Dynamic mobile agents – name of the patent

Figure 21: Example of one patent at the database

If you are technology buyer, Delphion is right choice for you. The largest IP database available over the Internet allows you the most powerful search. Unfortunately, it is not so good for inventors.

Second, not so good characteristics, is lack of negotiating and agreement support, meaning that you can only get contact information of potential partner, and nothing more.

Also, consultant support is insufficient.

However, Delphion.com is young company who showed great improvement over last few months, so progress is expected in all features.

11.6.3. Yet2.com

11.6.3.1. Introduction

URL address at which yet2 can be accessed is http://www.yet2.com/.

Yet2.com was founded in February, 1999. as the first on-line Technology Transfer company. In January, 2000 yet2.com announced $20 million in funding commitments from Venrock Associates, 3i Group, The Procter & Gamble Company, and Honeywell International. Besides these companies, partners and clients of yet2.com are number of Fortune 1000 Companies.

11.6.3.2. Basic Characteristics

Searcablity of database is good, fast and efficient. Since Yet2.com updates his database with user provided technologies for license, database is not huge as at Delphion, but big enough to satisfy needs of average user. All technologies are listed anonymously, which is better than at Delphion.com. Unfortunately, Yet2.com is unique if consider exclusivity. It is only company we have observed, which demand that same technology cannot be listed at any other web site. Charging is $50 per month.

11.6.3.3. How to Register?

Registration is much complicated then at Delphion.com. Full graph of registration process can be seen at Figure 22. Notice that there are two ways to register. First is to register as company member and join existing account, and second is to open a new account. After creating the account, next step is providing company information. It is not necessary, but is highly recommended, to add account and credit card data, in order to use all services of yet2.com. After finishing these steps, in one way or another, you are registered member and ready to do a business.

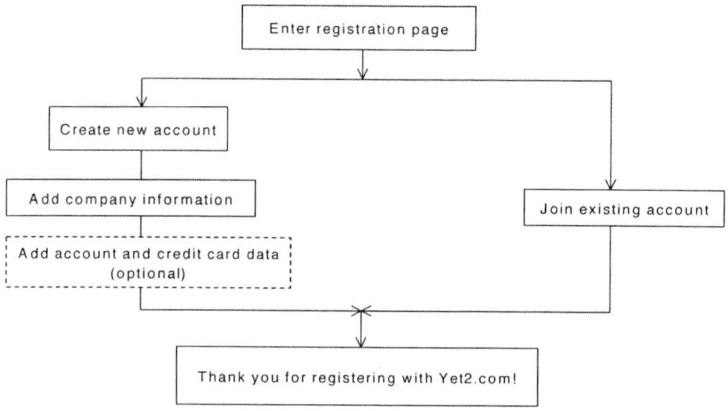

Figure 22: Registration process

11.6.3.4. Services

11.6.3.4.1. Offer a Technology

Each technology is presented as TechPak. TechPak is unique package for better technology organization, listing and search. TechPak is set of MS Word Documents and additional files, who describes technology, such as images and movies of prototype. TechPak can be in one of following stages: In Draft (Not ready for licensing), In Action List (Ready for commercialization), and Archived (Redrawn from action).

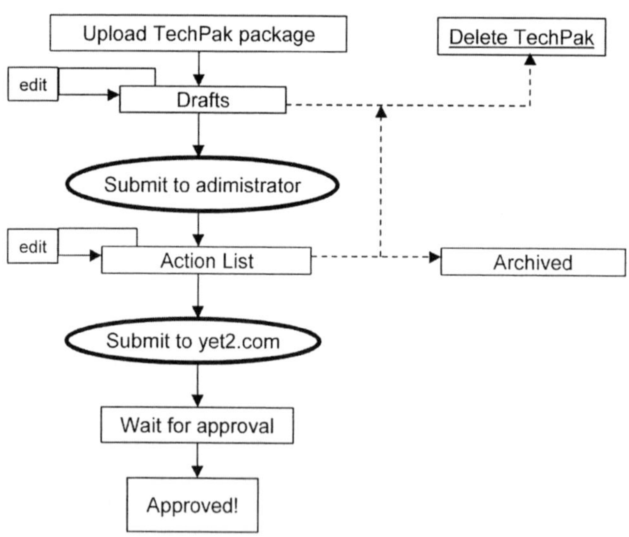

Figure 23: TechPak management flow chart

All information about technology is listed in TechPak, unique package for better technology organization, listing and search. TechPak is set of MS Word Documents and additional files, who describes technology.

The first step is uploading TechPak to database. Notice that there are five states, of TechPak: In Draft, In action list, Archived, Waiting for approval, Approved.

Technology is placed into drafts at the time it is posted. While in draft it can be edited or even deleted. When user get satisfied with his TechPak he puts it to action list. Still, no other user can access the TechPak. Yet2 administrator checks technology for quality, legal issues or similar. If it satisfy yet2 criteria, it is approved, and offered worldwide. While in action list, TechPak can be edited, deleted or archived, which means that technology is sold or under negotiations. This procedure ensures buyer that offered technology is world class.

11.6.3.4.2. Search for Technology

There are three ways of searching for technology, that is available for commercialization. One can either search for TechPak, which contains keywords provided by user, search for patent in yet2.com database, or create technology want add, and wait for contact from inventor.

11.6.3.4.3. Make a Proposal

After investor finds technology which is interesting for him, he can ask for an introduction to Intellectual Property owner.

In the first column it can be seen four ways for searching for available technology. Investor then asks for introduction to inventor. Request is proceed to technology owner by yet2.com. The inventor has 48 hours to respond to the request. After positive response potential investor has 5 days to respond and start negotiations. Yet2.com must be updated with advancement in negotiations.

11.6.3.5. Yet2.com Conclusion

As can be seen, yet2.com is highly powerful for Technology Transfer, equally good for buyers and sellers. Except help in legal issues, like composing the contract, it provides help in all steps of Technology Transfer process, discussed before. It is important to emphasize that customer support is one of the best.

On the contrary, request for exclusivity, that does not allow advertising the same IP at any third party web site, is extremely unpopular, and may, in some cases, result in deciding not to use yet2.com. It is highly important that one can advertise his invention at all sites he chooses in order to get more opportunities to realize his ideas.

11.6.4. Technology Connect

11.6.4.1. Introduction

TechnologyConnect (TC) can be accessed at www.technologyconnect.com. The company is founded in 1998. and officially formed in 1999. TC is market for licensing, consulting, research, and new in area of technology. It is important to emphasize that in Scientific Advisory Board are two Nobel Laureates: Robert Richardson and Jerome Friedman.

11.6.4.2. Basic Characteristics of TechnologyConnect

Searching at TechnologyConnect is simple as it can be, very fast and efficient. Size of database is not huge as at Delphion but large enough for a good business. Technologies can be listed anonymously. Also, TC does not require any exclusivity, so you can offer your technology at other web sites, too. Good thing about charging, is that it is free for the first six month, and bad is that, after, it's $250.

The main characteristics is that TC is the most comprehensive internet-based Technology Transfer company, meaning that all the job concerning transfer can be done on-line.

11.6.4.3. Types of an account

There are three types of account at Technology Connect.

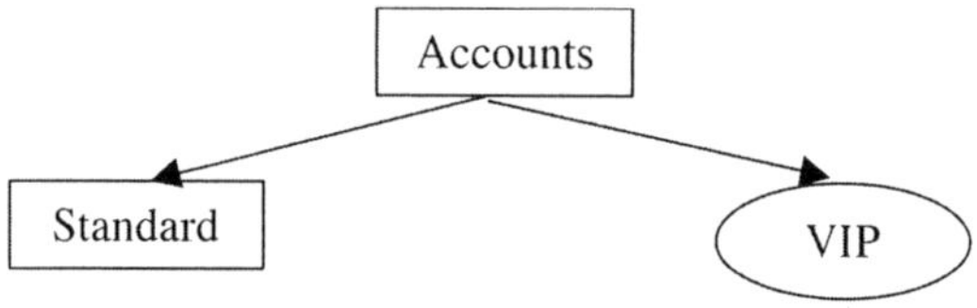

Figure 24: Account types at TC

Standard Program provides an on-line process in which buyers, sellers or consultants create profiles used by unique IntelliMatch System.

VIP Program provides enhanced support service in order to maximize the client's results in terms of buying or selling technologies.

11.6.4.3.1 Standard Program

Standard program uses unique system IntelliMatch, to join sellers and buyers, in order to maximize profit, and to provide contact to consultants, to improve business. A profile hosting fee is $250/per each profile, fee for disclosure is $100 and fee for hosting of product $100/month.

The Standard client can perform unlimited anonymous searches on the TC database in order to find potential partner for joint venture. Company specific information is used only by IntelliMatch System. That information helps for better search. The client can ask for company information but other side must approve it and also seeker must pay disclosure fee.

Online proposals are provided to allow a client to request the sale of a technology, or make an offer to sell a technology.

Technology Connect highly reduces time-to-market. Also, small companies get opportunity of connecting to Fortune 1000 companies.

Sellers get international exposure of their products. Buyers get access to international market of ideas, products, and patents. Consultants get opportunity of offering their services worldwide.

11.6.4.3.2. VIP Program

As VIP client one gets services of standard program and more.

All users assigned as VIP have their own support team provided by TechnologyConnect in order to get help in various issues, especially in science and law. Every VIP user gets its own manager who helps the client with all necessary services.

VIP Manager assigned to each user does following: works closely to user in order to understand its needs, provides education in using VIP Program features, provides education in updating TC Database, works as connection between client and TC.

Special services include: dedicated program managers experienced in VIP clients technologies and industries to facilitate deal closures, discounted research reports provided by a TechnologyConnect strategic information partner, qualification of potential licensees and partners, strategic marketing and technology expertise for VIP clients' technologies/products, negotiation and deal closure expertise.

VIP user has increased chances of finding buyers/sellers, and of closing deals, through efforts of TC VIP Manager, staff, management, and partners. Access to third-party consultants is also provided. VIP clients receive invitations to forums, organized by TC, to boarden awareness of market events/trends, and access to research report written by undefended consultants, for TechnologyConnect.

11.6.4.3.4. Technology Connect Conclusion

Technology Connect is most comprehensive .com company for providing on-line services for licensors and licensees VIP Program provides large companies with services in license management. IntelliMatch ensures best match between buyers and sellers.

11.7. Conclusion

As shown before, money and information are the key factors in technology progress. Technology Transfer allows scientist to find money for their projects, but also, investors to reach for information about trends in technology. It is shown, that before the Internet this process was highly complicated, and thus technology progress slow.

The newborn Technology Transfer companies make the process faster and effective. The Internet helps investors to find interesting projects they want to invest in, and allows scientists to find money in much easier way, using computers and the Internet. Communication is improved and negotiations accelerated.

Predictions are that further improvement is in area of legal issues on the Internet. It will be possible to reach and execute agreement on-line. Also, it is expected for companies to improve consultant services

11.8. Problems

1. What are factors for technology progress?
2. What is Intellectual Property (IP)? Name all types of IP.
3. Explain the purpose of WIPO.
4. What is technology transfer?
5. What is technological activity? What is the most important factor of technological activity?
6. Explain the concept of Genetic Algorithms (GA).
7. How GA can be used for search at technology transfer web sites?
8. What are the most important features of technology transfer companies?
9. Compare all three presented companies with attention to features defined in problem 8.
10. Suggest new services that can be provided by technology transfer companies

REFERENCES

[UK2001a] Intellectual Property: What is an Intellectual Property? http://intellectual-property.gov.uk/ip.html, July 2001.

[UK2001b] Intellectual Property: What is a Patent? http://intellectual-property.gov.uk/patent.html

[UK2001c] Intellectual Property: What is a Trademark ? http://intellectual-property.gov.uk/tm.html, July 2001.

[UK2001d Intellectual Property: What is a Copyright? http://intellectual-property.gov.uk/copyright.html, July 2001.

[Wherry95] Wherry, Timothy Lee. Patent Searching for Librarians and Inventors. American Library Association, 1995

[WIPO2001] World Intellectual Property Organization, http://www.wipo.org, June 2001.

[Mirkovic99a] J.Mirkovic, D.Cvetkovic, N.Tomca, S.Cveticanin, Lj. Nesic, S.Slijepcevic, V.Obradovic, M.Mrkic, I.Cakulev, L.Kraus, V.Milutinović "Genetic Algorithms for Intelligent Internet Search: A Survey and a Package for Experimenting with Various Locality Types", IEEE TCCA Newsletter, 1999.

[Mirkovic2000] J.Mirkovic, D.Cvetkovic, N.Tomca, S.Cveticanin, Lj. Nesic, S.Slijepcevic, V.Obradovic, M.Mrkic, I.Cakulev, L.Kraus, V.Milutinović "A Software Package for Experimenting Genetic search on Internet: Static versus Mobile Agents", IEEE 7th International Workshop on Enabling Technologies: Infrastructure for Collective Enterprises, Stanford University, California

[Milutinovic] V.Milutinović, L.Kraus, J.Mirkovic "A Genetic Algorithm for Internet Search Using a DB-Oriented Topic Sorted Mutation", to be published

E-Business and E-Challenges
V. Milutinović and F. Patricelli (Eds.)
IOS Press, 2002

CHAPTER 12
DENIAL OF SERVICE ATTACKS ON THE INTERNET

Bratislav Milic, Milan Savic and Veljko Milutinović

The main idea of this chapter is to give an introduction to Denial of Service (DoS) attacks. It covers basic types of the DoS attacks (UDP flood, ICMP flood, Smurf attack, etc.); evolution of DoS tools, from simple, easy to stop tools to complex distributed systems; overview of some of DDoS (Distributed DoS) tools, and finally, defenses against the DoS attacks.

12.1. Denial of Service Attacks, Basics

First of all, what is denial of service attack? The CERT/CC (Computer Emergency Response Team/Coordination Center) defines it as "attack in which the primary goal of the attack is to deny the victim(s) access to a particular resource" [CERT97]. This is a very broad definition, and it covers lots of ways to deny some service.

We will focus to a subclass of denial of service attacks: only the ones committed from outside of victim's system and whose goal is to reduce network connectivity and bandwidth. Or, following the CERT's definition of denial of service attack, it can be said that critical resources of our interest are network connectivity and bandwidth; and victims are the users of targeted systems.

Frequency of denial of service attacks is over four thousand per week [Moore00]. And according to [CSI00], a survey among security professionals showed that during the year 2000, 27% of them detected denial of service attack. Despite this fact, media coverage of DoS attacks is poor. This comes for two main reasons:

- Affected companies often hide the fact that they have been attacked in fear of negative publicity, especially in the case that company is e-oriented.
- Intensity of attack is small and it is more a local problem for some network.

But, from time to time, big companies become victims of attacks. As a good example, we can look at February 2000 attacks: On 7th and 8th February Amazon.com, Yahoo, eBay.com, Buy.com, and CNN Interactive were attacked. Method of attack was bandwidth consumption. All three companies are Internet-oriented and have high-speed links, but that did not help them: Buy.com had 100 Mb/s link, and the stream going to their routers was about 800 Mb/s.

The influence of those attacks was not limited only to the attacked sites - because of increased traffic over the Internet, overall Internet performance fell as shown in Figure 12.1. The increase in Internet traffic was partly because of the traffic produced directly by attacks, and partly by Internet users who were searching more information about the attacks.

The intensity and duration of the attacks lead us to a conclusion that lots of time was devoted to organizing the attacks. Also, it is highly likely that those attacks were committed by a group of people. Or, if it was not a group of attackers responsible, if attacks were act of a single man, that is even more frightening - a single man in control over so many resources.

Before committing an attack, an attacker has to find suitable systems - systems with weaknesses that will allow the attacker to infiltrate into them and later use them at its own wish. This is a necessary step - no one would use personal account for attacks. The use of stolen accounts hides the attacker and makes tracking down of the attacker very difficult.

Date	PPW	PAW	CPW
February, 7th	5.66	5.98	5.7% slower
February, 8th	5.53	5.96	7.8% slower
February, 9th	5.26	6.67	26.8% slower
February, 10th	4.97	4.86	2.2% faster

Legend: **PPW** - Performance in previous week (seconds), **PAW** - Performance in attacking week (seconds), **CPW** - Change from previous week (percent)

Comment: Used data is from The Keynote Business 40 Internet Performance Index. It is the average response time of accessing and downloading the home pages of 40 important business web sites by T-1 and T-3 links.

Explanation: In the table are compared times of normal week and of week in which attacks occurred.

Implications: Because of denial of service attacks, the whole Internet experienced slowdown.

Figure 12.1 Overall Internet performance degradation [KEYNOTE00].

One way to find suitable systems is done by exploiting errors in operating systems. There is not a single operating system without errors. Errors can be more or less dangerous for system security. After detection of an error, operating system vendor will make patch to fix that error. The attacker will use time gap between discovery of weakness and publication of patch. The attacker will also use negligence of some system administrators - experience shows that most of patches are never applied.

Process of finding vulnerable systems is automated. Usually it is done by some script, but generally it can be done by any kind of tool. Operation starts by scanning the network in search for systems with set of vulnerabilities that can be exploited. Once found, vulnerable system becomes compromised. It is best for the attacker to gain administrator privileges but in the case it is not possible, the attacker will be satisfied with ordinary account and privileges. The following step is the installation of desired tools. In most cases, the script will transfer itself together with denial of service tools. The next step is the installation of root-kits, in case that stolen account has administrator privileges. Root-kits can hide files, processes, network connections and can make detection of intrusion very difficult. Finally, after installation of the root-kit, newly compromised system can be used either for further scan of the network to compromise more systems or for denial of service attacks.

Another way of compromising systems is using Trojan horses and worms. This idea is used mostly on Windows based systems. In most cases it relies on neglectful users - worm is spread through email as attachment, and user has to start it manually. Worm is usually disguised as something else, e.g. screen saver, but sometimes it is seen as executable file or script - without any disguise. After it is started, worm creates back door for attacker, alters some system files and then sends itself to all persons from users address book. Of course, this pattern follows only one group of worms, some of them have destructive payload, some of them just spread through the Internet, some of them start automatically, some do not use mail to spread themselves, etc.

In July 2001, CodeRed worm gave good illustration of everything previously mentioned. Organization eEye Digital Security discovered security flaw in Microsoft's Internet Information Server (IIS) in late spring same year and notified Microsoft about their discovery. Microsoft made patch and put it on their technical support pages. One month after discovery, eEye published what they have found out. In mid-July, the worm struck the Internet. Total number of infected web servers was between 250000 [CERT01] and 359000 [Moore01]. During infection peak, some slower parts of the Internet experienced form of denial of service attack - because of large traffic created by the worm trying to infect more and more servers. Payload of the worm was: spreading itself, defacing web pages on infected server, and denial of service attack against *http://www.whitehouse.gov*. CodeRed had some design errors, so damage caused by it was not big:

- The worm was present only in system memory so in order to remove it and make system immune to future attacks, administrator should apply patch and reboot system.
- IP address of White house's site was hard coded in the worm so denial of service attack was avoided by changing IP address of the site.

It can be said that whole Internet community was lucky but in future we cannot rely whether worms will be made with errors or not. The whole event showed that most of system administrators did not apply Microsoft's patch. CodeRed infected even some Microsoft's servers and some of them were responsible for updates and support [Lemos01]. Lots of administrators did not even know what is going on until they heard on media.

Like mentioned before, it is highly likely that after infiltrating into a system, the attacker will install root-kit. Inexperienced administrators do not know either to deal with them, or how to detect presence of root-kit.

Easy "solution", which is often applied, is reinstallation of whole operating system. This is bad for several reasons. If system showed weakness once, and attackers found way to exploit it, installation of same version of operating system without additional security measures, patches or updates does not help. System will remain prone to intrusions.

Reinstallation also destroys all evidence of intrusion. This makes any analysis impossible. After reinstallation tracking back the attacker or finding out how the intruder got in is not possible any more.

The goal of all this preparations was the attack. It can be done in several ways, and those ways will be described in the following sub-chapters.

12.2. Teardrop and Ping of Death attacks

Teardrop and Ping of Death are now obsolete, and all mayor operating systems can handle them. Nevertheless, it's good to know basic facts about them for two reasons. The first one is need to learn from past and to avoid similar errors in future. The second is to clearly see evolution of DoS tools. Teardrop and Ping of Death are very simple. They were made in early days of DoS attacks. Latest denial of service tools are state of the art distributed applications.

Both of those attacks are based on implementation bugs of the Internet Protocol (IP). It is very important to understand that error is in implementation, not in standard and that protocol is clearly defined without any ambiguity.

IP's specification allows maximum size of packet to be 65536 bytes. Of those, header minimum size is 20 bytes and optionally it can be longer - up to 24 bytes. Remaining packet space is used for data.

Attacker's idea is to send packet longer than 65536 bytes. This can be easily done by using one part of IP - Internet Control Message Protocol (ICMP). ICMP is used for transmitting error and control messages between systems and it must be part of every IP implementation.

There are two specific instances of ICMP of our importance: ICMP ECHO_REQUEST and ICMP ECHO_REPLY. They are used for network testing: one machine sends to another ICMP ECHO REQUEST and waits for ICMP ECHO_REPLY. In case that network is functional, first machine will receive response (assuming that there are no firewalls or other blocking software installed in network). Usually, this is done by "ping" command. The "ping" command can send ICMP packets of different size, and it's user's task to define size. So, malicious user only needs to send oversized ICMP packet using "ping" command to some host, and it was highly likely that the host will crash, hang or reboot. That is why this attack has such name "Ping of Death" - the attacker can crash some system with only one packet.

Fortunately, protection against this attack is quite simple, only small change in IP implementation. Today, all modern operating systems are immune to this type of attack.

Similar to "Ping of Death" is "Teardrop" attack. Same as in the "Ping of Death", origin of this attack is in bad implementation of IP. One of many IP features is a possibility to fragment packets on sending side and to reassemble them on receiving side.

Each fragment has its identification number and offset address. Identification number is needed to resolve situation where one node receives several fragmented packets in the same time - in that case, without identification, it would be impossible to determine the right way for reassembling of fragments. Offset address determines order in which the packet is reassembled. Offset is relative to the beginning of message and it is given in 8 byte units.

The "Teardrop" creates fragmented packet with overlapping offsets inside every fragment. Series of such improper fragments can crash system.

This problem is corrected for older systems through patches. Newer versions of operating systems do not have problems with the "Teardrop".

12.3. The SYN Attack

To understand SYN attack one should know the basics about TCP connection.

First of all, TCP connection can be established only between two sockets. Socket is determined by IP address and port number. In order to open TCP connection, there must not be already opened connection between those two sockets. Usually, these sockets belong to different machines, and we will use the term "machine" instead of "socket". Also, both machines must agree to the connection and must have adequate resources to service the connection. Since victims of DoS attacks are publicly available services, it is assumed that both of machines are willing to connect to each other.

TCP connection is established through three-step handshake. In the first step, one of machines (client) request TCP connection by sending a SYN signal to the second machine (server).

The server responds with a SYN acknowledgement (SYNACK) signal and keeps track of this request. This is the second step.

In the third and final step, the client, after receiving acknowledgement from server, responds with another acknowledgement (ACK).

Once the handshake is finished, it is said that the connection is established. During the handshake, connection is half-opened. In case that server does not receive ACK, it will drop connection request after some timeout.

SYN attack is based on opening lots of half-open connections. For every half-open connection, server has to allocate some memory to store it. Usually the server has limited amount of memory for this purpose. This means that the server can keep only limited number of half-open connections, and once that number is reached, the server will refuse all connection attempts. Number of half-open connections can drop as time passes, as they get timed out or if connection is established.

Attacker prevents establishing of connection between its system and server. If connection is established, the server will refuse another one - and that would be the end of attack. To avoid this, attackers system sends its requests with spoofed source address. Server will then send SYN acknowledgement signal to some system that has not requested TCP connection and will never get ACK signal back.

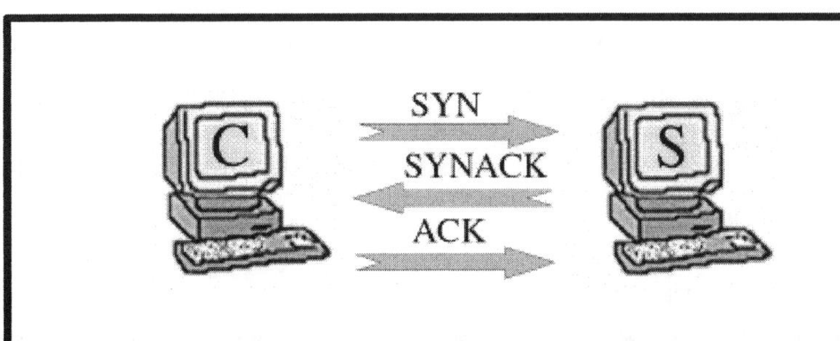

Legend: C -client, S - server

Explanation: Client is trying to establish TCP connection with server. To establish connection, it must pass through all three steps in SYN handshake. Server has to keep client information after receiving SYN package. For those purposes, server has limited amount of memory.

Implications: Large number of SYN packages can fill server's memory used for storing of half-open connections data. In that case, other connection requests cannot be accepted until some memory space is freed. Attacker sends SYN packages with spoofed source address. Server will respond with SYNACK package, but server will never receive ACK. Space used for keeping data on half opened connections will be always full, and legitimate users cannot access server.

Figure 12.2 The TCP Handshake

With all this false connection requests, the server will not be able to send acknowledgement to real user, since it's resources for keeping track of half-opened connections are full, and there is no place to put real request.

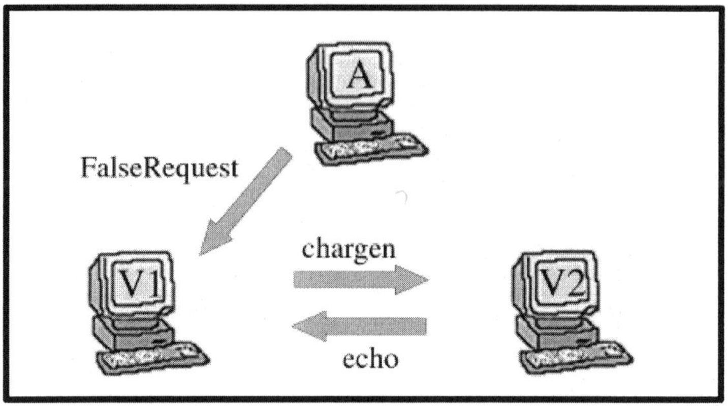

Legend: **A** -attacker, **V1** - victim one, **V2** - victim two

Explanation: Attacker sends request to **V1** asking for chargen service. In this request, source address is spoofed, so chargen service will be connected to **V2**'s echo service. Echo sends data generated by chargen back to **V1**, and so on.

Implications: Endless flow of useless data goes between **V1** and **V2**. This does not consume whole bandwidth, so before it is discovered, the attack can last for days.

Figure 12.3 "Smart" UDP flood

This attack is a good example of asymmetric attack and attack based on reducing network connectivity. Network connectivity can be significantly reduced, or, in worst case, victim system can even be totally inaccessible. It is asymmetric because the attacker has no need to send large amounts of data (like in some other flood attacks) to block targeted system - only quite small TCP connection requests.

In early days of this attack, it caused severe problems - some of targeted systems even crashed. To reduce damage of this type of attack, systems allocated more memory for storing of half-open connections and reduced timeout. Although this helped, it is not final solution of this problem. No mater how much memory is allocated, attacker can send more requests. Reducing of timeout looses sense after some limit, if timeout is too small, legitimate user will be timed out. However, these improvements help in case of small and medium size attacks.

12.4. The UDP Flood

UDP is User Datagram Protocol. In TCP/IP model it is in the same layer as TCP, one layer above IP. Like IP and unlike TCP, it is connectionless protocol. Connectionless means that it does not provide reliability. Sender has no way to find out if the message arrived at source address. Also, connectionless protocol has not got error-recovery capabilities. They must be defined either in upper or lower layers. But in case that we really need reliable protocol, it is logical to use TCP. So, UDP has specific purposes, where its simplicity and speed is more important that TCP's reliability. UDP is used as transport layer for TFTP (Trivial File Transfer Protocol) and RCP (Remote Call Procedure).

UDP flood can be done in two ways. One is by sending large quantities of data and that is brute force approach. It is difficult to stop, but attacker has to have lot of resources to do such attack.

The second way is more sophisticated and more deceitful. Also, it is easier to stop than brute force attack.

The idea of this attack is to connect UDP echo service with UDP chargen service. Chargen is UDP service designed for network testing, it sends character stream to specified socket until it receives request to stop. Echo service, like its name says, echoes all data back to sender.

The attack can be achieved by sending malformed request to chargen service of first victim. The request has spoofed source address and port number, so all chargen traffic will be directed to second victim's echo port. Echo will send all data back to sender. This doubles traffic intensity and the flood of useless data travels between two systems.

This kind of attack creates two victims. Its sophistication lies in fact that with only one packet, attacker consumes significant part of network bandwidth for two victims. Its deceitfulness is in fact that bandwidth is reduced but not completely consumed. Users will notice network slowdown, and before real cause of that slowdown is found, lot of time can pass.

12.5. Smurf attack

The "Smurf" is brute force and asymmetric attack that uses IP's direct broadcast addressing to generate huge amount of traffic.

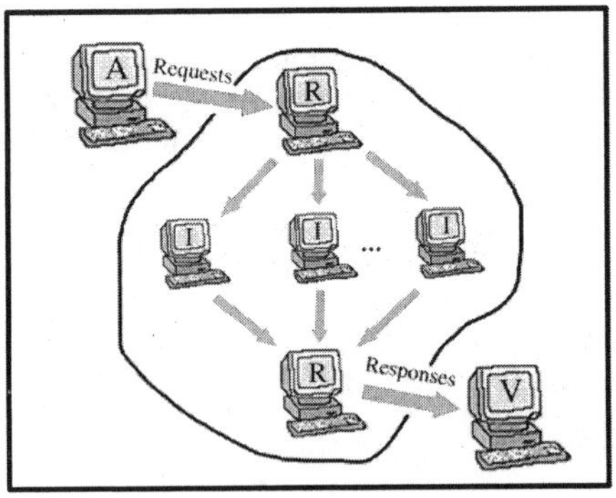

Figure 12.4 Smurf attack

Legend: **A** -attacker, **R** - router, **I** - intermediate, **V** - victim, **Requests** - ICMP ECHO_REQUEST packages, **Responses** - ICMP ECHO_REPLY packages

Explanation: Attacker sends stream of broadcast ICMP ECHO_REQUEST packages with spoofed source address to intermediate network (it consists of intermediate machines **I**). Router broadcasts those packages to intermediate machines, which send ICMP ECHO_REPLY packages to victim **V**.

Implications: Intermediate network works as multiplier so the attacker can overwhelm system with much higher bandwidth than his. Also, it is important to notice that victims are both victim **V** and intermediate network since both networks have bandwidth reduction.

In IP, there is a feature to broadcast a message to all networks and all hosts by specifying IP address of 32 ones (actually, this is correct for later TCP/IP implementations; in early BSD implementation of TCP/IP, for broadcast were used all zeros; since using ones is later and in use now, we will follow that convention). Also there is possibility to direct broadcast to only one network. For example, message to address 147.91.255.255 (galeb.etf.bg.ac.yu) will be sent to all devices in network 147.91.

The "Smurf" attack uses this feature to make a sort of multiplier. It sends ICMP ECHO_REQUEST to a whole network using direct broadcast addressing. Router will broadcast this ECHO_REQUEST to all hosts in the network, and in case that network has lot of hosts, this will generate large ECHO_REPLY traffic. Attacker can send a series of these requests to a network, and each of them creates multiplied response. Off course, all ICMP ECHO_REQUEST packages have modified source address, so the replies will not return to real sender (attacker) but to victim, whose address is put as source address.

This type of attack creates two victims, similar to UDP flood: one is network that receives broadcast requests and responds to them, and the other is system that receives all ECHO_REPLY traffic. Both victims can experience significant bandwidth reduction due to huge number of ICMP packets.

Prevention of this attack must be done on two sides. On the multiplier side, all broadcast requests coming from outside that network must be blocked. And on victims side, router should block all ECHO_REPLY traffic, or even better, reduce this traffic to some small percentage of all traffic.

12.6. Evolution of DoS Attacks

As time passed, defenses against previously mentioned attacks improved, system administrators educated themselves, technology improved bandwidth, etc. All these factors reduced effectiveness of attacks and, logically, attacks evolved.

Classical bandwidth consumption became more and more difficult, especially against commercial sites - they tend to have expensive and high-end equipment, the fastest on market.

That is why data floods were altered a bit. Attackers realized that limiting factor of most routers is not bandwidth but the packet processing rate. From attackers point of view, it is better to send 10 smaller packets than one large packet.

For the SYN attacks, as one solution it was proposed to allocate more memory for data structures responsible for storing of connection requests. This did help a bit, but then CPU's processing abilities showed up as a limit. Remember, in order to open new connection, there must not be already opened connection.

Legend: **A** -attacker, **I** - intermediate system, **V** - victim

Explanation: Attacker sends packet to intermediate system **I**. Packet has source address of victim **V** and is formed in such manner that it will be dropped. **I** will then send ICMP packet to **V** to notify it.

Implications: By sending stream of such packets at random addresses, attacker can make ICMP flood of victim system. This kind of attack is difficult to stop. Tracking back of the attacker is almost impossible.

Figure 12.5 "Reflected" flood

To determine whether connection already exists or not, memory must be searched both for opened connections and for half-open connections. It is well known that memory searches are time consuming operations. So, attacked machine can have enough memory to store all requests but it will not have time to work properly.

Attackers keep taking care of their security in fear of being caught. They have come to interesting idea: creating of packet in which instead of real source address stands victims IP address; the packet is created in such way that it will be rejected after reaching its destination (e.g. it addresses some rarely used port). Stream of this packet is sent to random IP addresses. After the packet was rejected, intermediate system will notify "sender" with ICMP message that packet was rejected.

A victim will suffer flood of ICMP packets coming from different sources. "Reflected" flood is difficult to stop because it is impossible to filter out only false ICMP packets and pass the useful ones, due to randomness of source addresses of false ICMP packets. Complete blocking of ICMP is out of question: there is no IP without ICMP. And without IP, there is no service, too.

Making of distributed denial of service (DDoS) tools and making those tools open-sourced turned this evolution into revolution. The DDoS tools inherited all types of attack from ordinary DoS tools.

The strength of DDoS tools is in hierarchical organization of networks they create. It's good to know methodology used for description of DDoS networks:

The uppermost layer is CLIENT layer. Clients are used by attackers for controlling DDoS networks. Usually clients are console programs with simple help and several commands needed for orchestrating of attacks.The lowest layer is AGENT layer - this layer is responsible for floods. It is controlled by intermediate, HANDLER layer. Handlers are used to make de-

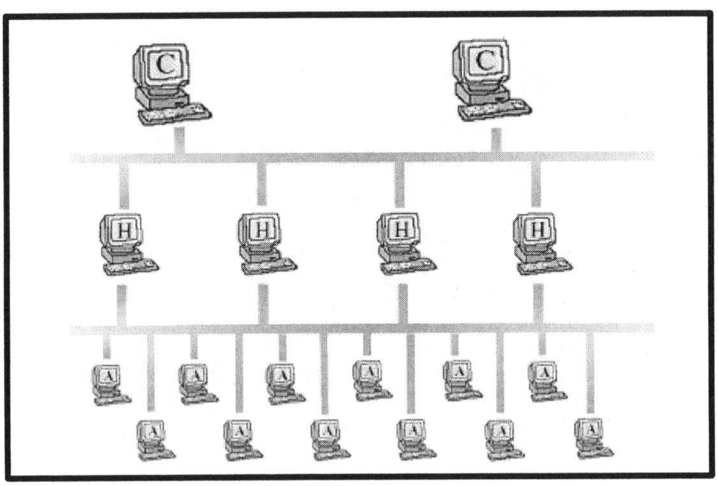

Legend: C -client, **H** - handler, **A** - agent

Explanation: Control goes from clients to agents. Agents do "the dirty work" - they are responsible for flooding. Handlers are mid-layer, put to make control easier. Each client can control several handlers and each handler can control several agents. Client is easy-to-use, menu operated program.

Implications: Attacker can orchestrate large-scale attacks with several commands. Tracking back of attacker is very difficult

Figure 12.6 Distributed denial of service network

tection of attacker almost impossible - attacker uses client to control handlers, and handlers control agents who are responsible for flooding. Additionally, agents try to hide themselves by spoofing of source address or by "reflected" attacks.

Each client can control several handlers, and each handler controls several (up to hundreds) of agents. So, with only one client, attacker can control thousands of systems.

During the attack, one set of agents will be either blocked by the victim or discovered on systems they were planted in. That means the attacker can simply change handler whose agents are not functional with new handler and new set of agents.

Exact communication between network's parts depends on tool implementation. The same goes for types of attacks (some DDoS tools can only use one type of flood, some can automatically alter between several different types).

Source code of DoS and DDoS tools is open. This makes analysis easy. But attackers do not lose anything with this - after some time, their tools would be eventually discovered and analyzed. Attackers gain, on the other hand, is great - all benefits of open source: large population make suggestions for improvements, code reusability, bugs are found and quickly fixed, and the tool gets better and better. It is interesting that indirect suggestions for improvements come from people who are fighting the DoS - they will publish all weaknesses of some tool and direct tool creators what to change in the tool.

Spreading of DDoS networks is basically the same as in case of ordinary DoS tools. The only difference is in the forming of the network: handler has to know what its agents are, and client has to be aware of its handlers or vice versa.

To understand better how DDoS tools are working, three most common DDoS tools will be described.

12.7. Trinoo

Trinoo (also known as Trin00 Distributed Denial of Service Attack) is a distributed tool used to launch coordinated UDP flood denial of service attacks from many sources. The first rumors about Trinoo existence could be heard in mid-1999, when Trinoo was used in some DDoS attacks in Europe.

The Trinoo network consists of clients, handlers and agents. Attacker, using already compromised systems, scans the network for potential agents. Once a suitable system is found, the attacker installs software needed to launch the attack and hide his/her presence. When numerous agents are found, the real attack can begin. In the first phase of the attack, the client connects to handlers via a TCP connection. Handlers form a list of live agents (communication between handlers and agents is via UDP packets), and when the list is transferred to the client, the second phase; UDP flooding of the victim may be initiated.

There are a few innovations that Trinoo introduces: first, passwords are installed to prevent unauthorized access to handlers and agents. Otherwise, in case if there are no passwords, system administrators or even other attackers could access the Trinoo handler or agent. In both cases, that system is lost for the attacker, but consequences for the Internet community are different: if system administrator discovers the password the whole Trinoo network could be dismantled, and in case that another attacker discovers the password, one could create even more damage than the first one. The second important innovation is one that encryption is used to hide communications between nodes of Trinoo network. This is important because there is a large amount of data that are transmitted between nodes of Trinoo network, and it could be possible to listen to the traffic on specific ports that are used for communication and to discover Trinoo presence and even to find the attacker. Like other

DDoS tools Trinoo is easy to use (e.g. there is simple help included) and its efficiency and actions are controlled via numerous options.

Nevertheless, there are a few weaknesses that can be used for detection. Encrypted passwords are visible on both agents and handlers binary image. This allows identification whether one has found Trinoo handler or agent and maybe even possibility to disable the Trinoo network. Another weakness is that the agent password is transmitted as plain text (not encrypted). Therefore if one carefully listens to the traffic, it is possible to capture this password.

When Trinoo is identified on a system, the whole Trinoo network can be disabled: at first, if agent is identified, one should extract the list of handlers that always exist on agent computer, then all handlers should be contacted, and notified that they serve as handlers. On the handler side the list of other agents should be extracted, and all agents should be sent a shutdown command. Also, system administrators that are responsible for these agents should be contacted. Also, on the handler side the traffic should be listened to, since there is a chance the attacker is still connected. If the handler is identified, two last steps should be repeated.

12.8. TFN/TFN2K

TFN (Tribe Flood Network) is a distributed tool that can launch multiple types of Denial of Service attacks. Attacks that can be launched with TFN are ICMP flood, UDP Flood, SYN flood and Smurf.

As with Trinoo, a TFN attack begins with the attacker compromising suitable systems, both handlers and agents and installing necessary software. Much of this work is automated, done with simple scripts, there for comprising numerous systems in a short period of time should not be a problem. When a TFN network is installed, the client sends the list of agents and target's IP address to available handler. The handler passes this address to all agents, which send acknowledgement and start flooding the target system.

TFN evolves earlier Trinoo approach (easy to use, menu controlled, etc.) and adds some more innovations. In TFN environment generated packets have spoofed source IP address and the list of addresses that the handler receives from the attacker may be encrypted with the "Blowfish" encryption. With this innovations, creator of TFN tool tried to improve attackers security and security of TFN network, in general. Also, the interesting thing in TFN is a possibility of launching different types of Denial of Service attacks.

To detect and disable TFN we can use a few weaknesses that were spotted during the TFN analyses (more about DDoS analyses can be found in [Dittrich99]). First, on the handler side there is always a list of available agents with their IP addresses. If this list is not encrypted, then the agents can be identified from the list. Also, considering that communication between handlers and agents uses ICMP_ECHOREPLY packets, we can configure router to disallow ICMP_ECHOREPLY packets. This solution has one negative consequence – any other communication that uses ICMP_ECHOREPLY packets will be blocked and it will not work. If one suspects that there is TFN installed on a system, there is a chance to dismantle TFN network. It is sometimes possible because agents do not check the source of ICMP_ECHOREPLY message. Therefore, in order to shut down agent program, one should forge ICMP packets and send appropriate command.

TFN2K (released in December 1999) is the advanced version of TFN that fixes some of the weaknesses of TFN.

Unlike its predecessor, the TFN2K agent is completely silent – it does not acknowledge the commands it receives. Instead, the handler repeats each command 20 times, relying in probability that the agent will receive at least one. For communication purposes between handlers and agents ICMP, UDP and TCP packets are used. All commands are encrypted with CAST-256 algorithm (RFC 2612). Also, the handler can specify using random TCP/UDP port numbers and source IP addresses.

Beside usual methods of detecting and disabling DDoS tools (described in separate part of this chapter), detection of TFN2K can be done with scanning the process list for the presence of agent processes, in case that no rootkit is installed.

12.9. Stacheldraht

The word Stacheldraht comes from German language and it means "Barbed wire". Stacheldraht is a distributed tool used to launch SYN FLOOD attack, UDP flood attack, ICMP flood and Smurf attack.

Like Trinoo and TFN/TFN2K distributed tools Stacheldraht, also, supports:

- Client/server architecture (for communication between attacker and handler TCP is used, and ICMP_ECHOREPLY packets for handler-agent communication)
- Easy to use interface (Stacheldraht always contains simple printable help system)
- Ability to change type, duration and intensity of the attack

Unlike other DDoS tools Stacheldraht has few features that make it unique and more dangerous. Stacheldraht includes automatic agent update. It means that with a simple command from a client, agents delete current agent software, and download new copy from specific site. Using this feature, Stacheldraht agents are easily developed and all bugs that are noticed can be fixed. Next important feature, from the point of the attacker's security, is that encryption is used for communication between handlers and agents (using "Blowfish" algorithm). Stacheldraht incorporates a possibility of determining if the network on which the agent is running allows packets to be created with forged source. In case it is possible, victim of the attack cannot recognize real agent's IP address, so it is hard to configure router to block flood of useless data from that agent.

Beside usual methods for protection maybe the best way to detect Stacheldraht agent on a computer is to listen to the communication on incoming traffic, especially the ports that are used for updating agents.

12.10. Defenses

As it can be seen from previous, Denial of Service Attacks can be launched by any one, from anywhere, at anytime which makes them almost impossible to prevent. As far, there is no universal solution for this problem. Anyway some things can be done in order to minimize possibility of launching DoS on the Internet.

Things that should be done to prevent DoS are:

- Install good firewall on the router of ones network

This should be done very carefully; otherwise impact of DoS would not be reduced (Figure 12.7)

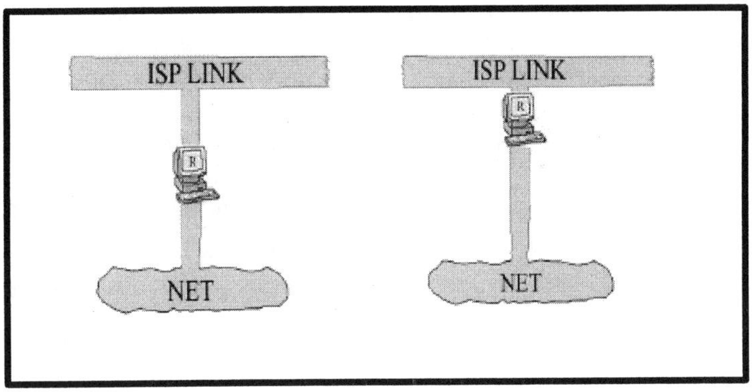

Legend: **R**-Firewall, **NET**-ones network

Explanation: Two ways how firewall can be installed. On the left side of the figure it can be seen that the firewall is installed on the user's side of the link, and on the right side of the figure it can be seen that the firewall is installed on the connection between ISP link and user's link.

Implications: If the firewall is installed like on the left side of Figure 12.7 it will not reduce damage from DoS because all traffic will go through user's link – bandwidth consumption is not prevented. In the other case, there will be no bandwidth consumption because the firewall will not allow undesired packets to go through.

Figure 12.7 Properly and improperly installed firewall

If the firewall is well installed, it should be also well configured. This means that the firewall should:

- Deny invalid source IP addresses (from ones network)
- Deny private and reserve source IP addresses
- Disable IP direct broadcast on all systems
- Disable chargen and echo services
- Disable and filter all other unused UDP services
- Keep systems up to date on patches
- Follow CERT/CC Security Bulletins
- Information about all dropped packets should be logged
- System administrators should be given time and support for training and enhancement of their skills
- Systems should be periodically checked to determine presence of malicious software

If one suspects that the system is infected with handler or agent software he/she should:

- Look for evidence of intrusions in log files
- Look for distributed tool footprints (to recognize them one should visit the official website of CERT/CC)
- Enable detection of unsolicited ICMP_ECHO_REPLIES
- Monitor traffic levels – unusually high traffic level could represent the existence of handler or agent software

If presence of handler or agent software is detected on a system, there is a chance to dismantle whole DDoS network. At first, one should identify whether the system serves as handler or agent.

If the agent software is identified, it is highly likely that on the system one can find a list of handlers (this list may be encrypted). This list should be extracted and all handler system should be notified that they serve as handlers. On a handler system, a list of all other agents should be found. All agents should be sent a shutdown command.

If the handler software is identified, the last two steps should be repeated.

Of course, system administrator should notify IRT (Incident Response Teams), ISPs and law enforcement.

More advices on this topic can be found in [DSIT99].

12.11. Conclusion

So far we have seen what is Denial of Service attack, how can it be done and some hints how to prevent the attack or how to minimize the damage. Yet, no matter how good infrastructure is built, and no matter how good administration staff one has, there is no guarantee that the attack will be prevented or stopped in time. Reason for this is in fact that often it is someone else's fault - poor security allows the attackers to overtake systems and use those systems for attacks.

Situation tends to get worse: rapid development of DSL and cable modems allows home users fast link to Internet. And ordinary home user is far away from security professional, so the attackers will have a large base of systems with poor security to build their networks and gain resources for attacks.

Fortunately, situation is not completely black. The Internet community works on prevention of attacks and realizes the threat of the attacks. The number of related literature grows, so it is not difficult for administrators to get educated, the only thing they need is good will and support for their efforts.

No matter how the problem of DoS attacks will develop, there is definitely one thing all must do: do not allow that your system becomes source of attack. If global security rises, then the attackers will have limited resources. And that can be easiest solution of DoS attacks problem.

12.12. Problems

All exercises that are mentioned in this chapter, must be done on a system that is used only for testing purposes - do <u>not</u> try to attack or modify configuration files on servers already in use.

1. Try to make Ping of Death attack. What happened on both sides (attackers and attacked)?
2. Search the Internet for information on new DoS tools. Try to get source code of some of those tools.
3. In case that source code was obtained, try to understand how it works and try to find some weakness.

4. Make a tool (in programming language of your choice) that will allow you to open TCP connection from specified socket to specified socket. Try to make two connections between same sockets. What happens?

5. Find out how to enable/disable echo and chargen services on your system.

6. Try to block all UDP and TCP ports bellow 255. What services have been lost with this action? Enable all ports below 255 and then block only the unused ones.

7. Check your systems for latest patches and anti-virus updates. In case that some patches are not applied, do it yourself, or consult your system administrator.

REFERENCES

[CERT97] "Denial of Service Attacks," CERT® Coordination Center, USA, 2001, *http://www.cert.org/tech_tips/denial_of_service.html*

[KEY00] "Keynote Systems press release," Keynote Systems, USA, February 2000, *http://www.keynote.com/press/html/00feb12.html*

[Moore01] Moore, D., "The Spread of the Code-Red Worm," , USA, 2001, *http://www.caida.org/analysis/security/code-red/coderedv2_analysis.xml*

[CERT01] "Code Red Worm Exploiting Buffer Overflow In IIS Indexing Service DLL," CERT® Coordination Center, USA, 2001

[Moore00] Moore, D., Voelker, G., Savage, S., "Inferring Internet Denial-of-Service Activity", USA, 2000

[CSI00] "Computer Security Institute and Federal Bureau of Investigation. 2000 CSI/FBI Computer Crime and State Security Survey," Computer Security Institute, USA, 2000

[Lemos01] Lemos, R., "Virulent worm calls into doubt our ability to protect the Net," CNET News, USA, 2001

[DSIT99] "Results of the Distributed-Systems Intruder Tools Workshop," CERT® Coordination Center, USA, 1999, *http://www.cert.org*

[Dittrich99] Dittrich, D.,"The TFN distributed denial of service attack tool," USA, 1999,

http://staff.washington.edu/dittrich/misc

E-Business and E-Challenges
V. Milutinović and F. Patricelli (Eds.)
IOS Press, 2002

CHAPTER 13
HOW A PSYCHIATRIC CASE CAN RUIN YOUR E-BUSINESS

Milan Simic, Sonja Mrvaljevic and Veljko Milutinović

Only 60 years form the birth of computer, technology has brought many good things to our everyday life: huge amount of easily accessible information, increase of work productivity, and efficient communication. We live in the Internet time and a new dimension of human experience is occurring. Each year more and more people get connected (see Figure 1.1). They are able to access information from any point in the world (even Antarctica) and that creates a whole new world of opportunities for the mankind. But, like all other things, the Internet has a bad side, too. It opened up back doors for attacks to many criminal, unethical, and ill individuals and groups.

13.1. Introduction

The Internet lets you easily access your own data or to collect new information, but it lets others to get your private information or to track your behavior.

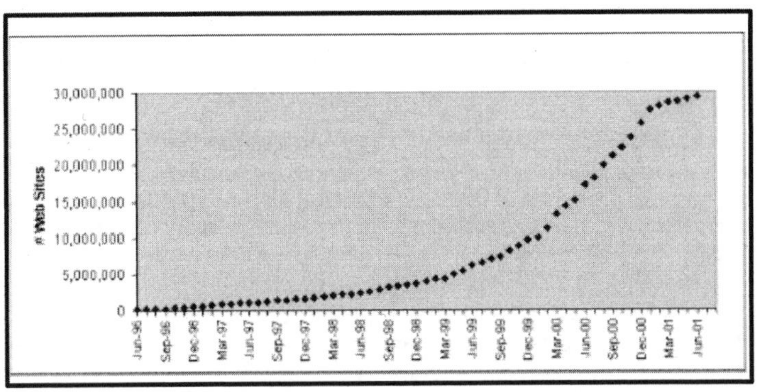

Figure 1.1 Growth of the Internet during last few years

"Clearly you are aware of when you cross the border between Germany and Poland, walk out your front door, or retrieve a document from a filing cabinet inside a law office. Those physical boundaries are clear and we base our experience on them – what we know about the physical world and its boundaries. There are such distinctions in the electronic world" [Geer2000].

The major factor that determines human behavior on-line is the" online disinhibition effect" [Suler2001]. People loosen up, feel more uninhibited, express themselves more openly on the Internet and do things that they never would do in physical world. In online communities (chat rooms or mailing lists) they write about personal things or show unusual acts of kindness and generosity. On the other hand, people think that nobody sees them or nobody knows who they are, so they can do things that are not allowed.

13.2. Backgrounds And Terminology

E-business includes the use of computer and telecommunication technology in business. Technology makes e-business possible and the driving force is in the Internet. The growth of e-business is closely connected with growth of the Internet.

The Internet traffic doubling each tree or four mounts and, by 2004, Internet population will grow to 700 million. According to Metcalf's law network has value in proportion to the square of the number of participants so value of the Internet is approximately 490 billions of $.

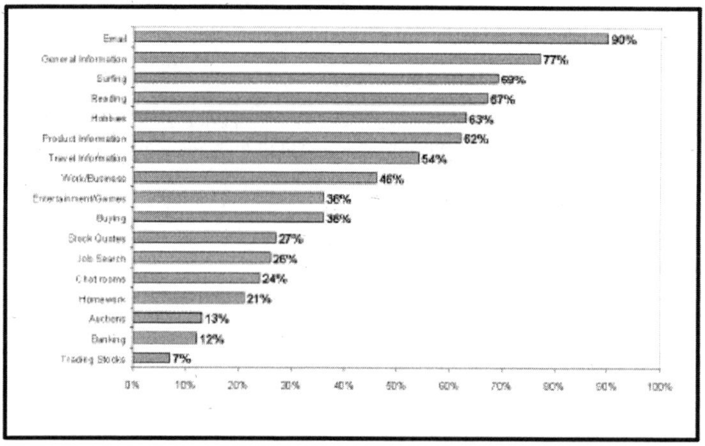

Figure 2.1 What users do on the Internet? For e-business the most important activities are e-mail and banking

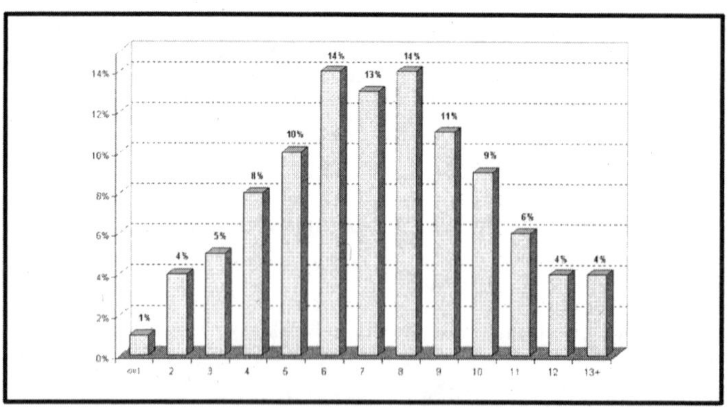

Figure 2.2 Illustrate the number of different activities done by the Internet user. The average number of activities is 7.4 [Stanford2001]

Moor's Law doesn't just affect processor capabilities. You can also observe similar growth acceleration in Internet traffic and global telecommunication bandwidth. As you can see in figure 1 the function is of S-type. Last few months the results of recession are visible.

As people become more dependent on the Internet the need for computer security has more and more importance. Users of the Internet want secure network. When somebody logs on the machine, he (or she) wants to know that my information is not shared with others. When somebody send e-mail, he (or she) wants to know that it is not been copied or stolen during crawling trough the net. When somebody buys things on-line, he (or she) wants to know that no other transaction is happened.

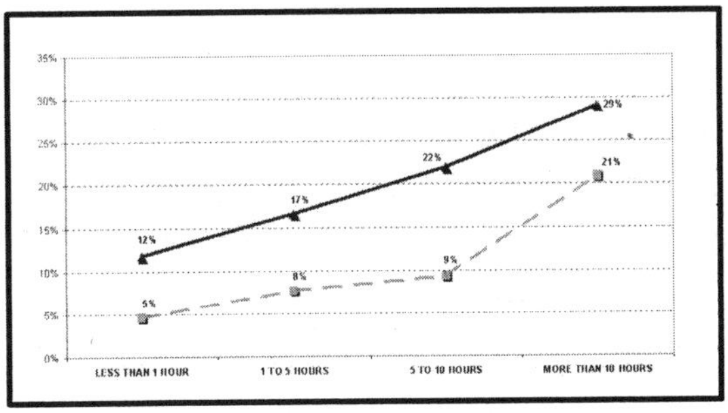

Figure 2.3. Time spent using the Internet (hours/week)
People spent more and more time connected to the Internet and that changes their shopping habits [Stanford2001

If there is some more skepticism about usage the Internet or computer security system, these are some facts provided by Computer Security Institute (Poll of 2001):

- 25% (of respondents) detected system penetration from the outside.
- 27% detected denial of service attacks.
- 79% detected employee abuse of Internet access privileges (e.g., downloading pornography or pirated software or inappropriate use of e-mail).
- 85% detected computer viruses.
- 273 organizations (that were able to quantify their losses) reported the total loss of $265,589,940.

The attack on the computer security problem can be done from two sides: technical and social and medical one. The major technical problems are developing of security module of operating system, handling denial of service attacks and solving some cryptography problems.

On the other side you can't successfully prevent people deviant behavior on The Internet or "You can't solve social problems with software ". The thinking of common web crawler about Internet crime must be changed. Like in the Wild West days of the US, kids want to be gunfighters instead of the town sheriff, because of picture made by media. Instead of that people must be educated about what is criminal and what is legal behavior on the Internet [Ranum2000].

All these problems can be solve with more success by using synergy of this two side, social-medical and technical, of security problem. The attack on the computer security problem can be done from two sides: technical and social and medical one.

13.3. Some Problems And Solutions

By the measure of damage "possible dangerous people for the e-business" can be divided in four categories:

- Clueless newbies
- Employees with psychical problems
- Time stealers
- Hackers

Clueless newbies are users who entering your e-business environment for the first time. They can be confused by the most basic aspects of the your site. The most common problem is some kind of blocking when the users simple don't know what to do. Internet users speak different languages so the Tower of Babel effect is visible. Clueless newbies usually don't require actions but rather a little help. All you need to do is to provide some kind of personal assistant for e-business service. That assistant must be:

1. Personalized. Program should learn the clients name and address. Called by name client is feel more known and he (or she) will be more leisure with unconditional
2. Positive regards. The program always values and respects the basic human worth of the client, no matter what the client says or does.
3. Reflection. Assistant must be able to read between the lines.
4. Universal wisdom. The program can have a large database of universal "truths" about life - aphorisms, sayings, and stories. The trick is having the program know WHEN to intelligently present a truism to a client

The natural application architecture that can support all of the above requirements is three-tier architecture with the little help of the software agents. Three-their architecture makes a strict distinction between the user's interface and the data storage part of the application.

The first level is the presentation level, client side. The most popular solutions for implementing this level are combination of HTML-JavaScript-DHTML or Java Applet. The second level contains logic of the program and should be implemented in JSP-Java Beans, ASP-COM or PHP-PERL technology. The third level is the level of data storage usually implemented by some kind of database server.

The software agents are small piece of code that usually has some (or all) of following characteristics: autonomous, adaptive/learning, mobile, persistent, goal-oriented, communicative/collaborative, flexible, active/proactive.

The agent technology is receiving considerable attention in the press. Even popular press has many column lines devoted to it

Employees with the psychiatric problems are nit easily recognized because they usually act normal. But statistic says that over the 15.4 % of all employees has some kind of the mental illness. They can make damage with: absence from the work, lover productivity at the work, and physical damages to the work. For them company must provide both types of the solutions: technical and social. From technical side CCTV, spy software and hardware for movement control can be used. Of course other worker can observe him, too

Time stealers have more of free time than they need, and they spend it on the Internet by asking unnecessary questions. That's the way they feel wanted and noticed

They have an antisocial character and ask for attention

For this kind of people e-mail may be the most important, method for communicating and developing relationships. First of all, it is easy to use. People also find it familiar and safe because it is similar in many respects to writing letters In figure 2.1 can be seen that it is the most common activity on the Internet "It is a more private, more reliable, less chaotic way to talk. Even when other methods improve greatly by becoming more effectively visual and auditory - as in video teleconferencing - e-mail will not disappear. Many people will prefer it BECAUSE it is a non-visual and non-auditory form of communication. After all, we don't see people rushing out to buy video equipment to accessorize their telephone - even though that technology has been available for some time." [Suler2001]

The main problems in this field are junk e-mail and spam. Junk e-mail and spam are both terms for advertising and e-mail sent to you which you did not ask for and which you do not want. Those two activities consume more than 15% of the Internet bandwidth. And each day more than 25 million spam messages are sent Spam costs customers as well as Internet Service Provider (ISP).

The facts by CIX (Commercial Internet eXchange Association) are:

- 94% reported that spam irritates their subscribers.
- 80% reported that UCE (unsolicited commercial e-mail) slows system performance.
- 76% stated that it increases operating costs.
- 34% said it creates system outages.
- 59% reported daily or more frequent performance impact.
- 28% reported weekly performance impact.

If the spam came from a known individual, you can write the spammer that you charge for use of your facilities to transmit and store unsolicited junk email. Many ISP use some unti-spam database so spammer can be reported to that database. On the personal computer filter of junk mail can be used. The authors of this text made small Java based mail filter and they can be contacted for further information.

Figure 3.1. Receiving messages without and with mail filter

The hacker is someone who illegitimately brakes into the system in order to access restricted privileges or data. They are usually antisocial and abusive and they have a sense of accomplishment, Mastery, and power from doing what others can't or opportunity to impress others are basic motives for hackers.

These 10 weaknesses of computer system are the most frequently attacked by hackers:

1. BIND weaknesses
2. Vulnerable CGI

3. RPC
4. RDS security hole
5. Sendmail buffer overflow
6. Sadmind and mountd
7. File, information sharing
8. User ID9. IMAP and POP buffer overflow10. Default SNMP communit For the e-business the most dangerous hackers are password stealers and credit card number stealers.

In January 2000, CD Universe's server was hacked by an intruder named Maxus, who tried to extort $100,000 after copying more than 300,000 customer credit card files. The hacker then posted 25,000 of the files on the Internet (a site that has since been shut down) after the company refused to pay blackmail. The case is under investigation

Or, In December 2000, a hacker stole 55,000 credit card numbers from Creditcards.com, a company that serves small and midsize merchants. The hacker published the information on the Internet after an unsuccessful extortion attempt. At press time, the FBI was still investigating the case.There are many more cases like this one.

Credit card stealing can be done in many ways:

Make Your Own Credit Card Online anyone can download credit card account generators.

Skimming Retail and restaurant employees typically use skimmers, pocketsize battery-operated devices that cost $300 to $500, to steal customers' credit card information.

Site Cloning (or Spoofing) With this tactic, the fraudsters clone an entire site or just the pages from which you place your order.

False Merchant Sites These are usually porn sites set up solely for the purpose of capturing personal data.

Triangulation A fraudulent merchant offers an item like a video camera at a deeply discounted price.

- And there are many ways to protect your E-Business site from credit-card stealer:
- Ask for a card verification value, or CVV—the three-digit number above the signature panel on the back of a credit card.
- Ask customers only for information that is crucial to complete the transaction—but always verify their billing addresses. And never store payment information in a readable form on your own servers. Once the purchase is completed, delete payment information or transfer it to an offline system.
- Use transaction-risk scoring software to trace historical shopping patterns and raise red flags for unusual shopping behavior. Some good bets are systems from ClearCommerce, CrediView, CyberSource, Digital Courier Technologies, HNC Software, and Mindwave Software.
- Contact organizations like the Better Business Bureau Online, TRUSTe, and WebTrust to make sure your site meets their security requirements.
- Limit employee access to sensitive data and payment systems.

If you are client in e-business process you can protect yourself by thinking about:

- Make sure the site's security is bulletproof.

- Use a separate credit card with a low limit exclusively for online shopping.
- Clean out your wallet.
- Order a copy of your credit report to check for fraudulent activity.
- If you fall victim to identity theft-or even if you're just paranoid-slap a fraud alert on your file.

On other side hackers are very important for developing of Internet security. After every attack new ways of defense are developed and site–security is more fortified or as Nietzsche once said "That which doesn't kill me, makes me stronger."

13.4. Online Therapy – Automation of Help And Prevention

Online therapy is new frontier and, just like all other frontiers, it's connected with promises and risks. The major benefit of online therapy is the opportunity to reach people who are unable to visit psychotherapists due to geographical, physical, or lifestyle limitations. Because of online disinhibition effect, computer-mediated therapy also may be an important initial step in the establishment of an in-person treatment.But online therapy has many unsolved problems: the legal and political dilemmas of online clinical work (If a therapist in Serbia is working with a client from Chile in a chat room located on a server in France, where is the therapy taking place?), problems with training and credentials (Online therapist must have good knowledge in communication and technology), and ethical problem. Maybe the biggest problem is the problem of online authentication. Neither client nor therapist is able to 100% verify the identity of the other side. For identity checking secure networks, encryption or user verification software can be used.

Therapist can use complex communication channel (such as video conferencing or multimedia chat) to collect valuable information about patient (like physical appearance, body language, and tone of voice).

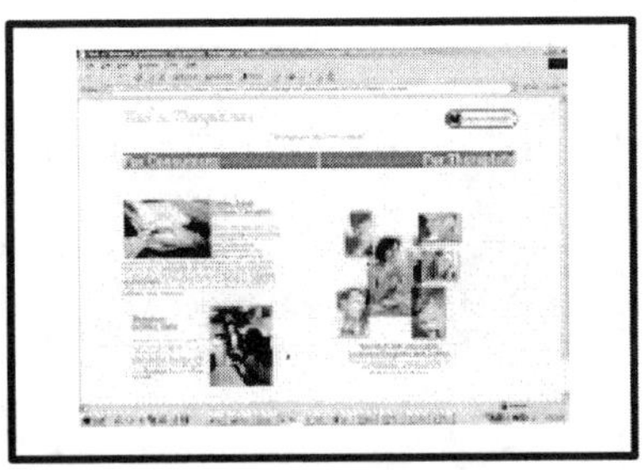

Figure 4.1 Interface of web site www.findatherapist.com for online therapy

The next step in evolution of online therapy is computer as a therapist. Or, the next question that should be answered is: " Can computers do psychotherapy all on their own, with little or no assistance from a human?" First steps in this field were done in 1960s by researchers at MIT. They pioneered the development of an interactive psychotherapy program. In 1976, Weizenbaum tried to write software to understand natural language. This early and unsuccessful attempt to simulate language and therapy resulted in Eliza. In response to the user's questions and statements, Eliza applies basic counseling techniques such as reflection, focusing, clarification, and open-ended inquiry. There are various versions of Eliza, (see Figure 4.2) some more sophisticated than others and every year there is a competition to find the best.

Computers carry out certain tasks efficiently, precisely, reliably, and fast and with the necessary peripheral equipment, they are capable of detecting changes in voice, body language, heart rate, skin conductance and blood pressure. But on other side there are some things almost impossible for a machine to do, like noticing sarcasm in someone's voice.Some people may feel MORE comfortable talking with a computer and computers can be programmed to look like they have feelings, but how intuition can be simulate?Computers are very limited in their ability to adapt to changing or new psychotherapeutic situations and cost for developing of a very sophisticated computerized therapist can be too large but once developed and installed, a computer program will probably work for the less than the average psychotherapist.

And finally, computer is more accessibly. If a computer program is placed on the Internet, anyone anywhere in the world can set up an appointment at any time.

In this moment, computers can do very well at structured intake interviews, administering and scoring quantitative psychological tests, memorizing results, and calculating diagnostic protocols. Using multimedia stimuli, Q&A interaction with the client, and perhaps even a biofeedback interface, the computer could guide the client, step by step, through almost any conceivable relaxation program. They can help clients develop new skills for managing their cognitions, emotions, and interpersonal behaviors.

13.5 Virtual Reality and Psychotherapy

A Virtual Environment (VE) can be defined as interactive, virtual image display enhanced by special processing and by non-visual display modalities, such as auditory, to convince users that they are immersed in a synthetic space. VR is an application that lets users navigate and interact with a three-dimensional, computer-generated environment in real time. According to different authors the essence of VR is the inclusive relationship between the participant and the virtual environment. VR provides a new methodology for interacting with information.

Figure 5.1 Equipment needed for VR

Exposure therapy involves exposing the subject to anxiety producing stimuli while allowing the anxiety to attenuate. These stimuli are generated through a variety of modalities including imaginal (subject generates stimulus via imagination) and *in vivo* (subject is exposed to real situations). For example, if the patient is afraid of heights, therapy sessions might begin by looking through a third floor window with the therapist present. But on other side, exposure therapy is expensive and logically difficult to arrange.

A team of therapists and computer scientists led by Drs. Hodges and Rothbaum conducted the first controlled study of virtual reality exposure therapy in the treatment of a psychological disorder. Virtual Reality Exposure Therapy is be very effective in reducing acrophobic subjects anxiety and avoidance of heights, and in improving attitudes toward heights. Current work by Hodges and Rothbaum includes designing a virtual reality airplane and conducting preliminary studies on the use of virtual reality exposure in the treatment of fear of flying

REFERENCES

[Geer2000] D. Geer, "Security and Privacy," IEEE Concurrency, vol. 8, no.5, pp. 70-72, **April/June, 2000**.

[Suler2001] J.Suler, "Psychology of Cyberspace," www.rider.edu/users/suler/psycyber/psycyber.html, **October 2001.**

[Stanford2001] Stanford University, www.stadford.edu, **November 2001**.

[Ranum2000] M. Ranum, "Security and Privacy," IEEE Concurrency, vol. 8, no. 5, pp. 73-75, **April, 2000**.

E-Business and E-Challenges
V. Milutinović and F. Patricelli (Eds.)
IOS Press, 2002

Chapter 14
Remote Surgery on the Internet

The Internet has become ultimate tool for surgical applications in recent years. The idea is to use the Internet for help in all phases of surgical procedure: education, diagnosis, planning, operation, and post-operational phases.
Educational tools are extremely important, since education of surgeons is hard and long lasting. Also, there is not, still, developed infrastructure to exchange information and experience between surgeons worldwide. Image guided surgery is a new trend in surgical procedures. The goal is to help surgeons perform operations, using different images, taken before and during the procedure. Tele-surgery is step beyond image guided surgery, allowing surgeon to remotely operate on patient.

14.1 Education of surgeons via the Internet

The Internet was widely used in education in past few years. The Internet is useful due to it's ability to provide user with information, but also ability to connect people in easy and efficient way. Education of surgeons becomes more and more computer-based and thus suitable for the Internet. The main problems that designers of such systems are facing is how to create system that is easy to use and distribute and, what is of upmost importance, that presents surgical problems in manner similar to medical practice. The interface between machine performing some surgical educational task and trainee surgeon must be plain. On the other hand, since the human body is complex and not entirely understud yet, the simulator, in order to truthfully represent patient, must be complex and must have dynamic structure.

14.1.1 New trends in surgical education

Surgeons never end their education. Learning process starts at the beginning of medical school and last until surgeon retires. It includes both education in human anatomy, and variety of disturbance in human bodies, and also education in performing procedure.

Currently, surgeons are trained during actual operations or on an animal in laboratory. Training in the operating room increases risk to the patient and slows the operation, resulting in greater cost. Animal training is expensive and cannot duplicate human anatomy. Computer-based training has many potential advantages. It is interactive, yet an instructor's presence is not necessary, so students may practice in their free moments. Any pathology or anatomical variation can be created. Simulated positions and forces can be recorded to compare with established performance metrics for assessment and credentialing. Students could also try different techniques and look at anatomy from perspectives that would be impossible during surgery.

Before the Internet became the ultimate source of information education of surgeons and other medical staff was quite complicated. Anatomy issues were studied from books and atlases, from 2-D images, and other conventional ways. Real-time education was only provided by video tapes, but students and surgeons was not able to participate in process actively. Thus, education was restricted on passive learning, without practical training. It is believed that adequate training is the most important part of surgical education.

The idea of new hi-tech tools for education of surgeons is to provide users with various types of simulators and digital information. Also, the goal is to make such technologies that can be widely distributed, possible over the Internet, so the surgeons worldwide can access advanced technology and thus improve their performance. During the first decade of introducing new technologies to medical education, these products were way to expensive, even for world's top institutions. Students rarely had opportunity to use this systems, so they were used only by surgeons to practice difficult procedures.

The new trends in area of education of surgeons include: body simulators, virtual simulators, and e-education.

14.1.1.1. E-education

E-education is new trend in education, allowing students to keep track with lectures over the Internet. Idea is to provide all services of universities or other schools on-line. This is, also, extremely important in collecting information about procedures worldwide, and making it available to all surgeons and students.

Training process is very important in education of medical doctors. Standard e-educational systems, besides on-line courses and tests, do not give enough possibility for training. Thus, standard systems must be redesigned, in order to include some specific features of medical education. The main difference between standard Internet educational tools and surgery educational tools is highly multimedia orientation of medical applications. Also, it is highly important to allow good and efficient feedback from user and also dynamic structure of system, to simulate changes in patient's condition due to specific interventions. Thus, e-education is usually combined with virtual simulators.

14.1.1.2. Body simulators

Body simulators are made of mechanical parts, to represent structure of body, and also of electronical parts to simulate body processes, e.g. blood flow. They were the first step in introducing technological achievements in education of surgeons. Figure 1 shows comparison of real surgery and simulation.

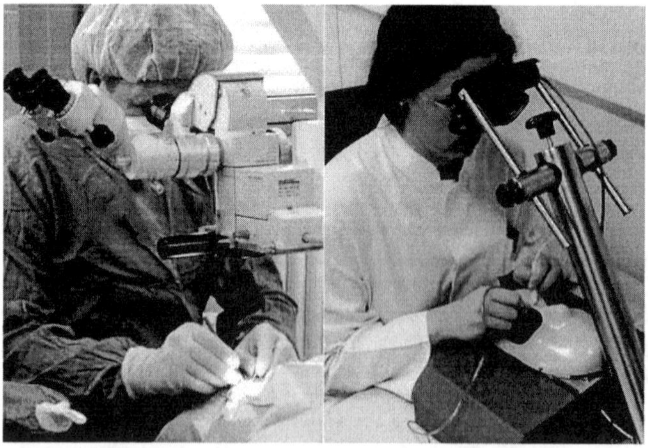

Figure 1: The example of body simulator developed by VRMagic

For simple operations simulation, or just for simulation of body processes, simple "artificial body" is designed. In cases where surgical procedure is complicated virtual reality tools, e.g. gloves or helmets are introduced.

The main drawbacks of body simulators are their high price, but also incompatibility with new communicational technologies, such as the Internet. Price is high due to expanses of plastic polymers, of which is simulator made. Internet incompatibility is connected to fact that simulator cannot be used remotely.

14.1.1.3. Virtual simulators

Virtual simulators are computer simulators, that create virtual reality environment for the trainee surgeon. Virtual simulators are completely software oriented and usually can be used at standard PC computers. The images used in creating such simulators can be real images from operation, or can be drawn by designers. In most cases, combination of this techniques is used. As for body simulators, various virtual reality tools are used, in order to represent to surgeon authentic operation environment.

Unfortunately, large number of now available simulators, do not allow feedback from surgeon. Also, number of simulators are provided with feedback, but usually such feedback is not sufficient enough. The main problem is to implement real time reaction for user and quick response from system.

The formats of this simulators are usual movie formats, e.g. mov, mpeg, or avi. The new technique, recently very popular is Virtual Reality Markup Language (VRML), the most suitable for Internet applications.

Advantage of virtual simulators is their extremely low cost. Also, virtual simulators are easy to distribute over the Internet. Virtual simulators are heart of every successful surgery educational web site.

14.1.2. The Visible Human Project

14.1.2.1. Introduction

The idea of Visual Human Project is to create dataset of human anatomy, called "digital atlas". The atlas represents two specimens, male and female, in structure of digital images. The initial aim of the project is to make series of CT, MRI, and cryo-section images of representative male and female cadaver at the average of one millimeter. Those images are grouped in male and female data set.

The idea was born in National Library of Medicine, in response to growing needs of medical students and practicing surgeons, for digital library of human anatomy.

For ages, students worldwide were teached anatomy on cadavers. Medical schools were faced with problems of finding enough bodies for all students, which was impossible. The idea of the Visible Human project is to create reusable body, that can be used time after time, at schools worldwide, by using the modern digitizing and visualizing techniques. Imaging systems that were used are: Computerized Tomography (CT), Magnetic Resonance imaging (MRI), and digital photos.

14.1.2.2. Finding and digitizing the bodies

Finding the suitable male and female body for the project was 2 years lasting process. Team that was responsible for the project had task to find two bodies, matching following criteria:

Size. For efficient imaging with conventional systems (CT and MRI) the height of specimens was restricted to below 6 feet (1,8 m), shoulder-to-shoulder distance less than 22 inches (56cm), front-to-back distance less than 14 inches (36cm).

Hard implants. It was not allowed for candidate to have any kind of hard implant, e.g. artificial hip.

Anatomy distortion. It was not allowed for candidate to have any kind of anatomy distortion, e.g. extensive surgery procedure performed, death by trauma, widespread cancer, infectious disease.

During two years, over 2700 bodies were extensively examined. It resulted in 232 suitable candidates for digitizing the body.

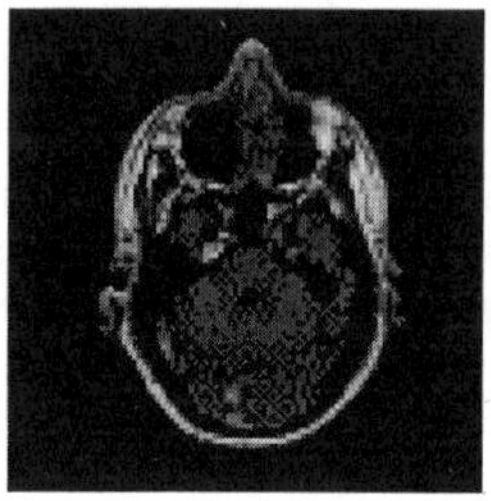

Figure 2: CT head image of male cadaver

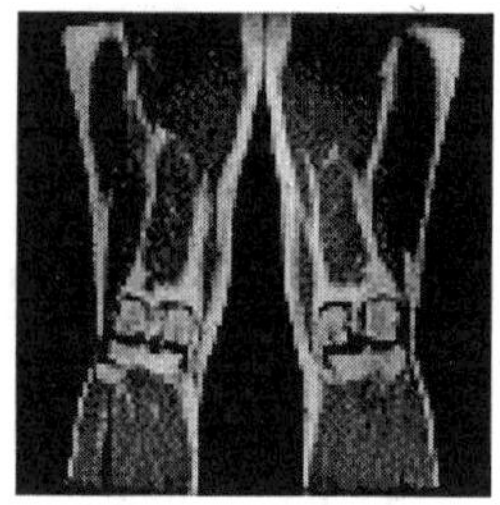

Figure 3: CT image of female cadaver

Finally, two cadavers were chosen. The male donator was 39-year old convicted murderer, executed with lethal injection. The female donator was a woman, died of heart disease. Her husband wrote an article about the project, and requested that his wife's body to be digitized.

Male cadaver was CT and MRI imaged 4 hours after execution of capital punishment. After, the body was divided into 4 parts, for easier manipulation. All parts were frozen to –70C. Next step was to start milling process, during which, in each iteration, a section of body was removed. Photo of each section was taken by high resolution digital camera. Thus, although the body was destroyed, the digital data about it was preserved for eternity. The same process was executed on woman body.

14.1.2.3. Achievements

In November 1994. the complete data-set containing CT, MRI, and cryo-section images, in size of 15GB, was made available worldwide via the Internet. Thus, digital human atlas was obtained, together with anatomy tool for medical students.

Since 1994. the images from visible male and female were widely used in education, but also for designing various virtual simulators. As an example, simulation of gastroscopy was created, using only images from visual male data-set.

Figure 4: Gastroscopy simulation as a par of project (re)Animating the Visible Human, done at Institute for Mathematics and Computer Science in Medicine, University of Hamburg

The advantage of this simulators is that they are made of real images, not only CT or MRI, but also cryo-section photos.

The next step, as promised at NML, is digitizing images from fetus and pre-menopausal woman.

The main drawback of the project, is it's inapplicability in teaching diseases, since both cadavers were of excellent health.

14.1.3. Virtual Orthopedic European University (VOEU)

The data of two healthy persons, provided from Visual Human project, as said before, is partially useful for pathological education. The next step should be collection of data, provided from patients with different diseases. The idea of VOEU project is to collect information about pathological cases and imaging material of various orthopedic interventions, generated for purpose of Computer Assisted Orthopedic Surgery (CAOS).

The problem with surgical training is education about rare diseases. Students and fresh surgeons do not have opportunity to meet with such diseases. The goal of VOEU project is to make information about all cases prosecuted at European Community available to all surgeons and students. Also, small hospitals encounter with organizational and financial difficulties, concerning gathering and maintenance of surgery information. Thus, idea is to centralize data bank, that will have mission to collect information from local centers and maintain database.

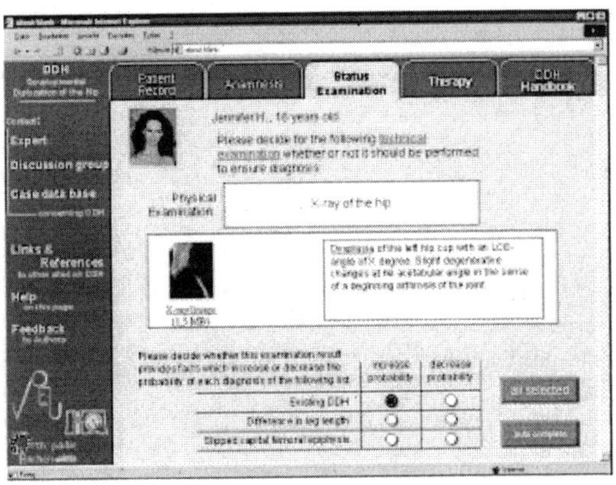

Figure 5: An example of patient information page

The result of VOEU should be standardization of orthopedic surgery procedures and education in Europe.

The project is sponsored by European Community (EC), and involves number of institutions in Europe: Helmholtz Institut RWTH, Aachen, GE, Université Joseph Fourier, FR, The University of Hull, UK, University of Exeter, UK, Royal College of Surgeons, UK, M. E. Mueller Institute for Biomechanics, SW, Scuola Superiore di Studi Universitari e Perfezionamento Sant'Anna, IT, Gesellschaft fuer Medizintechnik und Organisation mbH, GE, MEDIVISION, SW, SOFAMOR SNC, FR.

14.1.3.1. System concept

The heart of VOEU is, so called, Virtual Observatory (VO). The VO is a database containing large number of anonymous case reports and DICOM datasets. Figure 6 shows the concept of VO.

The systems is web-based client-server dB system. It contains central server, and distributed data collections located at different clinical centers, all over the Europe. Thus, each clinical center, e.g. hospital or medical school, can collect information about their cases, so the information is available to all users. Distributed database allows quick and efficient adding of new user institution, without rebuilding existing central database. Also, distribution of database reduces storage requirements.

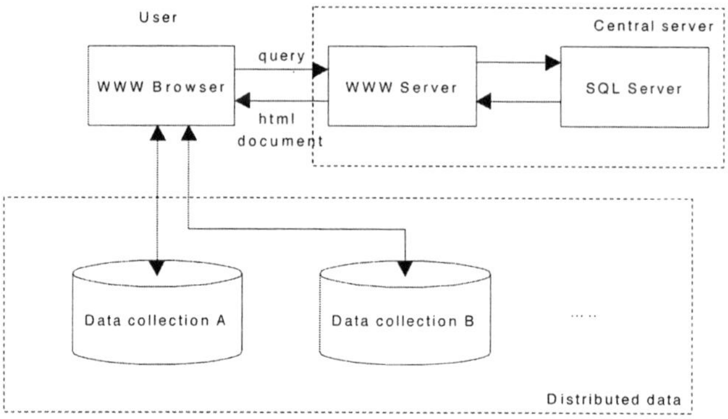

Figure 6: VOEU concept

The central server contains a WWW server and an SQL server, which hosts the central relational VO database. The WWW server provides an interface for users, in order to access VO database. Data submission is done by XML files. A DDT standard is defined in cooperation with orthopedic surgeons all over the Europe. At the users side interactive HTML forms are used, and than converted into XML files according to predefined DTD, and translated into VO database.

14.1.3.2. Achievements

The main goal of VOEU is to collect data about orthopedic procedures all over the EC. This information will be used for designing education modules for medical students and surgeons. Various topics will be included, such as: knee and shoulder anthroscopy, spine surgery, pelvic traumatology, and hip surgery. Emphasize will be on CAOS, and techniques used in it.

Next step in building multimedia educational system for orthopedic surgery is creating training simulators. Simulators, that are under development, will provide user with visual, acoustic, as well as optional haptic feedback. Again, CAOS will be specially focused.

As said before, the main part of system is Visual Observatory (VO) containing data about number of orthopedic cases. Information that will be included in database is: CT and MRI images of patient, anamnesis, surgical planning and execution, and post-operative data, such as images and rehabilitation information.

On contrary to Visible Human project dataset, which is digital representation of two healthy persons, the goal of VOEU project is to build database of various kinds of diseases, from large number of patients, in order to help surgeons in educational or diagnosis purposes. VOEU project surmounts problem of variation in human anatomy. On contrary to Visible Human project, that is just for educational purposes, VOEU dataset can be used in medical practice, as well for education.

14.2. Image guided surgery – IGS

IGS is procedure in which surgeon operates directly on patient, using images of patient presented on the screen during the procedure. Those images are: pre-operative and intraoperative images from patient, and anatomical atlases. Thus, surgeon operates in classical way, but uses imaging systems and computers during the procedure, in order to obtain better information about patient and operating area.

The images presented surgeon during the operation are: CT (computer tomography), MRI (magnetic resonance imaging), endoscopic images, and images taken by digital camera. Good IGS systems, besides plain images displaying, have quality to show merged images, e.g. taken before and during the execution, or to show exact position of surgical instrument in patients body. Also, some image guided systems contain robots, that usually performs some simple task, using images of patient and intraoperative feedback from surgeon.

14.2.1. System requirements

For successful IGS, some hardware and software requirement must be met. Most of requirements are connected to image processing systems, from obtaining images to image recognition.

For taking images, following systems are used in IGS: CT (computer tomography), MRI (magnetic resonance imaging), and PET (positron emission tomography).

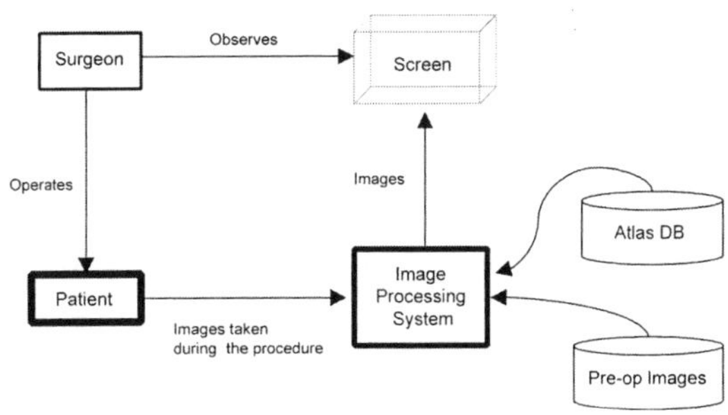

Figure 7: IGS system concept

For intra-operative imaging, optical camera and trackable instruments are used.

Software system for image processing must be accurate, able to recognize important parts of images, but also simple for use for surgeons during the preparation and operation.

14.2.1.1. Computerized Tomography – CT

The CT scan is a procedure in which the brain is X-rayed from many different angles. The greatest advance in neurological diagnosis since the discovery of X rays occurred in the early 1970s when CT scanning, conceived by William Oldendorf and developed by Godfrey Hounsfield, became generally available.

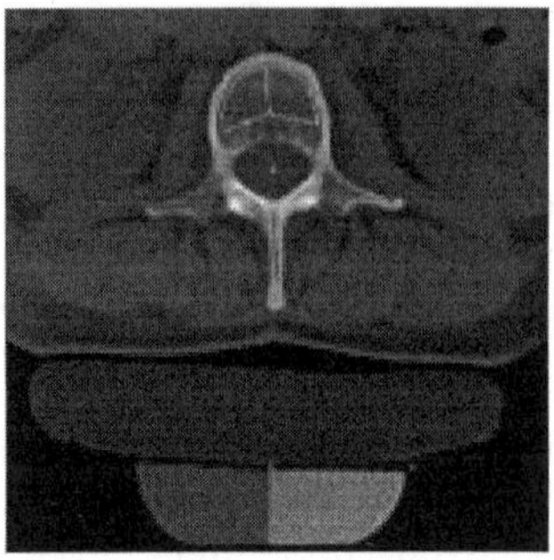

Figure 8: CT osteoporosis

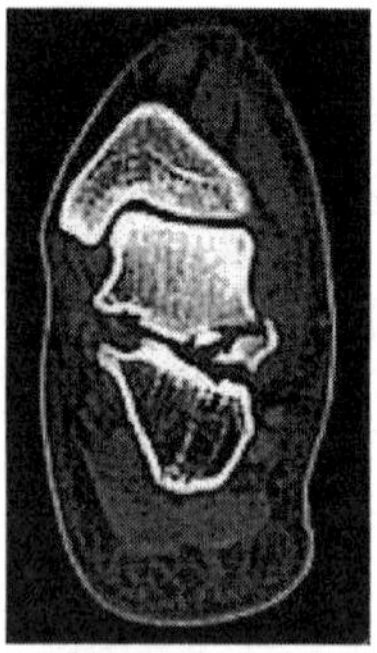

Figure 9: CT broken ankle

In CT scanning a narrow beam of X rays is rotated around the patient, who is surrounded by several hundred X-ray photon detectors that measure the strength of the penetrating photons from many different angles.

The X-ray data are analyzed, integrated, and reconstructed by a computer to produce images of plane sections through the body onto the screen of a elevision-like monitor. Computerized tomography enables more precise and rapid visualization and location of anatomic structures than has been possible with ordinary X-ray techniques. In many cases, lesions can be detected without resorting to exploratory surgery.

14.2.1.2. Magnetic Resonance Imaging – MRI

MRI is also known as Nuclear Magnetic Resonance (NMR). By the early 1980s nuclear magnetic resonance techniques had begun to be used in medicine MRI presented a hazard-free, noninvasive way to generate visual images of thin slices of the body by measuring the nuclear magnetic moment of ordinary hydrogen nuclei in the water and lipids (fats) of the body.

MR images are formed by the computer processing of signals that are emitted by body tissue. These signals are generated using a safe magnetic field in combination with radio waves of specific frequency. Different tissue characteristics are revealed through this process and translated into different contrast levels on the image.

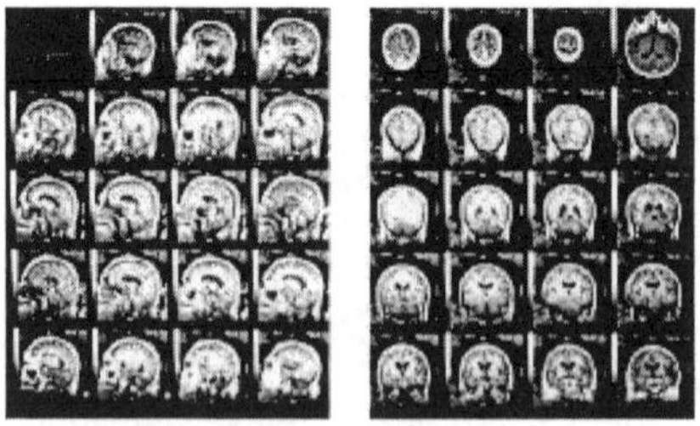

Figure 10: MRI head dataset

14. 2.1.3. Positron Emission Tomography – PET

This imaging technique permits physicians to determine patterns of blood flow, blood volume, oxygen perfusion, and various other physiological, metabolic, and immunologic parameters. It is used increasingly in diagnosis and research, especially of brainand heart functions.

A positron is a positively charged particle with the same mass as an electron. After being emitted from the nucleus of an atom, it travels for a short distance, in the case of PET, through surrounding tissue, losing energy as it collides with other molecules. As the positron comes close to a stop, it combines with an electron, and the mass of both particles is converted into energy. This is called an annihilation. The resulting energy is dispersed in the form of two high-energy gamma rays or photons, traveling outward and in opposite directions from each other.

PET imaging systems detect these events with several ring of gamma-ray detectors that surround the patient. When a detector "sees" a photon from an annihilation event, the detector opposite it looks for a matching photon; and if two matching photons are recorded within nanoseconds of each other the detectors register a coincidence along the line between the detectors.

Using PET surgeon can view activity of body, while MRI and CT provide structural image.

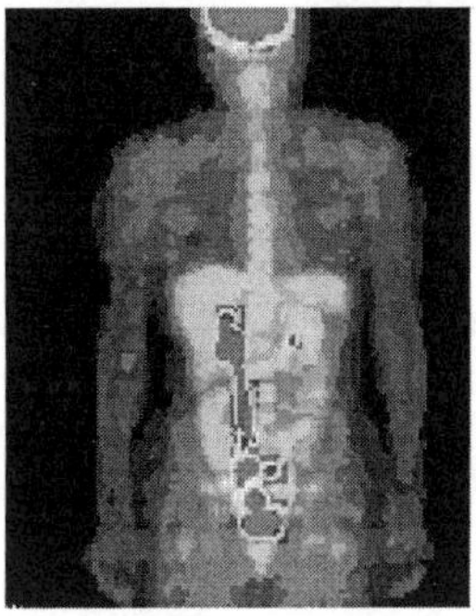

Figure 11: PET image of patient with ovarium cancer

14.2.1.4. Optical camera and trackable instruments

Optical camera is used to take real-time pictures during the operation. An optical camera is stationed in the operating room to receive signals from special digitized instruments equipped with light emitting diodes (LEDs). During surgery the camera receives and sends the signals to a high-speed computer. The signals are received from both the instrument (its position) and the patient (anatomy). Thus, surgeon is able to know exact position of tool within the patients body.

The specialized imaging system displays images showing the body and also the surgical instruments. This images can be merged together with pre-op images, e.g. CT, in order to track lesion.

14.2.1.5. Software requirements

Together with imaging systems, image processing systems must be present in operating room, for purposes of processing and displaying images. A software system must be fast and reliable. The surgeon can not wait for the computer to process signals, e.g. from optical camera. The information must be instantly available. Also, an interface to surgeon must be the simplest possible, allowing surgeon to freely operate without thinking about the computers. All this requirements lead to sophistic system, accurate and reliable.

In cases where robotic system is involved, it is important to develop image recognition systems, e.g. computer must segment the image, and find distinguish border between soft tissue and bone. For the purposes of building "intelligent" robot-surgeon, designing of image recognition is key part of development, together with implementation of machine learning process.

14.2.1.6. DICOM

Medical imaging has experienced enormous growth in the last 20 years. Distribution of these images is time-consuming and cost-effective task. The main problem with standard image storage, such as films, is with it's distribution. Also, film images need large space for storing.

DICOM (Digital Imaging and Communications in Medicine) is the medical imaging standard developed to meet the needs of users and manufacturers of medical imaging system. DICOM is a document which defines a method of communication for the various equipment of digital medical imaging devices/softwares. This standard is now in use by the majority of medical imaging hardware manufacturers. It represents a progress in that it makes it possible to predict the interconnection of various imaging modalities, through a Document of Conformity or " Conformance Statement " emitted for each machine/software following this standard.

Thus, the standard makes it possible for the equipment to communicate remotely through a network or a media (disk or tapes). By ensuring the compatibility of the equipment and by eliminating proprietary formats.

14.2.1.6.1. Image formats

Radiology departments at health centers worldwide produce number of images daily. It is not suitable to keep those images in some classical format, such as jpeg and gif, because it is important to keep other information beside the image itself, such as patients name, type examination, hospital and date of examination. The DICOM Standard allows to make each produced image single and to associate specific information to them. Thus each image is autonomous, if it is lost, reproduced or re-elected, it is always possible to identify formally its origin, the patient, the date, the series from where it comes, parameters of acquisition, etc.

The format is not rigid, it contains obligatory information and other optional ones. Several single identification numbers UID ("Unique IDentifiers") are automatically generated by DICOM modalities and mandatory in each DICOM file or transfer. It cannot exist two identical UID that indicates different information, for example the machine and its localization, the UID of a series of images which is specific to a date, a patient, a study, a hospital and a given machine. This identification is necessary not only for medical and medico-legal reasons, but also to allow the devices for the formation and the management of hospital or imaging databases.

Standard DICOM is used at the applicative " level " i.e. it allows the communication of a program another, this imply that connect them of low level, cablages and protocols networks are drawn up. It is significant that from one machine to another the vocabulary either identical thus, one identifies the data in a universal way the some or machine. DICOM uses standard SNOMED developed by the anatomo-pathologists (Systemized Nomenclature for Medicine).

Standard DICOM was emitted by the ACR (American College of Radiology) in partnership with the NEMA (National Electrical Manufacturers Association), it is currently updated by these 2 committees to which joined different committees of international experts the such JRIA Japan, the ANSI in the USA, the CENTC251 in Europe.

Sop Class Uid	Identify the type of Service for which the image is intended . - Storage Class Service - Query/Retrieve Class Service.
Study Authority Uid	Identify a whole examination, in time and place.
Series Authority Uid	Identify a series of images within the examination.
SOP Authority UID or Image UID	Identify the image associated with the file.

Figure 12: DICOM identifiers

The ACR is responsible for the technical and medical instructions, the NEMA is responsible for the publications and the legal problems, to avoid conflicts of interests or a possible infringement with the antitrust loies.

Without DICOM, it was almost impossible to build IGS systems or Internet communication between the surgeons, e.g. VOEU.

14.2.3. IGS procedure

The procedure of image guided surgery contains following parts: patient modeling, surgery planing, surgery simulation, surgery execution, and postoperative documentation maintenance. In most cases IGS system does not provide all this services, but they are essential for full image guided system.

14.2.3.1. Modeling

Under the term patient modeling it is meant making the full image model of patient, or which is usual of part of the patient interesting for surgery. The first step in modeling process is to obtain all necessary images, as explained in previous sections. Next step is to use this 2-D images for making 3-D model of target part, e.g. hip. This models must be clear and precise, easy to use by surgeon. Intelligent modeling systems are not just presenting the images, but give explanation and segmentation of image. For example, intelligent system for ontological applications should recognize the tumor from the CT or MRI images. Also, learning process could be implemented. For example, software system could learn from surgeon what is a tumor, during the usage of system. Thus, the computer enter years lasting process of learning. Usually modeling takes place before the surgery. Sometimes, it is important to model the target part of the body during the procedure, since something could be changed, due to intervention.

14.2.3.2. Planning and simulation

Planning is a process during which surgeon plans operation, using the model obtained in previous phase. As said before, this model is usually 3-dimensional, allowing to surgeon good visibility and veracity.

During this phase surgeon first examines the images, in search for possible lesions. If the lesion is found, the next step is to take some measurement of it, e.g. size of tumor. Measurement must be provided from system and must be accurate. After complete observation, the following step is actual procedure planing. Surgeon must be provided with simulator that simulates surgical instruments and also their impact to human tissue. The system must provide such feedback, that is similar to one in real operation. As for planning, intelligent systems could be provided with leering mechanisms. In some cases, planing can be done during the operation.

14.2.3.3. Execution

In most cases execution is classical with usual tools and instruments. However, IGS system can be equipped with additional robots. This robotic systems can be used to operate, using the images obtained before and during the operation. So far, robots performed simple tasks. Planing of such interventions is, mostly, intraoperative.

14.2.3.4. Documentation maintenance

Since IGS system is involved in all steps of process, it is able to collect all information needed. This data is important for hospital documentation and rehabilitation process of patient. Also, as mentioned before this data can be distributed via the Internet, and thus support education of students and surgeons.

14.3. Compact Robot for Image Guided Orthopedic Surgery CRIGOS

The goal of CRIGOS project is to design multipurpose surgery robot for orthopedic procedures, also including additional tools for special surgical applications, and software for planning and execution, with focus on imaging and image processing of various medical images, e.g. CT and X-ray.

CRIGOS is EC project involving following partners: Kreiskrankenhaus Marienhöhe Würselen, Germany, Université Joseph Fourier Grenoble Institut Albert Bonniot/IMC-Lab, France, Centre Hospitalier Universitaire de Grenoble Département de Traumatologie et Orthopédie, France, GEMETEC Aachen mbH ,Germany, Praxim SARL, France, SOFAMOR SNC, France, Catharina Ziekenhuis Eindhoven Afdeiling Orthopaedie en Traumatologie,

The Netherlands, Princess Margaret Rose Orthopaedic Hospital Edinburgh, U.K., Universitätsklinikum der RWTH-Aachen, Orthopädische Klinik, Germany, with coordinator Helmholtz Institut, RWTH Aachen, Germany.

14.3.1. CRIGOS concept

The system contains three large subsystems for following three phases in preparation and execution of procedure:

Intra-operative image acquisition and calibration. The idea is to calibrate position of surgical tools according to x-ray image. The core of system is robotic manipulator movable under control of user interface, e.g. joystick, that provides link between x-ray image taken before and surgical tool movement.

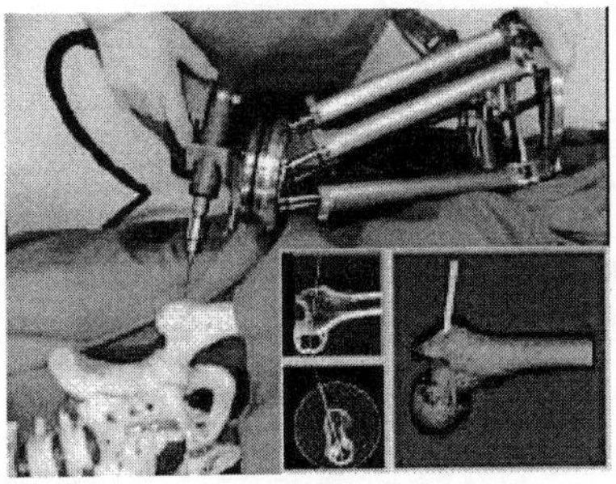

Figure 13: Planning system

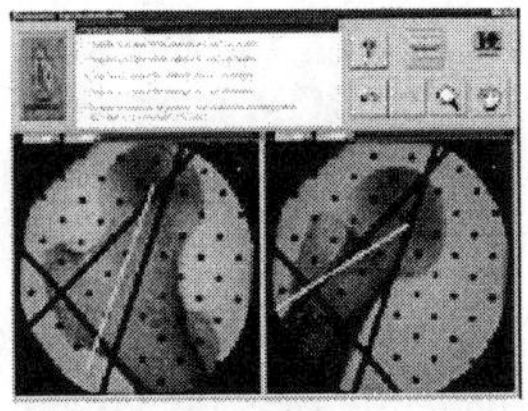

Figure 14: Laboratory setup and first tests on robot

Intra-operative planning. System allows semiautomatic positioning of linear tools, using planning software.

Intra-operative semiactive or active execution. Robotic system is able to perform or help performing parts of whole procedures, by using information obtained during planning phase.

14.3.2. Results

After 3 years of research and development two parallel robotic systems were designed. Both systems, suitable for different surgical procedures, have accuracy better that 1mm and 0.5 and load-to-weight ratio of about 1. Also software systems is developed, for all phases of planning and execution. The basis of imaging system is X-ray, CT, and 3-D localizer information.

14.3.3. Advantages and benefits

In Europe there are about 1 000 000 patients treated for orthopedic disorders. Total cost is estimated to 3 000 000 EURO/year. However, there are number of procedures that are highly complicated and difficult to plan and execute without help by computer. CRIGOS provides surgeon with accurate planning of interventions. Also, the system allows surgeon to accurately control position of surgical tools and to track their movement at real time images. Accuracy of such procedures minimizes invasiveness to patient, and thus makes rehabilitation process faster and easier. Also, this kind of systems allow standardization of procedures.

One of the main advantages of CRIGOS is that it reduces exposure of medical staff to X-rays.

14.4. Research at Carnegie Melon university, Center for Medical Robots and Computer Assisted Surgery (MRCAS)

14.4.1. Introduction

The center for MRCAS was formed in 1993. The group's goal is to foster the application of robotic and computer technologies within medicine and surgery.

14.4.2. MRCAS Projects

The MRCAS group works in framework of following projects:

NipNav. HipNav(tm) is the first computer-based surgical assistant which helps surgeons more accurately plan and place the socket portion of a hip implant

HipROM. HipROM is a preoperative planning system which helps surgeons choose the proper orientation of a hip implant prior to the patient entering the operating room.

Image Overlay. X-ray vision has always been the dream of surgeons. The image overlay system is the next best thing.

Biomechanics. Engineers at MRCAS and COR are developing software simulations to test joint kinematics and are creating Finite Element Analysis models to predict bone stresses during hip replacement surgery.

Microsurgery Error Compensation. Learning algorithms and precision hardware are being developed to solve the problem of imprecision in microsurgery due to physiological hand tremor.

Sonic Flashlight(tm). Research in real-time tomographic reflection allowing a simple intuitive visualization of Ultrasound data.

Two projects will be presented here: HipNav and Image Overlay.

14.4.3. HipNav project

The Hip Navigation or HipNav system is being developed by Shadyside Hospital and Carnegie Melon University to help reduce the risk of dislocation after total hip replacement surgery. The system allows a surgeon to determine the optimal, patient-specific location for an acetabular implant, and guides the surgeon to achieve the desired placement during surgery.

HipNav reduce dislocations following total hip replacement due to acetabular malposition. It determines and potentially increase the "safe" range of motion Also wear debris resulting from impingement of the implant's femoral neck with the acetabular rim is reduced. HipNav allows track in real time the position of the pelvis and acetabulum during surgery.

14.4.3.1. HipNav components

HipNav consists of following components:

– Pre-operative planner

The preoperative planner allows the surgeon to specify the alignment of the acetabular component within the pelvis, based upon preoperative CT images.

– ROM Simulator

A kinematic range of motion (ROM) simulator determines range of joint motion based upon the specific bone and implant geometry and alignment

– Intraoperative Tracking and Guidance

Several devices are used during surgery to allow the surgeon to accurately achieve the implant alignment specified in the preoperative plan, such as: Optical tracking camera, LED targets that are attached to the pelvis and to conventional surgical tools to allow accurate (0.1 mm) and high-speed (100 Hz) tracking of these objects.

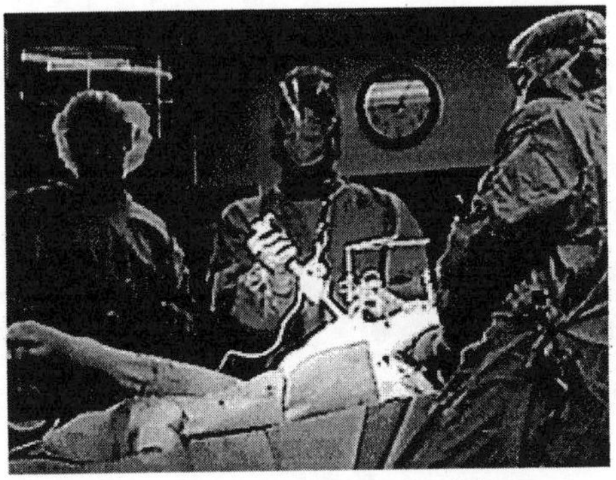

Figure 15: System trial

14.4.4. Image Overlay

Image overlay, a visualization method, combines 3D computer generated images with the user's view of the real world. In contrast with other image overlay systems, this system provides the observer with an unimpeded view of the actual environment, enhanced with 3D stereo images. The system has the ability to track changes in the observer's view point and transform the computer images to appear in the appropriate location.

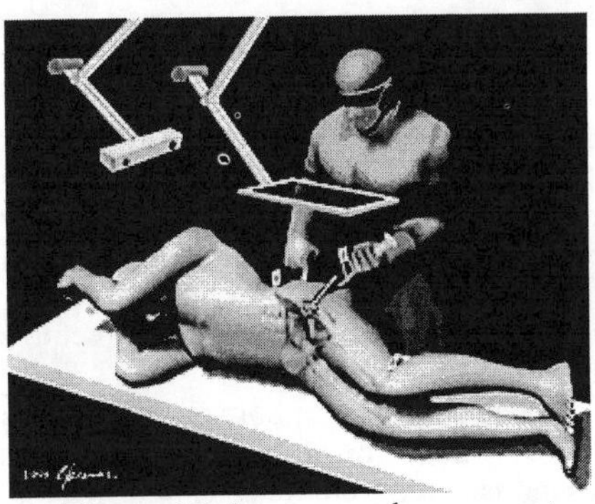

Figure 16: Image overlay concept

The user views the patient through a beam splitter which is both transparent and reflective. Positioned above the beam-splitter is a display device. The user sees the patient directly through the beam-splitter, plus a reflection of the video display which appears to float within the workspace. A six degree of freedom head tracking system is integrated with the overlay device allowing the user to change the view point while maintaining the correct view.

This system can be used in IGS , as well as in tele-surgery.

14.5. Tele-surgery

Tele-surgery is a procedure in which surgeon operates remotely, using pre-op and intra-op images of patient, and robots. The idea is to allow surgeon to operate from distance, by controlling robotic systems. All parts of IGS are included in tele-surgery: imaging system, 3-D visualization, and trackable instruments.

14.5.1. Tele-surgical concept

Figure 17 shows an outline of tele-surgical system. The core of the systems are computers and networks, connected to surgeon and patient via interface technology.

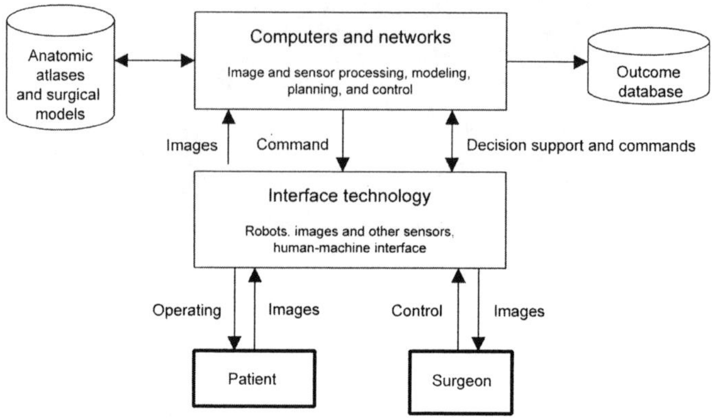

Figure 17: Tele-surgical concept

Computer system is used for image processing, as well for modeling, planning and control. Interface technology includes man-machine interface, sensors, and robots. As can be seen at the Figure 17, the images taken from patient are processed and that displayed for surgeon, same as in IGS.

The main difference between IGS and tele-surgery is that in tele-surgical systems surgeon controls robot from distance. The surgeon can be in the same room with patient, but also can be miles away.

First step is to make patient specific model from images and other information taken from patient. This model is used for planning the procedure. Intra-operative steps include updating the model, since conditions can be changed, updating the plan, and what is the most important, computer execution. Finally, information obtained before and during the operation can be used for assessment of patient.

In the mid 80s, the idea of tele-surgery was born in the research labs. By the end of 90s, first commercial systems were created. One of the first were: da Vinci system, Robodoc, and CASPAR. Few ten of thousand patients were treated so far with great success.

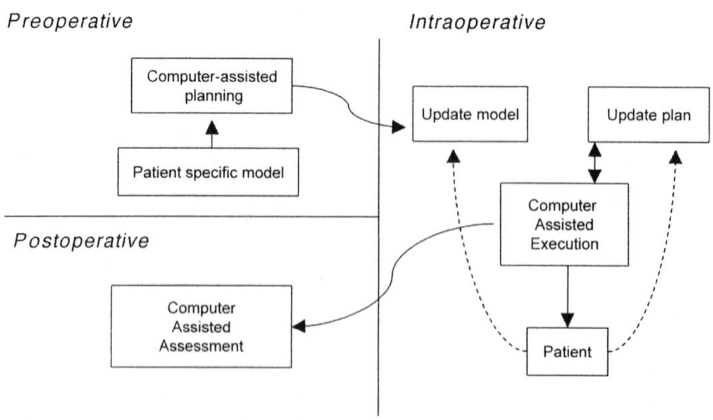

Figure 18: Tele-surgical procedure

14.5.2. Da Vinci surgical system

Da Vinci^{TM} is first commercial complete system for Computer Aided Surgery, constructed at Intuitive Surgical, Inc.

Using the da Vinci™ Surgical System, the surgeon operates while seated comfortably at a console, viewing a 3-D image of the surgical field. The surgeon's fingers grasp the instrument controls below the display with wrists naturally positioned relative to his or her eyes. The technology translates the surgeon's movements into precise, real-time movements of surgical instruments inside the patient.

14.5.2.1. System concept

Da Vinci surgical system consists of following parts:

Surgeon Console. Surgeons console is the place where surgeon sits, controls surgery tools, and performs remote surgery. Surgeon has ability to observe operation site with 3D images received from many cameras and controls surgical instruments. InSite™ Vision System display is in the orientation of open surgery. Instrument controllers transpose your fingers to the tips of tiny instruments. Navigator™ Camera Control quickly repositions your view, from inside the patient, without procedure interruption. Motion scaling and tremor elimination maximize surgical precision. Foot pedals control key system functions, maintaining procedure flow.

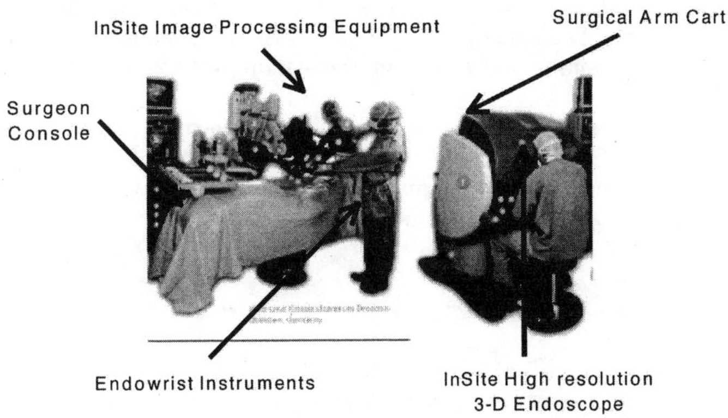

Figure 19: da Vinci system and it's components

Surgical Arm Cart. Surgical Arm Cart is set of operating instruments, that are controlled by surgeon from surgeon console. Surgical Arm Cart consists of following parts: two instrument arms designed for responsiveness and agility, one endoscope arm designed for steadiness and strength, built-in pivot on each arm that is minimizing tissue and nerve damage, and multiple positioning joints to access patient anatomy. Surgical Arm Cart is mechanically and electronically balanced for safety.

EndoWrist. EndoWrist^{TM} is part of Surgical Arm Cart. Modeled after the human wrist, these instruments allow surgeon to operate through 1cm ports Like the tendons in surgeons hands, the internal cables maximize dexterity and responsiveness. EnoWrist enable complex endoscopic manipulations, including suturing, with precision and ease.

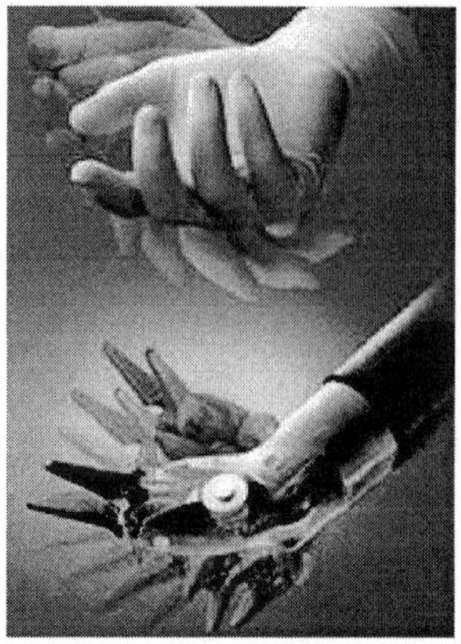

Figure 20: Endowrist tool

InSite™ High-resolution 3-D Endoscope. Dual lens design enhances depth perception and maximizes resolution. Two 3-chip cameras - one for each eye, eliminate blurring of images and ensure accurate color balance 0 degree and 30 degree tips optimize view of anatomy and minimize required ports.

InSite™ Vision System. InSite™ Vision System is the system that allows surgeon to observe surgical site. An 3-D display , takes surgeon "inside" the patient. Navigator™ Camera Control allows image zoom in and zoom out, translation, rotation, or any other image operation.

InSite™Image Processing Equipment. Two high-intensity illuminators ensure a bright image of the operative field. Two camera control units enhance color and contrast of image. Focus controller re-focuses the image quickly and easily at the touch of a foot pedal. Two image synchronizers maximize clarity and resolution of image.

14.5.2.2. Advantages and applications

Da Vinci™ makes existing Minimal Invasive Surgery (MIS) easier and faster. Da Vinci™ makes difficult MIS operations routine. More surgeon and more institutions will be able to perform such procedures. It allows new surgical procedures, mostly one with high risk to patient, since da Vinci supports surgery through 1cm port.

The systems was used in Europe, US, and Japan in past few years for following surgery applications: general, cardiac, plastic surgery, spinal gynecology, thoracic, neuro surgery, vascular, orthopedic.

14.6. Research at University of California, Berkeley

The goal of Medical Robots department at UC Berkely is to create advanced tele-surgical system for minimal invasive surgery (MIS). The idea is to use accuracy of robot in order to reduce operation port and thus reduce stress for the patient. The main drawback of such system is problem with making such interface which will be simple enough for surgeon but also comprehensive in terms of robot movement.

For the purposes of such system various tools for sensing, manipulation, and human interface were developed by University of California at Berkley and University of California at San Francisco. This tools can be used both in the operating room for classical operations but also in a tele-surgical system.

The complete telesurgical workstation will incorporate two robotic manipulators with dexterous manipulation and tactile sensing capabilities, master devices with force and tactile feedback, and improved imaging and 3D display systems, all controlled through computers. The goal is to design a system which is both highly dexterous and intuitive to use, allowing complex surgical operations to be performed with minimally invasive techniques.

14.6.1. Manipulators

Manipulators are tools for executing the operation, from the robot side. This tools are mainly the part of robotic system for actual operation but also for imaging the patient.

Endo-platform. Endo-platform is used for positioning of endoscopic tools. Endoscope is a tube used for imaging inside the body. This platform allows moving endoscope in large radius, enough for any operation. The control is automatic, allowing surgeon fast response.

Laparoscopic manipulators. Laparoscopic manipulators are executing the operation. The moves of the surgeon are transferred into moves of laparoscopic tools. This tools are usually used for grasping, needle holding or similar manipulation. The current design includes tools with 2 degrees of freedom.

14.6.2. Human interface

As said before, human interface is the delicate part of tele-surgical concept. The moves of surgeon must be transferred into moves of surgical instruments with accurately and fast. Following parts were designed so far:

Surgical master. The surgical master is primarily part in interface between surgeon and robot. It has 7 degrees of freedom and provides surgeon with force and tactile feedback. The master was built upon commercially available joystick.

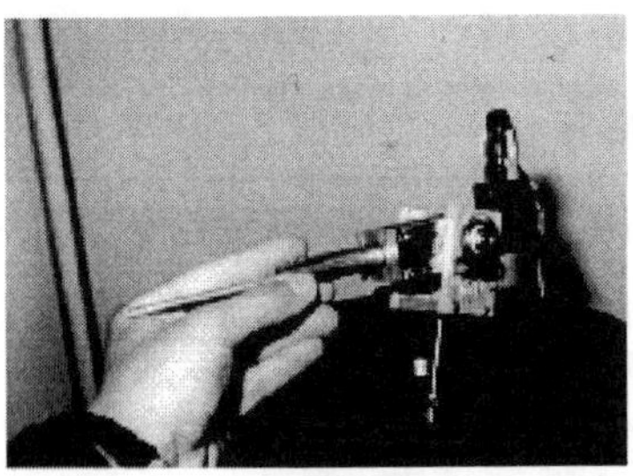

Figure 21: Surgical master tool is transferring moves of surgeon to computer signals

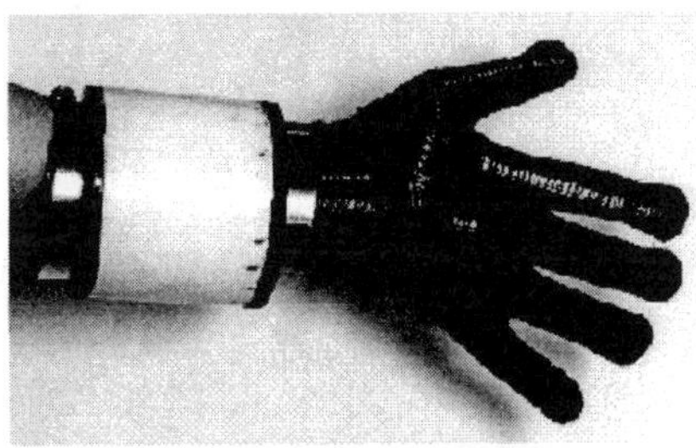

Figure 22: Glove is used for simple control without feedback

Surgical glove. The surgical glove transfer surgeons moves, by sensoring finger position, thumb and wrist rotation . This glove does not provide feedback, so it can be used in application where it is not needed.

Visual display. Visual display is used for displaying various images from inside of patient and operating area, e.g. MRI and CT. Development of new 3D direct interfaces, including holographic video and volumetric scattering displays, and depth cameras is the subject of another joint project (between UC Berkeley, UC San Francisco and MIT). Another area under study is the integration of images and data obtained from multiple sources, such as previously obtained X-ray, ultrasound, CT and MRI images, to the video display. This would be useful, for example, to show the surgeon the location of a tumor hidden inside the tissue.

14.6.3. System concept

All previously presented tools will be used in tele-surgical system. Surgeon is physically remote from the operating site inside the abdomen and interacts through visual display and manipulators. Surgeon is in two ways interaction with master components: master manipulators, human interface parts (glove or surgical master), and various sensors for sensing move of surgeon. On the patients side are manipulators for final execution .

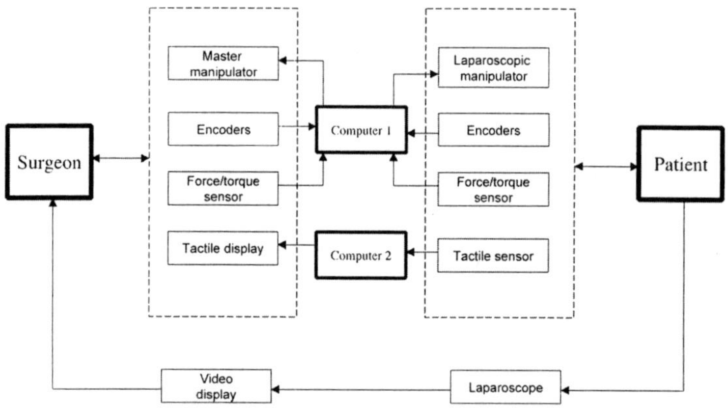

Comment: Two computers are used for control

Figure 23: system concept

14.7. Project Lindbergh

The project Lindbergh is the first transatlantic tele-surgery, performed on 7th September, 2001. A surgical team was stationed in New York, while patient was in Stassbourg, France. Figure shows an outline of intervention. Connection between the surgeon team an the patient was terrestrial cable, provided by France telecom.

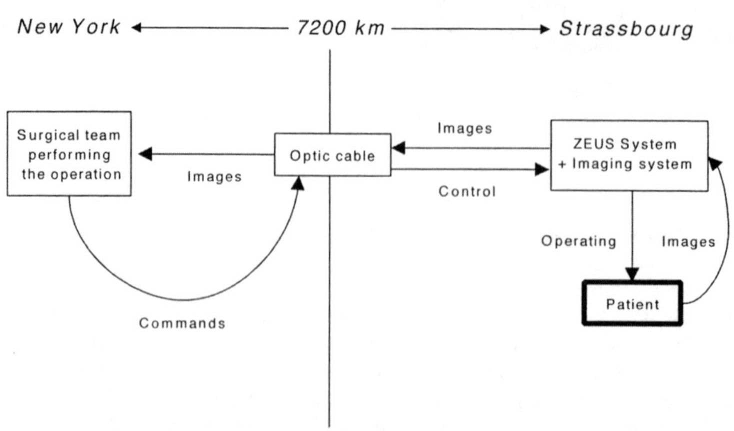

Figure 24: Description of Lindbergh operation

Operation Lindbergh was a vision of Professor Marescaux, president IRCAD/EITS (European Institute for Tele-surgery). Idea was to perform the world's first complete remote surgery. Project officially started in January, 2000. It was named by Charles Lindbergh - first person who made solo, nonstop flight across the Atlantic, flying from New York to Paris aboard his plane "The Spirit of Saint Louis".

14.7.1. System requirements

For the purposes of operation Lindbergh, some requirements had to be fulfilled. Since it was the-state-of-the-art project concerning hi-tech surgery, lot of people, from various profession were involved. Also hardware and following software used is one of the best, available these days.

First issue was team of surgery experts. It was important to collect not just good surgeons, which was required, but also one's that are familiar with computer assisted surgery. Thus, the main surgeon was Prof. Marescaux of IRCAD, with assistance from Dr. Michael Gagner, of Mt. Sinai Medical Center, NY. Also, the surgical team situated in Strassbourg was ready to intervene in case of system mall function or brake of connection. The head of backup team was Prof. Leroy of IRCAD.

The second problem, which design team faced is obtaining secure, fast, and reliable network, connecting patient and surgeon. An ATM fiber-optic terrestrial connection, provided by France Telecom, was used. ATM was chosen for its quality of service (QoS) and constant bit rate (CBR), guaranteeing readily available bandwidth of a 10 Mbps bandwidth of which 7 was allocated to the endoscopic video, and the remaining bandwidth was shared among the ZEUS® TS robots, the videoconferencing system and an IP phone.

The toughest challenge was to provide a robotic system capable of translating surgeon's hand movements in New York to the instruments inside the patient in Strasbourg, France. The robotic system was the only part of the project, that needed to be developed as none existed in the market. For the purposes of project Lindbergh system developed by Computer Motion ZEUS® was modified. Modified system was called ZEUS® TS. Constraints were placed on the team to not change the standard ZEUS® product that the ZEUS® Tele-surgery System (TS) was to be built upon.

14.7.2. Trials

The first prototype system was built in September, 2000. The system was trialed, in order to correct potential errors and to try robotic system for accuracy. While the first trial both surgeon and patient was in the same room in Strassbourg, France. Further improvement had to be done in order to test the system for transatlantic operation. Almost a year after, the first transatlantic test was performed in July, 2001. It was not actual operation but just final validation of system.

As said before, the first transatlantic surgery was performed in September 7., 2001. Let us repeat words of Prof. Jacques Maresxaux: *"It lays the foundations for the globalization of surgical procedures".*

Figure 25: Robot operates in France

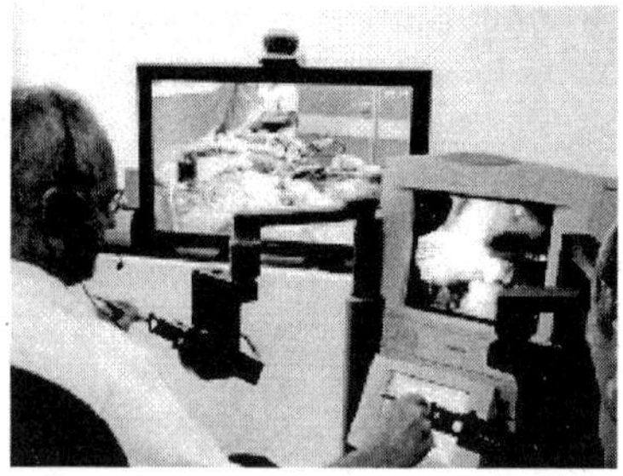

Comment: On the left side of Prof. Mareschaux is image of operating area; in front of him-image from patient's abdomen

Figure 26: Prof. Mareschaux operating from NY

14.8. Research at Johns Hopkins University

Research at Johns Hopkins University inlude all aspects of modern surgery: Internet education, IGS, and tele-surgery.

14.8.1. Image-Guided Therapy

Advances in the field of interventional radiology have led to the development of minimally-invasive therapies that can reduce morbidity and mortality for the patient and reduce complications when compared to conventional therapies. At Johns Hopkins, a team of two interventional radiologists, an interventional radiology technologist and an interventional radiology nurse is facilitating the development of minimally-invasive image-guided treatment centers worldwide. They do this by providing high quality, on-site training for all members of the healthcare team, headed by radiologists Lawrence Hoffman, M.D., and Aravind Arepally, M.D. The training program covers the complete range of image-guided procedures, pre- and post-procedural care, the different products available to perform these procedures, and equipment and inventory optimization guidelines.

A typical 5-day, on-site program involves daily lectures and cases with the attending physicians at the host institution; the nurse and technician also deliver lectures to their respective counterparts on patient sedation, patient monitoring, image optimization and inventory. When the training is completed, the host institution has the option of having the entire or part of the team return in six months or a year to ensure that the newly developed interventional radiology program is functioning safely and properly. The topics covered in the training, which are based on the needs of the host institution, may include: treatment of peripheral arterial occlusive disease with angioplasty and stent placement; endovascular treatment of aortic aneurysms and aortic dissections; image-guided surgery for liver cancer; treatment of vascular malformations; tunneled central venous access catheter placement; percutaneous biopsy techniques; treatment of portal hypertension; embolization techniques; and other procedures.

14.8.2. Robotics Overview

Research group addresses design, analysis, simulation, and implementation of novel robotic devices.

Research issues include: efficient formulation and representation of robotic manipulator kinematics and dynamics, real-time simulation of complex mechanical systems, design of novel surgical instrumentation, computer control of electro-mechanical devices, development of novel sensing algorithms and devices, particularly vision and haptics, design of "smart" electro-mechanical systems, geometrical issues in manufacturing, and analysis of "minimalist" robots for dedicated industrial tasks.

A robotic system for precise needle insertion under radiological guidance has been developed at the Urobotics Laboratory in collaboration with the Medical Robotics and Quantitative Medical Computing Laboratory and the Dynamical Systems and Control Laboratory at JHU. The system pertains to percutaneous access for surgical interventions and for delivery of therapy. The system presents a modular structure comprising a global positioning module, a miniature robotic module (RCM), and a radiolucent needle driver module (PAKY). The RCM is the newest member of a growing family of modular surgical robots under development at JHU. The system may be operated stand-alone under joystick control making it readily adaptable to anyoperating room, under full image guided computer control, or may be remotely operated through standard telephone lines. The RCM exhibit an extremely low profile offering compatibility with portable X-ray units for OR environments and CT scanners. Its miniaturized construction weighs only 1.6Kg while presenting relatively high mechanical stiffness.

The system is comprised of a seven degree of freedom passive mechanical arm mounted on the OR table, a novel RCM (Remote Center of Motion) robot and the radiolucent needle injector, PAKY. The overall system exhibits three motorized degrees of freedom: one translation accounting for needle insertion (T) and two rotations (R1, R2) allowing needle orientation in imager space.

Inserting a needle at an arbitrary location requires six DOF. If the skin insertion site of the needle is prescribed, however, one may observe that only two rotations are necessary in order to orient the needle and only one translation is necessary to insert it. Therefore, a total number of three DOF are necessary and sufficient to aim any anatomical target while initially positioning the needle tip at the desired skin entry point.

The system addresses safety by employing a low DOF robot, by decoupling needle orientation from the needle insertion, and by using non-backdrivable transmissions. Percutaneous needle access implies only 3 DOF. Our system implements all and only these DOF, such that the system has a minimal architecture and restricts arbitrary movements. Furthermore, needle orientation and insertion are implemented by different mechanisms, which are independently activated by safety buttons on the joysticks. For needle alignment the surgeon activates only the RCM and orients the needle using the two-dimensional joystick while the needle pivots around the skin insertion site. When properly aligned, the RCM is deactivated. Needle insertion is then enabled by activating PAKY. Using this scheme, the system prevents the needle to be inserted before being properly aligned and prevents changes of orientation while inserting it. In addition, the robot uses worm transmissions rendering a non-backdrivable mechanism. This preserves robot's configuration when deactivated or in the event of a power failure.

The system has been clinically used for several cases at the Johns Hopkins Hospital. In addition, a percutaneous renal access case has been performed remotely between Baltimore, MD and Rome, Italy. For renal access the system offers an unquestionable improvement of needle placement accuracy and procedure time as compared to the classic manual procedure while reducing radiation exposure.

Unlike traditional open surgery, percutaneous (through the skin) needle access procedures offer several advantages, including reduction of patient pain, recovery time, and morbidity. Successful percutaneous procedures require enormous skill — the surgeon must manually insert a needle to a desired point in a patients's body, guided only by feel and by grainy fluoroscopic x-ray images, all while avoiding collateral injury.

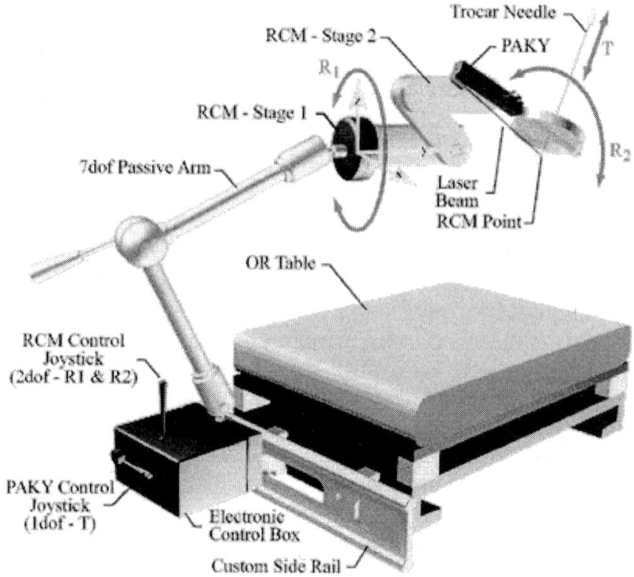

Figure 27: PAKY System

The goal was to develop a system to improve the accuracy and precision during percutaneous renal access. The result is a robotic surgical device called PAKY (Percutaneous Access of the KidneY). PAKY mimics the urologist's manual procedure yet increases its safety,speed, and accuracy.

A passive arm was emplyed and the novel needle insertion mechanism, 'PAKY' (Percutaneous Access of the Kidney). The passive arm is a seven-degree of freedom manipulator that may be locked in the desired position. A custom designed rigid side rail is mounted on the operating room table to provide a sturdy base for the arm relative to the patient during needle passage. The active injection mechanism, PAKY, is attached to the distal end of the arm. PAKY is a unique miniaturized radiolucent construction which provides motorized needle actuation. The needle injection is powered by a DC motor which the surgeon regulates via a proportional joystick.

14.9. Conclusion

Internet leads to globalization of medical information, such as diagnostic procedures, surgical data, etc. Globalization of medical information, allows surgeons to access numerous data over the Internet, but also overloads doctors with many unuseful information. The concept of Internet education of surgeons is not just to provide information, but to design such modules, that are easily to use, and above all that are useful and educative. The task is to collect information, decide what information should be used, and finally make educational tools, as explained before. For this job, various experts must be involved, from medical doctors to engineers.

New standards in medical imaging, such as DICOM, help in designing educational modules and exchanging information between medical doctors. The essence of DICOM is to keep in single file information about image itself, but also about date and place of examination, name of patient, type of acquisition, etc. Thus, all relevant information can be easily distributed and accessed.

The goal of current projects concerning Internet education is to collect data from various hospitals worldwide. Different developing infrastructures are Web oriented, with core database and various distributed databases in remote centers. Upon this information are build virtual simulators and other educational modules.

Surgery is one of the most delicate and thus most complicated tasks in medicine. It demands accuracy that is sometimes impracticable for human doctor. Thus, it is important to build systems that will use accuracy of computers and knowledge of surgeons. Concepts where surgeon plans procedure and computer performs it has shown it's quality in various systems now operating all over the world. Also, possibility to remotely control robotic system is widely used it surgical technology.

IGS systems must incorporate advanced imaging systems, such as CT, MRI, ultrasound, etc. Also, special image processing systems must be available, in order to display accurate images to patient. Image processing is the most challenging task in IGS. Images are used for constructing 3-D model of patient, but also for tracking tools during the procedure. Standard surgical tools must be modified, in order to be used by robot.

The next step might be to "teach" computer to plan and execute operation on his own, without direct help by surgeon. Future designers of such systems will face numerous problems, from building up efficient machine learning algorithms to legal and standardization issues.

Tele-surgery concept is new paradigm in surgery. The idea is to allow surgeon to operate from distance. Since robots are used, position of instruments is extremely precise. For tele-surgery system all part of IGS are used. The main problem in designing such systems is interface between man and machine. Surgeon must be provided with manipulators that are extremely easy to use and natural, letting her/him to concentrate to operation. Usually, some joysticks are modified for both arms. Also, electronic gloves, that transfer surgeon moves into computer signals, are used. Sometimes, as in da Vinci system, surgeon controls operation robot by hands, and controls imaging system by his feet.

Tele-surgery leads to globalization of surgical procedures. Surgeon can be miles away from patient, but still able to operate even.

E-Business and E-Challenges
V. Milutinović and F. Patricelli (Eds.)
IOS Press, 2002

CHAPTER 15
CANCER PREVENTION, DIAGNOSTICS, AND THERAPY ON THE INTERNET

Aleksandra Jovic-Vranes, Nikola Milanovic, Momcilo Inic and Veljko Milutinović

Cancer is the second one, next to heart diseases, as the leading cause of death in the modern world. According to some statistics, there are more than a million of new cases of cancer each year. In 1904, only 1 out of 24 Americans had cancer in his/her lifetime. Today, the cancer rate is 1 out of 2 for men, and 2 out of 3 in women. More than 50% of the population will be diagnosed cancer during their lifetime and the percentage is steadily climbing.

15.1 Introduction

The most important facts about cancer are that prevention and early diagnostics may reduce fatal outcomes. Therefore, educating people is probably by far the most efficient method to fight cancer, as well as the cheapest one. The idea is to disseminate knowledge, prevention information, and guidelines using the Internet. Also, preventive interventions on the Internet, involving counseling and patient education are safe, inexpensive, and unlikely to induce patient discomfort.

15.2 Preventing and Educating

It is not enough only to spread prevention information, but to educate various social layers, too. And which media would be better suited to that peculiar task than the Internet?

On the Internet, one may find two types of resources regarding the cancer:

- Government or non-government health-care related organizations (hospitals, societies, groups)
- University projects

Both aim at the same target group, but use different approaches. Universities, through their projects, experiments, and trials, are trying to offer concrete solutions, such as calculating risk factors or determining right diets, while the official organizations tend to have a broader, but less a efficient approach.

Let us look more closely at three examples of such approaches. We will examine the Harvard Center for Cancer Prevention web site, the OncoLink web site of the University of Pennsylvania Cancer Center, and the Cancernet, the biggest provider of cancer related material on the Internet.

15.2.1 Harvard Center for Cancer Prevention

Harvard Center for Cancer Prevention (HarvardCenter 2002) is a good example of one successful university project (www.yourcancerrisk.harvard.edu). It enables a user to estimate his/her risk of cancer and provides some advanced personalized tips for prevention.

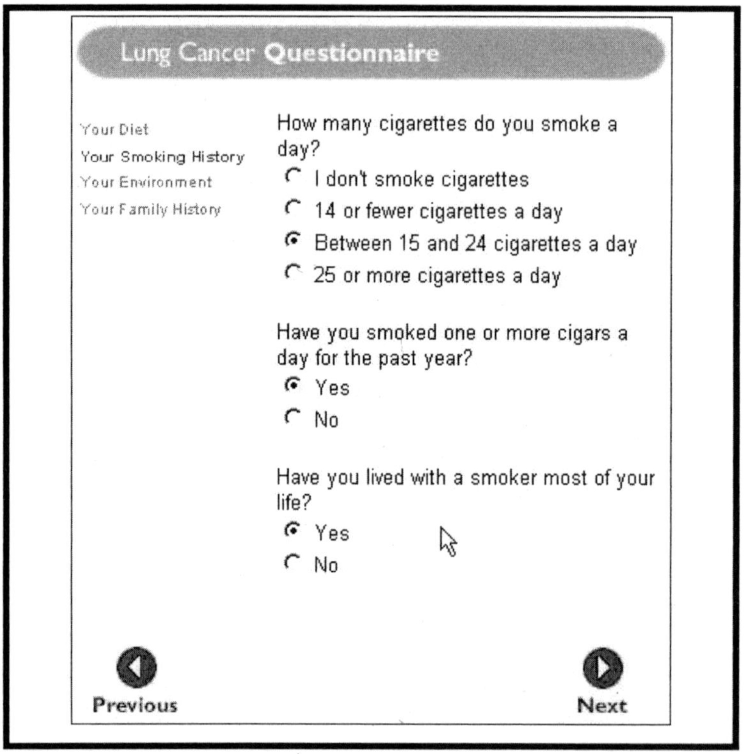

Figure 1: Harvard Center for Cancer Prevention Questionnaire

It is very important to notice that this is an educational Web site for information purposes only. It does not substitute the regular medical check-ups.

User first selects one of the various types of cancer: breast cancer, prostate cancer, lung cancer, colon cancer, bladder cancer, etc. Almost, all types of cancer are included. After that, user is guided through the systematic and comprehensive questionnaire (Figure 1). The questionaire consists of several groups of questions:

- Preliminary question (sex, age)
- Cancer history
- Questions about dietary habits
- Questions specific for the chosen type of cancer (for example, smoking history if lung cancer is selected)
- Working environment
- Family history

At the end, risk results are presented to the user. Calculated risk factor can be in one of the following areas: low, average, and high (Figure 2). But, if someone's risk is above average, it does not mean they will get cancer. It is just an estimate based on your risk factors, some of which we are not able to change. Also, there is always a screening tip present. There are additional pieces of information available, which may help user drop his/her risk. These are the advanced prevention information, which can include advices about diet, smoking, working etc.

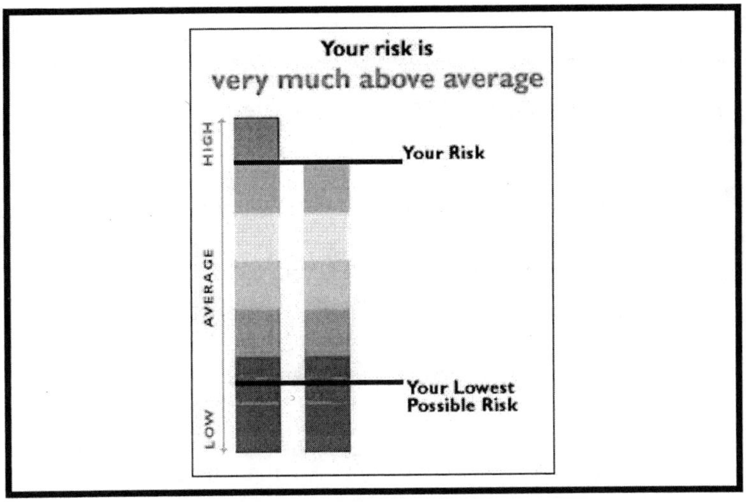

Figure 2: Harvard Center for Cancer Prevention risk results Limited additional information

The site is easy to navigate and to use. The related database is one of the biggest on the Internet. Also, there is additional cancer related information available: what is cancer, what is the risk, what is the risk factor, and what is a screening test. These are very important, because they build the educational component of this web site.

Therefore, we can summarize the following impressions.

Pro:

- By far the most comprehensive database
- Many types of cancer included
- Easy to use
- Detailed results
- Prevention tips

Contra:

- Valid only for people 40 years old and over
- Limited additional information
- Intended for calculating the risk factors only

This otherwise great site has only one major downside: it does not have any other cancer-related information besides this feature of calculating risk factors. And no links to the related sites are included. Even though, this is a university project that cannot aim to become a global cancer resource; it should by all means include links to some major web cancer sites.

15.2.2 OncoLink

OncoLink (http://www.oncolink.com) is the official web site of The University of Pennsylvania Cancer Center (Oncolink 2002). The site structure is similar to many other web sites covering this topic:

Types of cancer, treatment options, coping with cancer, cancer resources, ask the experts, OncoLink library, and the list of sponsors. This site also provides Onco Tip of the Day, which means that every day some different problem of cancer is explained in particular on this web site (Figure 3).

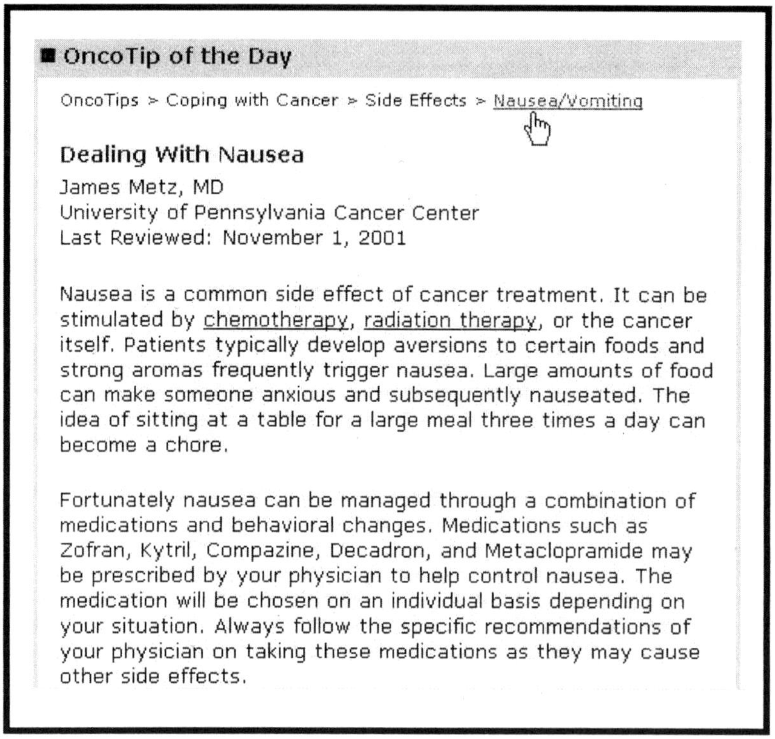
■ OncoTip of the Day

OncoTips > Coping with Cancer > Side Effects > Nausea/Vomiting

Dealing With Nausea

James Metz, MD
University of Pennsylvania Cancer Center
Last Reviewed: November 1, 2001

Nausea is a common side effect of cancer treatment. It can be stimulated by chemotherapy, radiation therapy, or the cancer itself. Patients typically develop aversions to certain foods and strong aromas frequently trigger nausea. Large amounts of food can make someone anxious and subsequently nauseated. The idea of sitting at a table for a large meal three times a day can become a chore.

Fortunately nausea can be managed through a combination of medications and behavioral changes. Medications such as Zofran, Kytril, Compazine, Decadron, and Metaclopramide may be prescribed by your physician to help control nausea. The medication will be chosen on an individual basis depending on your situation. Always follow the specific recommendations of your physician on taking these medications as they may cause other side effects.

Figure 3: An OncoLink Tip of the Day

Items can be searched by type and time. Many types of cancer are included with information about the treatment process. User is encouraged to read through all of these pieces of information, or if preferred, the user can go directly to specific sections by simply clicking on the title link below.

OncoLink provides the following resources about cancer: Causes and prevention, NCI resources, Cancer news, Conferences, Financial information for patients, Global resources, OncoLink TV, and OncoLink University.

In the OncoLink "Ask the Experts" section, user can send a question to some of the medical experts online. If a question is chosen, the answer will be posted on the OncoLink site, in hope that it will be useful to others as well.

OncoLink provides big library with books and Video Reviews, Journal scans, OncoLink reading room, Oncoserve, and Peer-reviewed journals... An Interesting thing is OncoLink Art Gallery, done by artists, who are somehow inspired by cancer.

Good sides of this web site are the user friendly interface, easy to use, lots of general information, but lack of comprehensive prevention and diagnostics information, and it does not provide risk assessment.

15.2.3 CancerNet

CancerNet (http://cancernet.nci.nih.gov/) is a joint project of the National Cancer Institute,

National Institute of Health, and FirstGov, sponsored by USA government (CancerNet 2002).

This is one of the largest cancer resources on the Internet. It aims to cover all cancer-related issues. The site structure is very complex as follows (Figure 4):

- Types of cancer and statistical data
- Treatment options (information, chemotherapy, radiation therapy, alternative medicine)
- Clinical trials (cancer trials, finding and understanding cancer trials, resources)
- Genetic causes, risk factors and prevention (information, testing, search for genetics professionals)
- Testing for cancer (detection/screening information, mammograms, PSA test)
- Coping with cancer (side effects of treatments, complications caused by cancer, emotional and other concerns)
- Support and resources (support organizations, hospice and home care)
- Cancer literature

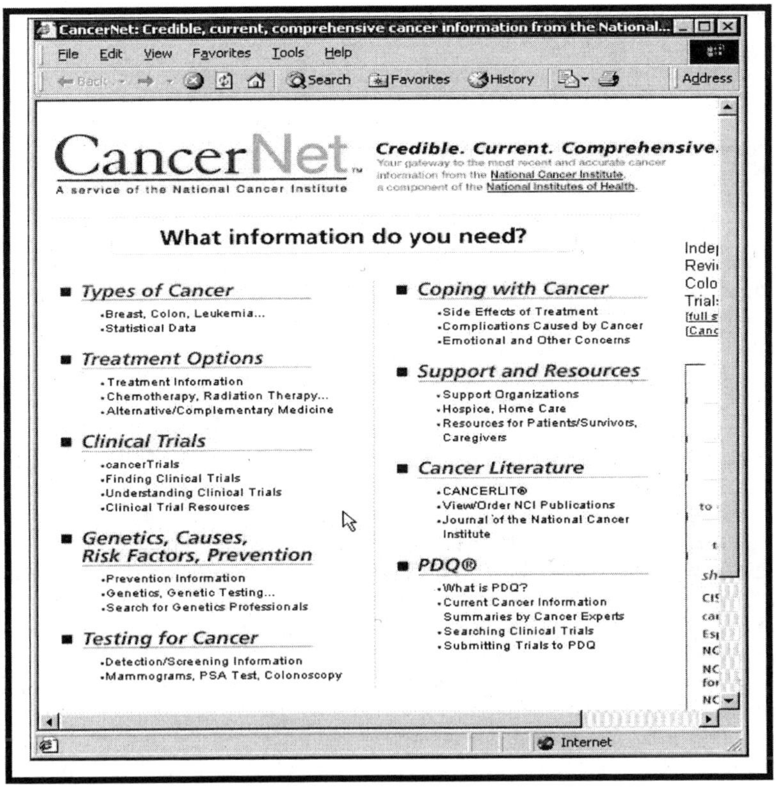

Figure 4: Cancer Net structure

Almost every aspect of cancer related issues is covered. But, this enormous site has one major problem: interface inconsistency. It seems that every part was designed by a different team, which presents great difficulties while navigating and using the content. It is understandable that for the project of this magnitude many people must be involved. However, this is not an excuse for such a lame and uneasy interface. So, as far as usability is concerned, this site does not satisfy the lightest criteria,

Summarized impressions are listed below.

Pro:

- Big database
- Almost all types of cancer included
- Detailed results
- Tips
- Info on current clinical trials
- Generous treatment options
- Cancer tests
- Comprehensive literature and links
- Additional support – living with cancer

Contra:

- Slow and inconsistent navigation and appearance
- Bad usability

15.3 Future Developments

So, we have seen that there are several problems that need to be addressed when presenting cancer related information on the Internet.

First, one must go in depth without superficiality. Being runner-up does not count when cancer is in question. All information must be available, without restriction. Because of the big databases, response must be optimized – you cannot leave user waiting. The example of a well designed and optimized site is Harvard Center for Cancer Prevention – although the database is relatively big, questions are sorted in an organized manner and the response is quick.

Second, always provide links! No site is good enough to stand for itself, alone. The CancerNet provides numerous links to other related resources. Unfortunately, the same does not imply for the Harvard site which makes it the greatest weakness, despite their unbeatable data base and great site optimization.

Next, there is a question of usability. Cancer does not affect only one social or ethnic group – we are all equally susceptible. Therefore, when designing a cancer related site, great care and effort must be made in making it usable. The goals must be simplicity, efficiency, and consistency. Although the quantity of information related to cancer is huge, advanced web techniques, such as XML, provide an easy way to present data in a uniform and descriptive manner.

Beside hard facts and information, the Internet presents a great opportunity to provide additional support to patients and their families. Due to social, moral, and other inhibitions, many patients refuse to attend group therapy. It is important to notice that Internet can solve these problems: newsgroups and chartrooms can be organized for cancer victims. So, if a personal contact is a problem, one can skip it, and meet other participants when they feel that it is the right time.

15.4 Conclusion

Internet gives us a new and powerful weapon that we can use to fight cancer. But, like with many other weapons, when in the wrong hands it can do more harm than good. Therefore, the prime issue here is: doctors and developers must cooperate and work together when designing a cancer related Web site. Only then the information presented would have a true value.

REFERENCES

[Harvard2001] Harvard Center for Cancer Prevention, www.yourcancerrisk.harvard.edu, September **2001**

[CancerNet2001] CancerNet, http://cancernet.nci.nih.gov, September **2001**

[OncoLink2001] OncoLink, www.oncolink.com, September **2001**

[eTForecasts01] www.eMarketer.com, April **2001**

[Vincent] Cancer: Principles & Practice of Oncology, Vincent T., Jr., MD Devita, Samuel, MD Hellman; Lippincott Williams & Wilkins

[Leland] Prostate Cancer: Biology, Genetics & the New Therapeutics, Leland W. K., Ph.D. Chung, William B., Phd Isaacs, Jonathan W. Simons; Humana Press

[Berger] Principles and Practice of Supportive Oncology, Ann Berger, Russell K. Portenoy, David E. Weissman; Lippincot-Raven

E-Business and E-Challenges
V. Milutinović and F. Patricelli (Eds.)
IOS Press, 2002

Chapter 16
E-Success on the Internet

Miloš Cvetanović, Andreja Cvetanović and Veljko Milutinović

E-Success is far more complex then any other website project. It is a successful e-Commerce.
There is no special formula for e-Business success - good idea can turn into insanely great thing. Moreover, there is still no consensus on how best to approach e-Business. Is spending more important, or is there a mix of business practices that can make an enormous difference? What role does partnering play in achieving e-Business success? Acquisition? Spin off? These are issues and strategies even the most advanced E-biz-ambitious companies are grappling with.
Success in e-Business may be in the eye of the beholder, but most of the metrics are objective. Page views, click-troughs, and online transactions are some of the measurable criteria. Yet, these do not begin to capture the range of aspirations executives hold about their e-Business investments or what they hope to achieve. Three of the most common achievements reported by companies engaging in e-Business are difficult to measure, though it is generally obvious (at least to company officials) when they are amiss.
We will try to define various aspects of e-Commerce in the first part of this chapter. That will help us to better understand information from the research on the best e-Business practices in second part of the chapter. We will than explore real-world e-Business examples and their different ways of selling through Internet as well as techniques or technologies through which those sites are adding value. We will also try to explore the value of site metrics in planning and analyzing the e-Commerce. Finally, we will summarize with some e-Commerce secrets and the ways to survive in this business.

16.1 Essence of E-Commerce

Electronic Commerce is an emerging concept that describes the process of buying and selling or exchanging of products, services, and information via computer networks including the Internet. Four ways in which e-Commerce could be perceived are: Communications, Business Process, Service, Online [Hui00].

Communication Perspective: EC is the delivery of information, products/services, or payments over telephone lines, computer networks or any other electronic means.

Business Process Perspective: EC is the application of technology toward the automation of business transactions and workflow.

Service Perspective: EC is a tool that addresses the desire of firms, consumers, and management to cut service cost while improving the quality of goods and increasing the speed of service delivery.

Online Perspective: EC provides the capability of buying and selling products and information on the Internet and other online services.

According to the market segment or field in which it is engaged e-Commerce could be categorized like:

Business-to-business (B2B), most of EC today is of this type. It includes the electronic market transactions between organizations.

Business-to-consumer (B2C), these are retailing transactions with individual shoppers. The typical shopper at Amazon.com is a consumer, or customer.

Consumer-to-consumer (C2C), Consumer sells directly to consumers. (e.g. www.classified2000.com, and selling residential property, cars, furniture, advertising personal services on the Internet and selling knowledge and expertise.

Nonbusiness EC, an increased number of nonbusiness institutions such as academic institutions, not-for-profit organizations, religious organizations, social organizations, and government agencies are using various types of EC to reduce their expenses or to improve their operations and customer service.

Intrabusiness (Organizational) EC, it includes all internal organizational activities, usually performed on intranets, that involve exchange of goods, services, or information. Activities can range from selling corporate products to employees to online training and cost-reduction activities.

Figure 16.1 sheds more light on the different dimensions in financial services that could emerge through the use of e-Commerce.

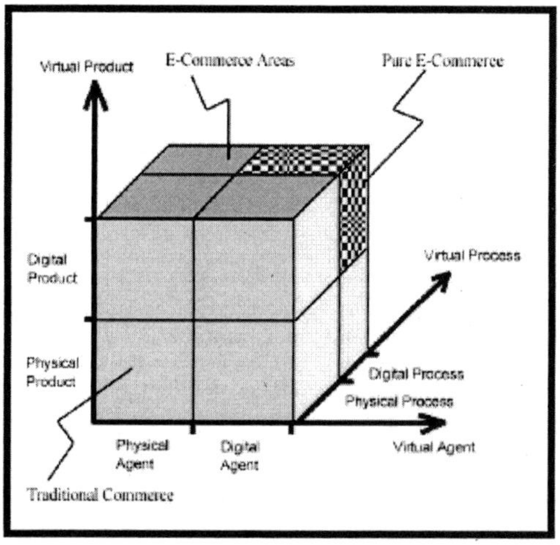

Comment: E-Commerce and its advantages open up a new dimension in financial services.

Figure 16.1 Dimensions of e-Commerce [Hui00]

E-Commerce could be used for numerous functions inside companies. Following are some of the examples that show the scope of e-Commerce: marketing, sales and sales promotion; pre-sales, subcontracts, supply; financing and insurance; commercial transactions: ordering, delivery payment; product service and maintenance; co-operative product development; distributed co-operative working; use of public and private services; business-to-administrations (e.g. customs, etc); transport and logistics; public procurement; automatic trading of digital goods; accounting; dispute resolution [Schneider00].

Important aspects from which e-Commerce could be defined are benefits that it e-Commerce brings to businesses. Some of the major ones are:

- Enabling and supporting changes on a global scale
- Enabling companies to be more efficient and flexible in their internal operations, to work more closely with their suppliers, and to be more responsive to the needs and expectations of their customers.
- Allowing companies to select the best suppliers regardless of their geographical location and to sell to a global market.

Additional benefits could be:

- **Reduce advertising costs** by providing timely information in response to specific question, customer can easily click on the online ad and immediately find more about the advertised product or service.
- **Reduce delivery cost**, notably for goods that can also be delivered electronically reduced design and manufacturing cost.
- **Improved market intelligence and strategic planning** by implementing personalization and other tracking techniques.
- **More opportunity for niche marketing** since company is responding to specific customers behaviors and preferences.
- **Equal access to markets** (i.e. for SMEs – Small and Medium-sized Enterprises and larger corporations)
- **Access to new markets** doesn't cost a lot and it might be sometimes built with few additional pages
- **Customer involment in product and service innovation.**

Some of the most common businesses where e-Commerce is being used are:

- **Financial services** (wide range of financial services from online banking, to online mortgage approvals, online investments, credit applications, bill payments, etc)
- **Real estate** (selling or buying house online is becoming more popular as customized search helps to reduce unnecessary visits or open house events)
- **Travel and transport** (no more waiting on the phone for agent to gather all customers preferences)
- **Automotive industry online** (it became very convenient to find your new or used car online instead of surfing dealers and car lots)
- **Online publishing** (they let you download your favorite books and carry your cyber library anywhere, anytime)
- **Online entertainment** (online video games, online radios, and online magazines are among the first to use Internet as their primary channel of distribution)
- **Healthcare industry** (getting advice about your health problem online could be faster than waiting for the appointment with your doctor)
- **Professional services online** (from lawyers to florists, there are numerous opportunities in which Internet could be used)
- **Online retail** (full range of retail selling from electronics to food)

16.2 E-Business Best Practices – Interviews

According to a newly released study by InformationWeek Research, the Redefining Business 2000: E-Success study, based on 600 interviews with IT and business-titled executives, reveals significant business improvements among companies that adopt at least three of four ambitious e-Business practices: implementing new customer-facing information systems; transforming legacy electronic processes to e-Business models; refining value or supply chains; and reinventing corporate culture around e-Business.

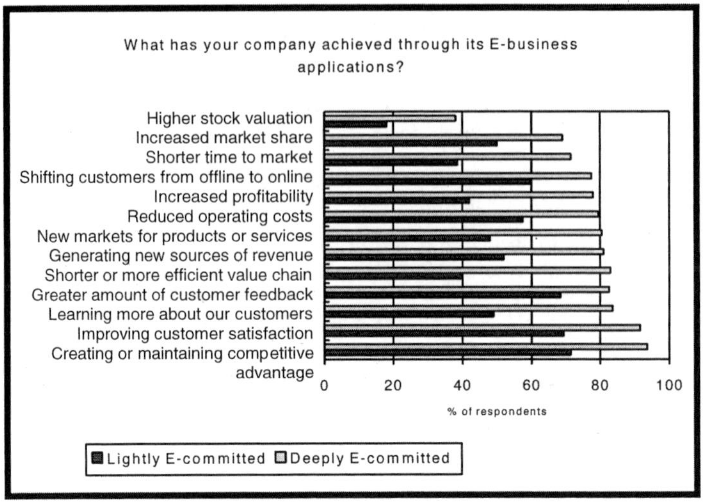

Comment: Based upon 111 Deeply E-Committed sites and 68 Lightly E-Committed sites. Both groups spend above average on IT products services. InformationWeek Research study of 600 executives. Multiple responses allowed.

Figure 16.2 Company achievements, through their E-Business applications [Chabrow00]

Above-average IT spenders practicing at least three of the four e-Business best practices and initiatives are designated in this study as "deeply E-committed," while "lightly E-committed" companies deploy two or fewer of these.

Does increased investment in e-Business pay off? In examining the differences between deeply E-committed companies and those that are lightly committed, InformationWeek Research found a wide gap in terms of results. Figure 16.2 shows questions and respective percentages of respondents in categories of lightly and deeply E-committed companies. Nearly four in five deeply E-committed sites say they achieved increased profitability through e-Business applications, while only 43% of those less committed claimed a similar achievement. The gap between the two groups also applies to establishing more-efficient supply chains (44 percentage points difference), learning more about customers (36 percentage points), achieving shorter time to market (34 points), creating new markets for products or services (32), and generating new sources of revenue (29).

Yet, the highest e-Business achievers are companies that combine above average IT spending with a deep commitment to e-Business best practices.

But one thing is sure, companies with Internet initiatives: get competitive advantage, improved customer satisfaction, reduced operating costs, generate new sources of revenue, create new markets for products, and most important, increase profits.

"There's a lot of buzz about the Internet giving businesses a competitive advantage, but I don't know if businesses can claim victory yet. The battle's still on," says Mani Subramani, an assistant professor of e-Commerce and knowledge management at the Carlson School of Management at the University of Minnesota in Minneapolis. "All the traditional measures come into play in the e-Business arena, such as the quality of business, the brand, the quality of fulfillment processes. They're as important to competitive advantage as a Web site."

The process of changing and evolving business models is unlikely to be smooth, even for well-managed companies. While business issues are significant, survey respondents say they trail the challenges posed by rapid changes in technology (83%) and adjusting to the pace of change (81%). Partnering with a dot-com business is a model more than one-third of the surveyed executives cite as an effective way their companies transform their businesses. Consider this pairing of a brick-and-mortar company and a dot-com partner.

Whether an e-Business unit remains inside or outside a company's walls, adopting an Internet solution to eliminate paperwork and other manual processes is one of the more successful e-Business efforts. Nearly six of 10 executives say their companies are instituting e-Business processes to replace analog or conventional procedures.

Using e-Business solutions to help make the customer experience simpler and more effective is a key concern for business and IT executives. Customer-oriented initiatives also scored high on the e-Success survey—utilizing e-Business applications to improve customer satisfaction (78%), solicit customer feedback (71%), learn more about customers (68%), and conduct customer research (63%).

The chart in the Figure 16.3 shows what are the most highly transformational efforts under way in the companies of the surveyed executives.

In terms of overhauling a company's strategy, the single most-effective effort is IT's more active role in the overall business, cited by 91% of the survey respondents. Using IT to create greater customer value was second, cited by 84% of respondents. More dramatic changes to a company's business model were cited by a smaller but still significant percentage, changes that range from partnering with dot-com companies (37%), to acquiring e-Businesses to improve offerings (33%), merger or acquisitions (32%), spinning out e-Businesses (30%), and equity offerings or IPOs (12%).

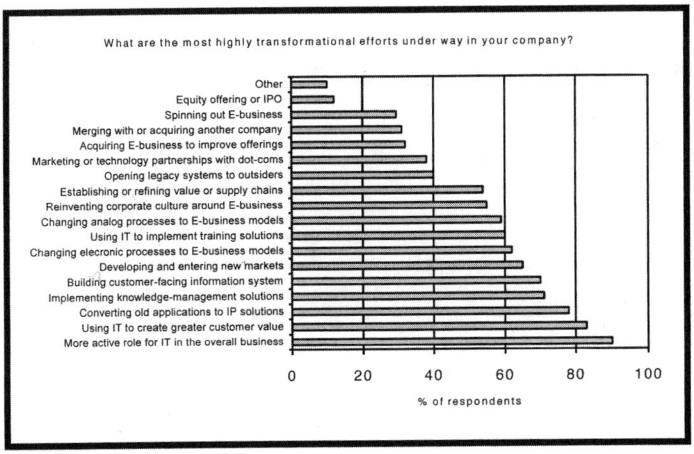

Comment: InformationWeek Research study of 600 executives.
Multiple responses allowed.

Figure 16.3 The most highly transformational efforts under way in companies [Chabrow00]

The early faith of e-Business innovators is bearing out through hard-won experience. Meanwhile, the rest of the business world is quickly embracing the Internet religion.

"We consider it more risky not to do anything," says Mark Klopp, Eastman's director of digital business ventures. "If we wait and watch what happens, the rules will then be dictated to us."

16.3 E-Success? Let Us Count The Ways to Sell, Sell, Sell!

How do you like to shop? Do you take all day and browse around until something catches your eye? On the other hand, do you march right up to the clerk and say, "I need a cheap widget with a whoziwhatzit Got one?" See, the product that you are seeking often defines how you shop for it. This is an important concept to remember when creating your online presence. What exactly is your product? Who is your target audience? How will they want to interact with your company, and how can your site enhance this interaction?

Many Web-based stores allow you to search through their stock by category or by keyword. These methods are, for the most part, derivatives of the technologies that make the software work; databases and file systems are quite effective at categorizing things. However, are the customers at your site going to find shopping by category intuitive? Is that the best approach for you?

Let us take a look at the different kinds of products that are out there and how actual companies are custom-fitting their websites for maximum effectiveness.

There are many different ways to sell your product on the Web, but most techniques tend to fall into one of the following categories:

16.3.1 Services

This category is some how different then others. Although it is hard to say it is product, its importance is growing everyday. We will take a look at the two companies with remarkable achievements and ideas in this field.

The first one is Verizon [Verizon01], Verizon Communications, (NYSE:VZ), formed by the merger of Bell Atlantic and GTE, and is one of the world's leading providers of high-growth communications services.

Verizon companies are the largest providers of wireline and wireless communications in the United States, with more than 112 million access line equivalents and more than 27 million wireless customers.

The Verizon web solution facilitates ordering, payment, reporting, and repair service by implementing industry-leading customer tours and unmatched on-line interaction [Shaygan01]. E-brochures, learning centers, troubleshooting, and other innovative features provide clients with thorough information that ultimately leads to smarter buying decisions. Besides offering products and services Verizon.com's home page features a clean look. Visitors can navigate the site more easily, clicking their way directly to the specific company service or selection required. Whether you are ordering a service or checking a bill, key interactions are generally no more than a few clicks away.

The second company in this field is Biological & Popular Culture Inc. (Biopop) [Biopop01] and its technology performance monitoring service, IsItWorking [IsItWork01]. IsItWorking is a low cost, high-utility telemetry service that monitors user technologies such as phones, faxes, websites, email, servers, routers, applications and other electronic and computer equipment. The service quickly notifies the appropriate contact when a problem or service outage is detected.

Biopop has developed a comprehensive service that will test and monitor the functionality of companies' most crucial technologies. As businesses have become dependent on technology, there is a huge market opportunity to help companies ensure that critical systems and devices are operating efficiently. Internet has become a perfect channel for providing this kind of services. Innovative services offered through IsItWorking bring lot of benefits to its customers:

- Single source for monitoring and reporting
- Allows IT staff to focus on development and support
- Allows executives to focus on core business
- Detects problems not visible to internal network
- Can be utilized as third party auditing and adherence to service level agreements
- Compliments existing internal monitoring tools
- Reduces downtime by customized notification when a problem is detected

- Fully customizable and allows system verification system status from anywhere at anytime

Biopop President and Chief Executive, Fred Darnell, does not release revenue for the private company, which is self-funded. While interested in funding, the company is not now actively seeking it. His company receives advice from a high-powered board of directors and a scientific advisory board. Beyond isitworking.com, he plans to introduce two Internet-based services to the market over the next 18 months. These expansion plans mean isitworking really works.

16.3.2 Gifts and Impulse Products

Sometimes you do not know what you want until you see it. Merchants who offer gift items are very familiar with this. If you are offering impulse buys, you may want to design a site that is easy and entertaining to explore; let them go Windows shopping.

Red Envelope [Billings01] makes its site as fun to explore, as it is to shop, creating impulses and ideas that drive sales. They started from a great idea that in Asian traditions, gifts are often presented in a simple red envelope – a timeless symbol of good fortune, love and appreciation. The company also shares a strategy: the creation of something called a "lifestyle brand".

One thing that RedEnvelope realized a gift ought to say is that the giver took the time to find something unique. Therefore, site design has to properly identify different gift giving occasions, recipients, lifestyles and shops. However, for a merchant, it is enormously complicated to provide such a service. You have to offer gifts for every occasion, from birthdays to bereavements, and from every category: games, gadgets, food, and flowers. This can create serious inventory problems, so RedEnvelope edits and updates their choices mercilessly. They also seize on universal sentiments, such as good luck, that can apply to many gift-giving occasions.

16.3.3 Commodity Products

Everyone knows what a CD or a book looks like. They are pretty low-risk purchases since you do not have to worry about whether they are the right color or compatible with your system. What matters is that the seller has them in stock at a good price. Merchants who offer commodity-type products are differentiated by their products' price, selection, and availability. CDNow [CDNow01] and Amazon [Amazon01] are working hard to be the killers in this arena.

Online selling (relative to traditional retailing) is a scale business characterized by high fixed costs and relatively low variable costs. This makes it difficult to be a medium-sized e-Commerce company.

Amazon.com passed many milestones in its short period of existence [Amzn00]. Up to the end of year 2000 they served 20 million customers, up from 1.5 million in 1997, yielding enormous revenue growth. Although their shares went down a lot, company is in a stronger position than ever. They served 20 million customers in 2000, up from 14 million in 1999 and their sales almost doubled to $2.76 billion in 2000 from $1.64 billion on 1999. Amazon early realized the need of content management and personalization. Their site stores previous customers choices and preferences and creates special offers according to other customers' reviews or sales volume.

But because competing on price alone would make their gross profits approach zero, these companies are focusing on adding value through personalized customer service and convenience. For example, music retailers have learned that many of their customers want to find albums based upon a half-remembered lyric. "You know ... the song that goes 'La la la la'? I want that one." So, in response, they extended their search capabilities to include song lyrics. Now that is convenience! The better you can cater to your customers, the more business they are likely to do with you.

CDNOW has 4.8 million customers and sells over 500,000 items including CDs, movies and digital downloads. Behind the company's success is a well-articulated, multi-point strategy: offer the most comprehensive selection of music in the world at great prices and with the best service and delivery; build communities of music fans; and strive to always stay at the cutting edge of music distribution technologies.

16.3.4 Considered Purchase Products

Some products require a lot of deliberation before a purchase is made. Expensive items that come in various models, each with different options and different pricing, require customers to consider a number of factors before they buy. We're talking about consumer electronics, cars, cellular phone service programs, and something you should be thinking about in the near future: e-Commerce software packages. There are now a number of middleman services popping up to help consumers make their buying decisions. Sites such as mySimon [MySim01] offer side-by-side comparisons of different products. MySimon's Internet e-Commerce hub is the largest comparison shopping site on the Web, with over 2,000 merchants in categories such as Computers, Books & Music, Electronics, Fashion, Flowers, Sporting Goods, Toys and many more. MySimon's shopping service offers unbiased information on products and merchants, including price comparisons, availability and other merchant information. MySimon's shopping service features its exclusive patent pending, Web-based intelligent agent technology. This technology powers the most advanced information retrieval engine, enabling accurate price comparisons from the greatest number of merchants on the Web.

16.3.5 Configurable Products

Sometimes a product is all about the options it comes with. A case in point is computer workstations and servers. The basic components are the same, but you can choose how roomy or fast each of those parts will be. Computer manufacturers like Dell [Dell01] and Apple [Apple01] enable their customers to design their own products, blending one-on-one marketing with customizing mass-market products: Their motto is, "Tell us what you want and we'll build it for you." Concept of this site has again deep retail analysis in its basis. Dell and Apple are trying to satisfy customers hidden needs, i.e. complete control over the configuration of the machine, by allowing customers to select different size machines, add or remove parts that are not important for their business. Behind this freedom of choice are years of careful site engineering since customer is in reality only selecting well-tested parts and none of the choices can be wrong. Finally, presentation is done in the way that customer feels superiority over purchased computer. It is the customer who controls the creation of one of those "super computers".

These techniques are now showing up in other fields as well. Take a look at Smith & Noble [SmNob01], where you can design your own window treatments by selecting and combining different attributes and features.

16.3.6 Categorized and Indexed Catalogs

OK, I will admit it. As much as I harp on the problems with the category/subcategory/sub-subcategory thing, sometimes that method of organization is convenient, especially when shopping for supplies. Office Depot's site [OfDep01] does a good job of organizing things so you can get in and out quickly. Office Depot, Inc., is the world's largest seller of office products and an industry leader in every distribution channel, including stores, direct mail, contract delivery, the Internet and business-to-business electronic commerce.

Grainger [Grain01], the industrial supply catalog, has thousands and thousands of items. For a company like that, categorization is a must.

You need to figure out what is right for your company and your products; not necessarily what is easiest to build. To be competitive, you need to understand how your customers want to work with you, what levels of convenience they desire, and what features they will value in your online store.

16.4 Adding value

In addition to the methods previously described, a number of companies have taken advantage of new technologies to deliver even better service and environments to their customers. These are not storefront solutions in and of themselves, but they can work as excellent supplements to other systems. Before that, we will tell something more about design of the previously considered sites.

16.4.1 The Design of a Storefront

All sites described above, have some common approach when we consider their design. They have design that is clever and straightforward. The design that is bright, clean, simple, and uncluttered. The quick, readable, intuitive navigation, and fast respond, results in smooth experience to the users. All sites present a clear, concise message. Portrays a consistent, strong brand image, and as you can see, it really sells.

When choosing a color for design careful thought must be given to the psychological effect these colors will have on your customers. All colors affect us psychologically, emotionally and physically. To some colors we will react in a positive way, and to others we will react in a negative way, but we will never react indifferently. Choosing the right color does not cost any more than choosing the wrong color, and it will have a dramatic affect on physical and mental well being, improving sales, and creating the right image for you and your company. The correct color combination can attract extra customers, compel them to enter the site, spend more money, and feel better about it. Therefore, the modern businessperson must learn how to use color effectively [Wiki01]. The correct colors must be chosen to reflect the type of business you are in. The range of colors used must correspond to the needs (real or imagined) of the buying public. These colors below the level of consciousness make customers choose one product over another. They will leave with a feeling of satisfaction and will come again. Any selling establishment must be an invitation to enter, to see and to buy, and the whole environment should be designed to give the merchandise or service offered a strong visual impact, which will enable people to identify themselves with the concept.

The sales philosophy that achieves this aim should try to make potential customers feel drawn inside and encouraged to buy or to partake of the service. First impressions are vital, and initial reaction will attract or repel trade, depending on the emotions of the individual. Color plays a large part in creating a good initial impression because it is an emotional thing. For example, red color denotes success, gives a sense of power, and creates strong image. Therefore, it is a very energetic color with stimulating and exciting effect. Opposite effect have a green color, a relaxing one. The green has some additional effects, which are very similar to the ones that we have with a blue. Psychologically blue is the color of tidiness. If blue incline towards a gray, it express stability and good organizational capacity. On the other hand, a mind perceives a yellow and orange color as colors of friendship.

Good taste is one thing, but it has little to do with effective merchandising, marketing or promotion. The correct use of colors is critical in today's extremely competitive business environment. It can literally, make or break a business.

Colors have an important role in the design, but other elements must not be forgotten. It means that what counts is a whole experience, and not only a separate moments.

The first part of the shopping experience enables customers to quickly find the products they want and add them to their shopping carts. The second part processes the orders and securely sends them to the fulfillment center, where they are packed and shipped to the customers. The third section offers a summary of their orders and functions as a printable receipt. So, a simple interface can hide a complex and powerful set of tools.

16.4.2 Content Management

With an end goal of building long-term, sustainable relationships with customers, businesses need to communicate with customers anywhere they are, on any device. And because customers expect to access information anytime, businesses must collaborate within and across internal and external enterprise systems to deliver on real-time customer demands. One way of approaching these issues is Content management. Figure 16.4 shows essential moments in Content management.

Creation	▪ Multiple sources ▪ Multiple formats of content/digital assets
Management	▪ Workflow ▪ Archive & storage ▪ Administration
Publishing	▪ Online publishing network
Distribution	▪ Multi site network syndication

Comment: Web content management is a set of tasks and processes for managing content explicitly targeted for publication on the web throughout its life from creation to archive.

Figure 16.4 Content management [Starw01]

Content management has to:

- Manage and aggregate content
- Provide behavioral insight
- Deliver personalization
- Integrate business processes

Content management is becoming necessity of a serious EC solution.

Vignette [Vignette01] builds one of the most comprehensive integrated content management solutions. Vignette tools have specialized in providing B2B, B2C, e-Marketplace and Information Portal solutions. Vignette solutions can help businesses achieve successes limit.

16.4.3 WAP

Mobility has become an essential part of today's business life. Constant availability is crucial for business competitiveness [Nokia01]. The WAP – Wireless Application Protocol is the leading standard for information services on wireless terminals like digital mobile phones. The WAP standard solves a number of problems in this area.

First, it implements a protocol stack that can deliver a reliable packet service over radio links with high bit error rate.

Figure 16.5 shows the order of the different stacks and their protocols. This includes the stacks responsible for the layout as well as the stacks responsible for the actual data transfer. This diagram compare WAP with TCP, because TCP is not well suited for a reliable packet service over radio links with high bit error rate.

Second, WAP protocol is used to display sites in WAP browsers through WML – Wireless Markup Language. Third, WAP specifies how integration with existing web services should be done: through a protocol gateway normally called a WAP gateway. This means that WAP service providers only need to have a web server to be able to serve WAP content. For some providers, it may be desirable to have a WAP gateway, and this is easily accommodated. Depending on the configuration access to content can be granted from any WAP gateway, or only from specific gateways.

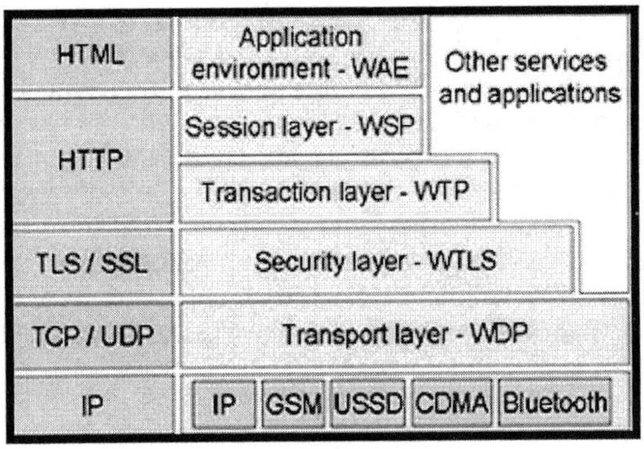

Legend: WAE – Wireless Application Environment
WSP – Wireless Session Protocol
WTP – Wireless Transaction Protocol
WTLS – Wireless Transport Layer Security
WDP – Wireless Datagram Protocol

Comment: The WAP stack is an entity of protocols that cover the wireless data transfer.

Figure 16.5 WAP Protocol stack [NetLig01]

In 1997, Ericsson, Motorola, Nokia and Unwired Planet formed the WAP Forum [WAP01], and they set out the way that WML would work, making it an industry standard. Since then hundreds of companies have joined the Forum. According to the WAP Forum, over 90% of mobile phone manufacturers worldwide are members of the Forum. Although usually simply designed, WAP sites are fully functional tools [Lewin01]. The future of WAP is still unpredictable. Some usability studies have raised few concerns about it. However, one thing is sure, mobile services are here to stay and it is only the question of standard that will take over the market.

16.4.4 Automated Answers and Advice

Brightware, a Firepond company (NASDAQ: FIRE) helps companies build better customer relationships, one interaction at a time. Brightware [Bright01] uses its 20 years of artificial intelligence knowledge to interpret natural language, magically allowing its system to answer customer questions. Brightware claims that, with some training, its system can automatically reply to 80 percent of common service and sales inquiries, regardless of how the questions are phrased. Brightware can then route the remainder of the questions to your customer service department for answering. Firepond-Brightware products transforms passive Web site content into a dynamic sales or service advisor that helps customers find the products or solutions they need. This kind of value will drive new revenue streams, increase margins and manage customer interactions across all channels and throughout the sales and service cycle.

This technology has also been used by financial, mortgage, and health care companies to determine their customers' needs and then actively recommend a prepared solution. Say goodbye once and for all to door-to-door insurance salesmen.

Similarly, Ask Jeeves [AskJee01] sells its question-answering software to other businesses so their users can get the answers they are looking for, which hopefully leads them to buy more products.

16.4.5 Automated Recommendations

Net Perceptions [Peterson01] is a purveyor of collaborative filtering, an automated merchandising technology that can cross-sell items to customers with similar purchasing histories. Say a customer wants to get caught up on his aquatic-adventure reading and buys 20,000 Leagues Under The Sea and Moby Dick. Meanwhile, someone else buys Moby Dick and The Hunt for Red October. These collaborative filtering tools will connect that information and recommend The Hunt for Red October to the first customer and 20,000 Leagues Under the Sea to the other customer. By using this system, you are basically letting your customers with similar interests make recommendations to each other. In addition, the more they buy, the more accurate the recommendations will become. Pretty cool, eh?

These are just few examples of ways you can add value to your site and stand out in a possibly crowded field. But before you start adding bells and whistles, you may want to begin simply and locally. Start by talking to your salespeople. Your front line knows a lot about what your customers need and, more importantly, how best to communicate with them. Find out what your sales team is doing that works most effectively.

16.5 Secrets of E-Success

Don't procrastinate	Implement a web site
Full Inventory	Customer go where the stock is
Searchable	First page search button
Fast	Connectivity and download time (8 seconds rule)
Low Prices	Offer value over cost
Availability	In stock and shipping time
Clean & Professional	Minimize frames and animated GIFS
Email the Customer	Keep apprised of order – reassure
Respond to Emails	The quicker, the better
Change	Dynamic site with new information
Exceptional Customer Service	Speaks for itself

Figure 16.6 Secrets of E-Success [Graham00]

16.5.1 Use those Log Files

Log files can give you valuable information about the shopping and surfing patterns of your customers, telling you how they found your site, which pages they visited, and who bought what. With careful tracking of the data generated by your log files (especially over the long-term), you can figure out which advertising and marketing tactics are the most successful with your customers. Information like this is valuable because it can tell you where to reinvest and how to change your media-investing tactics based upon what is performing and what is not.

One popular way to determine what marketing leads customers to buy your products is to track the sources of your sales leads all the way through to the order. Direct marketers have been doing this for years, long before the Web came into being. You will find source codes on almost everything they send out: postcards, coupons, the backs of the glossy catalogs, and that "address your letter to department AC8638" thing they do. By assigning a unique code to each coupon or postcard, marketers can keep track of which placement yielded the most customer interest.

You can do the same thing on your site. If you know the source of the lead, the customer who responded, and the orders that customer placed, then you have a gold mine of data with which to determine your ROI (return on investment). More important, you can improve upon it by fine-tuning both your marketing and site design.

Do users stop clicking once they hit a certain page? Perhaps that page needs to be simplified, rewritten, or even repositioned to make it easier for your customers to get to the key part of your site: the bottom line.

To make sure you are using the most cost-effective marketing for your site, you must not only determine which ads are generating the most orders but also quantify a return on that investment. You may find that your direct-mail campaign is bringing all kinds of visitors to your site, but they are not buying anything. At the same time, a banner ad may attract only a few visitors, but those that do come to your site via the banner ad tend to make purchases. Which form of marketing is the most cost-effective? To find out, take a closer look at how much money your site's making and how much you are spending.

16.5.2 Keeping track of everything

The websites that are running your banner ads are giving you clickthrough reports, showing you how many people came to your site during certain time frames. But you still need to figure out which advertisements actually make money [Hakman01]. It is a good thing you picked an open application architecture for the site, because now it looks as though you have an additional requirement: You need to start tracking.

To track your customers, you need to assign each banner ad a specific code and use that code in the referring URL that links your site to the ad. The URL in the link looks like this:

http://www.YourCompany.com/index.cfm?MC=WM001

If you click around, you will see that the site keeps track of where you came from. That is because MC=WM001 is a media code set up specifically for inquiries that will come from this page. The media code is tracked throughout a customer's session on the site, and if the customer places an order, that code is attached to the order for later reporting. You can embed unique media codes just like this in banner advertisements and outbound email messages.

You can also track customers that come directly to the site without the help of any specific ad. In this example, the media code "direct" shows that word of mouth is still the best resource for generating low-cost sales.

But that does not mean you should abandon all advertising and rely solely on word of mouth to keep your online business thriving. One fatal flaw of using log files to track user activity is that they make no allowances for customers who follow an ad simply to learn about your products and then, after doing some comparison shopping, return to your site to make a purchase. The tracking system will report this scenario as an advertising failure and a word-of-mouth victory, and that is just not the case. When it comes to site promotion, things usually are not all or nothing. Usually, the most cost-effective marketing for your site involves finding the right combination of a variety of advertising methods.

16.5.3 Staying in E-Business

To find the most cost-effective marketing for your site, experiment with your advertising while keeping a sharp eye on your sales. Try new things: Implement innovative banner ads, play around with things like affiliate marketing, consider sponsorships — and see how your sales are affected.

And keep at it. Your online storefront, like your business itself, must continue to grow and change to accommodate the evolution of your customers and products [Hakman01].

This flexibility is key to keeping your e-Business viable. Even if your products do not change much over the years, you need to constantly reevaluate and update your online presence. The quick and ever-changing nature of the Web can be daunting, but it can also bring customers, connections, and opportunities that never would have been possible otherwise.

As you set out to create your own e-Commerce site, keep in mind all that we have discussed here. With planning, hard work, and careful observation, you can build a site that is flexible enough to keep up with the ever-changing needs of your customers. And then you will really be in e-Business.

16.6 Conclusions

Although it did not define the exact formula for the e-Success, this chapter has presented the general principles and key ideas of adding values to your existent e-Commerce. One should look for an appropriate example among successful e-Commerce described here, and thoroughly examine the implementation of the ideas that were offered here. A full coverage of the topics introduced here would take another book about the size of this one. We refer the interested reader to the growing number of books on related topics. References appear in the next section.

REFERENCES

[Amazon01] "Earth's Biggest Selection", (http://www.amazon.com), Amazon.com Inc., P.O. Box 81226 Seattle, Washington 98108-1226, November 2001.

[Amzn00] 2000 Annual Report: Letter to Shareholders, (http://www.iredge.com/iredge/iredge.asp?c=002239&f=2006&fn=Jeffsletter2000__427.pdf), Amazon Com, 2001.

[Apple01] "Visit the Apple Store online", (http://www.apple.com/store/), Apple Computer Inc., November 2001.

[AskJee01] Ask Jeeves homepage, (http://askjeeves.com), Ask Jeeves Inc., December 2001.

[Biopop01] Biopop homepage, (http://www.biopop.com), Biological & Popular Culture Inc., 6646 East WT Harris Boulevard, Charlotte, NC 28215, December 2001.

[Billings01] Billings, H., "About Red Envelope" (http://www.redenvelope.com), November 2001.

[Bright01] "Firepond SalesPerformer products", (http://www.brightware.com), Firepond Inc., 2001.

[CDNow01] About CDNOw, (http://www.cdnow.com), CDNow Online Inc., 1005 Virginia Dr. Ft. Washington, PA 19034, 2001.

[Chabrow00] Chabrow, E., "Seeking The Deeper Path To E-Success", (http://www.informationweek.com/776/transform.htm), CMP Media LLC, March 2000.

[Dell01] Laptop, Desktop, Workstation, Server, (http://www.dell.com), Dell Computer Corporation, 2001.

[Grain01] Grainger homepage, (http://www.grainger.com), W.W. Grainger Inc., December 2001.

[Graham00] Graham, P., "The Net Effects of Web Recruiting", Talisman Technologies, November 2000.

[Hakman01] Hakman, K., "E-Commerce Tutorial", (http://hotwired.lycos.com/webmonkey/e-business/tutorials/tutorial3.html), Lycos Inc., 2001.

[Hui00] Hui, V., "E-Commerce: What/Where/Why/How", (http://alumni.cs.cityu.edu.hk/downloads/ecomm/), Tutorial, Department of CS Alumni, City University of HK, 2000.

[IsItWork01] Comprehensive Remote Technology Monitoring, (http://www.isitworking.com), Biological & Popular Culture Inc., 6646 East WT Harris Boulevard, Charlotte, NC 28215, December 2001.

[Lewin01] Lewin, J., "Converting applications to wireless", (http://www-106.ibm. com/developerworks/wireless/), May 2001.

[MySim01] MySimon homepage, "Compare products and prices from around the Web", (http://www.mysimon.com), CNET Networks Media Property, December 2001.

[NetLig01] WAP/I-mode, (http://www.netlight.se/wapimode.html), Net Light Inc., December 2001.

[Nokia01] Nokia WAP on Web, (http://www.nokia.com/wap/), November 2001.

[OfDep01] "Shop Online 24 Hours a day", (http://www.officedepot.com), Office Depot Inc., December 2001.

[Peterson01] Peterson, D., "About Net Perception", (http://www.netperception.com), Net Perception Inc., December 2001.

[Shaygan01] Shaygan, K., "Verizon Turns Up New and Improved Web Site for Online Customer Service", (http://biz.yahoo.com/prnews/011101/nyth078_1.html), Yahoo Finance, November 2001.

[Schneider00] Schneider, G., Perry, J., "Electronic Commerce", Course Technology, Cambridge, MA, 2000.

[SmNob01] Smith and Noble, "America's leading resource for custom home decor", (http://www.smithandnoble.com), Corona, California, 2001.

[Starw01] "Interlink, Web Content Management", (http://www.starwire.com), Starwire Corporation, December 2001.

[Verizon01] Verizon homepage, (http://www.verizon.com), Verizon Communications, December 2001.

[Vignette01] Vignette Solutions, (http://www.vignette.com/CDA/Site/0,2097,1-1-1515,00.html), November 2001.

[WAP01] Wireless Application Protocol Ltd., (http://www.wapforum.org), WAP forum, November 2001.

[Wiki01] Wikipedia, "Color", (http://www.wikipedia.com/wiki/Color), The Free Encyclopedia, November 2001.

Author Index